MULTINATIONAL ENTERPRISE

An Encyclopedic Dictionary of Concepts and Terms

Ankie Hoogvelt

with
Anthony G. Puxty

Consultant Editor
John M. Stopford

NP

NICHOLS PUBLISHING COMPANY: NEW YORK

First published in the United States of America by
Nichols Publishing Company
Post Office Box 96
New York, N Y 10024
U S A

Library of Congress Cataloging in Publication Data

Multi-national enterprise.
   Bibliography: p.
   1. International business enterprises – Dictionaries.
I. Hoogvelt, Ankie. M. M.   II. Puxty, Anthony G.
III. Stopford, John M.
HD2755. 5. M8337 1987   338. 8′ 8′ 0321 86-5136

ISBN 0-89397-249-5

Printed in Great Britain

CONTENTS

	page
Acknowledgements	vi
Preface	vii
Introduction	ix
How To Use This Dictionary	xi
Dictionary	1
Appendix I – References	242
Appendix II – Select List of Bibliographies	247
Apprendix III – Organizations	250
Index	251

Acknowledgements

Benedictions to all my relatives and friends for learning to tolerate the work on this Dictionary as a legitimate excuse for social neglect.

Joint ventures, whether in multinational business or in academic enterprise, are often fraught with difficulties and unstable. This dictionary is no exception. Work on it began as a joint project between Anthony Puxty and myself. In the event, pressures of other writing commitments meant that Anthony had to take a secondary role in its preparation. He has however contributed one-third of the text, chiefly in the fields of international business management, particularly international accounting and financial and risk management. I have also appreciated his exacting editorial comments.

I thank John Stopford for his encouragement, his expert advice, his willingness to lend his name to the work, and last but not least for being so nice and open-minded about the unavoidable clashes arising from our respective views. I owe a debt to Geoffrey Hamilton for his reading of and helpful comments on the entries relating to International Co-operation and Organizations, and to Anthony Rowell for doing the same with the entries on International Accounting, Corporate Structure and Management and Financial and Risk Management, but I hasten to discharge them both of any responsibility for the final text.

My very special thanks I extend to Frederick Clairmonte, for the deep commitment to the cause of popular understanding which prompted him to give, so generously and freely, much time to the work of a writer whom he had never met. The inimitable blend of his fulsome praise and roaring criticism has kept me struggling to get things right. But if they still are not, that is not his fault.

As this dictionary is the product of a word processor, there is – I regret to say – no debt owed to typists. Instead I want to thank Steve Brierley for making my computer so user-friendly that it almost completed the task by itself, leaving me time to go out and play!

Finally, I thank and give full praise to Sheila Macdonald, our copy editor, who tirelessly straightened the warps in my grammar and who so discreetly defended the right of the general readership to comprehend our esoteric jargon.

Ankie Hoogvelt
Sheffield, August 1986

Preface

The growth of the multinational corporation over the last 30 years has spawned a burgeoning literature of many varieties. Academics from many disciplines have turned their attention to understanding and explaining the economic, legal and political significance of such corporations. Others, concerned with managerial issues, have been asking increasingly searching questions about how operations across national frontiers alter the nature of the management process. At the same time, politicians and their advisers have become concerned about how the sheer size of these corporations has created new possibilities for exercising power. Different voices, using different languages of analysis, have been raised on the same subject.

To the uninitiated, this plethora of language and approach is confusing and potentially misleading. Assumptions made in one approach can lead to conclusions which seem to wholly contradict conclusions drawn by other approaches. Much of the problem can be traced to the difficulty most people have in understanding the terms used in the various technical arguments.

This dictionary represents a first attempt to provide a relatively simple guide to all the dimensions of the phenomenon of the multinationals. The two authors have done a splendid job of casting their net widely, consulting many authorities in different fields, and producing a text that can inform the general reader. As with any relatively new field, language is imprecise and often the terms defy precise definitions. The authors have consequently interpreted their task as that of defining those terms which can be pinned down precisely and of exposing the different arguments and perspectives involved in the use of other terms.

Quite naturally, in any work of this type there are two problems that can never be resolved wholly satisfactorily: defining the limits of the phenomenon and avoiding bias in interpretation. The first problem is addressed in the authors' introduction, where stress is rightly laid on the interdisciplinary and evolutionary nature of the concepts involved. The text is largely limited to terms commonly used in the Anglo-Saxon world and does not therefore attempt to cover all the terms required to describe conditions in the Far East and developing countries.

The second problem is more difficult to solve, for any study of the multinationals is wrought with political overtones and inferences. The treatment given to the more controversial terms will not be to everyone's taste. Early on in the editorial work, the impossibility of satisfying everyone with a summary statement became quite clear. Nevertheless, it also became clear that the divergent philosophical leanings of those involved could be accommodated in most cases. The dictionary represents, therefore, a serious attempt to provide as catholic an approach as possible. The risks of offending the few can be seen to be greatly outweighed by the benefits of helping the many to think more broadly about the issues raised by one of the most potent and least understood forces in the contemporary world of international affairs.

John M Stopford
London, July 1986

Introduction

Dictionaries are all of a season these days. They crop up in all sorts of discipline-straddling topics ranging from energy to environment. Their rapid proliferation is a sign both of maturity and of failure. It is a mark of the maturity of a given subject when knowledge of it has advanced enough and opinions have become sufficiently crystallized and commonly shared for someone to attempt to harvest the crop and bundle it in neat packages of one-liners and essayettes, ready for popular distribution.

But such dictionaries are also a record of failure: the failure of the relevant disciplines to transcend their respective boundaries and jointly examine real world phenomena in a cohesive whole. Our intellectual heritage dooms us to see the world about us in fragmented form, each fragment a view from the window of rigidly segregated academic disciplines. And so we resort to a second-best solution: an alphabetical listing of all the fragments.

But an A to Z does not add up to a complete picture. One is soberly reminded of the fable of the little blind men and the elephant. Clambering all over the beast, each blind man – using his exquisitely developed tactile skills – gave a description of the animal totally at odds with that of his fellows, depending on whether he had examined the smooth padding of the feet, the trailing length of the trunk, the ribbed mass of the back, or the cutting edge of the ivory tusk. Neither singly nor jointly did they ever get to see the real thing!

And so it is with our understanding of multinational enterprise. There is little doubt that the multinational enterprise is a jumbo in the jungle of world affairs. Today, some 200 multinational companies contribute about one-fifth of the non-socialist world's gross product. Each of the top 20, with an annual turnover of over 30 billion dollars, can outbid the gross domestic product of the majority of the world's 180 nations, and the very largest corporations can match dollar for dollar the economic strength of all but the very largest of national economies. International trade in the conventional sense of economic exchanges between independent producers and consumers in different countries is rapidly being overtaken by the intra-firm transactions of globe-girdling corporations. This means that the invisible hand of the market, which we habitually credit with the fine quality of efficient resource allocation, is in its turn being led by the global profit-seeking calculus of a handful of incumbents in the upper echelons of international corporate organizations. The spontaneous free market organization of our economic life is being supplanted by the planning and administration of global corporations. Whether this leads to greater or lesser efficiency and welfare for all of us is an issue of intense controversy, to which different disciplines and writers of opposing political views have contributed a rich variety of concepts and terms.

Efficiency is one of two central problems at the heart of the debate about multinational enterprise. Public accountability is the other. To contrast private corporate power with the size and economic strength of nation states is not to indulge in a frivolous statistical quibble. It is to point at once to the conundrum that multinational enterprise presents to the contemporary world and to the chief reasons why – like the elephant in the fable – it keeps eluding our full view.

The conundrum is that public accountability, such as it exists in a world of imperfect democracies, stops at the national frontier. But increasingly, decisions as to what shall be produced, where and by whom, for whom and at what price, are all decisions which are taken in cross-frontier boardrooms. And such boardrooms are beyond the reach of popular democracy. Universal suffrage is a fine thing, but people may be forgiven for thinking that there is not much point in casting their votes when the government of their choice cannot fulfil its electoral pledge of lower interest rates, or job creation, or the holding down of prices, because international capital can shift massive funds in and out of a country, relocate industrial activity to other nations, or mark up prices at will.

Corporate power is not just a function of size and market dominance: it also stems from inscrutability. Our rulebook of economic enterprise, including company legislation, the development of auditing practices and the delineation of the requisite categories of book keeping and disclosure, date from a time when the nation state had emerged as the historical companion to free market enterprise within one territorial state. But there is as yet no international rulebook accompanying the growth of international economic enterprise. Accounting practices vary between nations, and so do currencies, tax systems, trade regulations and so on. This permits multinational companies to develop and grow in relative obscurity, presenting less than meaningful profit and loss accounts of their segmented operations in different national locations, while consolidating the group accounts more meaningfully at a transnational level where they escape the public scrutiny of those affected by the segmented operations.

Few, if any, national authorities have a complete picture of the true benefits and costs of foreign operations in their country. Sometimes they have none at all. I remember once travelling all the way to an African country in order to study the socioeconomic impact of a British-owned iron ore mine (one of the country's major export earners) – only to find upon arrival that I needed to travel all the way back again to Companies House in London, where the company was incorporated and its accounts deposited for public inspection. Even the host country's tax inspector, much to his chagrin, had failed to obtain a copy of the company's accounts.

Furthermore, in a world of nations competing for international investments, the goal of harmonization of public scrutiny, of tax regulations and of other public policies *vis-à-vis* foreign investments, remains elusive. This is the reason why multinational companies have often been spoken of as 'invisible empires'.

I have emphasized this issue of public accountability because it is one of the aims of this dictionary to serve its quest. A great many entries in this dictionary deal with attempts – whether legislative, organizational, investigative, educational, or sometimes just consciousness raising – by national and international communities to embrace the multinational enterprise in some form of social and political grasp. In that sense, this dictionary is as much a dictionary of the environment in which the multinational operates as it is of internal corporate management, structure and accounting.

The attempts by the *international* environment to come to grips with multinational corporate power are very varied. They range from international codes of conduct solemnly declared (or in preparation) by august international bodies, which represent the world's nations, through the search for global solidarity by labour and consumer unions, to the campaigning cries of little-known concerned citizen groups. Because we wish to assist the process of making MNEs more transparent than they are at present, we have doubled up the relevant entries as a directory, giving addresses as well as details of aims, methods and achievements. We hope that this will assist the student of multinational enterprise to access quickly relevant organizations and sources of data.

The efforts by *national* communities to direct and control foreign operations on their soil have led to major changes in the organizational structure of multinational enterprise. Developing countries in particular have been at the forefront of the development of imaginative new cross-border collaborative ventures with multinational capital and a few of them have become skilful negotiators in the bargaining with multinational enterprise over its contribution to national economic goals. For their part, multinational companies have often been flexible and deft accommodators of such national aspirations. We have tried in this dictionary – often in lengthy essays – to deal with the plethora of practical terms, concepts and theories which have been engendered by this ongoing process of confrontation and collaboration between national aspirations and multinational capital's interest. We would like to think that our work will be seen by those working inside multinational companies as a useful guide to the national and international environment in which it operates.

As John Stopford says in his preface, we have cast our net widely. Many of the entries dealing with economic, financial, managerial, political and legal concepts and terms can be found in the dictionaries of conventional disciplines. But each time we have tried to tease out the significance of the concept or term in question in relation to the theory and practice of multinational enterprise. Thus, the reader will find that perfectly well understood concepts like rent, royalty, oligopoly, socialism, and systematic risk are treated quite differently in this dictionary than they are in conventional, academic subject-bound, dictionaries.

Though casting our net widely, we have also had to limit ourselves. Lack of space and knowledge have tied us, in the main, to concepts and terms current in the Anglo-Saxon world. Even so, the keen user of this dictionary may well be disappointed by serious omissions. Since it is our intention to update the text in future years, we welcome constructive comments, criticisms and suggestions.

How To Use This Dictionary

As said before, dictionaries offer an A to Z of bits of truth, of fragments of knowledge and ideas current in a variety of different disciplines. This dictionary is no exception. However, we have tried to go beyond the fragments and we encourage the committed reader to do the same. An intelligent use of our system of cross-referencing and index groupings will afford the reader an opportunity to zigzag across disciplinary boundaries and pursue a particular theme all the way to a fairly full summary of the present state of the art. To achieve this, four consecutive steps are involved.

1. Each entry is, where necessary, directly cross-referenced to those HEADWORDS which the reader may need to look up simply in order to understand the meaning of the entry itself.

2. At the end of each entry we will normally refer the reader to some other HEADWORDS which are most closely linked to the concept or term in question. But we have limited this exercise of direct inter-entry cross-referencing because lack of space does not permit full and comprehensive cross-referencing in this manner. Instead, comprehensive cross-referencing will be achieved indirectly by going through the Index at the back of the volume, page 251.

3. At the end of most entries, and after the direct entry cross-referencing, we name the index group to which the entry belongs, for example: *See* Index under Corporate Structure and Management, *See* Index under Regulation and Tax. The Index at the back of the volume lists all the headwords by index group. We have generated a system of 13 of such groups. The index group to which an entry refers should be regarded as its 'first-choice' index group. In some cases an entry will refer to two index groups and be listed under both.

4. While the entries listed within one index group are in some way related, some are of

course more closely associated than others. This closer connexion is in turn indicated by the way in which headwords in the index are cross-referenced to one other index group. They may or may not be listed in this index group. The cross-referencing to another classification merely serves to attract attention to the way in which concepts and terms within one index group may be seen to cohere in a special secondary dimension.

For example, if one looks up **Restrictive Business Practices (RBP) Code** one will find it indexed under International Co-operation. At the back of the volume, on p 255, the 'International Co-operation' index group lists over 90 headwords, the entries for which will all describe some form of action by the international community which is directly or indirectly relevant to multinational enterprise. But within this list, the headword **Restrictive Business Practices Code** is cross-referenced to the index group 'Dispute and Settlement'. This reflects the fact that the Code in question is related to efforts by the international community to resolve issues of conflict arising between nation states and multinationals. There have been more such efforts. Looking down the list, the reader will find other headwords cross-referenced to Dispute and Settlement. Together they yield a whole cache of international codes of conduct.

To give another example, the headword ARBITRAGE is listed along with nearly 80 headwords under Financial and Risk Management. But because of its theoretical treatment in the subject literature, it is – along with only 13 other headwords within this index group – cross-referenced to Theoretical Issues. A reading of these 14 entries will give the user of this dictionary a fair summary of the application of financial management theory to multinational enterprise.

There are a very few concepts which feature in more than two index groups. For example, TRANSFER PRICE has been indexed under Financial and Risk Management, and under Regulation and Tax, while in the index it is cross-referenced to two more groups. We have limited such multiple indexation, for the obvious reason that it would render the index useless as a cross-referencing tool. But the reader is reminded that where multiple indexation does occur, it is as likely as not a sign of the centrality of the concept or term in the study of multinational enterprise.

Lastly, a word about other books. While we have consulted a truly gigantic number of texts, we have felt that it would not serve a useful purpose to burden the reader with detailed references in every entry. We have limited our bibliographical references to those authors whose names are inextricably linked to a particular theory, concept or term, or whose work is actually quoted in our text.

However, in line with the encyclopaedic character of this dictionary, we have appended a list of bibliographies on multinational enterprise.

A

accounting principles. The basic rules that govern the way in which events affecting an enterprise are converted into the numbers in the financial statements. Although most countries are agreed on the basic conventions, such as conservatism in asset valuation and adherence to historical rather than current cost for those assets, the application of the basic ideas varies considerably in different countries: (a) in the extent to which they are explicitly formulated in company law, commercial practice or comercial codes; (b) in the extent to which they are uniform within the country itself; (c) in the extent to which they are helpful in aiding the reader of the financial statements to obtain a good picture of the status of the enterprise.

Issues concerned with principles should be distinguished from those concerned with extent of disclosure (*see* DISCLOSURE AND ACCOUNTS). In the US, the UK and in countries influenced by them (for example those developed countries that were once members of the British Empire), accounting principles are recognized as being important and are governed fairly tightly by a mixture of company law, pressure from government departments (for instance the SECURITIES AND EXCHANGE COMMISSION (SEC) in the US) and by independent or professional bodies that have strong persuasive power (such as the FINANCIAL ACCOUNTING STANDARDS BOARD (FASB) in the US and the ACCOUNTING STANDARDS COMMITTEE (ASC) in the UK). In other countries (such as West Germany and France) commercial codes have been developed that are concerned more with the form of the financial statements than their content. For example, they explicitly designate the headings under which items of the

income statement and balance sheet should be classified, but they make little or no reference to the way those items should be arrived at. Concern with the form of accounts has become more widespread with the adoption of the Fourth Directive by the EUROPEAN COMMUNITY (EC) and its incorporation into the laws of the member states. The Fourth Directive explicitly requires financial statements to be presented in the form of a standard set of headings. Concerned with harmonizing the practices of the Members of the Community, and improving the quality of information in those member countries with less developed accounting principles, this Directive is expected to have far-reaching effects.

The results of this diversity of practice between countries have been threefold. Firstly, financial statements that appear comparable on the surface because the descriptive terms and the form of the statements seem similar, are not in fact comparable because the means of arriving at the figures contained in them are different. Secondly, the statements of companies in some countries are of little use for decisions such as investment or divestment of the firm's securities since they are subject to considerable manipulation by the preparers for the purpose of concealing or distorting salient results from the general user, and frequently in order to reduce the firm's tax liability (since many countries require that tax assessments be raised on the published income figures). Thirdly, there have been pressures for the standardization or harmonization of accounting principles in order to avoid the problems these inconsistencies can cause (*see* ACCOUNTING STANDARDS COMMITTEE (ASC)). These variations in accounting principles have caused several problems for multinational enterprise. They can be confusing, time-consuming and expensive since the subsidiaries abroad will need to prepare results both in terms of local principles (for the local public authorities) and in parent-country terms (for the purpose of CONSOLIDATION). They can make the assessment of competitive position in foreign markets difficult, since the profitability of firms already established in those markets is open to misinterpretation. There is a tendency for managers to assume that apparently similar figures have a similar significance when they do not. They can be misleading when a multinational is considering the ACQUISITION of an overseas company as a means of penetrating the market, and needs to determine an appropriate price to pay. They can make the task of the audit of multinational corporations more difficult and expensive.

See AUDITING, and Index under International Accounting.

Accounting Standards Committee (ASC). A United Kingdom regulatory body set up in 1970 to regulate disclosure in corporate financial statements. Consisting entirely of part-time members backed by a permanent secretariat, the Committee is funded and its activities supported by the six major UK accountancy bodies. Its major function is to propose accounting standards through a process of consultation with interested parties. The standards are then issued by the six bodies, which become responsible for attempting to enforce conformity to the standards by pressure upon their members in positions of authority in reporting companies. The standards set by the ASC are not compulsory upon companies (in contrast to those of the FINANCIAL ACCOUNTING STANDARDS BOARD (FASB) in the USA) but are in most cases complied with.

The standard which is of most interest to multinational corporations concerns cur-

rency translation. Issued after three different exposure drafts, the current standard is SSAP 20. It distinguishes between two types of subsidiary: those carrying on a business that is essentially an extension of the operations at home, and those that are separate or quasi-autonomous. The results of the former are to be translated using the temporal method, charging exchange differences to the profit and loss account. The results of the latter are to be translated using the current rate method, with exchange differences being charged to reserves. The standard also requires companies to disclose the translation method used, the treatment of exchange differences, the net amount of exchange gains and losses, (showing separately those amounts that are adjustments to reserves and those that are included in or charged against profit), and the net movement of reserves that results from exchange differences. Either the closing rate or average rate method may be used.

See TRANSLATION, and Index under International Accounting.

ACP States. The independent black countries of sub-Saharan Africa, the Caribbean, and the Pacific brought together as a group only for the purposes of the LOMÉ CONVENTION. The most recent Lomé convention was signed in 1985 and its signatories included 65 ACP states.

See Index under International Co-operation.

acquisition. The taking over of one firm by another through the purchase of the targeted company's shares. Acquisitions or takeovers, MERGERS and CONSOLIDATIONS represent external expansion as contrasted with a firm's internal expansion: the building of new plant and facilities financed by sales of stock, loans or internal savings. When such external expansion through acquisition takes place in foreign lands, it is contrasted with GRASSROOT ENTRY or GREEN-FIELD INVESTMENT.

See Index under Industry Structure.

administered price. *See* TRANSFER PRICE; ADMINISTRATIVE FIAT.

administrative fiat. A process of making decisions and allocating resources within an enterprise which is derived from the political authority implied in the enterprise's hierarchical organization and not from determinants in the market in which it operates. For instance, investment decisions may be taken by subsidiary companies on the 'say-so' of executive personnel of the parent company, and the reasons why they are taken may go beyond or contravene the rationality of the market in which the subsidiary operates. More commonly, 'administrative fiat' simply becomes a method of establishing prices within the firm in the absence of, or in preference to, the market mechanism. Firms which have internalized commodity, factor and/or financial markets may fix administered prices for the exchange of goods and services between their subsidiaries without reference to market prices.

See also TRANSFER PRICE; ARM'S LENGTH, and Index under Corporate Structure and Management and under Financial and Risk Management.

ad valorem. Latin for 'according to value'. The term is used when TARIFFS or taxes are applied as a percentage of the value of a product, as distinct from those applied on the basis of weight.

affiliate company. In common usage, a company that is linked to another in some way, usually through ownership. A truly 'owned' company is usually described as a SUBSIDI-ARY, but the broader term 'affiliate' or 'affiliated company' may be used to include those linked companies that are not control-led by the MNC's parent. These include JOINT VENTURES and minority-owned affiliates. The US Department of Commerce describes a foreign affiliate as a foreign business enterprise in which the US parent has a direct or indirect ownership of ten per cent or more (*see* BENCHMARK SURVEY. For the UK standard accounting practice, *see* ASSOCIATED COMPANY and for the legal terminology *see* RELATED COMPANY).

See also Index under Corporate Structure and Management.

agency agreement. An agreement between a foreign company and a resident firm or individual in the buyer's country. The role of the agent is to promote, market and distribute the seller's goods. The agent usually does not bear financial responsibility but is paid a commission. The agent is normally responsible for entry/exit details and the necessary co-ordination with appropriate government authorities. The agreement normally covers a definite period of time, terms of sale and method of compensation, and it may be entered upon on an exclusive or nonexclusive basis. In less developed countries it is common for foreign companies to first penetrate the market by means of an agency agreement with politically well-connected residents who identify themselves for this purpose as 'business consultants'. On occasion, agents may act for the exporter's home government (e.g. the Crown Agents in the UK) and combine both selling and purchasing roles.

See also PURCHASING AGENT, and Index under Trade.

Agency for International Development (AID). An agency of the US State Department which administers economic aid under the US foreign assistance programme. The agency was created by the Foreign Assistance Act of 1962. About one half of the economic aid disbursed under the foreign assistance programme is in the form of loans, and nearly all of it carries tied purchase clauses which commit the recipient country to using the funds obtained on the purchase of commodities or technical services in the US. The aid programme is selectively targeted on the nations considered best able to use it.

AID also provides government insurance to US firms or subsidiaries making approved foreign investments in less developed countries. These INVESTMENT GUARANTEES do not protect the investor against ordinary business risks but are shields purely against adverse actions of foreign governments such as EXPROPRIATIONS or unanticipated restrictions on fund transfers.

See also OVERSEAS PRIVATE INVESTMENT CORPORATION (OPIC); EXPORT CREDITS GUARANTEE DEPARTMENT, and Index under International Co-operation.

agency problem. A recently rediscovered problem in the theory of corporate management and finance. It arises because of the opportunities that exist for corporate employees to siphon off a part of corporate RENT or profit. The problem is particularly acute in the case of multinational companies because of the diminution of social and legal control associated with transborder activities.

The agency problem may be solved by the owners in two ways: by providing incentives to the management to bring their interests into line with its own, and by investing in monitoring devices (such as accounting and other information). For his part the manager may provide an incentive for the owner to employ him by investing in guarantees as to his fidelity and willingness to act in the owner's interest. This is known as bonding. One device of the first kind is to provide management with the right to buy shares at below market prices (in particular stock options). However, this avenue is typically not open to employees of multinationals in

host countries as firms will seldom issue extra stock applicable to a subsidiary in a given host country. The implication of this may well be, in agency terms, a necessity to increase the monitoring devices so as to correct the absence of such incentives.

See Index under Corporate Structure and Management.

aggregate concentration. The share of some large segment of the economy (for example all manufacturing) controlled by the largest companies: the top 100 or 500 manufacturing firms, for instance.

See CONCENTRATION.

agreement corporation. A subsidiary of a US bank formed to conduct foreign or international banking, so called because the bank forming the subsidiary enters into an agreement with the Board of Governors of the Federal Reserve System concerning the type of activities that will be undertaken. Unlike the EDGE ACT CORPORATION (EAC), the agreement corporation is registered under US State rather than Federal law, and there are detailed provisions which restrict the activities the corporation may undertake. Nevertheless, such corporations are allowed to transact various kinds of business forbidden to domestic US banks.

See Index under Regulation and Tax.

agribusiness. At first used to describe the type of corporate farming that had expanded very rapidly in the United States during the 1960s and 1970s, the term has now acquired global currency through its use to denote the deployment of corporate power in plantation and non-plantation agriculture.

The essence of corporate farming is the vertical co-ordination of individual farmers' crop production with a company in the food processing and marketing business. Such co-ordination involves a long term contractual selling arrangement, based on futures market prices either of the crop concerned and/or of the food which is the end product: the price of livestock feed, for example, may be linked to the price of turkeys. But this vertical co-ordination is not simply a matter of the FORWARD LINKAGE of farmers' produce to the food processing chain.

In creating and catering for the sophisticated supermarket shelves of the giant retailers in the advanced countries, the food processing and distribution industry requires produce that is not naturally grown. Nature's potatoes are not suitable raw material for commercialized potato crisps, and nature's bananas will not survive the long journey to the supermarket shelves. As a consequence food companies supply their contract farmers with laboratory-developed hybrid varieties of seed and with other industrial farming aids such as fertilizers, herbicides, hormone forcers, specialized ploughs and other production and harvesting tools. In this way, the food processing industry, though it began as 'agro-based', has become industrialized agriculture.

Such agriculture, also known as 'corporate farming', has gone beyond the simple type of capitalistic farming which has been with us for centuries. Whereas capitalistic farming involved the application of man-made techniques of production to maximize output per man hour or per acre, corporate farming is now literally reshaping natural produce for marketing purposes. Corporate farming also alters the traditional capitalist relations of production: the contract farmer is not a capitalist entrepreneur, not an agricultural labourer, and not a feudal serf, but an amalgam of all three. While technically and legally still owning his land and carrying the risk of inclement weather and crop failures, the farmer has none of the decision making responsibilities which are normally the preserve of a capitalist entrepreneur. Yet he is not an agricultural wage labourer,

because his contractual commitments involve a tied relationship more akin to those of feudal land tenure than the free contractual relationship characteristic of the wage labourer and his employer in CAPITALISM.

The pure type of agribusiness firm is a CONGLOMERATE which integrates within its own organizational structure every activity in the chain from sowing and harvesting to marketing. Such vertical integration permits the conglomerate to make monopolistic profits (*see* MONOPOLY) by using TRANSFER PRICING techniques for all its internal transactions. An integrated agribusiness conglomerate will typically encompass, as well as the necessary plantations or contract farmers, divisions which supply seedlings, tractors, fertilizers and pesticides at the resource end and packaging, marketing and even maritime transport to carry food exports on the production end.

By the mid-seventies in the United States corporate farming had become a subject of increasing controversy and 'agribusiness' a term of abuse. Criticisms there centred on the capital- and energy-intensive nature of the new integrated approach, on the indebtedness of contract farmers – which has reached national crisis proportions – and on the deleterious ecological impact of the extensive and at times indiscriminate application of agrochemical products.

But the real groundswell of anti-agribusiness sentiment has followed the spreading of corporate farming into the developing countries. Today, 'agribusiness' is used more as a blanket derogatory term for all multinational food companies (whether they are of the pure integrated type or not) which are transforming traditional food producing areas in the Third World into luxury crop growing areas in order to service their huge markets throughout the world in the advanced countries. Agribusiness enterprises like Del Monte, General Foods and Lonrho contract Third World farmers to grow anything from asparagus to out of season strawberries and jojoba oil.

This extensive use of plantation agriculture by foreign investors in the Third World is of course not new. In the colonial period companies like Unilever produced export crops there for further processing and marketing in the metropolitan countries. But there are certain quantitative and qualitative changes in the vertical integration of Third World agriculture with First World consumption which are new, and it is these adverse changes which have made agribusiness a target for a growing number of activist groups in the advanced countries.

The scale of export crop production has been vastly extended. This has meant that many already hungry nations have shifted from cultivation of local staple food to export crops. For example, data collected by the United Nations Conference on Trade and Development (UNCTAD) (*see* UNCTAD, 1985) show that between 1970 and 1982 per capita food production in Africa declined at a rate of 1 per cent per annum, while the export of food crops increased by an average of 7.1 per cent per annum.

There has also been a shift in the type of crops exported. Throughout the postwar period, traditional export crops from the developing countries (sugar, vegetable oil, and so on) have suffered restrictions in market access to the advanced countries, partly because these countries have become major producers of traditional foodstuffs themselves and have embarked on protectionist measures (such as the European Community (EC)'s Common Agricultural Policy) and partly because of an overall decline in world market demand for such crops. In response to this situation, multinational food companies have directed Third World agriculture farther away from traditional crops and nearer to the production of non-essential luxury crops such as out of season vegetables, animal feed for the rapidly expanding meat requirements of the rich country consumers, and even houseplants

and flowers.

The social relations of international food production have altered too. Established international plantation firms such as the United African Company (a wholly owned subsidiary of Unilever) are removing themselves from the actual production of cash crops, leaving state-owned plantations to find the necessary capital through complex international borrowing arrangements. Yet the concentration of the processing, marketing and distribution of crops in the hands of these giant firms has continued at the same pace as their declining equity exposure in the poorer countries. Since the domestic market for most Third World exports is limited, Third World growers are dependent on the international agribusiness firms for the marketing of their crops. This dependency is magnified by the highly perishable nature of tropical produce. Their strategic position in the marketing and distribution system permits the international agribusiness firms to extract at least as much profit as they would have done if they had participated in the actual growing.

The international firms are contracting more and more smallholders into the production of tropical exports. Such contract farming is patterned on the postwar development of corporate farming in the United States which has already been described, and there are the same corollaries of bondage and indebtedness. In the Third World, however, this bondage and indebtedness, whether of state plantations or individual farmers, is expressed as a foreign exchange constraint. Such a constraint affects the national economy, pushing it deeper and deeper into expanded export-oriented production to service a growing debt burden.

The capital-intensive nature of corporate farming, with its large-scale plantations and mechanized farming methods, creates an unemployed rural proletariat with nowhere to go but the overcrowded cities. Since 1972, when Peru contracted with the American firm Leche Gloria to engage in extensive milk production from a vast dairy herd for export to the United States, no less than 65 per cent of the rural population has become redundant and has flocked to the cities (*see* Versluysen, 1981).

The ecologically damaging effects of extensive use of agrochemical inputs are considered to be greater in the Third World than in the advanced countries, if only because of the illiteracy of the farmers and the virtual absence of legislative and institutional arrangements limiting the use of agrochemical inputs.

A final critique of agribusiness is that it causes a reduction of the existing genetic pool of seed varieties. Extensive use of laboratory- produced seeds over time leads to a disappearance of the natural varieties. Hybrid varieties of seed (now the patented preserve of the agribusiness firms) do not reproduce in nature. They need to be re-applied every time. In this way, the reproductive basis of Third World lands becomes technologically dependent on the industrial and scientific might of the multinational companies of the advanced world.

See also CONCENTRATION; CENTRALIZATION, and Index under Industry Structure.

AID. *See* AGENCY FOR INTERNATIONAL DEVELOPMENT.

alternative technology. *See* APPROPRIATE TECHNOLOGY.

American Depository Receipt (ADR). A system devised to facilitate the ownership of non-US securities by investors in the United States. The issue of ADRs is normally required for a listing on the US stock exchanges and for registering with the SECURITIES AND EXCHANGE COMMISSION (SEC). Foreign companies wishing to internationalize their capital arrange for a US bank or trust company ('the agent', sometimes known as the depository bank) to take a number of their securities. The agent then issues ADRs that correspond to the underlying securities, though quite possibly not on a one-for-one basis: that is, there may be more or fewer ADRs than underlying foreign shares. ADRs are registered and not bearer securities, and investors trade in them just as if they were ordinary securities. Many foreign companies have taken advantage of the system and one, Jaguar, has 40 per cent of its equity in ADRs.

The advantages of the system are that the securities are priced in US dollars so that American investors do not need to assume exchange risks, and they can be easily traded within the USA. Also, they are preferred to US shares by the issuing companies because they avoid the onerous rules set by the SEC. In 1986 there was a proposal by the UK government to impose a five per cent tax on conversions of UK shares into ADRs. The ostensible reason for the tax was to protect the UK securities market by encouraging issues in the UK. However, it was successfully argued that the tax would end their creation, and hence jeopardize prices in the existing secondary market in the USA on the grounds that a lack of new issues would imply a fall in ADR tradeability. Prices subsequently fell in the UK market and the government amended the proposal to the actual tax now levied of 1.5 per cent.

See Index under Regulation and Tax.

American selling price. A price imputed to goods by the US customs for the purpose of assessing duty payable, based on the price of similar goods in the US domestic market. At the time of writing this applied only to a few categories of goods.

See Index under Trade.

Andean Group. *See* ANDEAN PACT COUNTRIES.

Andean Pact Countries. Group of countries in the Andean subregion of Latin America, set up in 1969 with the aim of expediting Andean economic integration within the larger structure and legal framework of the Latin American Free Trade Association (LAFTA). (LAFTA was succeeded in 1980 by the Latin American Integration Association, LAIA). LAFTA's failure to develop a common market along European lines prompted the smaller countries of the region to establish a subregional group by special Treaty. The basic aims of the group are to promote balance and harmonious development of member countries; to achieve a constant improvement in the standards of living of all the people in the Andean region; and to facilitate participation in the process of Latin American integration, with the aim of achieving equitable distribution of the benefits of integration amongst participating countries.

Although the Treaty was signed in Bogota, it is officially known as the 'Cartagena Agreement' in honour of the location where conclusive negotiations took place. At the time of the ratification of the Treaty in 1969 there were five member countries: Chile, Bolivia, Colombia, Ecuador and Peru. Venezuela joined in 1973. Chile, however, withdrew its membership in 1976 after a dispute on the common rules governing inward foreign investments. Indeed, it is these rules for which the Andean Group is best known throughout the world.

Conscious of the problem of technological dependence and anxious to ensure that direct foreign investment and technology transfer make an effective contribution to national and regional development, the Andean Group adopted Decision 24 in 1970 on the 'Common Treatment for Foreign Capital, Trademarks, Patents, Licensing Agreements and Royalties'. Decision 24 contains two sets of measures: those governing inward foreign direct investment and those regulating the transfer of technology. Among the former are provisions which limit the foreign ownership of local firms to

49 per cent and which set completion dates for the divestment of shares by those foreign owners wishing to benefit from tariff liberalization in intraregional trade; limit the repatriation of profits to 14 per cent of registered capital per year; prohibit reinvestment by foreign firms of more than 5 per cent annually without review and approval; limit the access of foreign firms to medium and long term local credit, and bind the members to create a network for the exchange of information relevant to direct foreign investment and technology transfer including data on the pricing of intermediate products. Among the latter are provisions which set up national agencies for the registration and review of all technology transfer contracts; require the identification of the value of each element in the technology package to be imported; prohibit restrictive clauses formerly incorporated in technology contracts, and provide for the development of a programme to promote the generation of APPROPRIATE TECHNOLOGY in the sub-region.

Decision 24 is generally seen as the most detailed example of intergovernmental HARMONIZATION of policies on foreign investment yet implemented and it is often presented in the literature as a model for other developing countries to adopt. However, research has suggested that the absence of social forces supportive of the regulation in all of the member countries has now led to attempts to modify Decision 24 and to divergencies in its implementation by national authorities (*see* Mytelka, 1976). Besides, one of the consequences of Decision 24 was to cause US divestment from the subscribing countries. This in turn led to the liberalization of much of their legislation with a view to attract US foreign investment back.

See CODES OF CONDUCT, TRANSFER OF TECHNOLOGY (TOT) CODE, and Index under Regulation and Tax and under International Co-operation.

Address: Paseo de la Republica y Andres Aramburo, PO Box 3237, Lima, Peru.

Anstalt. A form of organization in the principality of Liechtenstein that is popular as a vehicle for tax avoidance with non-Liechtenstein nationals, both corporate and personal. The Anstalt has limited liability and can trade as a body corporate: once registered by a Liechtenstein national it can be transferred to other ownership without the change being publicly registered. Liechtenstein is a TAX HAVEN, and the use of the Anstalt form may therefore have further tax advantages over the use of the normal corporate form *(Aktiengesellschaft)*.

See STIFTUNG and Index under Regulation and tax.

Anti-Trust Division. The Anti-trust Division of the US Department of Justice was established in 1903 and has responsibility for enforcing the Sherman Anti-Trust Act and, together with the FEDERAL TRADE COMMISSION (FTC), the CLAYTON ACT.

See ANTI-TRUST LEGISLATION, and Index under Regulation and Tax.

anti-trust legislation. Beginning with the Sherman Anti-Trust Act of 1890, there has been a series of Acts in the US, as well as a very substantial amount of case law designed to break up monopolies and curtail price fixing and other restrictive business practices with the aim of fostering competitive forces in a free market system.

While the term 'trust' refers strictly speaking to an amalgamation of firms, anti-trust legislation and court rulings have been directed towards both single firms who exercise monopoly power in the market and to groups of co-operating firms (which in other countries would be referred to as CARTELS). US anti-trust legislation specifically prohibits:

1. Contracts, combinations and conspir-

acies in restraint of trade;
2. monopolization, attempts to monopolize, and conspiracies to monopolize trade or commerce within the United States or between the United States and foreign countries;
3. price discrimination that substantially reduces competition or that tends to create a monopoly;
4. tying clauses and exclusive-dealing agreements that adversely affect competition;
5. mergers which substantially lessen competition;
6. interlocking directorates among competing firms.

Although there is some similarity between US anti-trust and British anti-monopoly legislation, there are both qualitative and quantitative differences. Much of US anti-trust legislation is principled and non-discriminatory; that is, it identifies certain practices and types of co-operation as illegal *per se*. UK legislation is pragmatic and discretionary, deciding on the merits and demerits of individual cases in the light of the public interest. US anti-trust policy is, moreover, very much greater in scope, not least because of its inclusion of the 'intent' clause. For instance, a company may be convicted of a criminal conspiracy to monopolize a market, even when it holds a relatively small share of this market, such conspiracy being inferred by the court on the grounds of observed 'non-normal' business practices. The only important exception to the anti-trust rules are rights conferred by PATENTS, but here too the exemptions are far from absolute.

It is sometimes argued that the success of US anti-trust policy has diverted US corporate growth into two directions: CONGLOMERATE expansion and foreign expansion. In the case of conglomerate expansion, the merging with or the taking over of firms across different branches of industry generally tends to fall outside the scope of anti-trust policy (*see* CLAYTON ACT and CELLER-KEFAUVER AMENDMENT). In the case of foreign expansion, the application of US anti-trust legislation in foreign lands has been restrained because of the principle of territorial limitation accepted in international law (*see* EXTRATERRITORIALITY).

While US anti-trust policy does not directly address the problem of FOREIGN DIRECT INVESTMENT, it nevertheless scrutinizes the restricting impact of such investments on US domestic commerce and import/export trade. A US parent, whose foreign subsidiaries' price-discriminating exports to the American domestic market cause a substantial reduction of competition there, may be deemed to violate anti-trust legislation just as surely as if it had served this market from its home base. Equally, the force of anti-trust legislation is applied to competition-lessening effects of inward foreign investments.

Since the Second World War, US anti-trust policy has developed a more resolutely international angle. Whereas before the argument that US firms should be free to participate in foreign cartels to claim their share of foreign markets had prevailed, this position was abandoned in two celebrated Supreme Court cases of 1945: *US v. Aluminium Company of America,* and *US v. National Lead Company et al.* The *per se* illegality of price-fixing, market allocation and other naked restraints on trade were deemed to apply to foreign commerce and not just domestic commerce. In the case of *US v. Imperial Chemical Industries* of 1951, the Court went further still, judging that a Canadian venture jointly acquired by ICI and du Pont unreasonably restricted du Pont's exports to Canada. ICI and du Pont were convicted of conspiracy to monopolize and their Canadian joint venture ordered to be dissolved.

Attempts on the part of the US Justice Department to extend the jurisdiction of anti-trust legislation to the foreign subsidiaries of American parent companies has on many occasions brought it into conflict with the national laws and interests of the countries in which US subsidiaries operate. Co-ordination of national anti-trust policies among concerned states may be one answer to this problem. The US has concluded formal agreements for co-operation in anti-trust matters with a few countries, including the Federal Republic of Germany, Canada and Australia. International anti-trust co-ordination under the auspices of the United Nations might be another solution. The UNITED NATIONS CONFERENCE ON TRADE AND DEVELOPMENT (UNCTAD) for example, in its draft TRANSFER OF TECHNOLOGY (TOT) CODE provides for notification of anti-trust investigations and cases and for consultation in such matters with a view to minimizing jurisdictional conflict. (*See also* EFFECTS PRINCIPLE.)

Like US anti-trust policy, that of the EUROPEAN COMMUNITY (EC) too is a policy based on principle, defining the *per se* illegality of certain anti-competitive practices (Article 85 of the Treaty of Rome) and of abuses of market domination (Article 86). Particular reference is made to four types of abuse of market domination:

(a) the imposition of unfair prices, or other unfair trading conditions;
(b) restraints on production, markets or technical developments to the prejudice of consumers;
(c) the imposition of dissimilar trading conditions so as to place certain trading parties at a comparative disadvantage;
(d) the imposition of supplementary obligations which have no connection with the subject of the contract as a condition of acceptance.

Cases of abuse may be taken by the EC Commission to the EC Court of Justice in Luxembourg, or they may be initiated by civil action on the part of companies which feel that they have been damaged by a dominant firm's (or OLIGOPOLY's) abuse of prevailing conditions.

Since the initial formulation of Article 86,

several Court judgements have extended the scope of the Commission's powers in respect of anti-trust actions. In a case involving Continental Can in 1973, the Court decided that attainment of dominance in itself may be considered an abusive practice within the terms of Article 86 if such dominance is obtained by external ACQUISITION instead of internal growth. Further, in the EC Commission's action against United Brands in 1978, the Court adjudicated that dominance could be defined at levels as low as 45 per cent of the relevant market, while in the Hoffman La Roche judgement a year later, the Court vastly expanded the range of anti-competitive or exclusionary practices indictable under Article 86.

The Commission's current battle against the abuse of unrestrained economic power is sometimes charged with being particularly targeted on non-EC giants; for example, cases have recently been brought against the American giant IBM and the Japanese conglomerate Pioneer. While this charge would be officially denied there is no doubt that efforts undertaken by other EC directorates to strengthen European industrial development – especially in advanced technology areas – generates both the documentation and the agenda for action to be considered by the directorate responsible for EC competition policy.

There is a further aspect of interesting historical significance. Much of the Commission's determination to safeguard competition within the common market is directed against collusive agreements by non-EC multinationals which have the effect of repartitioning the common market into separate national markets, for example export bans which hinder 'parallel imports' (i.e. from one EC country into another). Historically, the formation of the European common market has had the enthusiastic support of American multinationals. Some would even argue that it was in part the outcome of their intense lobbying during the formulation of the terms for the immediate postwar Marshall Aid programme for Europe. But today the profit strategies of multinational corporations are sometimes less influenced by the search for large integrated markets than by the desire to exploit location-specific differences between national markets (*see* INTERNALIZATION THEORY). Thus, the formation and the strengthening of the common market now pose a challenge to American multinationals which has emerged from the very aims that they originally sought to achieve.

See Index under Regulation and Tax.

appropriability theory. A theory of FOREIGN DIRECT INVESTMENT (FDI) developed by Magee (1977). By 'appropriability' is meant the ability of private originators of ideas to obtain for themselves the pecuniary value of the ideas to society.

The point of departure for the theory is that firms in industries in which demand for new products is high have to invest in the creation of five types of information: product creation; product development; production functions, markets and appropriability itself. 'Information' is an intangible asset, the returns on which the firm needs to protect in a market where this information may more or less easily become distributed as a public good. This is the problem of appropriability.

The general proposition of the theory is that the more uncertain the appropriability of the returns on information-investment, the more likely it is that the firm will wish to exploit the investment itself. This could explain the growth of firm size. At the international level (where variations in the efficiency of legal systems to protect private inventions lead to even greater uncertainty) this involves entering the foreign markets via direct international investments which ensure ownership and control over foreign operations, rather than through LICENSING and other forms of CROSS-BORDER TRANSACTIONS.

In its general proposition the theory has much in common with that of the theory of INTERNALIZATION THEORY. Appropriability theory however goes beyond the general internalization proposition in its specific and dynamic hypotheses. These are derived from the introduction into the internalization model of the two variables which most affect appropriability, namely the efficiency of the legal system in preserving appropriability (this varies with each type of information, it being typically less secure with process technology than with product creation, *see* PATENT) and the industry structure, which goes through a technology cycle parallel to that of Vernon's product cycle (*see* PRODUCT CYCLE THEORY). In this way Magee claims to have developed a model which predicts optimum firm size.

Of interest are the provocative policy implications for less developed countries on the issue of technology transfer and multinational corporations which the theory presents as logical corollary of its propositions.

First, it is pointed out that multinational corporations are typically firms that are specialists in the production of information that is less efficient to transmit through markets than within firms. They typically produce sophisticated, skill-intensive technologies because appropriability is higher for these than for simple, unskilled, labour producing technologies. For example superior labour-intensive organization of production functions which can easily be copied may be socially useful, but it is not of economic interest to a multinational. There is a contradiction in demanding of MNCs that they produce APPROPRIATE TECHNOLOGY for less developed countries, because of the low appropriability of such technologies. Instead, such technologies should come from government-financed research or from government tax-subsidy incentives. Second, Magee suggests that less developed countries should modify their patent legislation in line with their need for simple tech-

nology. Because of the simplicity of the types of information demanded in less developed countries, it is appropriate for them to have patents that are easier to obtain and of shorter duration than those obtaining in the advanced countries whose patent system the less developed countries have usually adopted.

See Index under Theoretical Issues.

appropriate technology. A set of specially designed techniques which make optimum use of available resources in a given environment to produce goods that are compatible with that environment.

The concept of appropriate technology is often used interchangeably with that of INTERMEDIATE TECHNOLOGY. Strictly speaking, however, appropriate technology has emerged as a sequel to intermediate technology, embracing not merely production technologies which would be relevant to the available resource mix in less developed countries, but also consumer products which are consistent with the physical environment, cultural capabilities and social needs. Dried baby milk, for instance, which requires literate mothers to use it as well as a clean water supply, is inappropriate in many less developed countries.

More recently, the concept of appropriate technology has been generalized still further to refer to the compatibility of *any* environment, including that of advanced countries where concern with conditions of work and environmental effects of technology have added new dimensions. Appropriate technology may thus be very widely defined as being sensitive to human needs, optimizing the use of indigenous resources, protecting the environment, minimizing frustrations and unpleasant aspects of work, providing for increased worker and consumer participation in decision processes, reducing physical risks to workers and encouraging equitable income distribution.

A large proportion of all technology acquired by the less developed countries is transferred through the global networks of multinational companies. Such companies typically standardize process and product technology on a worldwide basis, and often (though not always) ignore local conditions, and they have consequently been a main target of criticism in the appropriate technology debate. Academic interest in the subject has been reflected in the mushrooming of many voluntary, and some government-sponsored, appropriate technology research establishments in the advanced countries. The practical use of the appropriate technology idea is nevertheless in some doubt. This is not only because it is anathema to powerful commercial interests, but because the less-developed nations which are a market for exported technology display at least a political scepticism, if not outright rejection, of it. Many of these countries see appropriate or intermediate technology as a 'second-best' option designed to prevent them from catching up with fully industrialized countries.

Besides the term 'intermediate technology' one may also encounter the words 'alternative technology' and 'relevant technology' as synonyms for appropriate technology.

See Index under Technology Transfer.

arbi-loan. A term sometimes used to describe short-term finance that is raised abroad for a fixed period, the borrower simultaneously purchasing in the forward market the foreign currency that will be needed to repay the loan.

See HEDGING, and Index under Financial and Risk Management.

arbitrage. A means of profiting by the differences between prices in markets which has traditionally concerned markets for securities, commodities and currencies.

We take currencies as our example. The continuous transactions taking place in individual national financial markets lead to prices based on the forces of demand and supply in those markets. At any point in time these may differ: that is the exchange rates of the same two currencies may be different in two separate financial centres. Arbitrageurs buy a currency in the market where it is cheaper and sell it in the market where it is dearer. The result will be to equalize the prices in the different markets since the purchase in the cheaper market tends to drive the price up and the sale in the dearer market drives it down. Arbitrage operations continue until the two markets display equal prices.

Arbitrage operations are also possible where three or more currencies are involved, and profit can be made by buying and selling among the three, taking advantage of the fact that the bilateral exchange rates (for instance, A into B, B into C and C into A) are not perfectly in line.

It is generally argued that the existence of arbitrageurs is the force that makes financial markets so efficient, since they equalize information and prices.

Securities arbitrage takes place where corporate securities are traded on more than one stock exchange (whether within one country, or across different countries). If the price of the security changes on one exchange and not others, the arbitrageur can simultaneously buy and sell in different markets, thus making profit and equalizing the prices in the markets (subject to transaction costs).

Arbitrage operations are also crucial to various theories of international economics such as the INTEREST RATE PARITY theory (*see also* COVERED INTEREST ARBITRAGE). Traditionally they have also been significant for the theory of multinational enterprise, through capital arbitrage theory. This explained the existence of FOREIGN DIRECT INVESTMENT (FDI) by pointing to the different rates of return on capital available. FDI took place when higher returns could be earned abroad: and this implied a higher marginal productivity of capital abroad. *Ceteris paribus,* the arbitrage effect of FDI would be to tend to equalize the marginal productivity of capital among countries and hence equalize welfare. Evidence by Hymer and others (*see* OLIGOPOLY MODEL) has now discredited this theory.

Capital arbitrage differs from the other types so far described, because it involves an element of risk. Various kinds of risk arbitrage exist; for example, tendency arbitrage is a term that has been used to describe the operation in which an arbitrageur buys a currency in one market believing he knows of willing buyers in another market who will be prepared to buy at a higher price a short time after. This is still considered to be an arbitrage operation despite the risk element because it is concerned with profit making from market differences, and tends to equalize prices in such markets. More important today is merger arbitrage. In its simplest form this takes place when a bid is announced, the bid price differs from the market price, and the arbitrageur's analysis of the likely outcome leads him to believe he can profit from buying in the market for later sale to the bidder.

More recently, usage of the term has been extended to include tax arbitrage, which is the transfer of profit from one country to another so as to benefit from different tax rates or structures (although clearly the result here has been a number of attempts to obstruct the arbitrage operation rather than harmonize tax systems: *see* TRANSFER PRICE).

See also Index under Theoretical Issues, and under Financial and Risk Management.

arbitrage pricing theory (APT). A theory that purports to explain the pricing of any security by reference to a set of factors. Unlike the CAPITAL ASSET PRICING MODEL (CAPM) which takes the price to be dependent on two factors alone (the risk-free mar-

ket rate and the market portfolio), there could be any number of factors that affect the market price according to the APT. The model is abstract and does not specify what these factors are: they could vary from one security to another. Although proposed in 1976, the theory has presented considerable testing difficulties, and is still far more tentative than the capital asset pricing model.

See Index under Theoretical Issues, and under Financial and Risk Management.

arm's length. A term used to describe any transaction or relationship that is based on free negotiation between unconnected parties in a market. It is important to the multinational company, because a number of practices that the integrated multinational finds attractive may not seem so palatable to the countries across whose borders the practices operate. To counter this, such practices are judged by the countries concerned on the touchstone of what would have taken place between parties at arm's length rather than what actually happens when one (the subsidiary) is owned by the other (the parent). Chief among these is TRANSFER PRICING of goods and services where the acceptability of an administered transfer price (that is, the judgement as to whether it is manipulated), will depend on a comparison wherever possible with a price negotiated at arm's length in a free market. Other examples include management fees and ROYALTY payments.

See TRANSFER PRICE; ADMINISTRATIVE FIAT, and Index under Corporate Structure and Management.

ASC. *See* ACCOUNTING STANDARDS COMMITTEE.

Asiadollar. A dollar traded in the ASIAN CURRENCY MARKET in the same way that the EURODOLLAR is traded in the EUROCURRENCY market.

Asia Monitor Resource Center (AMRC). A non-profit making independent group based in Hong Kong, providing a research and information service on foreign economic activity in Asia. AMRC prepares organized and easy to use information on various industries, corporations, financial and natural resources and offers them to researchers in Asia and abroad.

Although AMRC files information on all major businesses it has more comprehensive records on the operations of US corporations in Asia, which have been monitored since 1976.

It publishes a bimonthly *Asia Labour Monitor* and two quarterly magazines: *Asia Monitor* and *Asia Book Monitor*.

See Index under Data Sources.
Address: 2 Man Wan Road, 18C, Kowloon, Hong Kong.

Asian Currency Market. A market based in Singapore that operates in a similar way to the EUROCURRENCY market. It is based in Singapore because of the absence of market restrictions such as those found in the other major Eastern financial centres, Hong Kong and Tokyo. Most of the dealings of the market are in US dollars.

See also ASIADOLLAR.

Associated company. A term defined by the ACCOUNTING STANDARDS COMMITTEE (ASC) as 'not being a subsidiary of the investing group or company in which:
(a) the interest of the investing group or company is effectively that of a partner in a joint venture or consortium, and the investing group or company is in a position to exercise a significant influence over the company in which the investment is made; or
(b) the interest of the investing group or company is for the long-term and is substantial and, having regard to the disposition of the other shareholdings, the investing

group or company is in a position to exercise a significant influence over the company in which the investment is made' (ASC 1971, revised 1982).

Until the Companies Act of 1981, UK legislation did not define associated companies. But the Companies Act of 1981 did introduce the term RELATED COMPANY, defining it in substantially the same way as the ASC's associated company.

See also AFFILIATE COMPANY; SUBSIDIARY, and Index under Corporate Structure and Management.

Auditing. The certification of a corporation's financial statements. In certain developed countries with extensive capital markets, a well-established accounting profession, and a recognition of the importance of the corporate audit by the government, it has become an accepted principle that auditing firms, legally separate from the clients, conduct an independent investigation of the truth of the accounting statements which a company proposes to publish. From their base in these countries (the UK and USA in particular, but also some countries of the 'old commonwealth' and certain European countries, particularly Holland) the giant INTERNATIONAL AUDITING FIRMS have developed to a size comparable to that of the major multinational corporations.

Audit varies between countries, and these variations may take account of
(a) the acknowledged purpose of the audit, which may variously include the detection of material error, the detection of fraud, and the efficiency of management practices;
(b) the kinds of business entity that statutorily or otherwise require an audit. Audit may be required only above a certain minimum size, or only for a certain type of legal entity, or only for entities quoted on a recognized securities market. It may or may not entail a report to the legal authorities;
(c) the duties of the auditor. These may be superficial or very thorough;

(d) the independence of the auditor from either the client company or any ancillary business of its own such as a management consultancy. Auditors may be prohibited from owning shares in a client company, for example. On the other hand, the auditors may, far from being independent, constitute an *ad hoc* group drawn from the ranks of the shareholders;

(e) the length of the audit report which may be just two lines or run to a number of paragraphs;

(f) the criteria that govern the way the audit report is framed. This may be in terms of 'generally accepted accounting principles', or conformity to the law; it may also incorporate commentary upon the quality of the management.

Creating uniformity in auditing practices and raising the quality of auditing to a minimum standard have been the main objectives of the standard-setting processes and pronouncement of the INTERNATIONAL FEDERATION OF ACCOUNTANTS and of the UNION EUROPEENE DES EXPERTS COMPTABLES ECONOMIQUES ET FINANCIERS (UEC). Uniformity has in fact been substantially achieved within the large international audit firms, which standardized their worldwide procedures in international practice manuals. Almost all the major multinational companies are now audited by these international audit firms and the growth of one has been parallelled by the growth of the other. However, sometimes a subsidiary of a multinational cannot be audited by an office of the group's auditing firm, either because its operations do not extend to what is perhaps a small country, or because local regulations preclude foreign auditors from practising. In such a case a local audit firm will be used which will report to the principal auditor.

See Index under International Accounting.

Australia–Asia Worker Links (AAWL). An independent, non-profit making information and resource group aimed at linking the workers of Australia and Asia. The group has carried out campaigns in support of Asian workers. It publishes two newsletters: *Asian Workers Organising* and *Australian Workers' News,* plus occasional case study leaflets focusing on a particular issue or company.

AAWL runs the Asian Workers Solidarity Links programme which identifies problems facing workers in the region, and is particularly concerned with the global policies of the multinational and their impact on local industry and employment.

See Index under Data Sources.
Address: PO Box 264 Fitzroy, Victoria 3065, Australia.

Autarchy. Policy of economic self-sufficiency which implies discouragement of imports including imports of capital and capital goods.

See also DELINKING; OPEN DOOR POLICIES; SELF-RELIANCE, and Index under Development Policy.

Authorization procedures. All countries in the world today require intending inward foreign investors to seek formal permission for their investment from the national authorities. Sometimes new direct investment by established resident foreign-controlled enterprises also requires prior authorization.

Authorization procedures vary in scope and restrictiveness. In some countries authorization is automatic and differs little from a request for prior 'notification', while in others inward investment proposals have to meet stringent performance criteria. But all countries prohibit investment in some sectors (the UK, for example, in nationalized industries) and limit foreign ownership in others.

See PERFORMANCE REQUIREMENTS, and Index under Regulation and Tax.

avoir fiscale. An imputation credit that can be claimed by recipients of dividends from tax-paying French companies (*see under* CORPORATE TAX SYSTEM).

B

back to back loans. A mechanism used by multinationals to make foreign currency available to their subsidiaries. The term is sometimes used interchangeably with PARALLEL LOAN, but strictly speaking it refers to a more complex arrangement which, unlike a parallel loan, involves a cross-border flow of funds. In such an arrangement, the parent companies of two multinationals based in different home countries lend sums to each other, each loan being denominated in the parent's home currency. Each parent immediately lends to its subsidiary in the other country the currency it has just borrowed from the other parent. Interest will probably differ depending on current conditions in the countries concerned. Each loan acts as (possibly partial) collateral for the other.

See also CURRENCY EXCHANGE AGREEMENT, and Index under Financial and Risk Management.

backward linkages. The stimulation of local supply and service industries as a result of the establishment of a domestically- or foreign-owned production unit. The linking of such industries is deemed to go 'backward' into a preceding stage of production, as when, for example, the introduction of a match factory stimulates the local wood processing industries. Backward linkages are often part of the PERFORMANCE REQUIREMENTS for new inward foreign investment.

See also FORWARD LINKAGES, and Index under Development Policy.

Badger case. A celebrated case of successful citation of the OECD guidelines on multinational enterprises in influencing multinational company behaviour (*see* DECLARATION AND DECISIONS ON INTERNATIONAL INVESTMENTS AND MULTINATIONAL ENTERPRISES).

The case was the first to be brought before the OECD's Committee on International Investments and Multinational Enterprises (*see* COMMITTEE ON INTERNATIONAL INVESTMENT AND MULTINATIONAL ENTERPRISES (CIME) by the TRADE UNION ADVISORY COMMITTEE (TUAC) of the OECD under the Clarification and Review Procedure of the Guidelines).

The dispute involved the closure – allegedly without reasonable prior notification or compensation to the workforce – of the Badger Company. This was a wholly-owned Belgian subsidiary of the American multinational Raytheon. The unions, and the Belgian Government, claimed that in such cases the parent company – according to the Guidelines – is obliged to help its subsidiaries fulfil their obligations.

While this view was not wholly accepted by the OECD IME committee, it did nevertheless express the opinion that in respect of closure, lay-offs and dismissals, the parent company did have obligations going beyond those required from them by law. In saying this, the Committee re-affirmed and clarified the meaning of Section 6 of the chapter on Employment and Industrial Relations of the Guidelines.

As a result of the pressures from the discussion within the OECD, from the Belgian Government and from other governments playing host to Raytheon subsidiaries, the parent company backed down and agreed a settlement in April 1977.

The Badger case is important since it lends support to the cause of those – within

18

EC policymaking circles, for example – who wish to redefine the legal status of corporate groups with a view to restricting the claim to limited liability of parent companies in relation to their subsidiaries.

See EUROPEAN COMMUNITY (EC), and Index under Dispute and Settlement.

balance of payments. A nation's balance of payments is a statistical statement summarizing all the external transactions in which it is involved over a given period of time. These transactions are usually divided into two groups, current account and capital account. The current account includes 'visible' trade transactions and 'invisibles' like payments for services such as insurance, shipping and tourism, but also transfers of interest, profits, royalties and dividends currently earned on assets. The capital account includes all inward and outward flows of money arising from investments and international grants and loans.

The impact of FOREIGN DIRECT INVESTMENT (FDI), most of which is generated by multinational companies, on the balance of payments is naturally of concern to home and host countries alike. Mirrored sets of controversies arise, depending on whether one examines the balance of payments position from the perspective of the home or the host country.

For capital exporting countries, the important questions are, first, if and when the outflow of capital is matched by a return flow arising from 'invisibles', that is, repatriation of profits and payment of royalties and payment of other technology and service payments. Early studies in the US have put these 'payout recoupment periods' anywhere between 10 and 20 years (*see* Bell, 1962). Over a longer period return flows will tend to exceed outflows. A recent study of British multinationals notes a similar positive effect (*see* Stopford & Turner, 1985).

A second and more contentious issue is whether capital exports are compensated by return flows arising from 'visible' trade transactions. While critics of the multinationals in the home countries point to the 'export displacement' effect of foreign direct investments, the multinationals have tended to defend themselves at home by arguing – in line with the PRODUCT CYCLE thesis – that at the time they make their foreign investments, competitive pressures abroad are causing a decline of exports, so that the only means of maintaining their market position is production in the relevant foreign market. They claim that by undertaking foreign production, they ensure a future flow of exports, as overseas subsidiaries are serviced and supplied by the parent company. And indeed, most of the economic evidence from the US, Sweden and the UK show positive net export effects.

Capital importing countries are concerned that a net inflow on the capital account should rapidly be offset by a net outflow on the current account, as repatriation of profits over time has an adverse effect on the balance of payments position, and the imports generated by inward investments also deplete the current account still further, although inward investment can also of course bring about new export trade which offsets this depletion – as in the case of the NEWLY INDUSTRIALIZING COUNTRIES.

On the first issue, multinationals will point to the re-investment of earnings locally, a re-investment which is usually the result of pressure from host countries. Today it is estimated that nearly 60 per cent of all global direct investments consist of such re-invested earnings. However, since very few countries record such re-invested earnings correctly as an outflow on the home country's current account and an inflow on the host country's capital account respectively, the distributional effects of such re-investments on worldwide balance of payments positions are impossible to assess. Even so, the less developed host countries worry about one logical consequence. Re-invested earnings increase the capital base of the subsidiary in the host country, which are denominated in local currency, and the ground is prepared for a larger volume of future repatriated profits, which are after all payable in foreign exchange.

The second issue is the trade-related effects on the balance of payments. Here too the MNCs are caught in the inter-nation zero sum game of their own strategies: the supposed export benefits to the home nation appear as import costs – and hence foreign exchange losses – to the host nation. Such apparent losses invite criticism and increasingly stringent import controls on the part of host nations, which of course lead ultimately to export displacement for the home nation.

Even if inward foreign direct investment has negative long-term effects upon the balance of payments of less developed host countries, a negative impact on the national income does not necessarily follow. Independent studies sponsored by the ORGANIZATION FOR ECONOMIC CO-OPERATION AND DEVELOPMENT (OECD) and the UNITED NATIONS CONFERENCE ON TRADE AND DEVELOPMENT (UNCTAD) in the 1970s examined manufacturing investments by foreign capital in developing nations, and although each assessed the impact on the national income in quite different terms, both concluded that such investments need not harm the home country's economy. The authors of the OECD study assumed that the alternative to foreign direct investment is no investment and no production at all, the so-called 'zero-hypothesis', and they assessed whatever LOCAL VALUE ADDED had resulted from foreign investment as a positive impact on national income (*see* Bos, Sanders & Secchi, 1974.) The authors of the UNCTAD study used a more sophisticated set of assumptions to calculate the national income impact of FDI. They compared the net benefits to national income not with a 'zero' alternative, but in relation to the net benefits of either importing the product or obtaining the capital in non-equity form (that is, indirect investments through bank borrowings). They found, in contrast to the OECD study, that the net effects on domestic income varied widely from country to country, depending on the nature of host government intervention. They concluded that projects must be viewed individually as far as their effects on the net social income are concerned, and that domestic policies play an important role in maximizing these net social income effects (*see* Lall & Streeten, 1978).

See Index under Development Policy, and under Regulation and Tax.

balance sheet hedge. *See* HEDGE.

The Banker. Leading English monthly magazine covering international finance and banking. A special issue in June carries a list of the top 500 banks ranked by various criteria.

See Index under Data Sources.

banker's acceptance. A draft or BILL OF EXCHANGE that has been accepted by a bank and thus may be bought and sold in the short-term money market.

Barcelona Traction case. A celebrated and controversial case of adjudication by the INTERNATIONAL COURT OF JUSTICE (ICJ). In the case, heard in 1970, the court held that Belgium lacked *jus standi* to present the claim of Belgian stockholders in a Canadian corporation allegedly put out of business by acts attributable to Spain. Its dictum upheld the traditional place of incorporation rule, by which the right of a corporate entity to diplomatic protection is attributed to the state in which it is legally incorporated and in whose territory it has its registered office (in the Barcelona Traction case, this state was Canada). In doing so, the Court appeared to deny the right of individual stockholders to diplomatic protection by their own national authorities – in this case, Belgium.

See also NOTTEBOHM CASE, and Index under Dispute and Settlement.

barriers to entry. A term used in the literature of economics and ascribed to Joe Bain (1956). It refers to the OWNERSHIP SPECIFIC ADVANTAGES of large firms dominating markets at home or abroad which exclude potential entrants into the industry because of the costs of duplicating the original innovation, or because of the expenditure required to achieve the same economies of scale, research and development, advertising and so on.

See Index under Theoretical Issues.

barriers to exit. A term coined by Caves and Porter (1976) to denote the opposite of BARRIERS TO ENTRY. Barriers to exit are assets which a firm is unwilling to liquidate because they represent non-recoverable costs owing to their limited marketability. Examples of such assets might be durable plant and equipment, advertising expenditures, human resources specific to the firm (such as management expertise) and expenditure on R&D. In other words, the firm is bound to its market because it is unable to divest.

In the case of multinational companies, it has been argued that because their foreign subsidiaries deploy assets created by their parents, the costs of liquidating such assets is relatively lower than for domestic firms.

See Index under Theoretical Issues.

barter. The exchange of goods and services without the use of a generalized medium of exchange, that is, money. While barter trade within national economies is generally speaking a thing of the past, and associated with primitive, cashless communities, inter-national barter trade has occurred throughout modern history whenever global liquidity problems have severely limited national capabilities to maintain vital imports or to service existing debts. Argentina, for example, resorted to barter trade extensively in the 1880s and 1890s, while Germany did the same in the reparations and debt repayment years of the 1920s. Hitler used barter to obtain strategic materials from his colonies, and the Japanese too – in the 1930s – engaged in barter-type transactions with South East Asian nations within their sphere of influence.

But such resort to international barter trade was intermittent and sporadic. In recent years barter deals have made a comeback on a very considerable scale. A combination of unstable foreign exchange markets, the debt explosion and chronic foreign exchange shortages on the part of Eastern bloc and less developed countries, have prompted the emergence of new and sophisticated forms of barter trade, today better known under the label COUNTER-TRADE.

See Index under Technology Transfer and under Trade.

base company. A subsidiary of a multinational corporation organized under the laws of a TAX HAVEN country which holds or controls the corporation's other foreign operating subsidiaries. For example, under the laws of Antigua, Barbados and Jamaica, as well as other tax haven islands, such a HOLDING COMPANY may be registered as an 'International Business Company' and is liable only to two and a half per cent income tax on investment income after deducting management expenses. Dividends paid to non-resident shareholders are also subject to a mere two and a half per cent WITHHOLDING TAX.

See Index under Financial and Risk Management.

basic needs. A concept that represents a new departure in development literature, because it defines the eradication of absolute poverty, and not national economic growth, as the central objective of development strategies. The concept has gained popularity in international organizations and in negotiating fora of international development assistance. The term was first coined by a group of Latin American scholars in a document spelling out an alternative development strategy for the THIRD WORLD (*see* Herrera *et al.*, 1976).

Since the late 1960s the rapid growth of some Third World countries has contrasted sharply not only with the stagnation and decline of others, sometimes called FOURTH WORLD countries, but also with the relative pauperization of large sections of the population within the successfully developing countries themselves. Consequently, development assistance organizations have become increasingly concerned about the failure of conventional 'growth'-oriented economic planning.

In the early 1970s, the WORLD BANK and various suborganizations of the UN, such as the ILO, emphasized *redistribution and employment* programmes. It was argued, contrary to mainstream development economic theory, that objectives of growth and of income distribution must be pursued simultaneously. The basic needs strategy was a logical next step and a radical extension of this programme. Instead of justifying the new poverty focus as a means to national economic growth, its aims were to eradicate absolute poverty and to meet the basic human survival needs of the world's poor.

Although the basic needs approach is neither a coherent theory nor a methodologically consistent development programme, a number of loosely-knit themes commonly surface. Basic needs are recognized as being of two kinds: (1) material needs necessary for physical survival, such as food, shelter, clothing, access to water, hygiene, and health, and (2) non-material needs, such as education, fundamental human rights and 'participation', which is conceived of in the widest sense so as to include employment, political decision making, and participation in national cultural life. Basic needs are ackowledged to vary in place and time: as countries become richer, so the definition of minimal survival will be adjusted upwards.

There is some consensus that basic need satisfaction requires policies of SELF-RELIANCE, selective disengagement from international production and marketing arrangements, redistribution of assets and incomes, employment-generating methods of production, and greater utilization of local resources. Basic needs development strategies may affect host country negotiations with inward foreign investors, since they tend to focus on the social income effects rather than on the economic growth and BALANCE OF PAYMENTS effects of foreign direct investment.

See also DEPENDENCY, and Index under Development Policy.

benchmark survey. Survey of US direct investment abroad carried out by the US Department of Commerce under authority of the International Investment Survey Act of 1976. The Act requires that a benchmark survey should be conducted at least once every five years. The first benchmark survey under this Act was carried out in 1977, and the results released in 1981. There had been earlier benchmark surveys, conducted under authority of the Bretton Woods Agreement Act of 1945 (*see* BRETTON WOODS MONETARY SYSTEM) but these were less frequent, and the types of information collected less comprehensive. The last such survey covered 1966.

The benchmark survey is a census, and reporting is mandatory. Its purpose is to obtain complete and accurate data on US direct investment abroad. Such investment was defined in the 1977 survey, as existing when one US person (US parent) has a direct or indirect ownership interest of ten per cent or more in a foreign business enterprise (foreign affiliate). The survey provides data that sheds light on the effects of such investment on the US and on foreign economies. In the 1977 survey, for example, three related types of data were collected: (1) foreign affiliate financial and operating data, (2) US parent financial and operating data, and (3) direct investment position and balance of payments data.

(*See* US Department of Commerce, Bureau of Economic Analysis, 1981.)

See also Index under Data Sources.

BERI. *See* BUSINESS ENVIRONMENT RISK INDEX.

Berne Union. The more commonly used name for the International Union of Credit and Investment Insurers, founded in 1934. The Union aims to promote the international acceptance of sound principles of export credit and investment insurance. Its membership includes private organizations, government departments and statutory bodies from 26 countries.

See Index under International Co-operation.

beta. A measure of the sensitivity of the movement in the price of a share to the movement of the market for securities as a whole. A key concept of the CAPITAL ASSET PRICING MODEL (CAPM), beta is measured in relation to the market as a whole, so that a security with a beta of one has the same systematic risk as the market as a whole. It follows that if beta is greater than one it has a greater risk, and if it is less than one it has a lower risk.

Formally, beta is measured as:

$$[COV(R(j),R(m))]/[VAR(R(m))]$$

where COV $(R(j),R(m))$ is the covariance of returns between the security j and the market m, and VAR$(R(m))$ is the variance of the market portfolio. Normally, the beta of a share on a highly developed securities market can be obtained from a 'beta service' which makes the betas of all shares in the market available monthly to investors on a commercial basis.

Because multinational corporations are more highly diversified, they would be expected to have a lower beta relative to the domestic securities market index and hence a lower cost of capital than their uninational counterparts. The empirical evidence on this has been ambiguous, partly because of the difficulty in specifying the tests involved.

See also PORTFOLIO THEORY; SYSTEMATIC RISK; COST OF CAPITAL, and Index under Financial and Risk Management.

BIAC. *See* BUSINESS AND INDUSTRY ADVISORY COMMITTEE.

big bang. Colloquialism for the DEREGULATION of some features of the London Stock Exchange in October 1986.

bilateral clearing arrangement. A government-to-government trade agreement designed to ensure bilateral balance in their international accounts at the end of the transaction. The agreement entails a COUNTERTRADE deal which in turn may involve a SWITCH TRADE transaction.

See Index under Trade.

bilateral investment agreement. More comprehensive than previously existing investment protection treaties, bilateral investment agreements are designed to promote as well as protect foreign direct investment. Pioneered by West Germany and Switzerland in the early 1960s, such treaties between home and host governments are designed to safeguard the interests of the investors in security of investment, NATIONALIZATION and compensation, repatriation of capital and remittances of income, dispute settlement mechanisms and subrogation rights. Although such treaties do not contain specific provisions relating to promotion of foreign investment on the part of home countries, they are nevertheless thought of as investment incentives as they establish conditions favourable to the flow of international investment.

See Index under International Co-operation.

bilateral tax treaty. *See* DOUBLE TAXATION AGREEMENT.

bill of exchange. The usual instrument employed to make payments in international transactions. Bills of exchange, also called 'drafts', are internationally recognized. The following description, though drawn from Anglo-American law, holds generally for all international trade.

In an international transaction where the goods are to be paid for by means of a bill, the exporter (or seller) is known as the drawer (or maker, or originator) of the bill. The person to whom it is addressed is known as the drawee. The bill instructs the drawee to make payment to the payee, who may be the drawer or may be a third party (such as the drawer's bank).

The drawee may be either a buyer or the buyer's bank. If the former is the case, it is a trade draft, if the latter is true, it is a bank draft.

If the draft is a 'sight' draft, it is payable on presentation. If it is a 'time' draft, payment is due later and in the intervening time it can be bought and sold. In this case it is necessary for the bill to be accepted by the drawee (signifying that he will honour it), which is done by the drawee signing the face of the bill. If it is a bank draft then the resulting bill is more easily negotiated

because of the creditworthiness of the bank.

Drafts may be 'clean' or 'documentary'. A clean draft is unaccompanied by any other form of documentation. It is frequently used by multinational companies to transfer goods between parts of the company. A documentary draft, in contrast, has a number of other documents attached which enable the drawee to obtain possession of the goods (for example, a BILL OF LADING or a CONSULAR INVOICE).

In the international use of a bill of exchange, the buyer is normally expected to pay or formally promise to pay before the goods are shipped.

The drawer sends the bill to the drawee: it takes the form of a request for the drawee to pay a specified sum to the person named on the front of the bill. If the bill is a time draft, once the drawee has accepted it by signing it on its face he becomes known as the acceptor.

Once accepted, the bill can be discounted; that is, the drawer can obtain cash by selling the right to receive the amount of the bill to a financial house or any other person. The amount received will be less than the face value of the bill to allow for the time value of the money and the discounting bank's profit (which will take into account the risk that the bill might not be honoured). The selling of this right is effected by the payee's endorsing of the bill on its reverse, thus assigning all rights in the bill to the endorsee.

The discounter of a bill becomes a 'holder in due course' and must be paid by the drawee no matter what dispute may arise between drawer and drawee.

Bills are particularly useful because they can be discounted with a financial intermediary, and because a bill can become a negotiable instrument if it is in writing signed by the drawer, it contains an unconditional promise to pay a definite sum of money, it is payable either on demand or at a fixed or determinable future date and it is payable to order or to bearer. Thus, since the bill is a negotiable instrument, the endorsee gains full title even though the quality of the goods concerned in the original transaction may later be disputed.

See Index under Trade.

bill of lading. A document used in the shipping of goods. It is issued by the carrier to the party sending the goods and has three functions: it is a receipt for the goods, a contractual document, and provides evidence of title. As a result it can be used as collateral by consignors to obtain payment from financial houses such as banks before the consignee has received the goods, and consequently before the consignor can issue receipt for payment.

A 'clean' bill of lading is given when the goods appear to the shipper to be in good condition. He is not expected to check beyond the external appearance for the bill to be clean. A 'foul' bill of lading is issued when the goods appear damaged.

An 'on-board' bill of lading is issued when the goods have been placed on board the ship. An 'on-deck' bill of lading is one where the goods have been stowed on the deck. Finally a 'received-for-shipment' bill of lading means that the goods may still be on the dock, and hence the time of loading is uncertain. The last two are not generally acceptable for the purposes of a LETTER OF CREDIT, although a 'received-for-shipment' bill may be specifically designated as acceptable by the letter of credit.

See Index under Trade.

binational enterprise. Enterprise where the ownership of the parent company is split more or less evenly between the nationals of two countries. Unilever and Shell, for example, are joint Dutch–British companies.

See Index under Corporate Structure and Management.

blocked currency. *See* BLOCKED FUNDS.

blocked funds. Restriction by a given government on the ability of private parties to transfer funds held in its currency out of the country. A fully blocked currency is one which is completely non-convertible. Normally this extreme case will not obtain, and funds will be exportable subject to the permission of the government in individual cases. Such permission is normally obtained through the central bank. The problem of blocked funds affects individuals such as expatriate managers and refugees as well as corporations.

Blocked funds are a source of tension in the corporate case for two reasons. Multinationals prefer centralized cash management so as to maximize the benefit they can obtain from, for instance, differential interest rates payable in different parts of the world; and dividend remittances are generally considered an essential aspect of the return to the parent company arising from its investment in a country. At the investment stage, therefore, it will take particular care to negotiate rights to funds transfers. Subsequently there are various strategies available to the multinational to sidestep the problem of non-remittable funds.

See UNBUNDLING; FRONTING LOANS; TRANSFER PRICING, and Index under Financial and Risk Management.

bonded warehouse. A strictly supervised and restricted territorial area within a country, near to air and sea ports, where imported goods may be stored and repacked prior to being re-exported free of duty or withdrawn for domestic consumption upon payment of customs duties. Where such bonded areas extend into facilities for handling, mixing and manufacturing the goods without customs intervention, they are termed FREE TRADE ZONES (FTZs) or free export processing zones.

See Index under Trade.

bonding company. US finance company which acts as guarantor to contractors for industrial or other development projects in third countries.

See PERFORMANCE GUARANTEE.

book entry security. US term for a security issued as an entry in an account at a bank rather than in the form of a certificate.

Bottin International. Biannual directory of major companies in the world by country and by economic sector.

See Index under Data Sources.

Address: Didot-Bottin, 28 Rue de Docteur, Finlay-F-75738, Paris, Cedex 15, France.

brain drain. The outflow of specialists, expert personnel or highly skilled labour from one country into another. Such a brain drain is thought to be critical in the case of developing countries, whose highly trained citizens are often attracted by the living standards obtainable in the fully industrialized countries.

Although the concept applies in the first instance to individual professionals such as medical doctors, teachers and lawyers, multinational companies are often accused of contributing to this brain drain by recruiting personnel from developing countries while they are still studying abroad, and by cultivating a 'corporate spirit' of cosmopolitanism which may imply neglect and disrespect for their home countries. There is a dilemma here for multinationals, for they are just as likely to be accused of discrimination if they do not promote local nationals.

The problem of the brain drain from less developed to more developed countries has been put on the agenda of global negotiations by the UNCTAD Secretariat, and it is to make proposals on what is now officially called 'the reverse transfer of technology'.

See UNITED NATIONS CONFERENCE ON TRADE AND DEVELOPMENT (UNCTAD), and Index under Technology Transfer.

branch plant. A foreign subsidiary of a multinational company which manufactures parts or components for the parent only. Compare RELAY SUBSIDIARY, a type of plant which also supplies third parties. The dependence of the branch plant on its parent for research and development and for managerial and marketing decisions means that the branch plant is often seen as an inferior, low-grade form of activity, and such prejudice inhibits independent industrialization and development. Some nation states are concerned lest the pattern of international investment should reduce their economies to 'branch plant economies'.

See Index under Corporate Structure and Management.

Brandt Commission. An independent Commission on international development issues, set up in 1980 under the chairmanship of the former Chancellor of West Germany, Willy Brandt. The Commission consists of experienced statesmen, high-ranking officials, distinguished academics and wealthy private individuals drawn from all parts of the world. Although independent of any nation or international organization, the Commission liaises closely with United Nations organizations and has the full backing of the UN Secretariat.

The Commission has added a voice of distinction to the wearied routine with which international issues of poverty and global inequality have been addressed by various international bodies. Its first two reports (*North-South, A Programme for Survival*, 1980; *Common Crisis*, 1983) have been successful in popularizing international development issues and liberal solutions to the word economic crisis against the backdrop of the monetarist response of the advanced countries. Spelling out the communality of interest between the rich and the poor world, the Commission has warned of the dangers of protectionism and has urged a far greater transfer of grant-type resources from the rich North to the poor South than has hitherto been contemplated. The Commission's political philosophy was critical of the distributional shortcoming of the contemporary system of international capitalism and anxious about its irrational resort to arms production as a way out of its recurring crises. In its most recent report (Brandt, 1986) however, the Commission has also become critical of many aspects of international capitalism as a system of production, and it devotes increasing attention to the need for reforming the role of multinational companies in the present world economy.

See Index under International Co-operation.

brass plate company. Name for a subsidiary of a multinational company or bank registered in a TAX HAVEN. The name is a reference to the minimal registration requirements for foreign companies and banks in these countries. For example, to obtain the tax advantages of Grand Cayman, a foreign bank needs only a brass plate on an office door, a secretary, a lawyer and a telex machine.

See Index under Financial and Risk Management.

Bretton Woods monetary system. System of internationally agreed principles and institutions governing international financial transactions and intended to provide a framework for international co-operation and development in the post-war period. The system arose out of the Monetary and Financial Conference called by the UN

Council for Monetary and Financial Relations in 1944. It was named after the village of Bretton Woods in New Hampshire, USA, where the conference took place. 44 nations attended the conference, 39 of whom signed the Articles of Agreement; the USSR was the most important exception.

The Articles of Agreement set up three important pillars upon which the post-war world monetary order was to rest:

a) an agreement establishing 'fixed but adjustable' exchange rates between currencies;
b) an INTERNATIONAL MONETARY FUND (IMF) destined to be a specialized though independent agency of the UN, whose main objectives were to promote exchange stability, to establish a world-wide multilateral payments system, and to provide monetary reserves to help member nations overcome short-term imbalances in their balance of payments;
c) an international bank for reconstruction and development (WORLD BANK). This was also to be a specialized but independent agency of the UN, whose main objectives were to be to provide long-term multilateral finance for investment and technical assistance in the member countries.

Under the Bretton Woods system, all currencies were linked together in a parity grid which defined the exchange rates of all currencies in relation to each other. Each currency was in turn linked to the US dollar, which was defined in terms of a gold content: US$35 was equated with one ounce of fine gold. Within the grid, currency values could fluctuate by one per cent above or below their central parities. Par values could however only be changed to correct a fundamental disequilibrium in the country concerned. Through this agreement the International Monetary Fund was assigned a stabilizing function: it provided a pooling arrangement whereby member countries could purchase foreign currencies with their own domestic currencies to tide them over periods of serious balance of payments difficulties.

For a long period after the Second World War, this system lived up to expectations: it provided a stable international monetary environment in which the post-war reconstruction of the major market economies was successfully undertaken and the trade between these economies expanded smoothly and rapidly.

The system had one major flaw, however, which eventually led to its partial dissolution in 1971. It operated a *de facto* 'dollar standard', and this led over time to an effective overvaluation of the dollar, and a massive outflow of American capital, mainly into Europe and particularly by American multinationals. The consequent prolonged US balance of payments deficit thus became the principal source of additional international liquidity, and gave rise to OFFSHORE (or EURODOLLAR) markets. The practical impossibility of reverting these offshore dollars into 'native' dollars, due to a combination of the restrictions of the Bretton Woods agreement (which prevented a proper reassessment of the value of the dollar) and political/diplomatic pressures by the US governments on the central banks of Europe, encouraged speculative movements against the dollar in these markets. These speculative currency transactions had reached such crisis proportions by 1971 that the US government in August of that year declared the dollar no longer convertible into gold, thereby effectively ending the Bretton Woods-based exchange regime. A devaluation of the dollar by ten per cent followed soon after, at the Smithsonian Conference in December 1971.

Although the Bretton Woods monetary system had thus come to an end, the need for a stable international monetary environment had not. If anything, the role of the International Monetary Fund became more critical, as it provided the only international forum for developing an internationally agreed reserve asset to replace the dollar/gold standard. By the late 1960s, contingency planning for just such replacement was already being undertaken and in 1969 the first amendment of the IMF Articles of Agreement since the Bretton Woods conference was ratified by the member countries. The new Articles made possible the creation of a Special Drawing Account, representing a new reserve facility from which member countries could draw.

See SPECIAL DRAWING RIGHTS (SDR), and Index under International Co-operation.

bribery. A general definition of bribery would refer to the secret and illicit payment of gifts in money or kind to any person in a position of trust with the objective of persuading such person to use his or her position to the advantage of the person offering the gift. In the case of multinational enterprises, the practice of bribery usually involves the illicit payment of monies to government officials for the purposes of securing business contracts or the tacit alteration of agreed-upon terms and conditions. The practice had become so widespread as a vehicle for political interference and distortion of market forces that the General Assembly of the UN in 1975 adopted a resolution condemning the practice and calling upon host and home governments to take appropriate measures. Subsequently, an *ad hoc* intergovernmental working group set up by the United Nations Economic and Social Council (UNECOSOC) has drafted a model national law and voluntary guidelines for enterprises, The Draft International Agreement on the Prevention and Elimination of Illicit Payments, and several governments have strengthened their machinery for disclosure and enacted legislation against bribery of foreign officials, for example the US FOREIGN CORRUPT PRACTICES ACT of 1977.

Britain's Top Private Companies, the First and Second Thousand. Annual publication from Jordan's, London. It includes an alphabetical register of companies and ranks them according to a number of criteria: pre-tax profits, profit margin, employment costs and levels, exports and so on.

See Index under Data Sources.

Brussels Tariff Nomenclature (BTN). A trade classification system of products according to their physical substance designed for customs purposes. The system is now applied in over 100 countries, accounting for two-thirds of world trade. Of the industrialized countries only the US and Canada continue to use their own tariff classifications.

See also STANDARD INTERNATIONAL TRADE CLASSIFICATION (SITC).

Burke–Hartke Bill. Controversial US bill, developed and sponsored by the American Trade Union Federation (AFL-CIO) in 1971, which sought to legislate major constraints on foreign direct investment abroad by American multinational enterprises. In particular Burke and Hartke wanted
(a) to increase the taxation on the companies' foreign income;
(b) presidential licensing of all foreign direct investment and exports of technology, taking the effect the investment would have on US jobs as one criterion for the license to be given;
(c) more complete corporate information disclosure on international activities;
(d) curtailment of US imports of goods produced abroad with American-made components.
Although the Burke–Hartke Bill did not reach the statute book, some minor elements of it were incorporated in the US tax code of 1975. The significance of the Bill lies rather in the expression it gave to American domestic dissatisfaction with and anxiety over American multinational expansion abroad.

See PEASE BILL, and Index under Regulation and Tax.

Business and Industry Advisory Committee (BIAC). Independent organization set up in 1962, and officially recognized by the ORGANIZATION FOR ECONOMIC CO-OPERATION AND DEVELOPMENT (OECD) as being representative of business and industry. Its members include the industrial and employers' organizations of the 24 OECD member countries. BIAC has a consultative status within the OECD, presenting to the OECD and its member governments the views of international business on issues such as investment, macroeconomic policy, taxation, environmental problems and transborder data flows. BIAC carries out its work through a committee structure which responds to and works with the different OECD directorates and committees.

See also TRADE UNION ADVISORY COMMITTEE (TUAC); COMMITTEE ON INTERNATIONAL INVESTMENT AND MULTINATIONAL ENTERPRISES, and Index under International Co-operation, and under Corporate Structure and Management.
Address: 13-15 Chausée de la Muette, F 75016, Paris, France.

Business Environment Risk Index (BERI). An index incorporating economic, political and social risk in one numerical measure. The single-scale index is developed from the assessments of a group of experts.

See also Index under Financial and Risk Management, and under Data Sources.

business reciprocity. A competitive strategy for expanding market shares available to the diversified CONGLOMERATE firm. It involves the reciprocal buying and selling of goods and services between the different subsidiaries.

See Index under Industry Structure.

buy-back deal. A provision in a technology contract between a foreign supplier and a local partner that requires the foreign supplier of the technology, plant and equipment of the project, to take as payment part or all of the output of the project. Buy-back deals are also known by the name of COMPENSATION TRADE.

See COUNTERTRADE; COUNTER PURCHASE; CO-PRODUCTION AGREEMENT, and Index under Trade and under Technology Transfer.

C

Caborn Report. The name frequently given to the *Report on Enterprises and Governments in International Economic Activity* which was adopted by the EUROPEAN COMMUNITY (EC)'s Committee on Economic and Monetary Affairs in April 1981 and subsequently submitted to the European Parliament. It was named after the rapporteur of the document, the European MP Richard Caborn.

The report discussed the attitude of the EC to multinational enterprise. While it recognized that multinational undertakings could be beneficial in their effects, it claimed that the possibilities for damage should be minimized by measures taken by the Community by means of legislation, guidelines, codes, multilateral agreements, greater co-operation between member states, and agreements between the Community and other nation states outside it.

It called specifically for the protection of developing countries; for groundrules in the areas of investment, and fiscal incentives to multinational investment; and for protection for workers' rights. It supported other international codes of conduct, and within the EC recommended specific measures concerning information disclosure, TRANSFER PRICING, merger controls, and greater activity in the field of competition policy to control companies with dominant positions. Finally, it called for the establishment of a monitoring group of the European Parliament to keep the situation under review on a regular basis.

See Index under International Co-operation.

CAD. *See* COMPUTER AIDED DESIGN.

CAITS. *See* CENTRE FOR ALTERNATIVE INDUSTRIAL AND TECHNOLOGICAL SYSTEMS.

Calvo Clause. A clause included in the constitutions of many Latin American countries which has bearing on their public contracts with foreign companies and citizens. Its purpose is to avoid intervention by foreign governments in the case of default or controversy. The clause is named after the Argentine jurist Carlos Calvo. In a book published in 1868, Calvo advocated that in the event of controversies arising under a contractual arrangement, the alien party agrees in the contract to rely solely on local remedies and not request diplomatic or other forms of support from his government. He argued that aliens who establish themselves in a country are entitled to the same rights of protection as nationals, but cannot claim any greater measure of protection.

The validity of the Calvo doctrine has never been fully established in international law, and international jurist and arbitral tribunals have disagreed about how binding such clauses can be said to be.

When in 1902 Venezuela defaulted on the public debt it owed to British, German and Italian nationals, it was subjected to a naval blockade by the creditor nations which violated the Calvo doctrine and led to its restatement as the Drago doctrine. The Drago doctrine held that the default on a public debt owed to aliens by a given state does not give another state the right to intervene forcibly on their behalf to collect that debt, or the right to occupy the territory of the debtor state.

The Drago doctrine, named after the Foreign Minister of Argentina who enunciated it in 1902, proved more viable as a principle of international law, not least because the United States defended it, since it accorded with the principle of European non-intervention in the hemisphere which the US had proclaimed in the Monroe doctrine of 1823.

On the other hand, there is a legal view suggesting that the inclusion in the United Nations CHARTER OF ECONOMIC RIGHTS AND DUTIES OF STATES of the right of the expropriating state to regulate the compensation to be given for the nationalized goods and properties according to domestic custom and law, rather than in accordance with international law, is itself an attempt to endow the Calvo Doctrine with status in international law.

See also UN DRAFT CODE OF CONDUCT ON TRANSNATIONAL CORPORATIONS, and Index under Dispute and Settlement.

CAM. *See* COMPUTER AIDED MANUFACTURE.

capital asset pricing model (CAPM). A widely accepted model for share valuation which suggests that the expected return on a share j $(E(Rj))$ can be found by the equation

$$E(R_j) = R_f + ß_j (E(R_m) - R_f$$

where R_f is the prevailing interest rate on risk-free securities, $E(R_m)$ is the expected return on the whole risky securities market, and $ß_j$ is the jth security's ß. Although most research and most practical application of the theory takes place in terms of a national securities market, with all the above expressions referring to a single country's markets, an international version of the theory has been proposed based upon a 'world market'.

See also SYSTEMATIC RISK; PORTFOLIO THEORY, and Index under Financial and Risk Management and under Theoretical Issues.

capital export neutrality. A principle con-

cerning the treatment of private investment by national governments which is sometimes advocated by international organizations such as the WORLD BANK. The principle involves the equal treatment of foreign and domestic investment. For example, in the field of taxes, true neutrality would mean that where foreign taxes are higher than domestic taxes, transnational corporations should receive a payment from the home country. Equally, the principle requires that host countries increase their taxes to the levels of home countries to avoid subsidizing foreign corporations and that TAX SPARING should be prohibited. In the field of risk insurance, neutrality would mean that all private investment receives guarantees against all political risks. In the field of domestic and foreign trade the application of the neutrality principle would not permit the discriminatory payment of subsidies to domestic firms or the protection of domestic industry by tariffs. Equally, it would forbid the use of incentive policies designed to attract foreign direct investment, but neither would it permit the imposition of PERFORMANCE REQUIREMENTS on such investments.

Supporters of the principle of capital export neutrality argue that even if it is not possible to implement neutrality fully, it can nevertheless serve as a guide in devising policies for controlling investment flows.

See Index under Regulation and Tax and under Theoretical Issues.

capitalism. A specific historical form of the organization of economic and social life. Characterization of its main qualities is made difficult by widely diverging ideological assessments of its nature.

Orthodox economists try to avoid the term altogether (preferring instead 'free market economy') and only use it when highlighting its presumed advantages over other organizational forms, such as SOCIAL-

ISM. They see it as a system of free enterprise and market exchanges where economic and social relations are ruled by contract and where individuals are free agents in seeking their livelihood. Sociologists like Weber (1927) and Parsons (1971) have sought the essence of capitalism not in any one aspect of its economic or social anatomy, but in a dominant cultural value system: a moving spirit lighting up the life of a whole epoch. This moving spirit they believed to be the profit motive, which in turn establishes economic rationality and means-end orientated behaviour, which links means to ends in a direct way, as the dominant forms of human productive behaviour.

In the Marxist view, capitalism is a system of generalized commodity exchange; that is, all goods and services are produced for the market instead of being produced to meet the immediate needs of those who produce them. It is also a system of relations of production which have consequently become organized by means of that exchange. Thus capital in all its forms – as money or as credit for the purchase of labour power and materials of production, as physical machinery or stocks of finished goods or work in progress – has become concentrated in the hands of a small class of capitalists to the exclusion of the mass of the population who have only their labour to sell. In the Marxist view the root of exploitation and the source of surplus value lies in these production relations. Under the guise of apparent contractual freedom the worker produces more than his wages' worth while the capitalist may appropriate this surplus because of his property rights to the final product.

In the Marxist view furthermore the process of the accumulation of surplus value builds up pressures of CONCENTRATION and CENTRALIZATION which turns the earlier historical phase of competitive capitalism into its opposite: MONOPOLY capitalism. Under monopoly capitalism the extremes of

wealth and poverty generated by capitalist exploitation result in crises of overproduction and underconsumption, in falling rates of profit for the capitalists and in their ensuing need to invest their capital abroad in search of higher returns. This is again reflected in the emerging phenomenon of multinational companies.

See IMPERIALISM; SOCIALISM, and Index under Theoretical Issues.

CAPM. *See* CAPITAL ASSET PRICING MODEL.

captive insurance company. An insurance company established by an industrial or commercial concern to insure all or part of the risks of that concern. If the insurance is restricted solely to the business of the parent the insurance subsidiary is termed a 'pure' captive. If the company underwrites risks for outsiders as well, it is described as a 'broad' captive.

As multinational corporations have grown and diversified through TAKEOVERS and MERGERS, so their insurance requirements have also changed. The purchase of insurance has become a major part of corporate finance, and risk management a major part of CORPORATE STRATEGY. Instead of insuring with an 'independent', the companies have thus started to self-insure.

Captives have in recent times become an important method of transferring funds to TAX HAVENS: while insurance premiums are considered in most countries as a legitimate business expense and hence tax-deductible, their accumulation in a tax haven carries the additional advantages of being subject to a minimum or zero income tax and to the minimal legislation prevailing in OFFSHORE centres. Offshore captives are distinguished from domestic captives, which are old-established companies based in and operated from the parent's own country.

See Index under Financial and Risk Management.

captive market. The opposite of a free market of independent buyers and sellers, a captive market is one for a good or a service which is wholly or largely encompassed within the internal trading circuit of a multinational company. This happens for example when the entire output of a mining subsidiary is sold to fabricating plants belonging to the same group of companies.

See INTRA-FIRM TRADE; ADMINISTRATIVE FIAT; TRANSFER PRICE, and Index under Corporate Structure and Management.

captive plant. Name for a plant subcontracted to produce for one overseas firm only.

See INTERNATIONAL SUBCONTRACTING.

Cartagena Agreement. Treaty establishing the group of ANDEAN PACT COUNTRIES.

cartel. An association of producers of goods which are the same or similar that seeks to obtain monopolistic advantages, including monopolistic profits, for its members (see MONOPOLY). These advantages are secured by practices such as prescribing conditions of sale, setting prices, allocating output QUOTAS and market shares, entering PATENT agreements, and so on.

A formal cartel has rules laid down in a formal document which may be legally enforceable, and where penalties may be incurred by firms violating it. Formal domestic cartels have been limited by ANTI-TRUST LEGISLATION both in Europe and in the United States.

Informal cartels have however proved to be much more difficult for anti-trust authorities to rout. Informal cartels involve no more than tacit agreements to follow certain policies, and such tacit agreements may be reached through *ad hoc* telephone calls, INTERLOCKING DIRECTORATES, and other intercorporate linkages such as JOINT VENTURES. In principle they may even occur without personal contact, as in cases where OLIGOPOLISTIC rivals learn through experience how to forecast and interpret one another's behaviour and engage in parallel conduct. The EUROPEAN COMMUNITY (EC)'s competition law as laid down in Article 85 of the EC Treaty has been judicially explained by two decisions of the Court of Justice to bring such informal 'concerted practice' within the scope of the Article. The Court has defined concerted practice as a 'form of co-ordination between undertakings which without going so far as to amount to an 'agreement', knowingly substitutes for the risk of competition practised co-operation between enterprises'. When concerted practices between undertakings result in the division of the community market into national markets, they are liable to affect interstate trade within the meaning of Article 85. In the case of multinational companies operating within the EC, Article 85 does not affect agreements between parent companies and their wholly owned or majority owned subsidiaries, even when the latter are legally separate entities, provided they have no effective autonomy as far as their market operations are concerned.

While domestic cartels have thus been restricted with partial success by anti-trust legislation, international cartels have often escaped legislation altogether. On occasion they have been encouraged by the domestic authorities: this was true, for example, of the inter-war period.

In the United States, the WEBB–POMERANE ACT of 1919 encouraged the setting up of export cartels (or 'trusts' as they are called in the US) between independent companies, although foreign subsidiaries were not to be included. It fostered the development of contractual international JOINT VENTURES, particularly in the oil and gas, iron and steel, and mining and chemical industries. These normally linked together a considerable number of competitors to negotiate collectively and control concessions over foreign supplies. Such international joint ventures are quasi-international cartels.

While international cartels in fact flourished in the inter-war period, most of them disappeared after the Second World War when American anti-trust legislation was more resolutely applied. (See ANTI-TRUST LEGISLATION). At times however the objectives of the anti-trust bodies themselves have run counter to national interests, and have as a result been thwarted. For example, in 1952 the FEDERAL TRADE COMMISSION (FTC) attempted to indict Jersey Standard, California Standard, Gulf, Texaco and Socony-Vacuum (now Mobil) for conspiring, since 1928 and together with two foreign oil companies (Shell and BP) to divide world markets, fix oil prices and limit imports of cheap foreign oil. Not only were these attempts frustrated on grounds of national security, but the American government openly supported the cartel's boycott of Iranian oil when it was nationalized by Premier Mossadegh in 1951, and it encouraged the 'defending' cartel members to operate the Iranian concessions on a joint basis (calling it a 'consortium') when Mossadegh had been ousted. So at the same time that the Justice Department was attacking the cartel, the State and Defense Departments were aiding it.

The term 'cartel' is used for associations of producing countries (such as the ORGANIZATION OF PETROLEUM EXPORTING COUNTRIES (OPEC)) as well as for those of large corporations.

See Index under Industry Structure.

cash management. The movement of liquid funds among the parts of a multinational so as to optimize its profitability subject to the need for readily-realizable cash by each part of the company (to pay creditors, for instance).

Managing the cash of a multinational is a more complicated business than managing the cash of a domestic company for a number of reasons.

One of these may be restrictions on fund transfers by host governments. These may be direct (see BLOCKED FUNDS) or indirect (limiting dividend remittances).

Another is the movement of foreign currency exchange rates, which can make the amount of cash available in the future uncertain.

Cash management may also be complicated by WITHHOLDING TAXES charged on dividend remittances and ROYALTIES paid by subsidiaries to their foreign holding companies. For example, West Germany imposes a 25 per cent capital yield tax on dividends to non-residents, who cannot offset the sum as residents can. The rate is slightly lower under the terms of bilateral DOUBLE TAXATION AGREEMENTS. Under the UK's imputation system, advance corporation tax is deducted from foreign dividend remittances, and the reliefs are even lower under tax treaties than those of West Germany.

In developing a corporate cash management policy, other considerations also need to be taken into account:

1) It must be decided where cash balances are needed. Positive holdings of cash may be needed by subsidiary or affiliate companies for any number of reasons: because of forthcoming investment opportunities, current drains on cash caused by capital expenditure on R&D or promotion of new products, or operating losses. They may also be required by local banks lending funds to affiliates, or by local creditors (since the cash constitutes a visible cushion). Larger subsidiaries will need larger amounts of working capital. Moreover, for a JOINT VENTURE or other enterprise with shareholders other than the multinational parent, there may be a need for cash to pay dividends to them.

2) The political risk of leaving cash in a country must be borne in mind in view of such possible direct action as expropriation.

This should be set against the political risk which might be experienced by taking funds out of the country.

3) There is an economic risk in leaving cash balances in a country, since any expected inflation will reduce its value.

4) The interest-earning potential on short-term funds, which will vary in respect of the rate offered, the availability of investment institutions that will take short-term funds, and the safety of those invested funds.

5) The TRANSACTION COSTS that will be incurred as a result of moving funds about the corporation, for example the commissions charged by banks.

6) There may be effects in terms of local management morale if cash is frequently taken from cash-surplus divisions to feed into cash-hungry affiliates.

7) There may be political pressures from other governments. In particular, the home government of the parent company may, for reasons of balance of payments, wish cash to be remitted to the home office wherever possible.

Where there are no penalties on the transference of funds and the currency concerned is freely convertible, cash management is straightforward. Moreover cash can be shifted about the company by using dividends; management and technical assistance fees; transfer prices; ROYALTY payments for head office overhead; FRONTING LOANS; and by LEADING or LAGGING payments and receipts both intra-company and inter-company.

As a result of these limitations, large MNCs tend to centralize the management of their cash. This will normally be done from a centre in a country with well-developed financial markets or one in a TAX HAVEN. When money is needed, therefore, funds will not be borrowed if they are already available elsewhere in the MNC's organization, and surplus funds will be shifted to that part of the company that can make the most profitable use of them (sub-ject of course to the restrictions noted above). Such a finance department needs good communications with the affiliates and sophisticated intelligence both about the opportunities available and the forecasts of future sources of, and needs for, funds in the various parts of the MNC. It will also, as with domestic treasury functions, set credit management policies (in terms of days of credit allowed, and so on).

See also CENTRALIZATION, and Index under Financial and Risk Management.

CD. *See* CERTIFICATE OF DEPOSIT.

Celler–Kefauver Amendment. An amendment to section seven of the CLAYTON ACT, which was passed by the US Congress in 1950. The Amendment closed the 'assets' loophole of the Clayton Act, making it clear that the Act applied to all MERGERS that may substantially lessen competition or that may tend to create a monopoly. However, the amendment also modified the law in a number of other important aspects and these changes rendered the Act ineffective in dealing with CONGLOMERATE mergers, even though it was now more effective in dealing with horizontal and vertical mergers.

See ANTI-TRUST LEGISLATION, and Index under Regulation and Tax.

centralization. Neo-classical and Marxist economic literatures use this term in entirely different ways.

In neo-classical literature the meaning of the concept is grounded in the vernacular: it refers to the bringing together in one central location (such as the head office) of the decision making and controlling functions of the enterprise. As firms become larger and more international, the decision to centralize or decentralize becomes more critical.

During the process of growth, diversification and overseas expansion of enterprises, both centralizing and decentralizing pressures become apparent.

Examples of pressures towards centralization are:

1) The standardization of products and of production methods due to advantages of economies of scale. The uniform specifications that such standardization implies necessarily involve greater central control.

2) Scale advantages to be gained from product and process specialization, leading to extensive intra-company trading marked by CROSS-HAULING of finished goods, sub-assemblies, industrial intermediates and components. The organic integration of the production process on a global scale that is implied by this extensive process of production rationalization requires in its turn centralized co-ordination.

3) The potential of co-ordinated allocation of financial resources to maximize profits on a global scale, and the possibility of central control over financial flows between component parts of a multinational firm. Variations in sources of funds, in interest and tax rates, and fluctuations in currency values, are generally so important that subsidiaries are seldom allowed to control their own finances.

4) Cost-reducing advantages of centralized overhead and servicing functions such as research and development, modernized data processing facilities, and the presence of scarce expert personnel.

Whereas the pressures contributing to centralization are commercial, those contributing to decentralization are more likely to be of a political, sociocultural or psychological nature.

Political pressures arise from host country demands for greater national control over foreign economic activities. Appreciation of, or submission to, such demands may lead to greater management autonomy of the local subsidiary in a wide range of operational matters. Sociocultural considerations in respect of local tastes and needs, and employment and market conditions, may likewise result in greater autonomy of the local subsidiary in product design, promotion strategy, recruitment policy and plant operations. Finally, there are sociopsychological considerations of staff motivation: it is generally thought that too much centralization destroys initiative and leads to a loss of able managers at subsidiary level.

In Marxist economic literature, the term 'centralization' has an entirely different connotation. Here it is seen not as a process internal to the firm, but rather as an inherent manifestation of the development of CAPITALISM as a whole. In Marx's own terminology, centralization describes the process of CONCENTRATION of capital ownership within an industry due to competition and credit. Competition destroys the weaker capitalists in an industry while the credit system enables the stronger to take over the weak, resulting in a small number of companies acquiring a larger market share. The combined processes of centralization and CONCENTRATION transform competitive market structures into oligopolistic ones. (*See* OLIGOPOLY). The profit levels which result from oligopoly are argued to force such companies into either overseas expansion or product diversification or both. In the Marxist analysis, therefore, the process of centralization of capital ultimately leads to internationalization of capital, and the formation of multinational companies.

See also CARTEL; CONGLOMERATE; MERGER; ACQUISITION, and Index under Corporate Structure and Management and under Theoretical Issues.

Centre for Alternative Industrial and Technological Systems (CAITS). Study centre in the Polytechnic of North London involved in research, publication and seminars on ALTERNATIVE TECHNOLOGY. It works closely with shop steward committees in companies under investigation, and can offer assistance in establishing shop stewards' combines (see COMBINE COMMITTEE). It publishes the CAITS Newsletter.

See Index under Data Sources.
Address: Polytechnic of North London, Holloway Road, London NY 8DB, UK.

certificate of analysis. An export document that is issued by a governmental or private institution guaranteeing the weight or purity of goods. It may be required either by officials of the importing country (especially in the case of food or medicines) or by the importer as evidence of the quality of what is being purchased.

See also BILL OF EXCHANGE; LETTER OF CREDIT; BILL OF LADING, and Index under Trade.

certificate of deposit (CD). A certificate issued by a bank, which acknowledges that it holds the sum of money stated on the face. Certificates of deposit are negotiable instruments and are traded in a substantial secondary market (that is to say that there is a thriving market in CDs once they have been issued). They have a very high security rating, and provide a means for the purchaser of the CD to undertake a short-term investment with a guarantee of repayment of the certificate's face value on its presentation at its maturity date.

The market for CDs began in the USA in 1961. The suspension of REGULATION Q (in respect of maturities up to 89 days from 1970, and in respect of maturities above 90 days from 1973) led to the rapid development of their market in the USA. EURODOLLAR CDs were introduced in London in 1966, and sterling CDs two years later. A limited market in yen CDs began in Tokyo in 1979. In 1980 some UK banks began issuing SPECIAL DRAWING RIGHTS (SDR) CDs.

CDs are of two types: tap and tranche. Tap CDs are the more common. A bank will offer CDs for sale in round denominations with a minimum amount (£50,000 in the UK; $25,000 in the USA; 5 million EURODOLLARS in the UK market; 1 million SDRs). Although very short-term maturities are possible (as little as 48 hours, for example) periods of three months, six months, and any number of years up to five are more normal.

Tranche CDs are issued in a way more akin to a share issue. They are issued in several equal 'slices' or tranches to make them more acceptable to smaller investors. Like share issues, they tend to be underwritten and to be issued for larger amounts and longer maturities than tap CDs. The tranches tend to be equal with respect to issue and maturity dates, interest rate, and dates on which payment of interest is due.

Forward forward CDs are London CDs in which a bank commits itself to the issue of a CD after a specified time for a specified period at a specified interest rate. These have been used to circumvent the five-year limit on UK CDs through the issuance of two CDs at once: a five-year CD and a forward forward CD which commences when the other matures.

More recently, CDs have been traded on the futures markets in both the USA and the UK.

See also EUROBOND, and Index under Financial and Risk Management.

Charter of Economic Rights and Duties of States. A Charter adopted at the 29th annual session of the United Nations General Assembly in November 1974. The Charter represents a codification of agreed principles of international economic relations upon which it was hoped that a NEW INTERNATIONAL ECONOMIC ORDER (NIEO) could be built. In particular the Charter introduced two new sets of general principles of international relations: those concerned with a state's economic rights, and those concerned with its economic duties. While the weight of the principles of economic rights favours the developing nations, the weight of economic duties rests upon the already developed nations. The economic rights of states include national sovereignty over natural resources, foreign properties and transnational companies; the right to NATIONALIZATION and the right to regulate the compensation to be given for the nationalized goods and properties. The section on economic duties of states, on the other hand, speaks of interventionism and discrimination in the world market in favour of the developing countries and places upon the developed countries the obligation to set right the existing inequalities in the organization of economic power by reorganizing the decision structure of international financial organizations such as the INTERNATIONAL MONETARY FUND (IMF) and the WORLD BANK by increasing net transfers of resources to the developing countries; and by ensuring the latter's access to science and technology in a manner appropriate to their development objectives and needs.

The adoption of the Charter in November 1974 had followed the adoption by the UN General Assembly of the *Declaration on the Establishment of a New International Economic Order* in a special session in May of the same year. The Declaration embodied a set of proposals, and was accompanied by a programme of action to redress the imbalances in international economic power, world market advantages, and distribution of income between the developed and the less developed countries. The purpose of the Charter was to give more weight to these proposals by underpinning them with a set of agreed principles. But all free market developed countries, with the exception of Sweden, New Zealand and Australia, either voted against the Charter or abstained, and it is therefore difficult to ascribe much legal significance to it.

See GLOBAL REFORMS, and Index under International Co-operation and under Dispute and Settlement.

cherry picking. The tendency of a wholesaler or other middleman to restrict his activities to those products that are already well established in the market. To the middleman this is economically sound because it minimizes the effort that he needs to exert to obtain a given level of profit. It causes difficulties for the multinational or exporter attempting to break into a new national market, since it means there is no incentive for the existing distribution system to promote the new product. Common solutions to this problem are either to temporarily set up a direct selling effort until such time as the product is established, or (again for a limited time period only) to subsidize the middleman, perhaps by paying the cost of those of his employees who are designated as concerned solely with the exporter's or multinational's products.

Chicago International Money Market. Part of the Chicago Mercantile Exchange, set up in 1972 to facilitate trade in foreign currency futures. Its starting date is connected with the demise of the BRETTON WOODS MONETARY SYSTEM of fixed exchange rates and the consequent instability of foreign exchange markets. As is the case with commodities, the future value of money became a subject of speculation. The market deals in the following currencies: Canadian dollar; Dutch guilder; French franc; German mark; Japanese yen; Mexican peso; Swiss franc; and UK sterling. The market is open to individuals and companies who cannot deal in the inter-bank market (because of restricted access and large denominations) yet wish to HEDGE or speculate in currencies.

See Index under Financial and Risk Management.

choice of law clause. A provision in an international trading contract by which the parties to the contract agree which national law will govern any disputes between them.

See Index under Dispute and Settlement.

CKD. *See* COMPLETELY KNOCKED DOWN.

classical corporation tax system. *See under* CORPORATION TAX SYSTEM.

clausula rebus sic stantibus. Also known as the change of circumstances doctrine, this rule in international law states that an essential change in the conditions under which a treaty has been concluded frees either one of the contracting parties from the treaty's obligations.

In disputes with multinational companies over mineral concessions, concluded in colonial times and for very long periods, developing countries have sometimes invoked the *clausula rebus sic stantibus* argument.

See CONCESSION; MODERNIZED CONCESSION AGREEMENT, and Index under Dispute and Settlement.

Clayton Act. US federal statute of 1914 revising and strengthening the Sherman Anti-Trust act (*see* ANTI-TRUST LEGISLATION). The Clayton Act was designed with the particular purpose of preventing those specific types of business activity 'leading to trusts, conspiracies and monopolies' which were already familiar: price discrimination, exclusive dealing, ACQUISITIONS and INTERLOCKING DIRECTORATES. Recognizing that in this area there is no limit to the 'inventiveness of the mind of man', Congress also enacted a general, or open-ended, prohibition of 'unfair methods of competition'.

The Clayton Act came in the wake of the celebrated break-up of Standard Oil into some 70 separate companies. This break-up had finally been achieved in 1911 as a result of the enforcement of the Sherman Anti-trust Act of 1902. It had, however, immediately been followed by a re-emergence of Standard Oil's monopoly. It had used the device of the HOLDING COMPANY to re-establish direct control over its severed subsidiaries.

The Clayton Act set up a separate agency charged with the supervision and enforcement of the Act, the FEDERAL TRADE COMMISSION (FTC). Under section seven of the Act, the FTC was granted the authority to prevent ACQUISITIONS of stock in order to deter takeovers which threatenened market competition, but the section failed to include the merging (*see* MERGER) of assets. This omission made the Clayton Act ineffective in dealing with the wave of mergers that occurred in the late 1920s. The omission was later partly corrected in the CELLER – KEFAUVER AMENDMENT.

See Index under Regulation and Tax.

clean draft. *See* BILL OF EXCHANGE.

Club of Rome. A non-profit making research and educational organization incorporated in Geneva under the Swiss Civil Code. It was founded in Rome in 1968 at a meeting of 30 prominent academics, industrialists, national and international civil servants. The meeting had been set up at the initiative of Aurelio Peccei, chief of the Italian Fiat concern.

The aims of the organization are to foster understanding of the varied but interdependent components – economic, political, natural and social – that make up the global system; to bring that new understanding to the attention of policymakers and the public worldwide; to promote new policy initiatives and action; to identify a new class of social problems, and to provide the language, the methodologies and the criteria of success appropriate for their solution.

Membership of the Club of Rome is limited to 100 prominent people from many countries. It publishes *Reports to the Club of Rome* on a variety of topics, each commissioned from experts in different fields. Eleven such reports have been published thus far, including the first and very popular *Limits to Growth* (*see* Meadows *et al.*, 1972).

As in the case of the TRILATERAL COMMISSION, the Club of Rome is of historical interest because it is an ideological and educational establishment, founded and funded by multinational corporate capital, and dedicated to some form of global transnational management of world economy and society.

See Index under International Co-operation.

Address: International Management Institute, 4 Chemin de Conches, CH-1211 Geneva, Switzerland.

CMEA. *See* COUNCIL FOR MUTUAL ECONOMIC ASSISTANCE.

Coase theorem. A theoretical explanation, hypothesized and tested by Ronald Coase in 1937, of the growth and equilibrium size of firms. Coase's basic idea was that the market is costly and inefficient for undertaking certain kinds of transactions. For example, there are costs associated with finding a relevant price, or defining obligations of contracting parties such as long-term buyers and sellers, and of enforcing such contracts. To overcome these costs, or 'market imperfections', Coase argued, firms will 'internalize' such transactions by bringing them within the socioeconomic and administrative organization of the firm itself, thus replacing the market mechanism with ADMINISTRATIVE FIAT. This explains the tendency of firms to grow bigger in size, diversifying into relevant productive and commercial activities.

While the Coase theorem was originally developed to apply to the firm with a number of plants but based in a single country,

the INTERNALIZATION concept has recently become a cornerstone of explanatory theories of FOREIGN DIRECT INVESTMENT (FDI) and the expansion of multinational firms. Thus multinational corporations can be expected to appear where it is less costly to allocate international resources internally than through the international market.

See Index under Theoretical Issues.

Code of Liberalization of Capital Movements. This Code, adopted by the ORGANIZATION FOR ECONOMIC CO-OPERATION AND DEVELOPMENT (OECD) in 1965 and amended in 1968, rests on decisions of the Council of the Organization for Economic Co-operation and Development. Under the Code, the member states of the Organization have undertaken to eliminate restrictions on the movement of capital. Measures to this effect are called measures of liberalization. Members are generally committed to the progressive abolition on movements of capital from one member state to another, the criterion being the extent necessary for effective economic co-operation. Under the Code, the member states have also agreed to endeavour to treat all assets owned by non-residents on an equal footing, and to permit the liquidation of such assets and the transfer of such assets or of the proceeds of their liquidation. But since no timescale for implementation has been fixed, the effect of the commitments is of questionable worth.

See Index under International Co-operation.

codes of conduct. Since the early 1970s, the world community has had international regulation of multinational corporations as one of its major concerns and objects of endeavour.

After two decades of expansion in relative obscurity, the power of multinational corporations was internationally recognized at the UNITED NATIONS CONFERENCE ON TRADE AND DEVELOPMENT (UNCTAD) III conference in Santiago in 1972. Here the first calls for international codes of conduct for the behaviour of multinational enterprises were made. Since that time various United Nations bodies and agencies, regional organizations and international business and labour organizations have all engaged in the formulation of international, regional or sectoral instruments which make standards and principles for the regulation and national treatment of international business clear.

Some of these codes, or guidelines, have been finalized and promulgated; others are still being drafted and are subject to intense negotiations. Some establish a comprehensive framework for all issues relating to the operation of transnational business, while others are limited to specific subjects, sectors of activity or regions.

Most codes or guidelines, particularly the comprehensive ones, are voluntary and therefore have no legally binding character. This has invoked disenchantment and scepticism on the part of those nations, principally THIRD WORLD countries, and sections of the community, such as trade unions, on whom the burden of international business 'misconduct' tends to fall. Yet voluntary codes cannot be dismissed out of hand.

Firstly, the drafting exercise carried out by intergovernmental groups of experts and the subsequent negotiations in international fora serve the practical purpose of creating an international climate of opinion which multinational business will in due course find it difficult to ignore. Already many of the larger multinational corporations have come to appreciate the advantages that the establishment of clear and stable 'rules of the game' may have for greater security of investments.

Secondly – and more directly – the drafting exercise has itself been instructive for many host governments, particularly in developing countries where there is a lack of resources and specialist expertise. It has equipped them with a growing battery of documents on the nature and scope of restrictive business practices, on the detailed requirements for information disclosure, and on the catalogue of multinational business practices that may adversely affect national economic and social goals. The voluntary codes and their preparatory documents have helped to inform the national statutory treatment of international business, and it is in this way that they will contribute to the international harmonization of the relevant domestic laws.

Thirdly, voluntary codes and guidelines themselves are not entirely without legal significance, as 'customary behaviour' is a source of international law, and resolutions adopted with regularity in international fora are quotable in a legal context. It is precisely this potential legal significance that has persuaded some multinational companies not to endorse publicly, for example, the ORGANIZATION OF ECONOMIC CO-OPERATION AND DEVELOPMENT (OECD)'s 'voluntary' guidelines in their annual reports, as they are being urged to do by the OECD Secretariat and their respective national governments.

Some sections of the international business community have responded positively to the code-making process, particularly because the process has over time been transformed from one which threatened the operation of multinationals to one which protects and legitimates it, but other sections remain antagonistic. The sheer proliferation of codes now penetrating specific industrial sectors, which have made the pharmaceutical and drug industries feel particularly threatened, has provoked a number of US multinationals into lobbying their government into resisting many of the codes promulgated by international organizations.

The most important international codes

of conduct which have been concluded are:

– DECLARATION AND DECISIONS ON INTERNATIONAL INVESTMENT AND MULTINATIONAL ENTERPRISES (OECD, 1976)
– TRIPARTITE DECLARATION OF PRINCIPLES CONCERNING MULTINATIONAL ENTERPRISES AND SOCIAL POLICY (ILO, 1977)
– EC CODE FOR COMPANIES WITH SUBSIDIARIES IN SOUTH AFRICA (EC, 1977)
– RESTRICTIVE BUSINESS PRACTICES CODE (UNCTAD, 1980)
– WHO/UNICEF CODE ON THE MARKETING OF BREASTMILK SUBSTITUTES (WHO/UNICEF, 1981).

The following main codes are still being negotiated:

– UNITED NATIONS DRAFT CODE OF CONDUCT ON TRANSNATIONAL CORPORATIONS (UN, since 1977)
– TRANSFER OF TECHNOLOGY (TOT) CODE (UNCTAD, since 1975)
– Draft International Agreement on the Prevention and Elimination of Illicit Payments (United Nations Economic and Social Council, since 1977).

For their part, anxious not to be overtaken by more stringent and hostile international measures on the part of governments and international organizations, some sections of international business itself have developed voluntary guidelines and codes. The most important of these are:

– the Sullivan Code (see SULLIVAN PRINCIPLES);
– the IFPMA CODE of Pharmaceutical Marketing Practices;
– the INTERNATIONAL CHAMBER OF COMMERCE (ICC) Guidelines on International Investment (1972), and Rules of Conduct on Ethical Practices in Commercial Transactions (1977).

See also EUROPEAN COMMUNITY (EC),

and Index under International Co-operation and under Dispute and Settlement.

collective self-reliance. An extension of the SELF-RELIANCE concept to include co-operation, solidarity and trade amongst the developing countries themselves.

In the course of the 1970s the concept has evolved from a Third World political idea into a guiding principle of both the UNITED NATIONS CONFERENCE ON TRADE AND DEVELOPMENT (UNCTAD)'s and the GROUP OF 77 (G-77)'s programmes of activities.

Starting with the third ministerial meeting of the Group of 77 in Manila in 1976 member states decided to begin pressing for the establishment of a separate UNCTAD Committee on ECONOMIC CO-OPERATION AMONG DEVELOPING COUNTRIES (ECDC). In the meantime a conference of developing countries on ECDC had been convened by the government of Mexico from which the ambitious Mexico City Programme of Action emerged, which was to serve as the guideline for UNCTAD's ECDC programme. It included:

a) the creation of a global system of trade preferences (GSTP) among developing countries;
b) the promotion of co-operation among state trading organizations (STOs);
c) the establishment of multinational marketing enterprises (MMEs).

In the following years ECDC moved to the forefront of developing countries' collective international development strategies. The fourth Ministerial Meeting of the Group of 77 at Arusha in Tanzania elaborated and revised the Mexico City Programme into what came to be known as the Arusha Programme for Collective Self--Reliance.

The inability of the Group of 77 to implement the Mexico City Programme of Action, which demanded substantial research, administrative and technical work, has sharpened a dilemma that has plagued UNCTAD since its inception. The dilemma centres around the question of how an organization with a universal membership (and largely financed by the developed countries) can respond to the wishes of the developing countries, such as those articulated by the Group of 77, in an area which is of primary, if not exclusive, concern to its less developed members.

Of the three priority areas defined in the Mexico and Arusha Declarations, UNCTAD at present is most deeply involved in the development of a global system of trade preferences. Within this area of priority it has moved furthest operationally by establishing a Trade Information System (TIS) on the foreign trade of developing countries.

See Index under Development Policy, and under International Co-operation.

collusion. Overt agreement between oligopolists (*see* OLIGOPOLY) to follow common policies in respect of market allocation, setting prices and so on.

See CARTEL.

combination export manager (CEM). A term used to denote a specialist exporting firm which acts on behalf of a number of manufacturers, thus saving them the expense of separately setting up an independent export department. It may or may not take title to the goods as part of its operations. In those cases where the CEM purchases the goods in its home country and assumes the risk involved in marketing the product abroad, it is generally known as an export distributor. Where it takes no title and hence no risk, it is generally known as an export commission representative.

See Index under Trade.

combine committee. Unofficial, inter-union, inter-site committee of shop stewards working within the same multilocal, uninational or multinational firm. Although the combine movement in Britain has waned somewhat after an initial spurt of enthusiasm in the 1970s, combines are still seen by some as offering potentially vital organizational links in the struggle for international union solidarity.

See INTERNATIONAL TRADE SECRETARIATS (ITS), and Index under Labour.

Comecon. The more frequently used Western name for the Eastern bloc common market countries.

See under COUNCIL FOR MUTUAL ECONOMIC ASSISTANCE (CMEA).

comfort letter. A letter which the European Commission may send to companies involved in collaborative agreements, expressing its view that (a) the companies involved do not contravene Article 85 (1) of the Treaty of Rome or (b) the Commission wishes to exempt the collaborative agreement under subsection (3) of Article 85, which bans cartels and restrictive practices liable to distort competition. It does however allow exemption in cases where agreements are likely to improve production, distribution or technical or economic progress, and where a fair share is passed on to the consumer. The advantage of the comfort letter is that it offers the EC commission a means of informing the companies of its view, without having to take a formal decision.

See ANTI-TRUST LEGISLATION, EUROPEAN COMMUNITY (EC), and Index under Regulation and Tax.

comity principle. Principle of goodwill and civility in international relations, founded on the moral right of each state to receive courtesy from others. The principle has become especially important in problems which concern conflicting jurisdictions in respect of subsidiaries of multinational enterprises. There is a view, expressed for example in the UNITED NATIONS DRAFT CODE OF CONDUCT ON TRANSNATIONAL CORPORATIONS, which argues that states should take account of the extent to which the conduct of their enterprises is acceptable under the applicable legislation or regulations in host countries. It is even proposed that the States of developed countries should take account of the financial and trade needs of less developed countries when framing legislation in respect of restrictive practices.

See Index under International Co-operation, and under Dispute and Settlement.

commercial letter of credit. *See under* LETTER OF CREDIT.

Commissaires aux Comptes. The statutory auditors required under French law for all Societés Anonymes and for Societés a Responsabilités Limitées with capital greater than FF300,000. Since 1966, all such auditors have had to be selected from a list of qualified persons or firms, and *experts comptables* (the members of the French professional accounting body) are included in that list. This has meant an improvement in French auditing, which is still in the course of development from the minimal requirements before 1966.

See Index under Regulation and Tax.

commission. *See* MOBILIZATION FEE.

Commission on Transnational Corporations. *See* UNITED NATIONS COMMISSION ON TRANSNATIONAL CORPORATIONS (UNCTC).

Committee on International Investment and Multinational Enterprises (CIME). A subcommittee of the ORGANIZATION FOR ECONOMIC CO-OPERATION AND DEVELOPMENT (OECD). Amongst other things the Com-

mittee is responsible for the promotion and the periodic review of the OECD's Guidelines on Multinational Enteprises (*see* DECLARATION AND DECISIONS ON INTERNATIONAL INVESTMENT AND MULTINATIONAL ENTERPRISES). The Committee has consultative meetings with representatives from employers (*see* BUSINESS AND INDUSTRY ADVISORY COMMITTEE (BIAC)) and with representatives from trade unions (*see* TRADE UNION ADVISORY COMMITTEE (TUAC)).

See Index under International Co-operation.

Common Fund. A proposed fund for the financing of bufferstock and other price stabilization measures for primary export commodities from developing countries. The Fund was one of the key proposals in the North-South negotiations following the adoption by the General Assembly of the United Nations in 1975 of the Resolution to establish a NEW INTERNATIONAL ECONOMIC ORDER (NIEO). Originally costed at US$18 billion and intended to cover 18 export commodities, the final agreement on the Fund reached in March 1979 under the auspices of the fourth UNITED NATIONS CONFERENCE ON TRADE AND DEVELOPMENT (UNCTAD) scaled down the size of the proposed Fund to US$6 billion, covering some 10 commodities only. The capital of the proposed Fund was to be raised partly through subscriptions by member countries, partly through international borrowings, and partly through access to resources of the International Commodity Agreements as and when these might become established.

Despite the initial global enthusiasm for the idea of the Fund, especially on the part of the developing countries, financial resources have so far failed to materialize. By January 1985 some US$750 million had been pledged to the Fund including US$280 million for a so-called 'second window' to be used to promote research into improving the productivity and competitiveness of primary commodities. The Fund can become operational only when at least 90 countries contributing not less than two-thirds of the capital have ratified it. By the end of 1984 over 70 countries had signed the agreement, but only just over 20 had ratified it. The failure of the Fund to materialize is conjoined by the failure of its counterparts, the International Commodity Agreements (ICAs) to be concluded successfully. At the time of writing only three such commodity agreements are in operation: tin, cocoa and rubber.

See Index under International Co-operation and under Trade.

Companies Registration Office. *See* REGISTRAR OF COMPANIES.

compensation trade. *See under* BUY-BACK DEAL. The expression 'compensation trade' is the more commonly used term in buy-back deals which are commonly made with the People's Republic of China.

See also COUNTERTRADE, and Index under Trade, and under Technology Transfer.

competence centre. A unit of a multinational company that has shown itself to have particular expertise in either manufacturing or marketing. Once designated as a competence centre, the unit will be used as as a resource for the flow of knowhow, and will advise on and help in the development of fledgeling operations in other parts of the world.

Since this unit may well be situated outside the home nation, the acknowledgment that such units can exist tends to break down the hierarchical thinking typical of the ethnocentric multinational (*see* ETHNOCENTRIC) which takes the parent company to be the natural repository of knowledge and expertise. In this way any new operation gains from the fact that advice is based on experience and the competence centre gains from the status arising from its expertise being recognized.

See Index under Corporate Structure and Management.

completely knocked down (CKD). A ready-to-assemble kit of fully built up components and fixtures of a mechanically complex final product (such as a motor vehicle, television set, or a refrigerator) which is transported to an overseas contractor or subsidiary for final assembly and sale. CKD transfers have become a regular feature of international production and trade since the economic nationalism of many developing countries dictated a policy of import-substitutive industrialization which typically discourages imports of finished consumer goods.

See Index under Technology Transfer.

compliance accounting. A term describing the accounting methods which major creditors, such as banks and international agencies, require those receiving loans or assistance to use.

compound duty. A mixture of SPECIFIC and *ad valorem* import duties.

comprador. A term frequently encountered in neo-Marxist literature on developing countries. It refers to that class of local entrepreneurs and national bureaucracy whose activities and social position are thought to serve the interest of foreign capital.

Originally the Portuguese word for 'buyer', the term's critical connotation is derived from the early mercantile activities of Portuguese traders in the Far East. Their unfamiliarity with strange customs, tongues and institutions encouraged enterprising natives to fulfil the role of *comprador* or agent of the foreign traders. In this sense the term is still widely, and perfectly respectably, used in China trade, particularly in Hong Kong.

Today the Western tastes and lifestyles, the economic interests and the political needs of the *comprador* bourgeoisie in many developing countries are argued to constitute the links that join the economic structure of their countries to those of the advanced countries, 'corrupting' the development process as they do so.

See also DEPENDENCY.

computer aided design (CAD). The implications of computer networks for multinational design and manufacture are still uncertain, but certain signs are already clear. Among these is their contribution to the localization of product research and development. Not only are sophisticated computer packages now available to aid in the design process, so that design takes place at the computer terminal, but the existence of communications networks also means that designs can easily and quickly be transmitted between countries and the design process shared among them. Developments such as these therefore permit the centralization of control over widely dispersed activities.

See also CENTRALIZATION; COMPUTER AIDED MANUFACTURE (CAM), and Index under Technology Transfer.

computer aided manufacture (CAM). The use of large computer systems to help with the scheduling and operation of manufacturing processes. Computers can assist in guiding re-order quantities for materials, scheduling the production process, and real-time running of the machinery used for production. The spread of CAM will bring about greater displacement of both skilled and unskilled labour than is made possible by mere mechanization for two reasons in particular:

a) the growth of expert systems (where computer software simulates the actions of physical labour or the decisions of mental labour) ;

b) the development of robotics, which displaces physical labour and allows work to take place under physical conditions (such as paint shops) that are difficult or dangerous for humans.

The extent to which it is economically desirable for a multinational (or any other firm) to displace human labour by computer or robotic systems will of course depend on the comparative cost of each, and currently many jobs are not considered replaceable by mechanized systems even in developed countries where labour costs are relatively high. The implications of these systems for the future demand for labour in any part of the world are far from certain.

See also COMPUTER AIDED DESIGN (CAD); CENTRALIZATION, and Index under Technology Transfer.

concentration. A concept with connected but different meanings in neo-classical economic literature and in Marxist economic literature.

In the neo-classical literature, concentration refers to the extent to which a small number of firms account for a large proportion of an industry's aggregate output, assets, sales or employment. High concentration ratios reflect oligopolistic or monopolistic market conditions, while low concentration ratios reflect competitive market conditions. (*See* OLIGOPOLY, MONOPOLY).

In Marxist economic literature, the concept has this same meaning in its static application, but it also has a primary relational and historical-dialectic dimension. Concentration of capital is seen as a capital process in relation to the labour process. The re-investment of profit in newer, more efficient methods of production results in a higher ratio of capital invested per worker and consequently in an increasing concentration of capital in relation to labour. In Marxist literature this is referred to as the increasing organic composition of capital, while in neo-classical literature it is referred to as the 'deepening' of capital. The process of concentration is in itself the outcome of free market competition, for competition forces entrepreneurs to reinvest their profits in new production techniques. Concentration of capital, in its turn, gives rise to a complementary process of CENTRALIZATION of capital when larger, more successful, firms swallow up their smaller and less efficient rivals. Concentration and centralization of capital constitute together historical evidence of the emergence of oligopolistic and monopolistic markets, referred to in the neo-classical literature as 'concentration'.

See Index under Theoretical Issues and under Industry Structure.

concession. A grant or lease of land or property by a government to a foreign company for a specified purpose and in exchange for a certain payment.

Concessions used to be the classical contractual framework within which foreign companies operated in the extractive sector of host countries. Under a traditional concession regime, a foreign investor was given the exclusive exploration and exploitation rights to a particular mineral resource, exercisable over a certain area of land and in exchange for a ground rent. Typically, it was also assured effective ownership of the raw material at the point of extraction, the right to dispose of (i.e. sell) the product being conceded in exchange for a ROYALTY.

In colonial times, under the combined weight of colonial government patronage, the application of brute force, and the illiteracy of local native communities, companies from the metropolitan countries often acquired concessions over vast areas of land with extensive exploitation rights for up to 50 or even 100 years, in exchange for modest royalties and a negligable rental. A typical concession would have no provision for the relinquishment of areas abandoned or untouched by the enterprise.

After independence, many governments of ex-colonial countries embarked on a series of attempts to renegotiate concession agreements and modify their terms. Typically, a tax on income would be added first, followed by an upgrading of rents and royalty provisions and the formulation of more precise terms of exploration, exploitation and disposition. Since conceptually the concession was classified as a species of contract and as such was underpinned by the traditional and internationally recognized principle of sanctity of contract (*see* PACTA SUNT SERVANDA) these renegotiation attempts led to many conflicts with the foreign companies. These conflicts in their turn often led to outright measures of EXPROPRIATION and NATIONALIZATION.

Today few if any traditional concession regimes remain. In their place have come many novel contractual agreements between host governments and foreign companies, ranging from JOINT VENTURES through MANAGEMENT CONTRACTS to PRODUCTION SHARING AGREEMENTS.

See also MODERNIZED CONCESSION; CALVO CLAUSE, and Index under Regulation and Tax and under Dispute and Settlement.

confirmed letter of credit. *See* LETTER OF CREDIT.

confirming bank. A bank which 'confirms' a LETTER OF CREDIT issued by another bank by guaranteeing payment to the exporter of goods.

confirming house. Term frequently used in the UK for an EXPORT BROKER. A confirming house may buy as agent for its overseas principal or as a principal itself.

confiscation. The taking of private property by the State without compensation. Whereas EXPROPRIATION in international law signifies lawful forms of interference with foreign property rights by a territorial sovereign power or any of its subordinate organs in accordance with international law, the term 'confiscation' is limited to any form of such interference amounting to an international tort.

See Index under Dispute and Settlement.

conglomerate. A multi-product, multidivisional enterprise. The term is frequently reserved for companies which have grown very fast by ACQUISITIONS and MERGERS in functionally unrelated industries. Today the largest conglomerates are also multinational companies spanning the globe. Because conglomerate mergers are typically those between any two companies that are neither direct competitors nor in a buyer-seller relationship with one another, existing ANTI-TRUST LEGISLATION both in the United States and in Europe has not generally been applicable or effective in stemming the tide of such mergers, which has been in evidence since the mid-1960s. (*See* CLAYTON ACT and CELLER–KEFAUVER AMENDMENT.)

Anti-trust legislation hinges to a large degree on the link between size and market power, but in the case of conglomerates a widely diversified presence in many industries does not necessarily mean a commanding presence in any. Nevertheless, once established, a conglomerate can – through practices of CROSS-SUBSIDIZATION and BUSINESS RECIPROCITY – lead to CONCENTRATION and perhaps reshape a competitive industry into an oligopolistic one.

Conglomerates vary in their possession and use of market power. Where a conglomerate operates essentially as a HOLDING COMPANY or a mutual fund, it may permit its portfolio of unrelated lines of business a far greater degree of autonomy than in cases where ultimate control of the conglomerate rests with the management of the parent company of the group.

See also OLIGOPOLY; FORBEARANCE, and Index under Corporate Structure and Management.

consolidated accounts. Also known as 'group accounts'. The accounts of a group of companies presented in such a way as to represent the economic activities of the group as if they were one unit, rather than a set of legally separate entities. Although required under company law in the UK, in many other countries they are optional, misleadingly presented, or unknown.

The technical problems and socio-economic implications of consolidated accounts are considerable in the domestic company: for the multinational they are far greater. Yet the nature of consolidation and the implications of presenting consolidated accounts are even more significant for the multinational group than they are for the domestic company. The domestic company has a choice of legal vehicle (it could bring all its activities under one corporate umbrella should it wish) and hence could avoid the problems of consolidation. This is not possible for a company with activities which span many economic and legal environments.

Any set of accounts is intended to represent the results of the activities of a business over a period of time (the income statement, or profit and loss account) and the state of the business at the end of that period (the balance sheet). The normal entity that presents accounts is the legal entity. Groups of companies are multiple legal entities in which one such company owns (directly or indirectly) some proportion of the shares of the other companies. Frequently these entities trade among themselves. For the group of companies as a whole such transactions are internal to the group, and hence must be eliminated in the accounting statements that report the progress of the group. This is the essence of consolidation: the elimination of all individual inter-company shareholdings, debts, and purchases/sales so that all that remains is a depiction of the entity's relationship with the external world.

This apparently simple task is complicated by a number of problems. These are:

(a) in any context (domestic or foreign) what are the criteria for including an AFFILIATED COMPANY among those that are consolidated? There are differences in treatment among the legal or professional rules of different countries so that their general treatment of consolidation varies. In addition, their criteria as to whether to treat foreign subsidiaries equally with domestic subsidiaries differs also. Thus in the USA and UK, there is effectively equal treatment: in Germany it is not normal to consolidate overseas subsidiaries at all.

(b) How customary is it for companies in any one country to consolidate accounts? This varies from consolidation being taken for granted to its being the rare exception. In addition, even though the companies of a country may customarily consolidate, the extent to which the consolidation shows a 'true' picture of the entity may vary with the quality of accounting practice more generally.

(c) The results of all foreign subsidiaries must be translated into the currency of the home country before they can be incorporated in the group accounts. This involves a number of technical problems. (*See* TRANSLATION.)

Problematic as these are, the alternative to consolidation (that is, showing the parent – and possibly also subsidiary – financial statements individually) is far less helpful to the user. The freedom of choice available to management to make management charges, settle TRANSFER PRICES, dictate sub-

sidiary dividend levels and apportion overhead costs (among other things) means that the unconsolidated parent company's results would be much less meaningful.

The criteria for exclusion from consolidation vary among rule-setting authorities. Thus multinationals based in different home countries will tend to have group accounts that are difficult to compare across borders. Codified requirements include the following:

UK. Statement of Standard Accounting Practice No.14, which like all UK accounting standards is strongly persuasive but not binding. Affiliates are excluded from consolidation if

(a) the affiliate's activities are so dissimilar from those of the company as a whole that the needs of the users would be better served by separate financial statements; or
(b) the holding company does not hold over 50 per cent of the voting rights or the rights to appoint a majority of the directors; or
(c) the control by the parent is severely restricted; or
(d) the control is only temporary.

US. principally from the Accounting Principles Board Opinion No. 18, 1971, which is authoritative and persuasive, though not binding. The basic criterion is the extent to which control can be exercised over the affiliate. Thus limitations of control will lead to non-consolidation, control being presumed where the parent owns more than half the voting equity of the subsidiary. A subsidiary will not be consolidated however if its business is considerably different from the rest of the business and its inclusion would distort the group results. Some US companies do not consolidate foreign subsidiaries on these grounds.

EC. Seventh Council Directive of the Euro-

pean Community (which has been passed by the community but has not been incorporated into the individual corporate legislation of any of the EC member states at the time of writing). Affiliates are excluded from consolidation if

(a) the parent does not have the majority voting rights; or

(b) the parent does not have the right to control the majority membership of the directors of the subsidiary; or

(c) the parent does not have a 'dominant influence' over the subsidiary's activities.

International Accounting Standards Committee (IASC). Accounting Standard No.3 (persuasive but not binding, this is intended to lead the rulemaking bodies of member countries): affiliates are excluded from consolidation if

(a) control is temporary or

(b) the subsidiary operates under conditions in which severe long-term restrictions on the transfer of funds impair control by the parent company over the subsidiary's assets and operations.

A final issue concerns the meaning of consolidation for a multinational company: to what extent can it be considered to be a single entity from the point of view of the parent's shareholders? This question is particularly significant if dividend remittances are restricted, or the risks of overseas holdings are substantially different from the parent's or each other's.

It may be argued that, on the one hand, so long as a subsidiary is the property of the parent, then despite these issues it is part of the group as a whole and hence should be fully consolidated. The restriction of funds remittances may be taken as temporary, because they encourage reinvestment by the multinational in its subsidiary operations. The value of the subsidiary in local terms will thus increase, and in the absence of evidence to the contrary it may be supposed that at some distant time funds will be remittable. At that stage the funds may be remitted if the parent wishes: and, subject to differential investment opportunities among countries, it may be supposed that their discounted present value will be equivalent to a current funds transfer.

The alternative view is that this eventual remittance is sufficiently uncertain for the company not to be assumed to be one entity. Hence to treat such subsidiaries on the same footing – so far as consolidation is concerned – as home subsidiaries or foreign ones that are not subject to these issues can mislead the user of financial statements. This difference of approach means that the question is not to be easily resolved.

See also DISCLOSURE AND ACCOUNTS; FINANCIAL REPORTS; HOLDING COMPANY, and Index under Corporate Structure and Management, and under International Accounting.

consolidation. *See* CONSOLIDATED ACCOUNTS.

constructed price. Tax authorities in the HOME COUNTRIES of multinational corporations have become increasingly concerned with the tax avoidance potential of a company's TRANSFER PRICING. The phenomenon of INTRA-FIRM TRADE and the associated need on the part of the corporation to attach an ADMINISTERED PRICE to transactions between different parts of the firm, makes it possible for the company to assign transfer prices in such a manner as to minimize profits in high-taxation countries and maximize them in low-taxation countries.

To come to grips with this problem, the US Internal Revenue Service (IRS) has issued detailed guidelines to resident corporations for the purpose of calculating 'constructed' prices for transferred goods and services. The constructed price is meant to be an approximation of the true ARM'S LENGTH price plus a fair markup profit adjustment.

See Index under Regulation and Tax.

consular invoice. A document issued by the consulate of an importing country for customs and statistical purposes.

contagion hypothesis. A sociological hypothesis which holds that technical innovations are most effectively copied when there is personal contact between those who already have the knowledge of the innovation and those who eventually adopt it. By this reasoning, multinational corporations can be seen as especially effective transmitters of technology from advanced to less developed countries. The thesis would seem to underline particularly the need for expatriate personnel in the overseas subsidiaries.

See Index under Theoretical Issues.

controlled foreign corporation. *See* SUBPART 'F' INCOME.

convenience financial statements. The financial statements of a company specially tailored for those of its shareholders who are resident in another country. The special preparation may take one of two forms.

(a) The text of the financial statements may be translated into the language of the recipient's country, possibly with some additional descriptive material explaining the meaning of technical terms unique to the company's own national accounting conventions.
(b) In addition to such textual translation, there may also be a translation of the financial amounts into those of the recipient's currency. This translation will not however amend the accounting principles underlying the preparation of those accounts, and hence must be used with care by recipients comparing the translated results with those of companies in the recipient's own country.

See also Index under International Accounting.

convenience translation. *See* CONVENIENCE FINANCIAL STATEMENTS.

Convention on the Settlement of Investment Disputes between States and Nationals of other States. The first and only multilateral instrument for the protection of foreign investments, this Convention was sponsored and signed by the WORLD BANK in 1965, and ratified by 20 member countries in 1966 when it came into force. To date 83 countries have signed the Convention, but many of those Latin American countries that have been in frequent dispute with multinational companies are not among the signatories.

Previously, the emphasis in international law relating to the protection of property had been on diplomatic protection and LUMP SUM SETTLEMENTS. The Convention established the first international arbitration and conciliation procedure to carry some legal force. It lays down minimum legal commitments in a form which leaves everything on the level of optional undertakings (including the decision whether or not to refer an investment dispute to the arbitration machinery). However, once the investor and host state consent to submit their dispute to arbitration, they are bound to carry out their undertaking and abide by the award. Unless a contracting state has reserved its right to require the prior exhaustion of local administrative or judicial remedies, the issue is taken out of its own jurisdiction. Correspondingly, the contracting state whose national is involved in the dispute must refrain from giving diplomatic protection to its national or from bringing an international claim in the matter against the other contracting party.

With this Convention it was hoped that the availability of clear-cut facilities for concilation and arbitration in capital-importing states would stimulate a larger flow of private international investment into countries in need of such capital. An attractive feature of the Convention is that capital-importing contracting states, in signing the Convention, can acquire some credit-worthiness, without thereby accepting any obligation to submit any particular investment dispute to conciliation or arbitration.

The conciliation and arbitration facilities established under the Convention are contained in the INTERNATIONAL CENTER FOR THE SETTLEMENT OF INVESTMENT DISPUTES, which, while closely linked to and partly financed by the World Bank, has its own distinct legal personality.

See Index under Dispute and Settlement.

convertible bond. A bond that may be converted into equity shares under specified conditions.

See Index under Financial and Risk Management.

convertible currency. A national currency that can be freely bought and sold for other currencies.

co-operative exporter. The exporting operation of a company that is used by other companies to sell their products in foreign markets. The co-operative exporter gains by making the full use of the export channels he has built up, and the other users of the service gain from the cost-effective use of an already-existing organization. He may or may not take title to the goods (compare export commission representative and export distributor: *see* COMBINATION EXPORT MANAGER. The operation is also known as PIGGY BACKING.

See Index under Trade.

coproduction agreement. A non-equity JOINT VENTURE first pioneered between Western multinationals and the FOREIGN TRADE ORGANIZATIONS (FTOs) of Eastern bloc countries, but now also common in other centrally planned economies, particularly the People's Republic of China. In a coproduction agreement, the co-operating parties to a project agree by contract to carry out complementary productive activities using Western techniques, know-how and equipment. The output is shared between them according to a varying formula measuring their respective particpation. Although no equity sharing is involved, coproduction usually entails the presence of Western management and responsibility for production and distribution on the part of the multinational.

See also RED MULTINATIONALS; SOCIALIST COMMON ENTERPRISE; COUNTERTRADE; PRODUCTION SHARING AGREEMENT, and Index under Technology Transfer.

Corporate Accountability Research Group. *See* MULTINATIONAL MONITOR.

Corporate Data Exchange. Independent, non-profit making research organization which investigates economic concentration and corporate control. It maintains a large database on industries and companies. It publishes a variety of handbooks to assist in the research of corporations, including the Stock Ownership Directory Series. It also undertakes extensive research on American multinationals in South Africa.

See Index under Data Sources.
Address: 198 Broadway, Rm 706, New York, NY 10038, USA.

corporate imperialism. A concept predominantly encountered in academic literature critical of multinational enterprise. The concept has its roots in Marxist analyses of the development of CAPITALISM and its highest stage, IMPERIALISM. As the concept of imperialism is generally understood to refer to a pattern of world economic relations where one or more nation states extend sovereignty over other nation states, a contradiction in terms seems inevitable in 'corporate imperialism', for here fundamental power and domination in world economic relations are attributed not to any one nation state but to owners and managers of capital, who are said to exercise this power over other groups and institutions in order to appropriate surpluses and accumulate further capital. The dominated and exploited groups include government bureaucracies and consumers, as well as those groups more commonly thought to be exploited, including peasants and workers. These hierarchical relationships of dominance and exploitation are institutionalized within the framework of large, integrated, multinational corporations. But while the multinationals as a group are seen to constitute the institutional base of the system, individual multinationals are its principal instruments of action. The corporations' self-proclaimed objectives of 'profitability and growth' represent the system's objectives of surplus appropriation and capital accumulation. The hierarchy of roles and the network of dominance/dependency relationships within the individual corporation are a microcosm of the roles and relationships within the total system of corporate imperialism.

The theory of corporate imperialism has been developed, for example by Norman Girvan (1976), in the context of the vertically integrated, multidivisional, multinational corporate structure of the large resource industries, such as petroleum, aluminium, copper, and bauxite. The many conflicts between governments of mineral-exporting developing economies and the corporations are said to attest to the imperialist organization of the industries. There are conflicts over the division of the total surplus generated by the local industry; over the role of that industry within the national as opposed to the transnationally integrated corporate economy; and over power and authority invested in expatriate personnel as opposed to nationals or the government itself.

See also POST-IMPERIALISM; NEO-IMPERIALISM, and Index under Theoretical Issues.

corporate tax system. Most countries assess the profits of corporations to direct tax (exceptions include the world's TAX HAVENS). This said, there is a great variety in the ways corporation taxes are assessed. Differences include the following:

(a) The type of corporate tax system. There are a number of different systems employed throughout the world, but broadly the most important are the CLASSICAL, IMPUTATION and DUAL RATE systems.

The *classical* corporation tax system is one in which net corporate profits are taxed (possibly subject to adjustments) and any dividends that are paid from the post-tax profits are subjected to a further WITHHOLDING TAX assessed on the recipient. Normally the withholding tax is deducted by the company at the time the dividend is paid, and credited to the recipient in any personal assessment. This system is used, for example, in Belgium, Denmark, Italy and the USA, and was used in the UK from 1965 to 1973, when it was replaced by the imputation system. The rates and imposition of the withholding taxes may differ as between residents and non-residents, and may be the subject of DOUBLE TAXATION AGREEMENTS.

The *imputation* corporation tax system is one in which net corporate profits are taxed (possibly subject to adjustments) at a rate that includes an element 'imputed' to the recipient of any dividends that may be paid out of those profits.

The amount of dividend received by the shareholder is grossed up for assessment purposes, and the imputed tax credited to the shareholder as already paid. Normally the imputed tax credit is payable to the tax authorities at an early stage by the company as 'advanced corporation tax', and can be deducted from the full corporation tax subsequently due. This system is currently in use in France and the UK. The tax credit may vary in rate and incidence depending upon the residence or non-residence of the recipient, and may in addition be the subject of special provisions in any double taxation agreements.

The *dual rate* corporation tax system is one in which net corporate profits are taxed (possibly subject to adjustments) at different rates depending on whether they are distributed as dividend or not. The normal system taxes distributed profits at a lower rate than retained profits: however, the dividends received by the shareholders are subject to a withholding tax before payment by the company, which is later credited when the recipient is assessed to personal income tax. This system is currently used in Austria and West Germany, for example. The rates and imposition of the withholding taxes may differ between residents and non-residents, and may be the subject of double taxation agreements.
(b) The definition of what is to be included in the definition of income, and what are judged to be expenses permitted to be set against that income in the calculation of corporate tax liability.
(c) The rate(s) of corporation tax.
(d) The treatment of worldwide income.

These factors are of considerable importance to the multinational in its tax planning. Firstly, there will be a multiplicity of bilateral tax treaties between the multinational's home country and the various host countries that may significantly affect the structure of the tax charge. Secondly, the capital allowance is a particularly significant expense allowed against tax: that is, the amount of capital expenditure that the authorities permit the company to charge against income in any given year. For the company with a high amount of investment in the early years, high rates of capital allowances in these years (which can rise as

high as 100 per cent or even higher for countries attempting to encourage inward investment) can approach the benefits of a TAX HOLIDAY and can be highly significant in the investment decision. Thirdly, not only are the rates of direct corporate tax important, but variations in the withholding tax that may be charged to the shareholder in addition are also significant. The rate of these may interact with the corporate tax rate, as in the imputation and dual rate systems. This in turn may be affected by some kind of double taxation agreement.

A final point of significance to the multinational is the treatment of worldwide income. Although there are countries which make no attempt to tax income arising outside their own borders, most taxing authorities when faced with multinational organizations will tax foreign income. There are two basic ways in which this can be done. The first is to tax all income arising in the subsidiaries of parents that are based in the country concerned, whether or not it is remitted to the parent. The second is to tax only remitted income. The former tends to be more common, since the latter allows considerable leeway for the multinational to avoid the payment of tax by restricting dividend remittance.

See SUBPART 'F' INCOME; UNITARY TAXATION; INTERNAL REVENUE SERVICE CODE 482, and Index under Regulation and Tax, and under Financial and Risk Management.

correspondent bank. A foreign bank that has links with a domestic bank in such a way that each acts on behalf of the other in international transactions. Examples would be the acceptance of BILLS OF EXCHANGE and honouring LETTERS OF CREDIT.

See Index under Trade.

corruption. *See* BRIBERY.

cosmocorp. *See under* MULTINATIONAL COR-PORATION/ENTERPRISE.

cost and freight (C&F). *See under* EXPORT-ING TRADE TERMS.

cost and insurance. *See under* EXPORTING TRADE TERMS.

cost centre. A part of a firm that is treated as one unit for the purpose of responsibility for costs (compare INVESTMENT CENTRE and PROFIT CENTRE). Because of their relative independence, foreign operations of multi-nationals are normally treated as invest-ment or (more commonly) as profit centres. Treatment as a cost centre would be most unusual, except for operations such as sales offices, where setting off costs against rev-enues to derive budgeted profits is not easily achieved.

See Index under Corporate Structure and Management.

cost, insurance, freight (CIF). *See under* EXPORTING TRADE TERMS.

cost of capital. The cost of funds to a com-pany. The concept of the cost of capital is fundamental to the theory of finance. Broadly speaking, the cost of funds bor-rowed at a fixed rate of interest (bonds, debentures, or bank loans) is the nominal interest cost less the tax shield that arises as a result of the deduction which taxing authorities normally permit for interest from taxable income. The cost of equity capital is based on the expectations that shareholders have of the future receipt of dividends from companies of a given risk class (although the CAPITAL ASSET PRICING MODEL (CAPM) claims to be able to derive the amounts of the shareholders' expected return from market rates of return and the company's BETA). The cost of retained funds is that of equity capital (since retained earn-ings are the property of the shareholders,

and the cost of distribution must be linked to its opportunity cost) adjusted for transac-tion costs and possibly tax. Most approaches to cost of capital then weight these costs of raising funds by assessing the relative significance they have in the com-pany's capital structure, and advocate using the resulting weighted average cost of capi-tal as a criterion for potential investment projects available to the firm.

There are two aspects of the cost of capi-tal that are important to the multinational in contrast to the company with solely dom-estic operations. The first concerns the mechanisms of raising funds abroad. Although other countries' capital markets are available to all companies, multi-nationals have a greater propensity to con-sider them, both because of their absolute size and need for capital and also because their awareness of such markets is enhanced by their having international operations. They can, moreover, use foreign markets not just for the securities of the parent but also, should they wish, for those of subsidi-aries. The second aspect concerns the resulting cost of capital for the multi-national parent compared with non-multi-nationals raising funds in the same markets. Given its access to multiple capital markets and its ability to diversify internationally, does the multinational have a lower cost of capital than the domestic company?

There is evidence that national capital markets are not fully integrated – that is, there are differences in the rates of interest, transaction costs, and so on, despite the apparent opportunities for ARBITRAGE. This is known as segmentation. As a result it may be advantageous for a multinational to raise capital in a securities market or markets other than those of the parent company. The extent to which a multinational can take advantage of this segmentation will depend on the parent's home government's willingness to permit the free flow of capi-tal. The extent to which it is worthwhile for the company to do so will depend on the degree of segmentation – that is, the extent to which funds can be more cheaply obtained in foreign capital markets. Exploiting such opportunities will add to corporate risk by adding the cost of FOREIGN EXCHANGE RISK to the cost of such funds.

It is possible that the multinational has a lower cost of capital than the equivalent domestic firm. As a result of segmented capital markets, differentiated political risks and differential risks in product markets, the multinational can take advantage of different opportunities throughout the world. The portfolio effect of this will reduce the company's SYSTEMATIC RISK. This diversification by the multinational is helpful to investors who may be personally unable to diversify worldwide (perhaps as a result of national legislation forbidding individual foreign PORTFOLIO INVESTMENT). Despite this ban they may invest in the multinational so as to gain this advantage indirectly (*see* PORTFOLIO THEORY). The empirical evidence is mixed, and indeed the proposition may for technical reasons be untestable, but it does seem that over a long period multinational companies have averaged a lower cost of capital than domestic firms, although the reasons for this are not clear.

See also Index under Financial and Risk Management.

cost-reimbursable contract. A relatively new contractual arrangement in the transfer of technology from advanced to less developed countries. It differs from a typical TURNKEY CONTRACT in that it gives the purchaser a far greater degree of responsibility, control and obligations in the development and implementation of the project. In a cost-reimbursable contract, the purchaser is responsible for the choice and purchase of plant, equipment and materials (although normally on the advice of the contractor) as well as the civil engineering and erection of the plant. For his part, the contractor supplies process license and knowhow, basic and detailed engineering and procurement, and inspection and expediting services at a fixed fee. In addition, he supplies training and supervisory services for erection, commissioning and start-up of the plant. The latter are paid for on a cost plus basis.

This type of contract is suitable for purchasers in countries that have some basic industrial and engineering skills but which lack the expertise to develop an industrial project completely without external assistance. It also enables the purchaser to become fully involved with all the activities in the implementation of the project and hence increase his knowledge and experience. It has a further advantage to the purchaser of UNBUNDLING the technological package, permitting the procuring of equipment and the like on the basis of international competitive bidding. For this reason it is sometimes preferred by international financial agencies (like the WORLD BANK and INTERNATIONAL DEVELOPMENT ASSOCIATION (IDA)) which may be involved in the financing of such projects.

See Index under Technology Transfer.

Council for Mutual Economic Assistance (CMEA). Better known in the West as COMECON, the Council is the major international organization of the socialist countries. It was set up in 1949 in piqued response to the US Marshall Plan for Western Europe and the founding there of the Organization for European Economic Co-operation, a forerunner of the EC. Until 1962 only European socialist countries could join. Since then Mongolia, Vietnam and Cuba have acceded to full membership.

The reponsibilities of the Council are to promote multilateral co-operation and integration amongst the socialist countries in economic, scientific and technical fields. It aims to promote a planned socialist division of labour among member states on a voluntary basis and without the creation of supranational organs; to accelerate economic and technical progress; to achieve greater industrialization in the less industrialized member states; to foster a steady increase in labour productivity, a gradual equalization of levels of economic development and a constant improvement in the welfare of its peoples.

The actual Charter of the Council was not adopted until 1959 and it has undergone substantial changes since. The supreme organ of the Council is the Assembly, consisting of delegations of all member countries and meeting annually in one of the capitals of the member countries. The Executive Committee is made up of one representative from each country at the level of deputy prime minister.

See also SOCIALIST COMMON ENTERPRISE, and Index under International Co-operation.

Address: Prospekt Kalinina 56, Moscow 121205, USSR.

Counter Information Services (CIS). Independent non-profit making organization of critical journalists researching British foreign investment, banking, and various industrial sectors within the UK to assist unions and community-based groups. It publishes a newsletter, CIS Reports, and regular monographs.

See Index under Data Sources.

Address: 9 Poland Street, London NW1, UK.

counter purchase. A commercial transaction involving several related sales and purchase contracts, whereby the seller agrees, as part of his contractual obligations, to purchase goods and services from the buyer up to an agreed percentage of his own deliveries to the buyer. Counter purchase agreements are increasingly common between Western multinational corporations and Socialist countries. They differ from BUY-BACK DEALS in that they involve the exchange of unrelated products. The transactions also tend to be smaller and to take place within a short time interval.

See COUNTERTRADE, and Index under Technology Transfer and under Trade.

countertrade. The modern term for international BARTER transactions involving any contractual arrangement which commits the seller of a commodity or service to accept as payment in part or in full goods or services from the buyer. Thus defined, countertrade is a generic term spanning a wide variety of international trade transactions, from commercial compensation transactions through to industrial compensation transactions, and involving either government-to-government, company-to-government or company-to-company deals.

The variation between types of countertrade dealing is explained firstly by whether or not the kinds of goods exchanged are related or unrelated. For example, in BUY-BACK DEALS the goods presented for payment are the 'resulting output' of the purchased machinery/equipment/technology, whereas in a COUNTER PURCHASE agreement they need not be related. A second cause may be that the transaction is not a once and for all occurrence, as in a simple BARTER or a swap commercial transaction, but a long-term technology/industrial development project involving the contractor and/or a third party such as an international bank in a loan agreement with the purchaser, whose repayments may stretch over a period of up to 15 – 20 years. An even more enduring organizational form of countertrade is achieved in COPRODUCTION AGREEMENTS and in PRODUCTION SHARING AGREEMENTS.

Countertrade has been practised for some considerable time both between socialist countries and in East – West trade. But since the oil price increases of 1974, and still more since the debt crisis of 1980, countertrade has become very popular worldwide, especially in trade with and between developing countries, and in trade with member countries of the ORGANIZATION OF PETROLEUM EXPORTING COUNTRIES (OPEC). In several countries countertrade is mandatory. For example, for the last three years any individual or institution selling more than US$500,000 in goods to Indonesia has been legally bound to accept Indonesian products in payment. Ecuador and Malaysia are preparing similar laws, while Mexico, Brazil and the Republic of South Africa, which have not elaborated pertinent legislation, are in fact large-scale practitioners of countertrade when such transactions serve to open up new markets.

Estimates of the share of countertrade in world trade vary considerably, from the OECD's cautious figure of 4.8 per cent of world exports in 1983 to figures of 20 or even 40 per cent regularly quoted in the press (see OECD, 1985, pp. 10ff.) The uncertainty exists because countertrade deals are not specifically recorded as such in national account statistics, and because several of these deals are shrouded in secrecy for political reasons. OPEC members have for example started to use countertrade deals as a means of subverting mandatory oil production quotas set by OPEC. For their part, Western governments and multinationals are often reticent about countertrade deals since they may contravene the trade liberalization principles of the GENERAL AGREEMENT ON TARIFFS AND TRADE (GATT). (See MOST FAVOURED NATION (MFN) CLAUSE.) International organizations such as the International Monetary Fund (IMF), the World Bank and GATT have openly opposed mandatory countertrade.

The issue of countertrade is all the more sensitive because of its built-in opportunities for DUMPING. Western trade unions, domestic producers and governments have become alarmed at the scale of dumping on Western markets of cheap manufactured goods, especially clothing and textiles, from COMECON countries under countertrade arrangements with Western multinationals. Western car manufacturers too are extensively involved in countertrade: Renault, Fiat and BMW have all received components and automobile supplies to be sold in their home markets under counter purchase conditions.

Countertrade is of obvious advantage to nations burdened with massive international debts which are denominated in international currencies, such as the US dollar, which have fluctuations in value that debtor nations cannot control. For this reason, it is expected to become more important than it already is. Furthermore, with the development of sophisticated computational facilities the TRANSACTION COSTS of countertrade deals have been declining to a level where countertrade can become competitive with the use of money as a medium of exchange. Most of the large multinational companies today have separate countertrade divisions, and the first international countertrade clearing houses have been established.

Countertrade is definitely a rising star in the firmament of international economic relations, but whether it will also fundamentally transform these relations, and North – South relations in particular, remains to be seen.

See also SWITCH TRADE; BILATERAL CLEARING ARRANGEMENT; FOREIGN TRADE ORGANIZATION (FTO); OFFSETS, and Index under Trade and under Technology Transfer.

countervailing duty. A charge on imported goods to counteract the results of specific export subsidies granted by other countries, whether the latter are direct or indirect.

See Index under Trade.

country risk assessment. A process that most multinationals undertake, in a more or less formal way, to judge the risk involved in investing in a foreign country. Country risk assessment is important both to multinationals contemplating initial or further direct investment, and banks contemplating loans to the countries' governments or to commercial interests within the countries. Only the former will be considered here.

There are four types of factor that affect the risk of a direct foreign investment: climatic, economic, social and political. The first is comparatively simple to deal with, since there is no reason to suppose that historical records will not furnish generally good predictors of future conditions (although clearly major disasters such as earthquakes defy precise prediction). The three man-made risks are more difficult to forecast.

Forecasting methods may be subdivided into two main types. The first relies on objective past statistical data and may use anything from a simple ranking of countries based on a set of indicators to a complex weighted system perhaps employing sophisticated multivariate statistical techniques. Its advantage is that once the indicators have been selected, it is objective.

The principal disadvantage is the time delay between the availability of the data and the date of proposed investment: social and political circumstances can change quickly.

The second type relies on subjective estimates, and writers have suggested that there are three way of attempting this. The first is the 'grand tour', in which senior managers visit a country, interview local officials and report back to headquarters. The second method is the 'old hands' approach, in which outside consultants with expertise in the country in question over many years are used. The third method is a 'Delphi' technique, in which consultants and internal executives work through a complex process of judgments interactively so as to come to a solution.

Most studies of country risk assessment have concentrated on the forecasting of sociopolitical risk. It is necessary to be clear what may be said to constitute a risk. At the extreme there is CONFISCATION. Lesser risks include EXPROPRIATION without adequate compensation and government interventions that reduce profits: price controls, minimum wage legislation, discriminatory taxation, renegotiation of the terms of entry of the company, demands to provide infrastructural improvements, and restrictions on imports which the company considers essential for efficient production. There are also non-legislative risks, such as consumer pressure on foreign companies and labour unrest.

Many of these factors are met in all countries: it is their extent that is in question.

Various methods have been used to forecast risk of this kind. Most have concentrated on assessing countries as individual units and ranking them in risk. To do this, various surrogates have been used for political and social risk: frequency of change in government, number of civil disorders ranked according to their seriousness (for example, riots, assassinations), and internal security forces per 1000 people may be used as political indicators; linguistic or tribal fractionalization and GNP per capita growth as socioeconomic indicators. All of these methods are of limited usefulness, since the indicators and weightings are subjective (though they may be tested on past cases for predictive power) and they fail to capture the richness of sociopolitical situations. For example, absence of rioting may mean social cohesion and content, or it may mean repression is very efficient on the surface, leaving discontent to ferment unseen.

Commercial risk assessment services are available for consultation, but a *Business Week* comparison of two major ones (1980) showed that they led to different conclusions. Taking each survey's list of the ten best and ten worst risks, only four countries appeared in both 'best risk' lists and only three in both 'worst risk' lists.

An alternative method devised by Knudsen (1974) was to define conditions in terms of frustration, on the grounds that a gap between the welfare of the population and its aspired welfare was the best indicator of likely unrest. Research for a short period on South America claimed to show a high predictive power for the method.

The ways that companies make decisions on direct foreign investment and risk vary. Some survey evidence indicates little formal analysis in the major US companies. Evidence on what methods are used suggests that there are four main means of assessment: (a) a 'go – no go' method by which a country is deemed safe or not, and then considering only countries regarded as safe; (b) an assessment of countries by demanding higher rates of return for those deemed more risky (the 'risk-premium' method, probably the most common); (c) a 'range of estimates' method identifying salient factors through managerial estimates and subjecting these to sensitivity analysis; (d) a risk analysis using a decision tree to apply probabilities to likely outcomes in the country concerned.

A criticism of most of the above methods is that they imply homogeneity within countries. Yet it has been observed that industries with higher profiles, key positions in the economy, or monopolies, are more likely to face expropriation than others, and this may be at least as important in assessing the risk of a direct investment as evaluating the country as a whole. As a result, there is a further form of risk analysis, project risk analysis, which uses country risk assessment as a starting point.

A final criticism of all the many studies of this kind is that they fail to take into account the reactions of the country to the company's own behaviour and treat the country as a static fact rather than a changing environment.

See Index under Financial and Risk Management, and under Theoretical Issues.

covered interest arbitrage. A technique that enables those dealing in the foreign exchange and financial markets to profit by differences in short-term money rates and forward exchange currency rates which, according to the theory of INTEREST RATE PARITY, should be in line with each other. The technique involves borrowing in one currency for a fixed time, exchanging the funds borrowed into the second currency, investing it for that same time period in the second country, and selling the expected receipts of money forward for the first currency. So long as interest rates are not in parity this will result (bearing transaction costs in mind) in a profit, until the forward exchange rates fall into line with the differential in the short-term money rates. This arbitrage technique is also, therefore, the means by which interest rate parity is maintained.

See Index under Financial and Risk Management.

covering. An operation in the forward foreign exchange market in which a seller of goods for a price denominated in a foreign currency, due to be received at a fixed time in the future, can insure against an adverse movement of that currency between the time of the sale and the time of payment.

A covering operation for an exporter might work as follows. The sale is made for a price fixed in the foreign currency to be received in one month's time. The exporter wishes to ensure that he does not lose as a result of a decline in the value of that currency relative to his own country's during that month. He therefore sells an amount of the foreign currency in the forward market exactly equal to the amount due to him. When he receives his payment, he uses it to discharge the debt he contracted in the forward market, receiving from the dealer the amount of local currency he contracted for one month earlier.

A second method of covering is to borrow

an amount in the foreign country equal to the sale amount and discounted for one month (that is, to borrow an amount that, at the interest charged by the foreign bank, will exactly equal the payment due on the invoice one month later). The exporter immediately converts it into local currency and invests it for one month. At the end of that period he uses the amount received from his buyer to pay the amount due to the foreign bank (both of them being denominated in the foreign currency) and collects the local currency deposit he made together with accumulated interest.

See Index under Trade.

credit swap. A term sometimes used to denote an agreement between a multinational and a bank (frequently the central bank) of a foreign country through which the multinational's head office can lend funds to its AFFILIATE COMPANY without incurring the FOREIGN EXCHANGE RISK that is particularly associated with developing countries. For example, the corporate head office in the UK may lend to the UK branch of another country's central bank. The head office of the central bank lends an equivalent amount to the UK company's subsidiary in local currency. At a specified future date the original amount of the loan is repayable to the parent company head office in sterling, so that the company suffers no foreign exchange risk. At the same time the SUBSIDIARY abroad repays its loan in the local currency. The bank bears the foreign exchange risk and may be compensated for this.

See Index under Financial and Risk Management.

creeping expropriation. Expropriation indirectly resulting from some governmental action: discriminatory or confiscatory taxes, fines, currency devaluation, limitations on profits or profit remittances.

See also EXPROPRIATION; NATIONALIZATION, and Index under Financial and Risk Management.

cross-border transactions. Eclectic term for various forms of joint production and trade arrangements between firms located in different countries. The term came into vogue when the traditional pattern of foreign production by multinational companies in wholly owned subsidiaries gave way to more complex forms of co-operation such as JOINT VENTURES, minority affiliations, MANAGEMENT CONTRACTS, INTERNATIONAL SUBCONTRACTING, and so on.

See Index under Technology Transfer.

cross-default clause. A clause often included nowadays in international loan agreements with sovereign borrowers from less developed countries. It stipulates that if a borrower defaults on any loan with any lender, this shall be regarded as an event of default and entitle all other lenders to consider outstanding loans as becoming due.

Cross-default clauses are also frequently inserted within the complex loan structure of a single project involving a mixture of private commercial lending and multilateral public lending, such as those from the WORLD BANK. Failure to meet debt obligations to one party to the agreement is considered as failure to meet obligations to all of the parties concerned. In this way the cross-default clause helps to link the authority of the public lender to the exposure of the private lender, thereby – it is thought – reducing the risk of that exposure and enhancing the willingness of private lenders to engage in the transaction.

See Index under Financial and Risk Management.

cross-hauling. The shipment of semi-processed and intermediate goods between geographically dispersed affiliates of a multinational enterprise.

cross-licensing. A contractual arrangement between multinational enterprises. A multinational enterprise may prefer to license a new product or technology to another multinational rather than produce it in its overseas facility itself. When companies in particular industries frequently need to do this, they may exchange technology as a matter of routine rather than compete with each other. This is cross-licensing. Its advantages are reduced start-up costs where licensees are able to use the licensed technology more efficiently. Cross-licensing is subject to severe anti-trust constraints both in the US and in the European Community (EC).

See LICENSING AGREEMENT; ANTI-TRUST LEGISLATION; PATENT POOL, and Index under Industry Structure.

cross rate. The exchange rate between two currencies as derived from the exchange rate between each and a common third currency. For example, if £1 = US$1.50 and £1 = FF10.50 then the cross rate between the US dollar and the french franc is US$1 = FF7.

cross-subsidization. A practice sometimes engaged in by multi-product multinational companies (*see* CONGLOMERATE) in which profits from one product line are at times used to subsidize the pricing of another product below the level of long-term total costs. Cross-subsidization may be part of a corporate strategy for enlarging market shares in a given sector by underpricing competitors, or by mounting lavish promotional campaigns, or both.

Cross-subsidization may be practised not only on a product or industry basis but on a geographic basis: that is to say, a company may finance losses in some geographic areas in which it has a small share of the market with profits made in other areas where it has a relatively large market share.

See Index under Corporate Structure and Management.

currency cocktail. A mixture of currencies which may be used as a basis for denominating bonds. Whereas traditionally bonds have been floated internationally as denominated in a single currency, the fluctuations that have become commonplace with the adoption of FLOATING EXCHANGE RATES have made this more risky for intending lenders who may find their own currency has moved substantially against the currency in which a bond is denominated by the time repayment is due. To reduce the risk, bonds may be denominated in a basket of currencies rather than one alone, since the fluctuations of such a basket will be less than the fluctuations of one currency alone.

The particular basket used will generally be one that has widespread acceptance such as the SPECIAL DRAWING RIGHT (SDR) of the INTERNATIONAL MONETARY FUND (IMF) and the EUROPEAN CURRENCY UNIT (ECU), although other baskets have been used in the past. As far as the denomination of the bonds is concerned, payment for them and interest payable on them will generally take place in a single currency.

See Index under Financial and Risk Management.

currency exchange agreement. A modification of the BACK TO BACK LOAN, sometimes known as a 'currency swap', in which two companies in different countries swap an agreed amount of funds in their respective currencies. A future date is specified at which time – either based on an option or an obligation – the same amount of those currencies shall be re-exchanged. Since normally one currency is stronger than the other, one party bears more risks, and currency exchange agreements normally therefore incorporate a fee paid by the company lending the stronger currency to the other.

See Index under Financial and Risk Management.

currency swap. *See* CURRENCY EXCHANGE AGREEMENT.

currency translation. *See* TRANSLATION.

customs union. An economic union between two or more countries involving (a) the removal of all barriers (TARIFFS and QUOTA) to the free exchange of goods and services provided by the signatories; and (b) the establishment of common external barriers against non-member countries.

See Index under International Co-operation.

D

Data Center. Independent and non-profit-making library and resource centre which collects and organizes information on political and economic issues. It has files on over 6000 corporations covering the period since 1970. Other files are organized under the headings of country, industry, labour, military and government. Profiles are completed on request.

See Index under Data Sources.
Address: 464 19th Street, Oakland, California CA94612, USA.

Data Star. Commercial organization 'hosting' several databanks of company and industrial sector information, including the New York Times Information Data Base, and the Financial Times Company Information. Publishes a monthly magazine, *Data Star Newsletter.*

See Index under Data Sources.
Address: D-S Marketing, 5th Floor Plaza Suite, 114 Jermyn Street, London SW7 6HJ, UK.

debt rescheduling. The change in the time period over which a debt has to be repaid, generally to a bank. Over the last few years the rescheduling of debt due from developing nations to international banks, particularly through SYNDICATED LOANS, has attracted widespread attention. Interest on such loans has in many cases risen to very substantial proportions of such countries' exports and GNPs, and repayment of the principal at the time originally agreed has proved impracticable. Rather than permit default to take place, bankers have agreed to reschedule the capital repayments. The probability that many countries will never be able to repay loans without a restructur-ing of the whole system is now accepted as very real, and already steps are being taken to find alternative means of settling loans, such as conversion of the debt into holdings of equity in debtor countries' industries.

See also DEBT SERVICE RATIO, and Index under International Co-operation and under Development Policy.

debt service ratio. The ratio of payments made by a national economy to service its foreign debt, that is, the interest payments and repayments of principal as a percentage of the economy's export earnings. The debt service ratio is one of the more important indicators used in COUNTRY RISK ASSESSMENT models.

See Index under Financial and Risk Management.

decapitalization.. The net outflow of capital from a country as a result of multinational corporate investment there. Such a net outflow is said to occur if the earnings generated by past investments and remitted abroad exceed the inflow of new FOREIGN-DIRECT INVESTMENT (FDI) over a specified period of time.

Decision 24. *See under* ANDEAN PACT COUNTRIES.

Declaration and Decisions on International Investment and Multinational Enterprises. In 1976, the governments of the member countries of the ORGANIZATION OF ECONOMIC CO-OPERATION AND DEVELOPMENT (OECD) adopted three related instruments for dealing with international investment and multinational enterprises: Guidelines for Multinational Enterprises, National

Treatment for Firms under Foreign Control and International Investment Incentives and Disincentives. Together these three instruments were intended to provide a balanced framework within which the OECD countries might organize their co-operation and consultation on issues relating to international investment and multinational enterprises.

1. Guidelines for Multinational Enterprises. Since the statutes of the OECD provide only for decisions, which are binding, and recommendations, which are not, to be addressed to member countries but not to private bodies such as multinational enterprises, the formulation of the Guidelines took the unusual form of a declaration by the member governments to 'jointly recommend' a code of practice to the multinational enterprises operating or originating within their territories. The Guidelines therefore are explicitly voluntary, but while they do not have legal force, they do have the authority of endorsement by the governments of all OECD member countries. This is in itself not without legal significance. Governments also committed themselves to active 'promotional' exercises, distributing the Guidelines to the business community, labour unions, professional federations and Chambers of Commerce, as well as individual companies. These promotional efforts were augmented by those of the international business and international trade union representative bodies of the OECD. (*See* BUSINESS AND INDUSTRY ADVISORY COMMITTEE (BIAC) and TRADE UNION ADVISORY COMMITEE (TUAC.)) Multinational enterprises, on their part, were asked to 'endorse' the Guidelines by making reference to them in their Annual Reports and other public presentations.

Because some of the guidelines go beyond existing legislation in the member countries, they may set in motion the creation of new laws, particularly if there are no express rules bearing on a specific case, and the use of the guidelines in preventing or resolving the conflict prefigures the shape of an equitable solution. The guidelines are thus also a source of law, and this indeed was the intention of the drafters of the declaration in 1976. Finally, the declaration included a commitment by the member governments to a process of consultation and review of all three instruments relating to international investment 'with a view to improving the effectiveness of international economic co-operation among member countries'. The particular significance of this for the guidelines was the resulting built-in process of clarification, review and revision (in 1979 and 1984) which was intended to preserve the evolutionary character of the guidelines as a source of law. In the early years after the declaration of 1976 this intention seems to have been realized: in the run up to the 1979 review, for instance, the OECD committee responsible for the guidelines (COMMITTEE ON INTERNATIONAL INVESTMENT AND MULTINATIONAL ENTERPRISES (CIME)) dealt with over 20 cases of disputes brought before it, 'clarifying' and 'interpreting' the wording of the Guidelines, though not actually 'settling' these disputes. Indeed, the actual resolution of disputes is beyond its brief or terms of reference. But out of this process of dispute, consultation and clarification emerged some of the revisions and amendments to the guideline document, adopted by the OECD member governments in 1979. To strengthen this evolutionary process still further, in the 1979 review member governments also agreed to set up NATIONAL CONTACT POINTS for undertaking promotional activities, handling enquiries and discussions on all matters relating to the guidelines with the parties concerned.

For all their sophistication as a voluntary, evolutionary code of practice, the Guidelines can only be as successful as the commitment of the interested parties. The worsening economic climate and the resulting competition between nations vis-à-vis foreign direct investment have sapped the energy and excitement originally invested in them. Governments, trade unions and the international business community have all shown signs of disenchantment and weariness in recent years, which have been expressed in reduced promotional activities, declining interest in seeking clarifications from CIME and in the decision by the member governments at the 1984 review to have a breathing space and to undertake no further reviews until 1990.

The substance of the Guidelines is contained in an introduction and seven chapters: general policies, disclosure of information, competition, financing, taxation, employment and industrial relations, and science and technology. The wording of the introduction and in five of the chapters is sufficiently abstract and non-specific to strike a fine balance between the COMITY PRINCIPLE and an evolving common philosophy which no more than charts an outline for further action. The idea behind the many passages which are hinged on 'having regard' or 'taking full consideration of' clauses is to commit neither governments nor multinational enterprises to specific forms of action, but nevertheless to express attitudinal sentiments which they are bound to take to heart and to find it difficult to disavow later on. Thus, for example, multinational enterprises should 'take fully into account established general policy objectives of the member countries in which they operate', and, in managing the financial and commercial operations of their activities 'take into consideration the established objectives of the countries in which they operate regarding balance of payments and credit policies', and 'endeavour to ensure' that their activities 'fit satisfactorily into the scientific and technological policies and plans of the countries in which they operate'.

The two chapters which offer specific and detailed recommendations are the chapter on disclosure of information and that on employment and industrial relations. But the recommendations on information disclosure fall in line with – or indeed arguably fall short of – domestic legislation already existing in many of the OECD countries and/or internationally binding codes of practice such as the EUROPEAN COMMUNITY (EC)'s Fourth Directive. In the case of the chapter on unemployment and industrial relations, the very nature of the detail coupled with the equivocal wording has prompted precisely the kind of controversies and 'clarification seeking' behaviour which the voluntary and evolutionary design of the guidelines meant to provoke. In one of the nine subsections of this chapter, the recommendation that multinational enterprises 'should respect the right of their employees to be represented by trade unions and other bona fide organizations of employees' has been one source of dispute, as has the phrase that enterprises should 'enable authorized representatives of their employees to conduct negotiations on collective bargaining or labour management relations issues with representatives of management *who are authorized* to take decisions on the matters under negotiation' (emphasis added). Both phrases were affirmed by CIME in the clarification procedures following the disputes. A third bone of contention, 'that enterprises, in the context of *bona fide* negotiations with representatives of employees on conditions of employment, or while employees are exercising a right to organize, not threaten to utilize a capacity to transfer the whole or part of an operating unit from the country concerned in order to influence unfairly those negotiations or to hinder the exercise of a right to organize', was clarified once by the CIME, and then again in the 1979 review, by the addition 'nor transfer employees from the enterprises' component entities in other countries in order to influence unfairly'. Finally, paragraph eight of the introduction to the Guidelines, germane to matters discussed in the chapter on employment and industrial relations, was also revised subsequent to the process of dispute and clarification. The original text states that 'the Guidelines are addressed to the various entities within the multinational enterprise (parent companies and/or local entities) according to the 'actual distribution of responsibilities among them on the understanding that they will co-operate and provide assistance to one another as necessary to facilitate observance of the Guidelines'. This was clarified as meaning that parent companies are expected to take the necessary organizational steps to enable their subsidiaries to observe the guidelines; *inter alia* by providing them with adequate and timely information and ensuring that their representatives who carry out negotiations at the national or local level have sufficient authority to take decisions on the matters under negotiation.

2. National Treatment Instrument. *See under* NATIONAL TREATMENT.

3. Incentives/Disincentives Instrument. This instrument consists of a declaration and a decision which, together, are aimed at strengthening co-operation between member countries in the field of international direct investment. Incentive and disincentive measures are used by member governments to influence the nature, location and size of direct investment for a variety of policy purposes such as industrial, regional, technology, employment and trade factors. Often these incentive and disincentive measures are part of the overall economic policies of member countries. The Incentive/Disincentive Instrument was designed to prevent 'beggar thy neighbour' policies developing between member countries in the keen competition for international direct investment. The instrument does not cover incentives and disincentives in respect of domestic investments.

The instrument consists of three main elements: a declared commitment by member countries 'to give due weight to the interests of (other) member countries affected by specific laws, regulations and administrative practices providing official incentives and disincentives to international direct investment'; a declared commitment by member countries 'to endeavour to make such measures as transparent as possible so that their importance and purpose can be ascertained and information on them can be readily available'; and a decision to provide for consultations in the framework of CIME 'at the request of a member country which considers that its interests may be adversely affected by the impact on its flow of international direct investments of measures taken by another member country specifically designed to provide incentives or disincentives for international direct investment'.

See also CODE OF CONDUCT; BADGER CASE, and Index under International Co-operation.

defensive investment. A FOREIGN DIRECT INVESTMENT (FDI) by a multinational company in a particular national or regional market intended to preserve for its exports an existing market share which is threatened by local or other foreign competition.

See under PRODUCT CYCLE THEORY.

delinking. A term used in literature on international trade and development describing the domestic policies of some THIRD WORLD countries which are designed to limit the dependent involvement of their economies in the world economy.

See DEPENDENCY; OPEN DOOR POLICIES; AUTARCHY, and Index under Development Policy.

delivered duty paid. *See under* EXPORTING TRADE TERMS.

demonstration effect. The impact on an individual of seeing a larger variety or superior quality of goods, which may lead that individual to increase expenditure to buy such goods even though his or her income has not changed.

In a similar way, the emulation of consumption patterns of the rich countries by the wealthy elites of poor countries, which is initiated through trade, travel and tourism, in turn acts as a model for the tastes and consumption patterns of the poor. This demonstration effect is reinforced by the investment patterns of multinational corporations and their marketing, advertising and communications techniques.

de novo entry. *See* GREENFIELD INVESTMENT.

depackaging. *See* UNBUNDLING.

dependency. In the widest, uncritical sense of the term, dependency refers to the degree to which a national economy relies on foreign trade, foreign capital and foreign technology for its survival and growth. In conventional economic usage nothing sinister or detrimental has been implied in the term.

The critical connotation of the term dates from the early 1960s and has two quite separate intellectual roots. First there was the work of the 'structuralist' school of writers associated with the UN Economic Commission for Latin America (including Raoul Prebisch and Celseo Furtado) who criticized the then prevailing conventional economic theory of international trade and comparative advantage. They argued instead that the position of less developed countries in the contemporary structure of the international division of labour, in which they were assigned the role of primary producers, caused their economic stagnation and underdevelopment. This was seen as the result of the deterioration of the terms of trade for primary commodities in the exchange with manufactures, inherent partly in the nature of the commodities traded (such as differential demand elasticities) and partly in the differential evolution of wages embodied in the commodities exchanged.

The second intellectual root came from neo-Marxist thinkers on imperialism, who examined the effects of imperialism in the colonial and ex-colonial countries, and who criticized both liberal theories of MODERNIZATION and orthodox Marxist theories of IMPERIALISM. Paul Baran in *The Political Economy of Growth* (1957) argued that 'development and underdevelopment' is a two-way street: the advanced capitalist countries developed by expropriating the economic surplus of overseas countries with whom they traded and which they later colonized, while the overseas countries became underdeveloped through aiding the ascendancy of the West. Interaction with the industrializing countries left the overseas countries with a narrowly specialized, export-oriented primary production structure which found its handmaiden in a frozen internal class structure dominated by a small, mercantile COMPRADOR elite. Even after political independence, the shared interests of the imperialist states and ex-colonial elites, and the specialization of production, blocked any attampt to industrialize or effect internal social transformation. The result was overall economic stagnation and the pauperization of the masses. In contrast to Marx's optimism about the historically progressive role of capitalism everywhere, Baran led the neo-Marxists in demonstrating the historical failures of the imported type.

André Gunder Frank's *Capitalism and Underdevelopment in Latin America* (1967) expanded and formalized Baran's notions into a theory of dependency and underdevelopment which postulated three laws of motion concerning the process of development and underdevelopment. He coined the term 'metropolis-satellite' to characterize the nature of worldwide imperialist economic relations, and became the best known dependency theorist.

The Baran – Frank dependency theories advocated a 'radical break' with world capitalism as a requisite for the development of the now underdeveloped countries.

Dependency theory has had a great influence on the political ideologies of many less developed countries, particularly in Latin America, where it helped underpin an already strong tradition of populist ideology (*see* POPULISM). It has been criticized by Marxist writers like Bill Warren (1980) for disarming the working class and the socialist movement inside the Third World, subordinating them to ideologies of nationalist, anti-imperialist unity and inducing them to bow to undemocratic regimes.

More recently, however, Latin American scholars of the same tradition (the *'dependista'* writers) have reformulated dependency theory in the light of the economic development which has quite obviously taken place in Latin America within the orbit of international capitalism. Recognizing that domestic industrialization and sustained economic growth have occurred during an imperial alliance between foreign multinational companies and the national state, they have concentrated on pairing apparent economic success with such social failures as rising inequalities, the increasing marginalization of substantive sectors of the population, deepening class conflict and mounting repression by authoritarian regimes. Early dependency models regarded the internal class structure as a lifeless victim of external domination, but the new dependency theory is more optimistic about the potential for internal class struggle, reform and even transition to socialism without a prior radical break with the world capitalist system being necessary. (*See*, for example, Cardoso and Faletto, 1967).

See Index under Theoretical Issues, and under Development Policy.

deregulation. The abolition of governmental, institutional, or professional controls on the behaviour of people or corporations in socioeconomic affairs. The perceived failure of market mechanisms over the course of this century has led to an increasing number of controls over such matters as food purity, employment policy (especially minimum wages), cartelization, restrictions on entry into institutions (such as the Stock Exchange) or professions (such as lawyers and accountants). Advocates of free market solutions have argued for the abolition of these controls on the grounds that the market mechanism is more efficient than administrative regulation in allocating resources. In the USA and the UK particularly it has become declared government policy to dismantle many restrictive practices and institutions, and both countries have gone some way to achieving this.

A number of aspects of deregulation have been important to multinational enterprise. These are:

(1) The abolition of exchange controls in the UK in October 1979. Before this, Bank of England permission was required for the export of funds, and the dollar premium was payable on capital purchases outside the UK. The freedom to move funds has had many effects, one of which has been a very high export of PORTFOLIO INVESTMENT funds from the UK in the period since 1979.

(2) A reluctance to pursue anti-trust actions in the USA. Although definite evidence is difficult to come by, some commentators have suggested that in the current political climate the willingness of the US administration to prosecute alleged violations of ANTI-TRUST LEGISLATION has declined markedly in recent times.

(3) The abolition of restrictive practices in the UK stock market on 27th October 1986. The so-called 'big bang' is expected to increase the holdings of international financial conglomerates in, for example, UK stockbroking firms.

The abolition of controls where they are perceived to be harmful to national interests is not a new phenomenon. For example, the US REGULATION Q was suspended in 1974.

See Index under Regulation and Tax.

DFI. Abbreviation for 'direct foreign investment'. *See* FOREIGN DIRECT INVESTMENT.

Dialog Information Services. American commercial concern affiliated to the Lockheed Company and 'hosting' a large number of company and industrial sector data banks. These include Standard and Poor's, Harfax Industry Data Sources, Predicast and others. Online and offline service offered.

See Index under Data Sources.
Address: PO Box 8, Abingdon, Oxford OX13 6EG, UK.

direct foreign investment (DFI). See FOREIGN DIRECT INVESTMENT.

Directory of Social Change. An educational charity which provides information, advice and help to charities and other 'good cause' organizations in fundraising, administration and promotion. It publishes the most comprehensive list of handbooks and guides aimed at all those who run or work for or advise charities. The second edition of its *A Guide to Company Giving* (1986) contains information on the donations of over 1000 leading companies, the donation policies of the 150 largest companies, details of over 100 grant-making trusts linked to companies, and advice on how to approach companies for charitable contributions and arts sponsorship.

See Index under Data Sources.
Address: Radis Works, Back Lane, London NW3 1HL, UK.

dirty float. A term sometimes used to describe a MANAGED FLOAT.

DISC. *See* DOMESTIC INTERNATIONAL SALES CORPORATION.

disclosure in accounts. The amount of salient information which an enterprise is required to disclose in its published financial statements varies greatly according to national accounting rules. This raises two main questions. The more important is the extent to which information is available at all, and in addition there is the extent to which reporting companies make such information easily accessible. The extent to which information is available at all is governed by the cultural attitudes to secrecy of the country concerned, the extent to which the government or other regulatory authority has specified disclosure in addition to what business would otherwise disclose, and the pressure upon reporting companies from institutions such as large investors and banks. The extent to which the regulations emanating from international institutions such as the INTERNATIONAL ACCOUNTING STANDARDS COMMITTEE (IASC), the UN, the ORGANIZATION FOR ECONOMIC CO-OPERATION AND DEVELOPMENT (OECD) and the EUROPEAN COMMUNITY (EC) are persuasive or binding in the country concerned must also be considered. Finally, there is the extent to which the company concerned is international in outlook: companies from countries that do not have extensive disclosure regulations but have their securities quoted on the markets of countries that are more rigorous, will generally be obliged to disclose more than others.

Certain core items will be disclosed in all countries: fixed assets, cash balances and shareholders' equity, for example. Few items are of this type, however. Gross asset values may not be distinguished from net values after depreciation; the basis of doubtful debt provision may be undisclosed, and so also may be the basis of depreciation or the capitalization of expenses such as research and development; even turnover may not be disclosed. Even where items are disclosed they may not be comparable (*see* ACCOUNTING PRINCIPLES).

Turning to the second aspect, the extent to which information is easily accessible, a number of barriers may be encountered. The notes to the accounts may be complex and difficult to unravel; comparative figures from previous years may be omitted: items may be concealed by the use of ambiguous language. A further, though not insurmountable, problem in international comparison is that the format of financial statements varies widely; assets may be on the right or left of a balance sheet (or above or below in the case of vertical formats), and the most liquid or least liquid may be listed first, depending on the individual country's traditions and rules.

The reason why accounts in some countries are so poor compared to others may be explained by the varying level of business sophistication; the different structures of capital markets (for instance, if banks have representation on corporate boards, other channels than published information are available to them); and by the structure of share ownership, since if a few family shareholders control a company they too will have other channels of information open to them. The problems of disclosure for multinational companies are similar to those discussed under ACCOUNTING PRINCIPLES. As multinational corporate enterprise spreads so that it originates from countries other than the US – UK axis within the developed world, the quality of disclosure between multinationals may become increasingly varied.

See Index under International Accounting.

Disclosure Incorporated. Commercial information service specializing in the sale of copies of all information that American companies are required to lodge with the SECURITIES AND EXCHANGE COMMISSION (SEC).

See Index under Data Sources.
Address: 516 River Road, Bethesda, Maryland MD 20816, USA.

discount house. A UK institution which specializes in discounting short-term securities such as BILLS OF EXCHANGE and Treasury bills: that is, buying them at a price lower than the maturity price and then normally holding them until maturity so as to realise a capital gain. Similar institutions exist in countries influenced by the UK financial system such as Singapore and South Africa.

discrimination. *See* NON-DISCRIMINATION RULE.

disinvestment. More gradual and less complete than DIVESTMENT, disinvestment involves the draining of investment funds away from a subsidiary operation: for example, when dividend remittance abroad exceeds the locally generated cashflows in any one accounting period.

displacement effect. An indirect effect of multinational corporate investment in a national economy, which occurs when indigenous production is undermined, diminished or eliminated altogether as a result of the presence of the foreign producer.

diversification. A key aspect of the large company is its ability to diversify its activities. This diversification can be an expansion, or a broadening of the product and area portfolio. The multinational company is particularly strongly placed to diversify and, indeed, it is its very diversity that gives it much of its character. The term refers to both to horizontal and vertical diversification.

Diversification for the multinational can take place through

(a) Product markets. Such diversification may be minor, as where new products are developed similar in many respects to existing ones, or major. The tobacco industry, which has moved into food and other product lines, is a case in point.

(b) Geographical markets or production. The multinational can sell in new national markets – whether or not it chooses to produce in the country concerned – and spread its production facilities among different plants in one country or among different countries of the world, thus reducing dependence on one ~ facility and hence reducing risk.

(c) Business sectors more generally. According to PORTFOLIO THEORY it is advantageous to diversify because of the imperfect interdependence among investment opportunities. Unlike the market-based rationales in (a) and (b) above, this is an entirely financially based theoretical justification for diversifying. Finance theory does not however advocate diversification by companies, recommending that they remain with one risk class of business and that shareholders diversify instead.

(d) Sources of finance. Because the movement of exchange rates is uncertain, the cost of any individual source of funds, whether in the country of the parent or otherwise, is also uncertain. Accordingly, the multinational can diversify its sources of equity and loan capital so that these risks are spread across a large number of currencies.

In most of these cases a further advantage of diversification is the flexibility it gives the enterprise in the face of environmental changes; whether in customer demand, political action, technological development or currency movement.

However, although various aspects of spreading risk are among the significant rationales for diversification, many other theories have been developed on the basis that companies have diversified in the past

through believing they have observed particularly fruitful market opportunities outside their own sphere, including the ability to capitalize on oligopolistic advantages. (*See* OLIGOPOLY MODEL, PRODUCT CYLE THEORY, INTERNALIZATION THEORY.) One particular argument against encouraging product diversification concerns the possible inability of the existing management to handle the problems that arise in any new sphere.

See Index under Financial and Risk Management, Corporate Structure and Management, and Theoretical Issues.

divestment. The closure, full or partial sale, EXPROPRIATION, CONFISCATION or NATIONALIZATION of an operation.

See also DISINVESTMENT.

dividend repatriation. The ability of a multinational company to make dividend payments from SUBSIDIARIES to the parent company freely.

The factors that may impede the repatriation of dividends fall under two classes.

(a) Direct barriers. Many countries have exchange control regulations which require the permission of the financial authorities before funds can be exported, or ban some classes of funds transfers entirely (*see* BLOCKED FUNDS).

(b) Indirect barriers. There may be political pressures (frequently tacit) which discourage a company from repatriating dividends. Where the government or national sentiment (expressed perhaps through the press) is sensitive to multinational enterprise in particular, or BALANCE OF PAYMENTS or similar issues in general, such pressures may exist.

In opposition to this, multinational companies see the issue as central to their operations, since a fundamental rationale for investment is the ability to receive a return on that investment. It has been suggested that a subsidiary cannot be considered part of the multinational group as a whole if fund remittances are blocked. Dividend repatriation is therefore an issue that will frequently be negotiated at the time of entry into or expansion in a country as part of a package.

See Index under Financial and Risk Management and under Regulation and Tax.

division. A form of organization that is commonly found in the diversified multinational corporation.

The essence of a division, in contrast to a department or other organizational unit, is that it operates in most respects as if it were a firm in itself, with autonomy in most spheres of decision making. The divisional head is responsible for production, marketing and financial decisions, and has line authority over all such functions. This decentralization will however be qualified in some respects; the finance function in most cases, for example, is relatively centralized. Similarly the marketing function will tend to be centralized in certain industries, such as consumer products.

The essence of the divisionalized form is that it enables decisions to be made closer to the ground where they will have effect. Moreover it is claimed that the divisionalized form has further advantages.

It increases the motivation of high-quality managers by giving them full responsibility for a defined area of the business, and this in turn aids the company by giving training for such responsibility to managers and also indicating those managers suitable for promotion.

It also avoids the problems of the large firm identified by Penrose (1959) and others, namely, that the very large firm is hampered by the complexity of the decisions to be made and by the high degree of expertise required for multiple areas of operations. To overcome such problems, the areas at which such decisions must be made are split into acceptably sized divisions. Divisional organization also enables greater integration of functions – for example, between procurement, production and marketing in any one country.

The whole matter of the structure of the multinational has been the subject of considerable debate. Various forms have been tried, including product-based structure, geographically based structure, and various forms of MATRIX ORGANIZATION; some companies have used the INTERNATIONAL DIVISION in the parent structure to bring foreign operations under one umbrella. There is evidence that certain types of structure are to be found more commonly in certain sizes of firm or certain industries.

See also CENTRALIZATION, and Index under Corporate Structure and Management.

doctrine of domicile. A doctrine that states that foreign individuals and enterprises must behave in accordance with the laws and customs of their host countries.

While originating as a principle of international law, today the doctrine is sometimes elevated to the status of an ideology eminently suited to the practice and scope of multinational enterprise. Some multinational companies claim that their global economic interests transcend their loyalty to any one particular nation. Hence, it is asserted they are 'above' nations and that this is what makes it possible for them to behave like good citizens in any country, whatever its political or cultural composition.

See POST-IMPERIALISM, and Index under Dispute and Settlement.

documentary draft. *See under* BILL OF EXCHANGE.

documentary letter of credit. *See under* LETTER OF CREDIT.

domestic international sales corporation (DISC). A special kind of favourable tax status for eligible companies in the USA. Enacted in 1971 to provide an incentive to encourage exports, the system operates on the principle that federal corporation tax is not charged on the DISC's profits as such but that tax is payable only on distributions to shareholders (either actual or deemed) on a complex basis. A DISC may be incorporated in any State; some States tax DISCs in just the same way as other corporations.

Five requirements must be satisfied for DISC status to be awarded to a company. It must not be engaged in manufacturing; it must receive at least 95 per cent of its gross revenue from 'qualified export receipts'; at least 95 per cent of its assets at the end of the year must be 'qualified export assets' as defined; it must elect to be treated as a DISC; and it must satisfy certain requirements concerning minimum capital and the types of security that constitute its equity.

See Index under Regulation and Tax.

domestic sourcing. *See* LOCAL SOURCING.

domestic value added. *See* LOCAL VALUE ADDED.

double sourcing. Multinational companies which have developed globally fragmented, yet organically integrated, production patterns will sometimes take the precaution of establishing duplicate plants in different geographic locations lest the entire network of production be endangered by a production failure in one plant in one country. Amongst other things, double sourcing offers the multinationals a degree of independence of and control over union actions such as stoppages and strikes in any one location by permitting speedy switching between sources of supplies.

See Index under Corporate Structure and Management.

double taxation agreement. A bilateral treaty between nation states establishing agreed methods of avoiding the taxation of the same business profits in both countries. In general, corporate tax philosophy differs depending upon whether or not the business is domiciled or headquartered in the country concerned. There are two main variants.

Where the company's headquarters is in the country concerned, the taxing authorities may hold to one of two basic principles. The first is to tax a company with international operations on its earnings in the home country alone. The second and more common approach is to raise an assessment on its worldwide earnings and then deduct from the assessment a sum in respect of the tax that has already been levied in the countries where the earnings originated. Frequently, however, this tax credit will not be as great as the foreign tax charge (for instance, if the corporate tax rate in that country is greater than the domestic rate).

Where the company is not domiciled in the country concerned, then tax will normally only be charged on income arising from the operations of the subsidiary in that country. An exception that has recently become controversial is the UNITARY TAXATION system which some US States have attempted to apply.

To avoid the problems of the system of deducting tax credits from worldwide income, a tax treaty or double taxation agreement may be signed between two nation states. These agreements are always bilateral. Because each treaty is individually negotiated there are no general provisions. However a frequent provision of such a treaty is that the country that has the right to tax each particular type of income is specified in the treaty so that the income is not taxed twice and hence no tax credit is needed. Because of the limits frequently applied to tax credits, this provision can be advantageous to the companies concerned.

See also STEPPING STONE COMPANY, and Index under Regulation and Tax.

downstream activities. Within vertically integrated production processes the term 'downstream' refers to production activities and commercial transactions at or near the mine-end of the integrated production chain, such as exploration and exploitation of mineral resources. Upstream activities, on the other hand, occur at the market end of the chain: refining, manufacturing, assembly.

draft. *See* BILL OF EXCHANGE.

Drago doctrine. *See* CALVO CLAUSE.

drawback. A refund of duties and internal taxes to the exporter of a product that was previously imported into the country.

See Index under Trade.

dualism. Probably the first theoretical concept invented to characterize the social and economic structure of underdeveloped areas. It originated in the 1930s with Boeke's analysis of the Dutch East Indies, now Indonesia (Boeke, 1953).

'Social dualism', Boeke claimed, was the clashing of an imported social system with an indigenous social system of another style. Underdeveloped societies of South and East Asia had a modern, capitalistic export sector and a traditional, pre-capitalistic, subsistence sector, with little direct contact between the two. The former was an 'enclave' in an Eastern land, 'not touching native life at any point'. Neither the capital nor the labour employed was indigenous, the land was waste land, the product was exported, and even the necessities of life for the workers were brought in from elsewhere. The reason was that Western and Eastern economic activity were entirely

different and could not be reconciled. Where the former was spurred on by unlimited needs, the latter was immobilized by the limitation of wants and needs. Where 'Western' man sought profits, the 'Oriental' avoided risks, disliked investing capital and offered his labour only long enough to meet immediate needs. Boeke concluded that Western marginal productivity theory was inapplicable to dualistic economies. Any policy attempting to superimpose Western economic markets, techniques of production and organization of industry on Eastern society would fail and cause retrogression and decay.

See Index under Theoretical Issues.

dual rate corporation tax system. *See under* CORPORATE TAX SYSTEM.

dual sourcing. *See* DOUBLE SOURCING.

dumping. The sale of a product in a foreign country for less than the marginal cost in order to gain a MONOPOLY in the foreign market, or in order to dispose of temporary surpluses without causing a reduction in price in the home market. The GENERAL AGREEMENT ON TARIFFS AND TRADE (GATT) prohibits the practice of dumping and provides for a defence against it through higher tariffs. Dumping is also prohibited under the rules of the European Community (EC), embodied in the UK in the Customs Duties (Dumping and Subsidies) Act of 1969. In the US the Anti-Dumping Act of 1921 gives the Tariff Commission the power to recommend retaliatory action. The practice of dumping is, however, difficult to prove, especially when the exporter receives an export subsidy from his own government or is otherwise assisted by his government through its foreign aid programme, for example.

See Index under Trade.

E

EAC. *See* EDGE ACT CORPORATION.

East-West Center Project on Women and TNCs. Independent, radical group researching the impact of transnational corporations (notably electronic corporations) on women.

See Index under Data Sources.
Address: 1777 East-West Road, Honolulu, Hawaii 96848, USA.

EC. *See* EUROPEAN COMMUNITY.

EC Code of Conduct for Companies with Subsidiaries, Branches or Representation in South Africa. A voluntary CODE OF CONDUCT adopted by the European Community (EC) Council of Ministers in September 1977. The Code is addressed to parent companies with operations in South Africa. It urges acceptance of black trade union representation, collective bargaining, minimum wages and equal pay, and of desegregation at the place of work.

While not outrightly condemning the system of apartheid, the Code nevertheless calls upon employers to alleviate as much as possible the effects of the existing system by assuming a social responsibility to contribute towards ensuring freedom of movement for black workers and their families, and by concerning themselves with the living conditions of their employees and their families.

Although the Code is voluntary and has been received with hostility by some sections of the multinational business community, it does refer to a follow-up provision which takes the form of annual reporting and review on the progress made in applying the Code. At present pressures are building up within the EC Commission and Parliament to make this follow-up procedure effective.

See also SULLIVAN PRINCIPLES, and Index under International Co-operation.

eclectic theory. Theory of INTERNATIONAL PRODUCTION put forward by John Dunning (1977), which attempts to synthesize the principal existing theories of FOREIGN DIRECT INVESTMENT (FDI). It proposes a formal model of international direct investment in which the main determinants of such investment identified by previous theories are integrated. There are three of these determinants: OWNERSHIP SPECIFIC ADVANTAGES as identified in the industrial economics approach to foreign direct investment (*see* Vernon's PRODUCT CYCLE THEORY); internalization advantages, which form the key elements of Buckley and Casson's INTERNALIZATION THEORY; and finally LOCATION SPECIFIC ADVANTAGES as originally proposed in various location theories of foreign direct investment.

The central hypothesis of the eclectic theory is that a firm will engage in either foreign direct investment or licensing, rather than serve foreign markets through exports, if it possesses ownership specific advantages which can be profitably internalized; but it will prefer foreign direct investment to licensing if there are at least some location specific factors of the foreign location that make it more attractive to do so.

See also LICENSING AGREEMENT, and Index under Theoretical Issues.

economic co-operation amongst developing countries (ECDC). *See* COLLECTIVE SELF-RELIANCE.

economic nationalism. Nationalism is the belief of a given people that they comprise a distinctive community with special characteristics that mark it off from others and place it a cut above those others. To this belief, economic nationalism adds the desire to be in control of national economic resources and the development of the economy, and to protect and enhance the national economy in a world of competing states.

Economic nationalism is reflected in domestic economic policies of NATIONALIZATION of foreign property, statutary limitation of foreign participation in the economy, government subsidies for key industrial sectors, and protection through TARIFFS and other import restrictions of certain economic activities.

See also INDIGENIZATION; EXPATRIATE MANAGEMENT QUOTA, and Index under Development Policy.

economic sovereignty. An elaboration and application of the concept of national sovereignty to the economic sphere. While the principle of national sovereignty conveys upon a state the 'absolute and undisputed right to make decisions and act accordingly', it was still felt by many newly independent countries that the effectiveness of this principle was undermined by other competing principles of international law. It was argued for example that international property rights, sanctity of contract, NON-DISCRIMINATION RULES and so on, helped perpetuate a colonial legacy of economic domination even after 'sovereignty' had been granted.

After decades of wrangles with foreign companies over such issues as EXPROPRIATION, renegotiations of CONCESSIONS and so on, the group of THIRD WORLD countries in the United Nations had become sufficiently numerous and united to have the principle of economic sovereignty enshrined in a formal UN Charter, adopted by the General Assembly in 1974. The CHARTER OF ECONOMIC RIGHTS AND DUTIES OF STATES recognizes amongst other things national sovereignty over natural resources, foreign properties and transnational companies, and the right to nationalize foreign property and regulate the compensation to be given for the nationalized goods and properties.

See Index under Dispute and Settlement.

ECGD. *See* EXPORT CREDITS GUARANTEE DEPARTMENT.

ECU. *See* EUROPEAN CURRENCY UNIT.

Edge Act Corporation (EAC). A subsidiary of a US bank formed to conduct foreign or international business. The authorization for the creation of EACs dates from the Edge Act of 1919, in which the US Congress amended Section 25 of the Federal Reserve Act of 1913.

Unlike the AGREEMENT CORPORATION, which is only permitted to undertake foreign or international banking, an Edge Act Corporation can make equity investments abroad and conduct other non-banking operations. The advantages of EACs were felt particularly after 1933 when the Glass – Steagall Act prohibited US commercial banks from directly owning shares in the stock of home industrial corporations. Thus US commercial banks could still act as multipurpose banks abroad even when they were prevented from doing so at home. But the advantage of both the Agreement and Edge Act Corporations declined after 1966, when another amendment to Section 25 of the Federal Reserve Act authorized banks to have a direct share in the capital of a foreign bank without having to go through an EAC or agreement corporation.

In 1978 the International Banking Act made Edge Act privileges available to non-US banks operating in the United States, but at the same time limited their abilities to conduct business in more than one US state.

See Index under Regulation and Tax.

EEIG. *See* European economic interest grouping.

effects principle. A principle in international law which requires significant adverse domestic effects as a basis for prescriptive jurisdiction over wholly foreign conduct. The effects principle is particularly relevant in the extraterritorial application of anti-trust legislation and some states, notably the US and West Germany, have at times used the effects doctrine in the extraterritorial application of anti-trust provisions in respect of foreign-owned companies.

The extraterritorial ambit of US anti-trust laws through the medium of the effects principle has led to many conflicts of jurisdiction with other sovereign states, which have sometimes turned to so-called 'blocking' legislation to protect their nationals and enterprises from the reach of American anti-trust laws.

See also extraterritoriality, and Index under Dispute and Settlement.

efficient market. A security or currency market that quickly and accurately impounds information, making it dificult or impossible to 'outguess' the market in predicting future prices.

The notion of market efficiency is one that has developed in the theory of finance over the past 30 years and is now well accepted. 'Efficiency' in this case is not a term of approbation, referring to the market's technical qualities rather than its value in a broader socioeconomic context. According to the 'efficient markets hypothesis', there are three forms of market efficiency.

Weak form efficiency supposes that the market price of a security at any point in time incorporates all the information contained in its past prices. As a result, no change in the price can result from any analysis of those past prices, hence security prices follow a 'random walk'. There are no 'patterns' in market price movements: none can be correlated to the previous movements in prices.

Semi-strong form efficiency supposes that not only do security prices incorporate the information of previous prices, but in addition also incorporate all publicly available information. 'Efficiency' here means that when new information is received by the market it is quickly and accurately reflected in the price of the security. Thereafter, no analyst can discover further information and 'beat the market' by superior interpretative ability.

Strong form market efficiency is similar to the semi-strong form except that as well as published, unpublished information is incorporated into a share price at any point in time.

Substantial research effort has concluded that, for large securities markets such as London and New York, the first two forms of the efficient markets hypothesis are true. The evidence for the strong form is less conclusive. It appears that foreign exchange markets in frequently traded currencies are also efficient: that is, no individual can consistently outperform the market by predicting more accurately the future exchange rates of those currencies.

See also capital asset pricing model (CAPM), and Index under Financial and Risk Management, and under Theoretical Issues.

EMS. *See* European monetary system.

EMU. *See* European monetary unit.

enclave economy. A term which describes the economic and social structure of many developing countries, in which one sector of the economy is completely integrated in the modern world economy while the rest of economy and society is relatively untouched and remains backward. The enclave is the foreign-dominated export sector and typically contributes a disproportionate share to gross domestic product in national account statistical terms. However, the absence of linkages (*see* FORWARD LINKAGE and BACKWARD LINKAGE) between the enclave and the rest of the domestic economy, together with the export orientation of this sector, its dependency on imported capital-intensive production techniques and its foreign ownership and/or control mean that little of the wealth generated in this sector benefits the national economy in any real sense.

See DUALISM, and Index under Theoretical Issues.

environment risk index. *See* BUSINESS ENVIRONMENT RISK INDEX (BERI).

EPC. *See* EUROPEAN PATENT CONVENTION.

estoppel principle. Principle in international and domestic law which states that a party is prevented by his own acts from claiming a right to damages from another party, who was entitled to rely on such conduct and has acted accordingly. In international business the estoppel principle may be justifiably invoked when a state invites (either by prospectus or general advertisement) foreign capital to invest in the development of certain industries or utilities, and the foreign investors who respond are subsequently subjected to an expropriation process without compensation by the state (*see* EXPROPRIATION).

In such a case, the expropriating state may be held estoppel in acting contrary to the reasonable expectations that it has itself created.

See Index under Dispute and Settlement.

Ethical Investment Research and Information Service (EIRIS). Set up in 1983 by a number of bodies including Quakers, Methodists, Oxfam and the Rowntree Trust, EIRIS provides a unique information service on the ethical and social aspects of investment for those holding shares or belonging to organizations or funds doing so. Upon request it provides subscribers with factsheets on companies in which they are interested. EIRIS covers major UK companies and each individual factsheet gives basic details of the company's involvement in any one of the following areas of social concern: advertising, alcohol, animals, arms sales to military purchasers, gambling, newspaper production and television; nuclear power, overseas interests, political contributions, South Africa/Namibia, tobacco, and trustee investments.

EIRIS also assists subscribers in listing companies acceptable to their own ethical or social criteria. It publishes the *EIRIS newsletter* with news and information on companies, investors, legal matters and recent events.

See Index under Data Sources.
Address: 9 Poland Street, London W1V 3DG.

ethnocentric. A term devised by Howard Perlmutter (1969) to describe a managerial attitude taken by certain kinds of multinational. The ethnocentric corporation views its domestic employers as superior to its foreign employees, its home operations as clearly distinct from those abroad and centralizes all important decisions at headquarters while applying home-country criteria to foreign operations. As a consequence he claims it lacks a global approach to strategy and problem-solving. The other types of attitude defined by Perlmutter are GEOCENTRIC, POLYCENTRIC and REGIOCENTRIC.

See Index under Corporate Structure and Management, and under Theoretical Issues.

ETUC. *See* EUROPEAN TRADE UNION CONFEDERATION.

eurobank. A bank in which EUROCURRENCIES are held. Eurobanks are the large international banks; the term refers to the type of transaction undertaken rather than the geographical location of the bank, which need not operate in Europe.

eurobond. A bond denominated in a currency other than that of the country where the issuer is situated and the country (or countries) in which the issue is being sold. Borrowers issuing eurobonds are always of very high standing – for example, governments of developed countries and large multinationals – and the bonds are invariably underwritten by international syndicates. Eurobonds tend to be in bearer form. The most popular currency in which they have been issued in the past is US dollars. More recently certain currency baskets (*see* CURRENCY COCKTAIL) have been used instead, but so far their popularity has been limited.

See Index under Financial and Risk Management.

eurocommercial paper. Also known as 'euronotes'. Short-term loan security issued by a blue-chip non-banking company and denominated in a EUROCURRENCY. Some UK companies began to use euronotes in 1984 and 1985, a development that resulted in the UK Government's 1986 announcement that it would abolish the restrictions on a sterling commercial paper market. The very largest companies have found the commercial paper attractive because it enables them to bypass the banks as issuers of short-term financial instruments. In this way they gain both flexibility and cheapness, since euronote coupons can be below the LONDON INTER-BANK OFFERED RATE (LIBOR), and underwriting fees are also avoided. These advantages will also apply to the new sterling market. Commercial paper carries no interest, and the profit from holding it arises from the discount at which it is issued.

See Index under Financial and Risk Management.

eurocredit. A medium-term bank loan denominated in EUROCURRENCY. The interest rate is normally the LONDON INTER-BANK OFFERED RATE (LIBOR) plus a premium.

eurocurrency. A currency held in a deposit outside its country of origin. Eurocurrencies are not bought and sold as such; they are claims on deposits held within the currency's country of origin. Thus they can be lent and re-lent either between banks (in the short term) or to corporate customers or governments (medium- and long-term).

The original eurocurrency was the EURODOLLAR, but now many of the world's major currencies have their euro-counterpart (euromarks, euroyen). The deposit can be held either in a bank that is not headquartered in the currency's country of origin, or in a foreign branch of a bank that is.

Eurocurrencies are not separate from the base domestic currencies, and they have the same exchange value. They are however more easily traded, since the banking restrictions imposed by domestic central banks may be avoided by trading outside the jurisdiction of the central bank.

The eurocurrency market is thought to have its origins in fears by the Soviet Union and its allies in the 1950s that their dollar deposits in the USA might be frozen or become the subject of claims against them by US citizens. They accordingly lent them to European banks. These banks in turn lent them to customers, and a market of lending and borrowing outside the USA developed.

As a result of restrictive US banking policies and the overvaluation of the dollar resulting from the BRETTON WOODS MONETARY SYSTEM the market grew rapidly and the original eurodollars were later joined by other currencies. Eurodollars now account for about 70 per cent of the Eurocurrency market, and euromarks constitute half the remainder.

See Index under Financial and Risk Management.

eurodollar. A US dollar that is deposited in a bank outside the USA. For the nature of the eurodollar market, see EUROCURRENCY. The term 'eurodollar' is often used loosely to refer to eurocurrency.

See also ASIADOLLAR.

euronote. *See* EUROCOMMERCIAL PAPER.

European Community (EC). The European Economic Community was set up under the Treaty of Rome in 1957 to create a union of European states. It formally merged with the European Coal and Steel Community and European Atomic Energy Community in 1965 to form the European Community (EC). The original six member states of Belgium, the Federal Republic of Germany, France, Italy, Luxembourg and the Netherlands were joined by Denmark, Ireland and the United Kingdom in 1973, by Greece in 1981, and by Portugal and Spain in January 1986.

The EC has two main aims. It is an attempt to establish a common market among the member states, which involves common legislation relating to business affairs and the abolition of all tariffs and barriers to the free movement of people, goods and funds within the community. It also aims over the long term to achieve political union.

Institutions. The European Commission has 17 members proposed by the member states, who are required to act in the interests of the community as a whole and not the nation from which they come. Each commissioner serves a term of four years. The Commission acts as the executive of the EC and the initiator of policy. The European Parliament has 518 members elected directly by the member states' citizens. It has a small number of significant powers, including the power to reject the Community budget as a whole, and to force the Commission to resign as a body. Its principal importance at present is as an open debating chamber. The European Court of Justice has 11 judges assisted by 5 advocates-general, and ensures that the founding treaties are implemented. It deals with disputes between member states, between member states and community institutions, and between community institutions and individuals, including firms. The Council consists of representatives of the member states' governments. It is the most powerful of the institutions and can enact proposals binding on member states, normally as proposed by the Commission.

Legislation. The four instruments available to the community are: (a) regulations, which are laws directly binding within the member states; (b) directives, which are instructions to member states which lay down the results required but leave the manner of implementation to the state itself; (c) decisions, which are addressed to specific member states, legal entities or persons, and are binding on them: (d) recommendations and opinions, which are not binding.

The EC does not distinguish in its legislation between multinationals and other companies. Nevertheless at various times initiatives have been taken that have a direct bearing on MNCs. These include particularly the LANGE – GIBBONS CODE, the EC CODE FOR COMPANIES WITH SUBSIDIARIES IN SOUTH AFRICA, the CABORN REPORT and the formulation of 'Guidelines' on multinational undertakings for purposes of European competition policy (*see* European Community, 1973). In addition, there have been proposals for breaking the ties between incorporation and national domicile, the most important of which have been the SOCIETAS EUROPAEA and the EUROPEAN ECONOMIC INTEREST GROUPING (EEIG). Furthermore there are four areas in which EC policy is of specific interest to the MNC: corporate disclosure of information; employment protection; anti-trust legislation and competition policy; and taxation policy.

EC Directives. The company law directives have been concerned with the harmonization of the legal provisions of member states. So far, ten directives have been formulated.

The First Directive is concerned with safeguards for members of the major classes of company. These include the disclosure of significant factors affecting the company (which are listed in detail, and include the company's constitution in particular); and measures of protection at the formation and dissolution of a company. Adopted March 1968.

The Second Directive extended the requirements of the first directive, but for public companies (or equivalent) only. It extended the disclosure requirements; it made further provisions for winding up; it specified minimum share capital requirements of 25,000 European units of account (*see* EUROPEAN CURRENCY UNIT) and it tightened the requirements for the preservation of share capital. Adopted December 1976.

The Third Directive sets out requirements that must be followed in the case of merger between public companies or their equivalents concerning disclosure and the procedures to be followed. Designed principally to protect shareholders, it requires that the terms of the merger should be drafted and made available to members; that independent experts must (subject to each country's laws) comment on the terms of the merger; that creditors must be protected; and how a merger might be prevented by a country's authorities. Adopted

October 1978. The Commission deferred the deadline for implementation of this directive until January 1986 so that it might be implemented together with the Sixth Directive.

Far more detailed than the previous three, the Fourth Directive governs the principles of construction, the form of presentation, and the minimum extent of disclosure in the financial statements of most types of company. The accounts are defined as the balance sheet, profit and loss account, and notes on the accounts. The layouts are defined precisely and in detail, with lower levels of disclosure being permitted for smaller companies. Size limits are precisely defined in the directive. For the balance sheet two layouts are presented, for the profit and loss account four: countries may select one or more of these and prescribe them as they wish. The principles of arriving at the figures in these statements (particularly valuation rules) are defined. A number of other disclosures in the notes to the accounts are prescribed. Finally, audit is defined and required. Certain provisions of the directive are not necessarily to be applied to dependent companies of groups. Under certain conditions there are also exemptions for dominant companies in groups. Adopted July 1978.

Proposed in 1972, the draft Fifth Directive has been the subject of considerable controversy: much debate led to a second draft issued in 1983. The directive would apply only to public companies and equivalents. Its principal requirements are twofold: for a two-tier board structure and for employee participation in aspects of the management of the company. As to board structure, it requires that countries either introduce a two-tier system (of management and supervisory board) or that they permit companies to choose between single- and two-tier systems. For each system detailed provisions are made by the directive. Employee representation must be permitted on the supervisory board (which elects the management board) unless alternative representation methods are prescribed. For single-board systems, rights to elect non-executive directors by the employees are likewise defined. Information rights of employees are also set out. As well as this, the directive also contains provisions for general meetings of the shareholders. The so-called VREDELING PROPOSAL also covers matters concerning employee rights; however Vredeling and the Fifth Directive are proposed independently of each other by the Commission. The Fifth Directive has not yet been adopted by the Council.

The comparatively short Sixth Directive is designed to complement the Third Directive by making provisions for those situations in which a company is wound up with its assets divided between other companies. The rights of various parties are protected by the directive. Adopted December 1982.

The important Seventh Directive is concerned with consolidated accounts (that is, the accounts for a group of companies as a whole). It effectively applies only to public limited companies or their equivalents. It defines the types of corporate relationships which make consolidation necessary, and the disclosure required in the CONSOLIDATED ACCOUNTS. Of particular importance to multinationals based outside the EC is Article 11 of the directive, which permits member states to exempt companies from the requirements of the directive if a parent within the member state is also the subsidiary of a company outside the jurisdiction of the member state provided that it is eventually included in a consolidation that itself meets the requirements of the directive. Adopted June 1983. Member states have until the end of 1987 to implement it, and need not apply it until 1990. It will be reviewed in 1995.

The Eighth Directive is concerned with the approval of persons responsible for auditing corporate accounts. The basic provisions of the directive detail the types of

auditing firms sanctioned, the knowledge and examinations required of auditors, and the extent to which cross-national approval of auditors acceptable to other member states shall be acceptable to any member state. Adopted April 1984.

The Ninth Directive had not been formally issued in draft form at the time of writing. It will be concerned with the creation of a harmonized legal structure for the 'unified management' of public limited companies that are controlled by other companies, and prescribe rules for the conduct of groups not managed on a 'unified' basis. An informal text has been circulated to member states and a formal draft is expected in 1988.

Proposed in January 1985, the Tenth Directive is concerned with the cross-border merger of public companies from different countries within the Community. (*See* EUROPEAN ECONOMIC INTEREST GROUPING (EEIG).) Explicitly intended as an extension of the Third Directive, it sets out the limitations on its operation; safeguards for employees; the methods by which cross-border merger can be achieved; requirements for publication of the terms of the merger; requirements for reports by experts on the merger proposals; measures for creditor protection; and means of solving problems of conflict between legal systems. Not adopted at the time of writing.

In addition to these measures, there is currently a draft proposal concerning the disclosure made in one member state by branches of companies registered in another member state or a non-EC country. This is undergoing preliminary discussions at the time of writing.

Other features. Two other aspects of the European Community are of particular importance to the multinational. The Acquired Rights Directive (1977) provides for the continuation of employment liabilities, terms and conditions, union recognition rights and collective agreements in mergers and takeovers. Buyers and sellers of companies are supposed to consult and inform unions of the implications of proposed changes. The UK version of this directive, the *Transfer to Undertakings (Protection of Employment) Regulations, 1981*, came into effect in 1982. It is a watered down version of the final directive and ambiguous in parts.

Competition policy is a cornerstone of the Treaty of Rome. The notion of a common market required that there should be no economic barriers among member states. At the individual corporate level, the Treaty provided that agreements between companies which would distort competition and are liable to affect trade between member states are prohibited (Article 85). Examples of this are price-fixing, agreement on market shares, production quotas and tie-in clauses. This applies to both horizontal and vertical agreements. However the European Commission can rule that such agreements may stand in certain cases where the harmful effects are more than counterbalanced by beneficial elements (See COMFORT LETTER).

The Treaty also specifies that abuses of their power by companies in a dominant position are prohibited (Article 86). Dominance can come about through high market share, or through other contributory factors to a company's power, such as access to raw materials. The dominant position must be in the Common Market or a substantial part of it. Evidence of abuse of that position can arise from unfair selling prices (whether high enough to be to the detriment of customers or so low that they are designed to eliminate weaker competitors); from discriminatory pricing between customers; from refusal without valid reason to sell to a customer; or from tactics for holding onto to customers that are deemed unfair.

To prevent or punish these abuses, the Commission can order companies to stop them and can fine companies up to either one million ECUs or ten per cent of their annual turnover. The rules surrounding

these basic provisions are detailed and complex, and a body of cases has now grown up around them.

The rules apply equally to all companies, including multinationals in non-member countries where their conduct has an appreciable impact within the Community. In addition, the Commission and the Court are prepared to impute the actions of a subsidiary to its parent, which can be significant if a multinational not based in the European Community has a subsidiary there. On occasion, the effects of these rules have been beneficial to foreign-based multinationals, but have also at times operated against them (*see also under* ANTI-TRUST LEGISLATION).

Information on EC competition decisions can be obtained from the annual *Reports on Competition Policy* issued by the Commission.

See Index under Regulation and Tax, and under International Co-operation.

Address: Rue de la Loi 200, 1049 Bruxelles, Belgium

European composite unit (eurco). A CURRENCY COCKTAIL developed by the international bankers Rothschilds in 1973 and based upon a weighting of European Community (EC) currencies. It is used for denominating bonds. Although popular initially, it has since been supplanted by other cocktails, in particular those based on SPECIAL DRAWING RIGHTS (SDR) and the EUROPEAN CURRENCY UNIT.

European currency market. *See* EUROCURRENCY.

European currency unit (ECU). A monetary unit of account used by the European Community (EC). Originally identical to the European unit of account (EUA) in composition and value, it was introduced in March 1979 as part of the EUROPEAN MONETARY SYSTEM (EMS) and replaced the EUA for all Community purposes in January 1981. It is now the only currency basket used officially by the European Community. As a basket currency, it is a reference point rather than a circulating currency.

The ECU is a mixture of the currencies of the first ten member states of the European Community, weighted to take the size of each member's economy into account. The currencies of Spain and Portugal are not expected to be included in the ECU until at least 1989. In addition to changes in its value resulting from the individual basket currencies' fluctuations, the weighting is reviewed every five years, or on request if the value of any one currency has changed by more than 25 per cent. At the time of writing, the weights are (approximately) 32 per cent for the deutschmark, 19 per cent for the French franc, 15 per cent for sterling, 10 per cent for the guilder, 10 per cent for the lira, 8 per cent for the Belgian franc, with the currencies of Denmark, Ireland, Greece and Luxembourg together accounting for the remaining 6 per cent.

In addition to its roles as the 'official currency' of the European Community and the base currency of the EMS, the ECU is used by the private sector as a CURRENCY COCKTAIL because as a composite currency it is less subject to fluctuation in value than any individual currency. It is at present used in two principal ways: for the issue of corporate bonds and for export invoicing. Italy in particular uses the second option extensively, nearly 50 per cent of her exports being denominated in ECUs.

ECUs can be traded forward, and there is the possibility that ECU futures contracts may be introduced on the London International Financial Futures Exchange. At the time of writing a clearing system for the inter-bank market in ECUs between 18 international banks was being set up, with the Bank for International Settlements acting for the system.

In its role in international bond issues the term may be used interchangeably with the term 'European monetary unit'. In these circumstances the investor may be allowed to denominate the EC currency in which he requires interest and repayment of the principal, and is thus protected from devaluations of his own currency while being able to profit from revaluations.

See Index under International Co-operation, and under Financial and Risk Management.

European economic interest grouping (EEIG). A proposal adopted by means of a Regulation of Council of the European Community in July 1985. It provides a means by which companies or natural persons in different countries of the European Community might group together for commercial purposes. An EEIG may not trade for profit itself: its purpose is to enable its constituent companies or individuals to make profits. The Council regulation enabling the grouping sets out the conditions under which it may operate, including details of its registration, publicity, and internal contractual arrangements. The regulation will come into force from 1st July 1989.

See also SOCIETAS EUROPAEA, and Index under Regulation and Tax.

European Investment Bank (EIB). A bank created in 1958 under the provisions of the Treaty of Rome with capital provided by the members of the EUROPEAN COMMUNITY (EC). The EIB is formally independent of the Community, and can lend to private and public enterprises, to states and such autonomous parts of states as local authorities and to financial institutions, provided that all are within the EC, as well as to projects outside the community in certain circumstances. It has two principal purposes: to make loans to advance the less developed regions of the EC and to finance projects enhancing the infrastructure of the Community as a whole, such as road and rail communications.

See Index under International Co-operation.

Address: 2 Place de Metz, Boite Postale 2005, Luxembourg.

European monetary system (EMS). A system developed by the countries of the European Community (EC) in 1979 to create greater stability in the EC currency markets. All EC states are members with the exception of the UK. The system is based around the EUROPEAN CURRENCY UNIT, which can act as an anchor point for the currencies of the EMS member states because member states are required to keep their currencies' values both within a band around the base rate, and within a certain limit of each of the other member countries' rates. Thus, where a country's currency moves outside of an allowed limit on either side of its base rate relative to the currency basket, the country must counteract such a move in the foreign exchange markets. Similarly, where a member country's currency deviates by more than a certain percentage from the base rate of another country's currency, both must act in the foreign exchange markets to bring the values back within the allowed limits.

See SNAKE, and Index under International Co-operation.

European monetary unit. *See* EUROPEAN CURRENCY UNIT.

European Patent Convention (EPC). A PATENT approval system by which a single application is made for a single patent, which thereby has the effect of a national patent in all contracting nations. The EPC became operational in 1977 and covers 16 countries in and around the European continent.

See Index under International Co-operation.

European Trade Union Confederation (ETUC). A confederation of trade union federations from the 18 countries associated with the European Community (EC) and EFTA. The Confederation was established in 1973 to succeed the European Free Trade Union Association, which had only included members from the original six EC countries.

The ETUC has influenced EC policy initiatives in multinational company legislation. Many of its core demands on multinational company law as formulated in its 1977 publication *European Action Programme – Multinational Groups of Companies* are reflected in EC proposals either already made or in an advanced stage of preparation. These demands include: new European rules for defining the status of groups of companies, protective measures for shareholders and workers in dependent undertakings of a group of companies, information disclosure, and direct employee participation in board-level decisions.

The ETUC has also been successful in putting on the EC's legislative agenda proposals for the control of TRANSFER PRICES and the monitoring of investments.

See also EUROPEAN COMMUNITY (EC); CODES OF CONDUCT, and Index under Labour, and under International Co-operation.

Address: 37 Rue Montagne aux Herbes Potageres, 1000 Brussels, Belgium.

European unit of account. See EUROPEAN CURRENCY UNIT.

exchange controls. Limits imposed and supervized by the central bank or government of a country on the exchange of that country's currency into a foreign currency. Most countries have exchange controls; among the exceptions are Canada, Germany, Switzerland, the UK and the USA . Under exchange controls permission must be sought, frequently by the bank involved in the transaction, for the foreign exchange to be purchased: generally there will be rules, varying from case to case, as to the types of transaction for which the central authorities do and do not grant permission. Capital movements are particularly prone to more or less strict supervision.

See also BLOCKED FUNDS; FOREIGN EXCHANGE RISK; FRONTING LOANS; UNBUNDLING; TRANSFER PRICE, and Index under Financial and Risk Management.

ex dock. (or ex pier, or ex quay) *See* EXPORTING TRADE TERMS.

EX-IM Bank. *See* EXPORT-IMPORT BANK.

expatriate investment. The investment of their personal savings by those temporarily abroad, such as the EXPATRIATE MANAGEMENT of multinationals or military personnel posted overseas.

expatriate management. Nationals of one country working in another. The term is usually restricted to managers of multinational corporations. The use of expatriates was very common at a time when the skill levels and attitudes of host country personnel were perceived to be inferior, but has declined in recent years for three main reasons: the mounting pressure by host nations for the employment of their own nationals in managerial positions; the increased educational level of elites in host countries, plus the increased awareness of the type of attitude that multinationals demanded in a local workforce; and the increased awareness by multinationals that many operations are best handled by locally-trained managements.

See also EXPATRIATE MANAGEMENT QUOTA, and Index under Corporate Structure and Management.

expatriate management quota. The statutory limitation of the number of foreign management staff who may be given a work and residence permit. Many developing countries have introduced such a limitation on the number of expatriate staff in enterprises on their territory controlled or owned by foreign interests in an effort to ensure the effective transfer of skills and ultimately of operational control over the business. It is common to find just three managerial positions reserved for expatriate staff: general manager, production manager and financial comptroller.

See Index under Development Policy.

Export Administration Act. American legislation (1977) prohibiting the boycotting of one nation in order to do business with another. It also limits the most favoured nation trade status to those countries not deemed to be human rights violators.

See MOST FAVOURED NATION (MFN) CLAUSE; GENERAL AGREEMENT ON TARIFFS AND TRADE (GATT), and Index under Regulation and Tax.

export broker. Normally a specialist acting in markets that involve little product differentiation (primary commodities, for instance), the export broker brings together buyers and sellers from different countries, receiving a commission fee as reward. The fee is usually paid by the seller.

See Index under Trade.

export commission representative. *See* COMBINATION EXPORT MANAGER.

Export Credits Guarantee Department (ECGD). A department of the UK government which assists exporters of goods and services and those who finance them. The Department was set up in 1919 and is presently governed by the Export Guarantees and Overseas Investment Act (1978).

The purpose of the Department is to encourage British exports by reducing the burden of risk faced by exporters. By doing so, it is claimed, exporters are able to pursue more aggressive marketing policies both through taking on new buyers and through entering new markets. Because the services it provides are at competitive rates (ECGD is not required to make a profit) it enables them to obtain contracts they might otherwise lose. Currently the Department covers around a third of all UK exports.

The ECGD has four specific functions. It insures exporters against the risk of not being paid for goods or services. It provides guarantees to banks lending to exporters so as to assure them of full repayment and hence facilitate export finance at favourable rates of interest. It also insures new overseas investment against risks of war, expropriation, and restriction of remittances and provides protection against currency fluctuations. In addition, the ECGD has in the past provided cover against cost escalations.

There are two types of cover offered by the ECGD. 'Comprehensive' policies are available for trade of a routine type, in standard or near-standard goods. For projects with high capital outlays that are non-repetitive, the Department offers specific insurance tailored to the specific project.

As well as cover for exporters, the ECGD offers cover to financial intermediaries. If the foreign importer borrows from a UK bank to finance purchases from a UK exporter (who thus receives immediate payment), the ECGD will provide cover for the bank.

The ECGD does not cover the whole potential loss but will cover up to 90 – 95 per cent in some cases. It may, however, reduce this percentage in certain circumstances.

The ECGD charges for its services and is supposed to break even over a period of years. Most of its business is based on commercial charge rates, but a small proportion is undertaken because it is judged to be in the national interest. Premiums charged vary not only as a result of the amount insured, but also on the basis of the Department's assessment of the risk of the particular market concerned.

Competitiveness in the provision of credit terms is recognized by the Department as a danger. Regulation of the terms offered is therefore seen as desirable and is the subject of continued discussion through the BERNE UNION, the ORGANIZATION FOR ECONOMIC CO-OPERATION AND DEVELOPMENT (OECD), and the EUROPEAN COMMUNITY (EC).

See also OVERSEAS PRIVATE INVESTMENT CORPORATION (OPIC), and Index under Financial and Risk Management.

Addresses: Aldermanbury House, Aldermanbury, London EC2P 2EL, UK/ Crown Building, Cathays Park, Cardiff CF1 3NH, UK.

export distributor. *See* COMBINATION EXPORT MANAGER.

Export-Import Bank (EX-IM Bank). Established in 1934, this US Government corporation guarantees private credit and makes direct loans to foreign and domestic firms so as to promote foreign trade. Originally set up to encourage US trade with the Soviet Union on the one hand and with Latin America on the other, the Bank's operations have since become worldwide in scope, although the bulk of its lending is still directed towards Latin America. Its operations are a classic example of 'tied' aid: its loans must be repaid in US dollars and normally the monies received must be spent on capital equipment purchased in the US.

See Index under Trade.

exporting trade terms. The terms of the agreement by which buyer and seller deal with each other in an export transaction. Those commonly recognized in international trade are:

cost and freight. The quoted price of the shipment includes the cost of transporting it to the named destination. The normal phrase used is 'C&F (name of destination)'. This type of nomenclature is standard for all the terms listed below.

cost and insurance. The quoted price of the shipment includes the cost of insuring it.

cost, insurance, freight. The quoted price of the shipment includes the transportation cost and the cost of insuring it en route.

delivered duty paid. The quoted shipment price includes all costs of getting the goods to a named place in the importing country, and the seller is responsible for obtaining all permits or licenses necessary.

ex dock (or ex quay, or ex pier). The quoted price of the shipment includes all the costs required to convey the goods to the named port of importation, including any necessary duty.

ex factory (or ex warehouse, ex plantation). The buyer takes delivery of the goods at the time specified in the contract. Title, and hence responsibility, passes at the seller's premises and the buyer takes possession at that point.

free alongside ship (FAS). In this case the price includes all costs and responsibilities up to the point where the goods are placed on the wharf by the ship within reach of its loading equipment.

free on board (FOB). The basic FOB terms are that the seller pays for all costs up to the point at which the goods are stowed on the ship at the port of departure. There are many variants of this.

franco delivered. By this arrangement, almost all aspects of the transaction are the responsibility of the seller. The only responsibility incumbent on the buyer is the obtaining of an import permit should one be necessary.

See Index under Trade.

export management company. Alternative term for a COMBINATION EXPORT MANAGER.

export merchant. A trader who identifies market needs in one country and fulfils that need through purchasing in another country. The activities of export merchants are normally to be found in unbranded, staple products.

export platform. *See* FREE TRADE ZONE (FTZ).

export processing zone. *See* FREE TRADE ZONE (FTZ).

exposure. The extent to which a company may experience gains and losses as a result of movements in the exchange rates of foreign currencies. There are three main types of foreign exchange exposure.

The most significant and all-embracing of the three kinds of exposure, *economic exposure* refers to a potential change in the economic value of the multinational firm resulting from unexpected changes in foreign exchange rates. By 'economic value' is meant the net present value of the future cash flows of the firm: that is, the standard measure of economic value. This can only be an estimate and hence suffers the problem of subjectivity in measurement. Despite the difficulty of measurement, it remains the most significant long-term effect of currency movements.

Narrower than economic exposure, *transaction exposure* is the risk of gain or loss that might result from a currency movement in a particular transaction involving foreign exchange. It may be a result of credit sales and purchases overseas, of buying or selling currency forward, or of corporate lending or borrowing which is designated in a foreign currency.

Translation exposure results from the need to consolidate the results of a multinational in group financial accounts before they are announced. (*See* CONSOLIDATED ACCOUNTS.)

To achieve this, overseas holdings must be translated into the home currency.

Translation into the parent company's currency may be at either historical rates of exchange or current rates. The former are not exposed in accounting terms, the latter are. Thus where an item is translated at current exchange rates, and those rates have changed, a translation gain or loss will arise.

A fourth but less significant type of exposure is *tax exposure*, since a change in currency values will have implications for the tax liability of the multinational's parent.

See also TRANSLATION, and Index under International Accounting.

expropriation. The taking of private property by the State with compensation.

From the mid-1950s up to the mid-1970s, THIRD WORLD countries tried increasingly to assert control over their economies by policies of expropriation of foreign capital. Often expropriation took place in the belief that it would not only enhance political and economic independence but would also minimize the costs of foreign involvement (for example through profit remittance abroad), while maximizing the benefits arising from such involvement – continued access to management expertise, technological skills, worldwide marketing arrangements, and so on.

The sovereign right to expropriate private foreign property has been effectively recognized in international law since 1962. In that year the UN General Assembly adopted Resolution 1803 which recognizes that a state has such a right, provided that it is exercised within the territory of the sovereign state, is carried out for reasons of public utility, security or in the national interest, and is accompanied by appropriate compensation. International law already in existence at that time had defined as unlawful those types of expropriations that are measures of retaliation or reprisal against another state, and those which discriminate against nationals of particular states or against members of particular racial groups.

The duty of the expropriating state to provide some form of compensation has been the most controversial aspect of the international recognition of sovereign expropriation rights. As often as not the 'legality' of what otherwise would have been considered 'illegal' expropriations has turned on the payment of prompt, adequate and effective compensation. Resolution 1803 determined that in the event of a dispute between expropriating state and the victim of expropriation, the INTERNATIONAL COURT OF JUSTICE (ICJ) would act as the final arbiter in settling the dispute and in deciding upon the level of compensation. Subsequently, the CHARTER OF ECONOMIC RIGHTS AND DUTIES OF STATES adopted by the United Nations General Assembly in 1974 recognized the sovereign domestic authority as the ultimate arbiter in respect of compensation too, thereby removing this from the jurisdiction of international courts.

To date, most developing countries have expressed their attitude towards NATIONALIZATION in various investment laws, in policy statements, or even in their constitutions. Many of those who write nationalization clauses into their constitution also give legal guarantees of compensation, using such terms as 'just', 'appropriate', 'equitable' and 'fair' to describe the intended level of compensation.

See also INDIGENIZATION; CONFISCATION; ECONOMIC SOVEREIGNTY; ECONOMIC NATIONALISM, and Index under Dispute and Settlement.

Extel Information Service. Commercial organization providing loose-leaf summaries of companies upon request. The Extel Statistical Card includes a ten-year financial overview, employment data and so on.

See Index under Data Sources.
Address: 37-45 Paul Street, London EC2, UK.

externalities. Costs or benefits, whether in consumption or production, which are not reflected in market prices. The consumer or firm creating the externalities does not take its effect into account. Examples are the costs to the community of air or water pollution created by chemical firms, or the benefits of employment creation by certain labour-intensive firms.

It has been argued by welfare economists ever since Pigou (1924) first systematically explored this phenomenon, that social welfare could be optimized if the private consumption or production decision were to be 'corrected' to take the external effect into account. Such corrections could be applied by three means.

Taxes could be levied on activities which create losses in welfare or increases in costs; or subsidies paid on activities which increase welfare or lower costs. Compensation for 'damages' could be allocated by the courts on the principle of property rights and common law as in the cases of claims by asbestos or thalidomide victims. The government could also impose prohibitions and regulations on the consumer or on the production activity itself (for example, meeting certain standards of safety and health regulations).

The concept of externalities is important in the study of multinational enterprise, because externalities create the imperfections in the international markets which firms either want to take advantage of, or want to avoid by internalizing across frontiers the activities that give rise to externalities in the first place. For example, stringent anti-pollution regulations at home may encourage chemical companies to transfer the smellier part of their production process to countries with less prohibitive government regulations. Companies may also want set up foreign productive establishments to benefit from a foreign government's 'corrective' subsidies to domestic producers, which might be protective TARIFFS, tax incentives, or government direct financial subsidies.

The study of how externalities give rise to international market imperfections has in recent years contributed to the INTERNALIZATION THEORY of foreign direct investment.

See also TRANSACTION COSTS; ECLECTIC THEORY; FOREIGN DIRECT INVESTMENT (FDI), and Index under Theoretical Issues.

extraterritoriality. The principle of territorial limitation, generally recognized in international law, holds that a state can only commit an act of sovereignty within its own territory. If it commits an act of sovereignty within the area of another state, it is acting extra-territorially. However, there are also internationally recognized exceptions to the principle of territorial limitation; one exception is the concept of diplomatic immunity, whereby an embassy is seen as detached from the country in which it is situated and diplomats sent there are freed from the jurisdiction of that country.

With the growth and spread of multinational enterprises, the problem of extraterritoriality has become a keenly debated issue in international law, and still more a source of conflict. The issue is whether or not the jurisdiction of the state in which the parent company of a multinational enterprise is located can extend through the structure of legal ownership and control of that enterprise to subsidiaries located in other territories. Sometimes a government treats foreign affiliates of multinational corporations headquartered in the country as its nationals, even though these affiliates are incorporated in the host country. Conflicts arise when such foreign affiliates are instructed to follow home country policies which contravene the policies of the host country. A recent case in point was that of the US trade embargo on the shipment of high-technology products to the USSR. In this instance subsidiaries of US companies in the UK and elsewhere were instructed to obey US law although this clearly contravened the domestic laws and policies of the countries in which they operated.

Conflicts arising from the application of the principle of extraterritoriality have been most common in the area of ANTI-TRUST LEGISLATION.

See Index under Dispute and Settlement.

F

facilitation fee. *See* MOBILIZATION FEE.

factor endowment. The possession by countries of a factor of production, such as capital, labour or natural resources.

factor mobility. The ability of factors of production to transfer to foreign locations. Classical theories of FOREIGN DIRECT INVESTMENT (FDI) and trade conventionally considered the relative mobility of only two factors, capital and labour, as being one of the variables which determine whether firms choose to produce abroad or to export. These classical theories were consequently referred to as 'two-factor' models. The so-called 'neo-factor' theories of trade introduced into discussion the mobility of other factors which affect the pattern of foreign involvement. Most notable among these are monopolistic advantages of process and product technology, managerial and technical skills, scale economies, and product differentiation.

See NEO-FACTOR TRADE THEORY; NEO-TECHNOLOGY TRADE THEORY; PRODUCT CYCLE THEORY, and Index under Theoretical Issues.

fadeout policies. Host country policies aimed at ensuring that JOINT VENTURE arrangements between nationals and foreigners will eventually evolve into full national ownership. The rationale for such policies is that initial foreign participation in joint ventures should improve the quality and potential of local enterprise, but that the quality subsequently developed will enable the host country to dispense with the continuation of such participation as the prime agent in the industries' growth and development. Fadeout policies have commonly been pursued in the ANDEAN PACT COUNTRIES. Fadeout policies are also sometimes referred to as 'phase-in' policies. The phrase looks at the same process from the point of view of the host country.

See Index under Regulation and Tax.

fair market value system. A formula for computing the price of a resource (petroleum, for example) for purposes of negotiating the distribution of gains from the exploitation and sale of the resource between producing host country and transnational corporation. This formula, in which the value of the resource is defined by reference to some market standard, is designed to counteract unfair transfer pricing policies by the transnational corporations.

See TRANSFER PRICE; NEGOTIATED PRICE SYSTEM; REFERENCE PRICE SYSTEM; REALIZED PRICE SYSTEM, and Index under Regulation and Tax.

Fair Trading Act. This 1973 Act replaced, extended and updated the provisions of previous anti-monopoly legislation in the UK, to wit: the Monopolies and Restrictive Practices (Inquiry and Control) Act of 1948 and the Monopolies and Mergers Act of 1965 – both of which it replaced – together with the Restrictive Trades Practices Acts of 1956 and 1968 and the Resale Prices Act of 1964, neither of which have been repealed.

The Act established a new Office in the Director General of Fair Trading, whose powers include both the reference of monopoly situations to the MONOPOLIES AND MERGERS COMMISSION and the monitoring and investigation of trading practices, which had previously been the responsiblity of the Registrar of Restrictive Practices.

Under the Act, registration is required of all agreements btween two or more firms which contain restrictions on prices, quantities or quality of goods and services traded, or on channels of distribution. It is the task of the Director General to review and identify any commercial practice or agreement which goes against the public interest. The DG may seek an undertaking from individuals or firms that any unfair trading practice they have committed will be discontinued, upon which the Office of Fair Trading publishes the undertakings and the relevant details in its publication *Trade and Industry*. Alternatively the DG may bring his recommendations to the Restrictive Practices Court or County Courts. The Act requires the courts to assume that each collusive agreeement or practice is against the public interest unless it may be shown to contribute to the public interest in respect of any one of seven explicit criteria, including public safety, substantial consumer benefit, export earnings and so on. Finally, the DG may recommend to the Secretary of State for Trade and Industry certain courses of action for dealing with new forms of unwelcome trade practices.

See also ANTI-TRUST LEGISLATION; MONOPOLY; OLIGOPOLY, and Index under Regulation and Tax.

FAO. *See* FOOD AND AGRICULTURE ORGANIZATION.

FAS 8. *See* FINANCIAL ACCOUNTING STANDARD NO 8.

FAS 52. *See* FINANCIAL ACCOUNTING STANDARD NO 52.

FASB. *See* FINANCIAL ACCOUNTING STANDARDS BOARD.

FDI. *See* FOREIGN DIRECT INVESTMENT.

federal chartering. A proposal for US corporate law reform, which would make the federal government, rather than any individual State government, the chartering authority for corporate business. This proposal, which is currently being pressed for by American consumer advocates like Ralph Nader and other social critics of the large corporation, has a long but so far unsuccessful history in American corporate policy. Although national banks are required to have federal incorporation, nationwide industrial and retail corporations are not.

The case for federal chartering rests on the argument that State incorporation is an anachronism in the age of the giant interstate and multinational corporation, and that it has encouraged competition between State legislatures in offering the most lax corporate laws, thereby rendering such statutes useless as a means of regulating corporate power.

A detailed proposal for a Federal Chartering Act was published by the Corporate Accountability Research Group in 1976. This proposed Act would cover all industrial, retail and transportation corporations in the US with an annual turnover of over $250m or employing over 10,000 people in any one of three preceding years. Sections in the proposed Act deal with measures to enhance corporate democracy and increase corporate disclosure of companies' social and financial performance; describe a programme of deconcentration; restore competition to industries now characterized by MONOPOLY and OLIGOPOLY, and detail a constitutional Bill of Rights for employees.

Federal Trade Commission (FTC). Established in 1915, the FTC is one of two federal government agencies which have primary responsibilities for enforcing the anti-trust laws. The other agency is the Anti-trust Division of the Department of Justice, established in 1903. The FTC has responsibilities for enforcing the Federal Trade

Commission Act, which overlaps and extends the Sherman Act and concerns itself with restraints on and monopolization of trade. Together with the Anti-trust Division, the FTC also enforces the CLAYTON ACT.

See ANTI-TRUST LEGISLATION, and Index under Regulation and Tax.

feeder factory. Another term for a BRANCH PLANT or WORKSHOP SUBSIDIARY.

fidelity contract. Another term for a guarantee insurance. It is a contract in which the insurer agrees to indemnify the insured against loss consequent upon the dishonesty or default of a designated person. Guarantee insurance used in its broad sense includes credit insurance.

Financial Accounting Standard No 8 (FAS 8). A regulation issued by the FINANCIAL ACCOUNTING STANDARDS BOARD (FASB) in October 1975 concerning the treatment of currency translation in the published financial statements of US corporations. The standard used the temporal method of TRANSLATION and required, among other things, that all gains and losses on currency movements be included in the calculation of profit in the year in which they took place. The result was a considerable volatility in the reported earnings of many multinationals as a result of the sharp changes in the currency markets at the time, and pressure was consequently brought to bear on the SECURITIES AND EXCHANGE COMMISSION (SEC) to have the standard rescinded. The SEC did so and the FASB issued a new standard, FAS 52, in December 1981.

See also FINANCIAL ACCOUNTING STANDARD No 52 (FAS 52), and Index under International Accounting.

Financial Accounting Standard No 52 (FAS 52). The standard in force in the USA at present on currency TRANSLATION in the published financial statements of major cor-porations. Promulgated to take effect for all fiscal years beginning on or after 15th December 1982, the standard requires that companies define the 'functional currency' of a particular foreign entity. Normally this will be the currency of the country in which the entity is situated, in which case the standard requires that the company use the current rate method of currency translation. In contrast to the earlier FINANCIAL ACCOUNTING STANDARD No 8 (FAS 8), this method requires gains or losses on currency movements to be included not in the net profit (income) but in a separate account, set off against each other accumulatively, and reported separately in the balance sheet. The only cases excepted from this rule are those where the FUNCTIONAL CURRENCY is the US dollar, and here the method required by FAS 8 applies.

See also EXPOSURE, and Index under International Accounting.

Financial Accounting Standards Board (FASB). An institution in the USA which issues regulations governing the form and content of the published financial statements of certain classes of US corporations. The FASB is claimed to be independent in its judgments and consists of seven eminent people who, supported by a permanent staff, issue financial accounting standards. Board members are required at the time of taking up their position to sever all ties with their previous employers so that objectivity is secured to the greatest possible degree.

The Board is financed by the Financial Accounting Foundation, which is itself funded half by business firms and half by public accounting firms, and operates with the support of the SECURITIES AND EXCHANGE COMMISSION (SEC). Most of its judgments to date have been accepted by the SEC, Congress and the business community, but there have been exceptions.

See Index under International Accounting.

Address: High Ridge Park, PO Box 3821, Stamford, Connecticut, USA.

financial reports. The accounting statements issued by companies. In most countries these are now required by law, although the extent of this requirement will depend on the type of company, on whether its securities have been issued to the public, and on its size. In many countries companies must disclose their accounts to the government as well as to shareholders, and the reports filed are frequently available from a government department. Financial reports vary greatly in the principles on which they are based (*see* ACCOUNTING PRINCIPLES) and on the extent of disclosure required (*see* DISCLOSURE IN ACCOUNTS).

See Index under International Accounting.

financial structure. The mix of different kinds of security that a company uses to obtain funds for its operations.

There are a large number of different sources of funds available to a company. These include: accounts payable (creditors); bank overdrafts or short-term fixed-sum bank loans; short-term unsecured notes (commercial paper); BILLS OF EXCHANGE (drafts); secured or unsecured debentures (bonds); reinvested funds from the profits of past operations; and shares, whether preference shares (rarely issued today) or equity shares. The mix of these employed by a company will reflect

(a) the timing of its need for funds. Overdrafts can be raised quickly, whereas long-term instruments issued to the public involve negotiations, publicity and a number of formalities with stock exchange authorities. Short-term sources of funds are also clearly appropriate where the need is temporary.
(b) the cost of the funds. The interest charge on different sources of loaned funds will vary depending on market conditions. The cost of reinvested capital will depend on the expected returns on equity; and the latter will in turn depend on market conditions (*see under* CAPITAL ASSET PRICING MODEL (CAPM) and under COST OF CAPITAL).
(c) the relative riskiness of the different types of instrument. It is more risky to have a highly geared (or highly leveraged) structure than its opposite. A high gearing is said to exist where the amount of debt, normally measured as long-term contracted debt only, is high in relation to the residual equity, which is measured as the sum of the issued share capital plus the reserves. This is more risky because when profits are low there is a danger that the interest charges cannot be met, whereas if the source of capital were equity rather than debt there would be no contractual obligation to pay a dividend.

All companies must make decisions concerning their capital structure. The decision is the more complex for the multinational because it tends to have access to more capital markets. Not only may the group of companies as a whole raise capital in different financial centres, but SUBSIDIARIES themselves may, with consent from headquarters, raise funds in local capital markets. This may give the appearance of being more expensive, since both TRANSACTION COSTS and returns demanded tend to be higher, particularly where the home country has very large efficient stock markets and the host country does not. However, there are some advantages. FOREIGN EXCHANGE RISK to headquarters is reduced, because any change in asset values and profits which results from currency movements is offset by the concomitant change in debt. The existence of local bondholders will give extra potential leverage if the company comes under threat of EXPROPRIATION. The risk of expropriation may indeed be diminished if there is perceived to be some local ownership interest in the subsidiary concerned.

See Index under Financial and Risk Management.

Financial Times International Business Yearbook. An annual publication giving essential facts about a representative selection of the world's largest 800 companies in industry, oil, transportation, utilities and retailing. It describes international economic groups, and gives statistics of relevance to business. Its national surveys include economic indicators, lists of companies, taxation and company law.

See Index under Data Sources.

Address: Financial Times, Business Enterprises Division, 10 Bolt Court, Fleet Street, London EC4A 3HL, UK.

First World. A term normally only used in the contrasting context of THIRD WORLD and SECOND WORLD. The First World consists of the advanced market economies (or capitalist nations) of Northwest Europe and North America. It was here that industrialization first took place.

Fisher effect. *See* INTERNATIONAL FISHER EFFECT.

fixed exchange rate. The value of a national currency fixed by the country's government. It will normally be permitted to fluctuate within a narrow band with reference to another currency or basket of currencies.

See also FREE FLOAT; MANAGED FLOAT, and Index under Financial and Risk Management.

floating lending rate. A rate of interest on a loan which varies at a fixed premium above a recognized rate such as the LONDON INTER-BANK OFFERED RATE (LIBOR).

'follow the leader' theory. Thesis of FOREIGN DIRECT INVESTMENT (FDI) in which it is argued that while some 'pioneer' companies go abroad to exploit fully any OWNERSHIP SPECIFIC ADVANTAGES they may possess, others follow the pioneers not so much because they possess clear advantages, but to keep up with the industry leader. The advantages that pioneering companies possess enable them to earn additional MONOPOLY profits in a new location. This threatens the competitive relationship between the firms in the industry and compels them to follow the leader in order to share in the gains and to re-establish some form of competitive equilibrium. The theory thus purports to help explain the 'bunching' of overseas investments that has been discovered in some empirical research. The phenomenon is also known as 'oligopoly reaction'.

See Index under Theoretical Issues.

Food and Agriculture Organization (FAO). An organization set up in 1943 under auspices of the United Nations Conference on Food and Agriculture, as an international co-ordination centre and information exchange. It became a specialized agency of the United Nations in 1946. Its aims are to work towards raising levels of nutrition and standards of living, to secure improvement of production and distribution of all food and agricultural products, to better the conditions of rural populations, and – as it says in the Preamble of its constitution – thus to contribute to an expanding world economy.

As is the case with other UN specialized agencies, the organizational structure of the FAO includes (1) a general conference of all member countries, which meets biennially, (2) an executive council, and (3) a secretariat. Membership of the FAO is upon application and requires a two-thirds majority decision. The membership now totals over 150 countries.

The FAO has special links with other UN specialized agencies, in particular with the UN Development Programme (UNDP), for which it acts as executive agency, and the WORLD BANK. To these and other international aid and development organizations, as well as national governments, the FAO renders technical assistance in the preparation and execution of agricultural development projects in the developing world.

Although the FAO has undoubtedly contributed to the progress that has been made in raising food production, especially in the Third World, it has also been criticized for maintaining over-close links with AGRIBUSINESS. For example, the joint FAO/Industry Co-operative Programme (ICP) for a time co-opted representatives of the world's largest multinational agrochemical and food companies as privileged consultants to the FAO's agricultural development work. In this way these companies were able – under FAO auspices – to promote and sell to many Third World governments highly profitable but, some argued, socially dubious high-technology projects. As a result of these criticisms, the ICP Bureau has been ejected from the FAO's organization, but the connections with agribusiness are not completely severed. Critics of the FAO argue that the organization's continuing preoccupation with technical solutions (as opposed to political and economic ones) to the world's food problems makes it a handmaiden of Western agribusiness interests in the Third World. On the other hand, there are also critics who feel that the FAO is becoming unduly politicized.

See Index under International Co-operation.

Address: Via delle Terme di Caracalla, 00100 Rome, Italy.

footloose investment. Derogatory term for what is seen by some as a new characteristic of multinational corporate investments in the manufacturing and services sector. This is the investment in SPLIT-SITE production facilities which may be transferred rela-tively quickly across borders in response to LOCATION SPECIFIC factors such as lower wage costs and more generous tax allowances. In some industries characterized by rapidly changing and highly competitive conditions – the electronics industry, for example – companies are especially likely to set up or close down operations anywhere in the world according to local conditions. During the 1960s, assembly plants in the semi-conductor industry typically moved first to Hong Kong, Taiwan and Korea. Searching for ever lower wages, the industry next moved to other Southeast Asian countries, Malaysia, the Philippines and Indonesia in the early 1970s. Today many of these plants are being shut down as constantly developing automated technology is introduced, permitting the return of production to sites in the advanced countries. This phenomenon is sometimes referred to as U-TURN INVESTMENT.

Because of the temporary nature of the investment and the transnational integration of production, some critics argue that such investment has no enduring developmental impact on the host economy (Frobel, Heinrichs and Kreye, 1980).

See also FREE TRADE ZONE (FTZ); NEWLY INDUSTRIALIZING COUNTRIES, and Index under Corporate Structure and Management.

forbearance. A term used to describe the tendency of CONGLOMERATES to avoid competitive attacks on each other's strongest product lines. Since conglomerates are multi-product companies and the importance of their various product lines as sources of profit varies among them owing to differences in cost, market shares and product acceptance, they are inclined to avoid mutual conflict. A conglomerate that launches a competitive assault in one industry which is an important source of profits to a rival conglomerate can logically expect a retaliatory attack in another industry which is an important source of its profits. To escape this, it will abstain from initiating a competitive move in the first industry. The greater the number of industries in which given conglomerates confront each other, the stronger the rationale for mutual forbearance.

See Index under Industry Structure.

Forbes. Fortnightly American business magazine published by Forbes Inc., New York. In April of each year a separate issue appears listing the 500 largest US corporations. These are ranked by turnover, profit, assets, share value, employment, productivity and capital intensity. The July issue publishes a survey of the 100 largest foreign companies with investments in the USA.

The magazine produces frequent background articles about companies and industrial sectors. The emphasis is on American business.

See Index under Data Sources.

foreign bond. A bond raised in a country other than that of the borrower. The currency of the bond is that of the country in which the issue takes place, and all the conditions surrounding the loan are those applicable to the country in which the funds are raised.

foreign content. The foreign content of a firm's production refers to the sum of its exports from the home country plus the total of its overseas or foreign production.

See also FOREIGN INVOLVEMENT.

Foreign Corrupt Practices Act. Legislation passed in the United States that prohibits US corporations from bribing the officials of a foreign country in order to get or keep business in that country. It does not however forbid payments to ensure shipments move swiftly through customs or to ensure permits are granted.

See also BRIBERY, and Index under Regulation and Tax.

Foreign Credit Insurance Association. An institution created to insure US companies against certain risks of exporting. It is an association of about 50 private insurance companies together with the US government's EXPORT-IMPORT BANK (EX-IM BANK).

See also EXPORT CREDIT INSURANCE; EXPORT CREDIT GUARANTEE DEPARTMENT (ECGD); OVERSEAS PRIVATE INVESTMENT CORPORATION (OPIC), and Index under Financial and Risk Management.

Address: 1 World Trade Center, New York, NY 10048, USA.

foreign direct investment (FDI). This term was originally used to describe the acquisition, through equity investment, of managerial control over an economic enterprise in one country by a citizen or a corporation of another country. Corporations that widely engaged in foreign direct investments were called multinational corporations or transnational corporations. Today the concept has become ambiguous owing to the growing variety of novel cross-border transactions.

The acquisition of a foreign economic enterprise may occur either through the takeover of an existing enterprise (in which case no new economic investment may take place) or through the setting up of a new enterprise (*see* GREENFIELD INVESTMENT) which does involve a new economic investment. In the latter case, capital may not necessarily be transferred from the home nation to the host nation. The multinational corporation may acquire real capital from local, or third party, sources or may utilize local or third nation sources of financing. Despite this ambiguity, the concept of foreign direct investment – both in its use as a statistical category and in theories of FDI – has been treated as a special case of international capital movements. The definition of foreign direct investment has hinged upon the exercise of foreign managerial control through ownership of equity capital or 'voting stock'. The concept has conventionally been distinguished from foreign indirect investments which involved the cross-border flow of interest-bearing loan capital not accompanied by managerial control (so-called PORTFOLIO INVESTMENT).

Starting from this definition of foreign direct investment centred on equity ownership, theories of FDI were developed which attempted to explain why companies should wish to invest abroad as opposed to exporting their products or licensing their production technologies. (Compare PRODUCT CYCLE THEORY; INTERNALIZATION THEORY; PORTFOLIO THEORY; APPROPRIABILITY THEORY; INDUSTRIAL ORGANIZATION THEORY).

But the centrality of the notion of equity ownership in the concept of FDI proved a liability. Exactly how much foreign equity investment is required to class an enterprise as a foreign direct investment because it is controlled from abroad?

Even before the recent wave of novel CROSS-BORDER TRANSACTIONS severed the link between ownership and control, national account procedures differed widely between countries, making estimates of worldwide flows of FDI unreliable. Some countries regard an enterprise with as little as five or ten per cent foreign equity participation as a foreign direct investment, others have a much higher floor limit of over 50 per cent. Some countries adopt a uniform percentage ownership irrespective of diffusion of investors and investing countries, while others adopt various minimum criteria according to the degree of such diffusion. Some countries include re-invested earnings in their recording of FDI flows, others exclude them.

A standard 'working' definition of FDI adopted by the INTERNATIONAL MONETARY FUND (IMF) since 1964 (*Balance of Payments Yearbook – Concepts and Defini-*

tions), and also followed by the ORGANIZATION FOR ECONOMIC CO-OPERATION AND DEVELOPMENT (OECD) refers to FDI as investment in enterprises located in one country but 'effectively' controlled by residents of another country. 'Effective' control is inferred from:

(i) ownership of 50 per cent or more of the voting stock by residents in an investor country;

(ii) ownership by a single holder or organized groups of holders of 25 per cent or more of the stock in an investor country, or

(iii) the existence of specific groups of residents in an investor country represented on the board of directors.

However, this working definition of FDI is of limited use today as the nature of foreign direct investment has been changing. It has moved from equity participation to the use of loans and suppliers' credits, and from direct parent control over management to participation in management through TECHNICAL ASSISTANCE AGREEMENTS, PRODUCTION SHARING AGREEMENTS, SERVICE CONTRACTS, MANAGEMENT CONTRACTS, LICENSING AGREEMENTS, supply contracts, and so on. In these new arrangements the umbilical cord between ownership and control has been broken. While foreign direct investment in the conventional sense has been diminishing (particularly in less developed countries) these new forms of private foreign economic involvement have been increasing. They make modifications to the concept of foreign direct investment necessary, both for the purposes of properly assessing international capital movements and of correcting conventional theories about such investment.

See Index under Theoretical Issues.

Foreign Direct Investment Program. A programme endorsed in 1965 together with the

Voluntary Credit Restraint Program. Targeted particularly on US multinational corporations, the programme requested them to improve their balance of payments position with the developed countries by 10 to 15 per cent. These guidelines were designed to counteract the growing external deficit of the United States at that time, and to restore international confidence in the US dollar. The programme was made mandatory in 1968 and administered by the Office of Foreign Direct Investment.

The effect of the Foreign Direct Investment Program was twofold: US multinationals began to encourage their subsidiaries to borrow abroad – particularly in the EUROCURRENCY markets – and US banks, to whom the programme did not apply, set up branches overseas to continue to service their clients. In this way, the programme indirectly fuelled the internationalization of American banks, as well as the growth of OFFSHORE FINANCIAL CENTRES.

See also TRANSNATIONAL BANKS, and Index under Regulation and Tax.

foreign exchange risk. The risk arising from a holding in a particular foreign currency at a certain time. This can be either a short or a long position (*see* EXPOSURE). The basic risk arises from speculative transactions, where a net holding or liability in a currency will result in a profit or loss depending on the movement of that currency in the foreign exchange markets.

See Index under Financial and Risk Management.

foreign freight forwarder. A highly specialized operator who acts for manufacturers and COMBINATION EXPORT MANAGERS, using his skill and knowledge of overseas customs regulations, import regulations, shipping rates and so on to aid exporting. US forwarders must be licensed by the Federal Maritime Commission.

See Index under Trade.

foreign involvement. In the literature on multinational enterprise, the extent of a company's foreign involvement is said to equal the total of its exports plus its foreign production, that is to say the production by its foreign subsidiaries.

See also FOREIGN CONTENT.

foreign portfolio investment. *See* PORTFOLIO INVESTMENT.

foreign tax credit. *See* TAX CREDIT.

Foreign Trade Organization (FTO). A trading company of Eastern bloc countries which has the monopoly over all international trade in a particular commercial or industrial sector. FTOs are the Eastern bloc countries' participants in joint ventures and COPRODUCTION AGREEMENTS with foreign multinationals. They are also central to East – West COUNTERTRADE.

See RED MULTINATIONALS; SOCIALIST COMMON ENTERPRISE.

forfaiting. A technique for export financing. Developed in Switzerland and subsequently taken up in London, the system involves a 'forfaiter' who pays an exporter at a very early stage for the goods sold, and recovers the advance from the importer over a specified period.

The advantage to the exporter is that the goods (usually capital goods requiring payments over several years) are paid for immediately. The risk to the exporter is also eliminated, since the forfaiter has no recourse to the exporter should the importer default. The exporter pays a fee to the forfaiter for the finance extended to him. It is normal for the importer to have the debt endorsed, or guaranteed, by his bank, thus reducing the risk to the forfaiter. The payment by the importer is generally by a series of promissory notes which mature at fixed intervals.

Having received the endorsed promissory notes the forfaiter may well subsequently sell them in the money markets.

See Index under Trade.

Fortune. Monthly American business magazine. Each year in the May issue the top 500 American industrial concerns are ranked by turnover and further data is given in respect of employment, profit, assets and dividend. The June issue ranks the top 500 companies in the services sector (commerce, transport and banking), while the August issue ranks the top 500 industrial concerns outside the US.

See Index under Data Sources.

forward exchange market hedge. *See* HEDGE.

forward linkages. The stimulation of local processing industries and services as a result of the establishment of a domestic- or foreign-owned extractive industry. The linking is deemed to go 'forward' within the mine-to-market chain of production, as in the case of a pig-iron plant being set up as a result of the extraction of iron ore locally.

See also BACKWARD LINKAGES; LOCAL VALUE ADDED; LOCAL SOURCING, and Index under Development Policy.

Fourth World. A concept which first gained currency in the early 1970s when it became apparent that THIRD WORLD countries differed markedly when it came to economic development performance. United Nations' resolutions began to speak of 'least developed' countries, while the World Bank introduced a distinction between 'middle-income' and 'low-income' countries in its literature. The Fourth World is not an officially designated group of countries, but the references to it which are beginning to appear in popular literature usually combine the World Bank low-income category with the UN least developed category. Most countries of sub-Saharan Africa are included, as well as some of the more populated countries of Asia, notably Bangladesh.

franchising. A specific form of a LICENSING AGREEMENT which consists of a 'package' combining access to a company's TRADEMARK and technology with technical, managerial and marketing assistance, as well as local exclusivity. In return for the franchise, the franchisor normally receives a downpayment fee, ROYALTIES and compliance with certain corporate regulations.

As is the case with other new forms of investment by multinational enterprises in less developed countries, franchising agreements have become very popular in recent years. They have however also mushroomed in the advanced countries, more especially in the retail and service industries.

The upward trend in franchising as a contractually established collaborative arrangement between legally independent firms is proving to be a problem for anti-trust authorities both in the United States and in the European Community (EC). The question at issue is whether franchising agreements are potentially pro- or anti-competitive. So far the anti-trust authorities have tended to adjudicate on a case-by-case basis.

See Index under Technology Transfer.

franco delivered. *See under* EXPORTING TRADE TERMS.

free alongside ship (FAS). *See under* EXPORTING TRADE TERMS.

free equity. A novel form of state equity participation in foreign extractive industries. Governments of poor countries wishing to participate in JOINT VENTURES with multinational mining companies, but not having the capital to do so, may demand a share of the equity in exchange for making available the ore body which is to be mined. Hence free equity is really 'resource' equity, that is, equity based upon the sovereign ownership over the resource.

free float. The abandonment of all controls on the exchange value of a country's currency by the financial and governmental authorities of that country.

See also FIXED EXCHANGE RATE, DIRTY FLOAT.

free on board (FOB). *See under* EXPORTING TRADE TERMS.

free port. *See under* FREE TRADE ZONE (FTZ).

free processing zone. *See* FREE TRADE ZONE.

free trade zone (FTZ). Originally this term and its synonym, free port, were used to refer to a specially designated 'bonded' area within a country, near air or sea ports. In such an area imported goods may be stored, distributed and re-exported without interference by the customs authorities, provided these goods do not cross the national borderline separating the zone from the customs territory.

In the past 20 years, however, a new dimension has been added to the concept of the free trade zone. Eager to attract foreign capital investments in export-orientated, manufacturing ventures, governments all over the world, but initially and more particularly in the so-called NEWLY INDUSTRIALIZING COUNTRIES of Southeast Asia, the Middle East and Central and Latin America, have added new functions and new privileges to the conventional free trade zones. These new functions are reflected in current synonyms of the FTZ, which may at present also be called an export processing zone, an export platform, or an industrial free zone.

In modern FTZs, foreign investors, including those in JOINT VENTURES with nationals, are offered physical, fiscal and customs incentives, and partial or complete exemption from national legislation on industrial relations and conditions of work.

Physical incentives include the provision of industrial building sites and other infrastructural facilities. Fiscal incentives typically include reduced tax liabilities, 'tax holidays' and preferential treatment on repatriation of profits; while customs incentives normally involve free importation of raw materials, semi-finished and capital goods for the purposes of manufacturing, processing or assembling export products. In addition, in many FTZs in newly industrializing countries, the application of pertinent industrial laws and regulations is relaxed or waived altogether. Cut off by barbed wire or walled fence, the zone often has its own authority to which government functions are relegated, and a zone 'police' who check the movement of labour and suppress labour disputes. This means that wages and conditions of work, including hours of work and health and safety conditions, may be below those prevailing elsewhere.

The proliferation of the new FTZs has greatly stimulated the internationalization of industrial production by multinational enterprises, allowing manufacturing industry to fragment on a global scale. Labour-intensive assembly operations are farmed out to FTZs in low wage countries and the finished products return from their global journey to the home markets of the advanced countries. The electronics industry provides the best but by no means only example of this new FTZ-inspired international division of labour. Electronic circuits are printed on silicon wafers and tested in California. Then the wafers are shipped or even transported by air to Asia for the labour-intensive process of cutting them into tiny chips and bonding them to circuit boards, to be returned to the US for final assembly.

While FTZs offer undoubted advantages to international capital, their role in national economic development is open to dispute. Marxist critics have often argued that FTZs are a mere vehicle for exploitation of local human labour, but liberal writers are also beginning to question the purported value of FTZs in boosting national economic activity. It is now argued in particular that the stated objectives of foreign exchange earnings, of industrial technology and skill transfer, and of employment generation, are eroded by the very structure of incentives offered. Tax incentives only serve to lower a country's share of the profits of foreign enterprise which will in any case be attracted more by factors like market share, political stability and growth potential. Technology and industrial skill transfer is negated by the fragmented nature of the labour processes and their lack of backward and forward linkages within the national domestic economy and market. Even job creation is prejudiced by the duty-free imports of capital and semi-processed goods.

See FORWARD LINKAGES; BACKWARD LINKAGES; SPECIAL ECONOMIC ZONES; *MAQUILADORA;* NEW INTERNATIONAL DIVISION OF LABOUR, and Index under Trade.

fronting loan. A loan from one part of a multinational to another (usually from parent to foreign subsidiary) channelled through a bank, usually a major international one, as intermediary. Instead of the parent lending to the subsidiary directly, it lends to the bank, which in turn lends to the subsidiary. The principal advantage to the MNC is that by using a bank to 'front' for it, it finds it easier to obtain permission from the country in which the subsidiary operates to pay the interest to a third party than it would if the payment were to be made directly to the parent. If made directly to the parent, it would probably constitute one of a number of payments such as royalties and dividends (*see* UNBUNDLING). A second advantage is that if EXPROPRIATION were to be threatened, the loan from a powerful international bank would be more likely to be honoured than one from a parent company.

Fronting loans may also be known as 'link financing'.

See also Index under Financial and Risk Management.

FTC. *See* FEDERAL TRADE COMMISSION.

FTO. *See* FOREIGN TRADE ORGANIZATION.

FTZ. *See* FREE TRADE ZONE.

functional currency. A term coined for the purposes of currency translation methods in a multinational's group accounts in FINANCIAL ACCOUNTING STANDARD NO 52 (FAS 52).

See Index under International Accounting.

fungibility. A characteristic and potentially beneficial indirect effect of the inflow of external funds invested in an economy. It results in the release of resources for other uses.

G

G-77. *See under* GROUP OF 77.

GATT. *See under* GENERAL AGREEMENT ON TARIFFS AND TRADE.

gearing. See FINANCIAL STRUCTURE.

General Agreement on Tariffs and Trade (GATT). An international organization dedicated to the expansion of world trade through the multilateral extension of reciprocal trade concessions. GATT began as a trade agreement arising from a tariff conference held at Geneva in 1947. At that time, the conference was meant to be the first of a series of such conferences to be held under the auspices of the International Trade Organization, which was itself being set up at the same time, at the HAVANA CONVENTION. However the Havana Charter was not ratified by the United States, and the General Agreement consequently became the founding document of what over the years was to evolve into a fully fledged international trade organization. One of the key provisions of the original agreement was that 'joint' action could be taken by the 'contracting parties'. This formula has permitted the participating countries to develop an elaborate institutional framework which includes within its structure the Session of Contracting Parties as the supreme decision making body, a Council of Representatives as the executive body, and a Secretariat.

The General Agreement incorporated many of the commercial policy rules of the ill-fated Havana Charter. The main aims of the General Agreement are to lower import quotas and tariffs and to eliminate other non-tariff restrictions on international

trade. The key principles through which this is to be achieved are the most favoured nation treatment and reciprocity. The most favoured nation clause ensures that tariff and other trade concessions negotiated between two contracting parties be extended to the other contracting parties. However, members of CUSTOMS UNIONS such as the European Community (EC), which have no tariffs amongst themselves, are exempt. The principle of reciprocity means that trade concessions should be mutually advantageous, that is that no member country should be asked to grant a trade concession without receiving adequate concessions in return.

GATT has sponsored seven 'rounds' of multilateral tariff negotiations and effected very substantial tariff reductions worldwide. Its Secretariat also assists bilateral trade negotiations, bringing about pragmatic solutions between contracting parties and generally ensuring that liberal commercial attitudes prevail. At present, however, in the wake of the severe economic recession of the 1970s, protectionist measures are being widely re-introduced in the form of NON-TARIFF BARRIERS, and no progress has been made within GATT to counter these, especially those which apply to the service sector.

Originally signed by only 22 contracting parties, the General Agreement's signatories now total 88 countries, with a further 30 countries participating under special arrangements. The chief non-participants are the Soviet Union and the People's Republic of China.

The success of GATT in attracting so many new member countries stems from the application of a flexible and pragmatic attitude to issues of international trade and development, which have allowed it to bend its key principles substantially to accommodate the needs of the less developed countries. A central provision added in 1965 for example states that 'developed contracting parties do not expect reciprocity for commitments made by them in trade negotiations to reduce or remove tariffs and other barriers to the trade of less developed contracting parties'. Nevertheless, the GATT negotiations are currently plagued by North-South disagreements, especially over non-tariff barriers.

See also GENERALIZED SYSTEM OF PREFERENCES (GSP); VOLUNTARY EXPORT RESTRAINTS, and Index under Trade, and under International Co-operation.

Generalized System of Preferences (GSP). Signed in 1971 first by the countries of the EUROPEAN COMMUNITY (EC), and later by nearly all other developed countries, the GSP is a trade agreement established under the GENERAL AGREEMENT ON TARIFFS AND TRADE (GATT) offering developing countries lower tariffs for their exports to the markets of the signatory countries than are required of developed countries. The novelty of the scheme when first introduced was that it departed from the two GATT-established norms of reciprocity and most favoured nation treatment.

The scheme was intended to stimulate trade with the developing countries, but it has been criticized for including in its coverage only agricultural commodities that do not compete with those protected by the EC's Common Agricultural Policy (CAP) and for failing to include a number of manufactures and semi-manufactures important to the developing countries, notably textiles, leather and petroleum products. In 1982, after 12 years of operation, GSP goods imported into the advanced countries accounted for just 23 per cent of dutiable imports and an even

smaller proportion of total imports (11 per cent). Moreover, the benefits of GSP have tended to fall unevenly between less developed countries. Those countries with a relatively wide industrial base and diversified industrial exports naturally benefit more than those relying on exports of agricultural products and raw materials. Roughly a dozen industrially more advanced beneficiaries supply 80 per cent or more of total preferential imports.

GATT has provided for periodic multilateral trade negotiations which aim to liberalize tariffs worldwide, and the benefits of GSP are automatically reduced each time such a multilateral negotiation is successful. Thus, the Tokyo Round of tariff liberalization concluded in 1980 has seriously eroded the GSP preferential margins, retrenching the benefits of the GSP still further by accepting the principle of 'graduation', which specifies that less developed countries requesting GSP treatment from developed countries should accept greater obligations with the progressive development of their economies and improvement in their trade situation. Under the GSP since the Tokyo Round, graduation is a means of moving successful developing countries towards full participation within the framework of rights and obligations under the General Agreement, that is the principles of reciprocity and multi-favoured nation treatment.

See also PEASE BILL; LOMÉ CONVENTION; MOST FAVOURED NATION (MFN) CLAUSE, and Index under Trade and under International Co-operation.

geocentric. A term devised by Howard Perlmutter to describe a managerial attitude taken by certain kinds of multinational. The geocentric multinational treats its home and foreign subsidiaries as increasingly interdependent, seeks universal standards of performance, integrates communications both ways between head office and the subsidiaries, has worldwide objectives, seeks the best managers regardless of national origin and is willing to place them in the most appropriate place, and attempts to be truly international while at the same time identifying with individual national interests. The geocentric multinational is the 'truest' multinational in the sense that it has taken the concept to its limits. The other types of attitude defined by Perlmutter are ETHNOCENTRIC, POLYCENTRIC and REGIOCENTRIC.

See Index under Corporate Structure and Management, and under Theoretical Issues.

global commons. Planetary resources considered to be the common property of mankind, as distinct from resources that are subject to national territorial claims. Examples include the electro-magnetic spectrum, the ecological environment, space, and the sea bed.

See LAW OF THE SEA TREATY.

global corporation. *See under* MULTINATIONAL CORPORATION/ENTERPRISE.

global efficiency. A concept which suggests that optimization of the world's raw material resources demands concessions to those developing countries where there are rich and accessible deposits of natural resources. This perspective gained some popularity amongst the advanced countries in the mid-1970s in response to the THIRD WORLD's demands for a NEW INTERNATIONAL ECONOMIC ORDER (NIEO).

See also GLOBAL REFORMS.

global industrial systems constellation (GISC). A phrase coined by Perlmutter (1972) to describe a new form of collaboration between nationally oriented enterprises from different countries which may form joint ventures for particular projects and product lines, with the object of achieving worldwide competitive advantage without losing their national identity. Examples of this type of collaboration are those between Dunlop and Pirelli, and British Leyland and Honda.

Such multinational corporate coalitions are quite different from the single enterprise whose global strategy is managed from a single corporate headquarters. They are a particularly popular form of collaboration among THIRD WORLD multinationals.

See Index under Industry Structure.

global reforms. Catch-all term for a wide variety of reforms in international arrangements demanded by the developing countries.

Since the mid-1970s, when these demands were first formally and comprehensively put at the Sixth Special Session of the UN General Assembly (*see* NEW INTERNATIONAL ECONOMIC ORDER (NIEO)) they have been the subject of periodic 'global' negotiations between representatives of the advanced world and representatives of the developing world, and they have appeared separately or together in numerous international conferences and meetings held by the various suborganizations of the United Nations.

See also CHARTER OF ECONOMIC RIGHTS AND DUTIES OF STATES; BRANDT COMMISSION, and Index under International Co-operation.

global scanning. The evaluation of the multinational's environment on a worldwide basis. The essential features of a good global scanning system are

(a) its assessment of all relevant features of the environment – political, economic, technical, financial, and social;
(b) its willingness to consider all opportunities and threats in the various countries relevant to the corporation; and

(c) its continuous nature. Good scanning is sensitive to environmental changes as or before they occur, rather than being tied to discrete planning periods.

See also GLOBAL STRATEGY, and Index under Corporate Structure and Management.

global strategy. An approach to multinational corporate planning which integrates the planning process for the corporation as a whole. A corporation taking this approach to planning assesses the alternatives available, and their consequences, without being limited by national boundaries: all interdependencies are considered. As with all strategic planning systems, there are a number of steps involved. These include setting corporate objectives; assessing the various national environments (*see* GLOBAL SCANNING); evaluating worldwide corporate strengths and weaknesses; scenario-building for global courses of action; selection of preferred actions; undertaking those actions, and monitoring the strategy's success, feeding back into the earlier steps where appropriate.

Given the increasing interdependence of political environments, technology, marketing plans and financial systems, it is sometimes argued that a global approach to strategy is essential to all multinationals and not merely those with integrated product lines.

See also Index under Corporate Structure and Management.

Gonzalez Amendment. A 1972 extension to the HICKENLOOPER AMENDMENT of 1962 requiring the United States to cease automatically all contributions to international lending institutions which provide loans to any country expropriating private US property without compensation or without taking the appropriate steps. The Gonzalez amendment has never been formally applied, although it has been used as a lever to strengthen the US case in investment disputes.

See EXPROPRIATION; NATIONALIZATION, and Index under Regulation and Tax.

grant back provision. A clause sometimes included in technology contracts, providing for a one way flow of technical information and improvements from the purchaser of the technology without a reciprocal obligation on the supplier. All technical innovations and improvements made by the purchaser following the agreement remain the supplier's property. The clause is also known as the 'retrocession' clause.

See RESTRICTIVE BUSINESS PRACTICES (RBP) CODE; TRANSFER OF TECHNOLOGY (TOT) CODE.

grassroot entry. *See* GREENFIELD INVESTMENT.

greenfield investment. Investments involving the establishment of new firms, especially new factories or other physical assets, as opposed to the acquisition of existing establishments. This form of investment is sometimes called grassroot entry, when it is a firm's first direct investment in a particular country.

See FOREIGN DIRECT INVESTMENT (FDI).

group accounts. *See* CONSOLIDATED ACCOUNTS.

Group B states. United Nations expression for the group of advanced industrialized countries represented on various intergovernmental working parties which are set up from time to time within the UN negotiating system. The term is a virtual synonym for OECD countries.

See ORGANIZATION FOR ECONOMIC CO-OPERATION AND DEVELOPMENT (OECD);

GROUP D STATES; GROUP OF 77 (G-77).

Group D states. United Nations expression for the socialist bloc countries, except China, represented on various inter-governmental working groups within the UN negotiating machinery.

Group of 77 (G-77). Established in 1967 at Algiers, an organization of developing countries whose objective it is to develop and present a THIRD WORLD perspective on the world economic situation, and define a unified response from the Third World in matters of economic development and trade within the international negotiating machinery of the United Nations. Its origins go back to the first UNITED NATIONS CONFERENCE ON TRADE AND DEVELOPMENT (UNCTAD) when the then 77 participating developing countries joined to form a caucus group. Since that time the term 'Group of 77' has stuck, even though its membership has swollen to 120 countries.

See also GROUP B STATES; GROUP D STATES; COLLECTIVE SELF-RELIANCE, and Index under International Co-operation, and under Development Policy.

Groupe d'études des experts comptables de la CEE. *See under* UNION EUROPÉENNE DES EXPERTS COMPTABLES ECONOMIQUES ET FINANCIERS (UEC).

GSP. *See* GENERALIZED SYSTEM OF PREFERENCES.

guarantee insurance. *See* FIDELITY CONTRACT.

H

hard currency. A currency that over a period of time has shown itself to be stable or increasing in value, and is expected to continue in the same way.

harmonization policies. Policies of national governments or institutions (such as professional accounting organizations) formulated to come into line with relevant legislation and policies in other countries. Examples relevant to multinational enterprise are the policies promulgated by the ANDEAN PACT COUNTRIES (such as Decision 24) and the EUROPEAN COMMUNITY (EC) Directives.

An important instance of harmonization has been the matter of financial reporting. The large number of different ACCOUNTING PRINCIPLES and disclosure policies (*see* DISCLOSURE IN ACCOUNTS) extant has led to steps for standardization and harmonization. The principal instigator of international standards has been the INTERNATIONAL ACCOUNTING STANDARDS COMMITTEE (IASC). Other institutions have also attempted to narrow differences in financial reporting. For the members of such institutions, the most important have been the European Community (EC) (particularly the Fourth and Seventh Directives); the ORGANIZATION FOR ECONOMIC CO-OPERATION AND DEVELOPMENT (OECD), whose Committee on International Investment and Multinational Enterprises set up a permanent Working Group on Accounting Standards in 1979; and the United Nations Economic and Social Council, which set up an *ad hoc* Intergovernmental Working Group of Experts on International Standards of Accounting and Reporting. This working group collaborated in the formulation of the UN DRAFT CODE OF CONDUCT ON

TRANSNATIONAL CORPORATIONS, and produced a report of its own in 1982. Because member states of the UN have disagreed about the policy of any UN action on multinational or international accounting, no further developments have yet been agreed.

See Index under International Co-operation and under Regulation and Tax.

Havana Charter. A suggested charter for an international trade organization submitted to the United Nations Conference on Trade and Employment held at Havana, Cuba, from November 1947 to March 1948, and attended by 55 member states of the United Nations.

The objectives of the Havana Convention, as it came to be called, were to expand world trade and remove trade barriers by means of the establishment of International Trade Organizations (ITOs); to foster industrial and economic development, particularly of those countries still in the early stages of such development, and to encourage the international flow of capital for productive investment.

The protection and regulation of foreign investment was dealt with in Article 12 of the Charter. It recognized the need to create good opportunities and adequate security for all foreign investment as a determining factor in the continuous flow of private capital to poor countries, yet it also acknowledged the rights of countries which imported capital to control it.

Although the agreements reached were duly signed by 54 of the attending states and came to be known as the Havana Charter, the US failed to ratify them, preferring the less stringent and less comprehensive agreements meanwhile reached in the GENERAL

AGREEMENT ON TARIFFS AND TRADE (GATT). Furthermore, the American business community also felt that the provisions on foreign investment were weak and unsatisfactory. Following the American lead, other major nations failed to ratify the Charter, and in consequence it remained a mere historical document.

See Index under International Co-operation.

Heckscher – Ohlin theorem. The core proposition of the 'neo-classical' theory of international trade. It is referred to as 'neo-classical' because it is based on Ricardo's theory of comparative advantage, but adds and modifies it to take into account existing differences in factor proportions between trading countries. The theorem is attributed to two economists writing decades apart. (Heckscher, 1919 and Ohlin, 1967).

The Heckscher – Ohlin proposition holds that under conditions of free competitive markets and international immobility of resources the commodity composition of trade between countries will be determined mainly by the correspondence between the pattern of FACTOR ENDOWMENT of the trading countries and the factor intensities of the production processes of the commodities traded. Specialization in accordance with the principle of correspondence between factor intensity and factor endowment is likely to lead to equalization of the returns to the factors of production, and hence to a more equal distribution of income between countries over time. For example a country relatively well endowed with labour will have low wages and will tend to export labour-intensive goods. Trade will raise incomes in the exporting country, and will thereby reduce or eliminate the wage differential between exporting and importing countries. In this way, the Heckscher–Ohlin theorem gave a positive theoretical underpinning to an existing international division of labour in which

advanced countries traded primarily capital-intensive commodities for the labour-intensive commodities exported by the less-developed countries. Since the theorem in its original formulation assumed that the factors of production (capital and labour) could not be moved on an international scale, it was not applicable to – or worse, was contradicted by – international direct investments. However, neo-classical theories of the international firm have managed to work within this tradition by relaxing the assumption of factor immobility between countries.

Thus, it has been argued that international capital movements should be seen as a substitute for trade. According to this view, capital exports are merely substitutes for capital-intensive commodities. This leaves the general propositions of the theory intact, including the equalization of returns between countries.

See FOREIGN DIRECT INVESTMENT (FDI); INTERNATIONAL PRODUCTION; NEO-FACTOR TRADE THEORY; NEO-TECHNOLOGY TRADE THEORY, and Index under Theoretical Issues.

hedge. An operation in the foreign exchange market to protect an exposed asset position. The term is often used interchangeably with COVERING, to describe the protection of a future receipt denominated in a foreign currency. More properly it involves the protection of an exposed asset position in a foreign currency.

The hedge is 'covered' or 'square' if the party selling forward either already possesses the currency sold or is due to receive it by the forward contract date. It is 'uncovered' or 'open' if the currency is not available in this way and will have to be bought at the forward contract date on the spot market.

A 'balance sheet hedge' is a means of reducing translation EXPOSURE. Most kinds of CURRENCY TRANSLATION used to consolidate financial statements result in an exposed risk. This can be reduced by attempting as far as possible to equalize the exposed assets and liabilities in the balance sheet, so that a change in one is automatically offset by a change in the other. The exposure risk can be avoided completely if the monetary/non-monetary or current/non-current method of currency translation is used (*see* TRANSLATION): it cannot if the current method of translation is used. Alternatively, the company may sell the amount of the exposed assets in the host country currency forward for delivery at the next balance sheet date. Any decline in the translated value of the exposed position will be exactly offset by the gain from buying in the spot market at that date to deliver the currency contracted for.

Although the term is usually concerned with financial hedging, physical hedging is also common, as when a manufacturer who uses a primary commodity buys it forward in the appropriate commodity market.

See Index under Financial and Risk Management.

Hertz-gap. *See under* INTERNATIONAL TRADE SECRETARIATS (ITS).

Hickenlooper Amendment. Congressional amendment to the Foreign Assistance Act of 1962. The Hickenlooper Amendment requires the US to automatically cease all bilateral aid to any country that expropriates private US property without fair compensation or without taking the appropriate steps. The amendment was broadened in the following year to include any case in which a government repudiates or nullifies an existing contract with a US investor.

The Hickenlooper amendment has been applied in only one case. In 1963, Peru saw its aid cut off for three years as a result of a dispute with the International Petroleum Corporation, a subsidiary of Standard Oil of New Jersey. The threat of its application has however been used as a lever to achieve US objectives in investment disputes.

See EXPROPRIATION; NATIONALIZATION; GONZALEZ AMENDMENT, and Index under Regulation and Tax.

high-context culture. A term coined by Edward T Hall (1976) (contrasted with LOW-CONTEXT CULTURE) to describe a particular set of cultural factors important both to international marketing and to the multinational personnel function.

The high-context culture, according to Hall, is characterized by a reliance upon personal relationships rather than the exact form of words when coming to a business agreement: it is so called because the context of the words rather than the particular form of the words themselves is the significant factor. In a high-context culture sales negotiations are lengthy because the buyer needs to trust the salesman personally; and the formal contract is less important because the personal word of the seller is more important than legal phraseology.

Hall suggests that Japan and the less developed countries are examples of high-context cultures, and the USA and northern Europe examples of low-context cultures.

See Index under Corporate Structure and Management, and under Theoretical Issues.

holding company. Normally the parent of a group of companies which owns directly or indirectly the other companies in the group. Within a group structure, however, a subsidiary may be set up which is itself a holding company for other subsidiaries.

A holding company in a group may undertake operations itself, or, more commonly, it may act only as a vehicle for ownership of the shares in other group companies. Frequently in the latter case it will be located in a major financial centre rather than being close to any of the individual operations. The domicile of a multinational's holding company is crucial since this will determine the laws under which the group as a whole operates, its 'nationality' for various purposes (such as government controls) and the principal taxing authority to which it is responsible.

In the beginning of this century, the invention of the holding company structure proved an efficient means for large corporations to bypass ANTI-TRUST LEGISLATION. Since 1968, US banks have also used a general holding company to avoid restrictive legislation. Much of US bank legislation in the past had been devised to separate banking activities from commercial activities, and to prevent banks from investing long term finance in industry. In practice, banks could get around that legislation by means of the trust laws which permitted the trust departments of banks to hold and manage the securities of third parties. In 1968, the First National City Bank came up with the idea of creating a structure which allowed it to escape from the strict rules of American banking legislation. A holding company was created which owned both the bank itself and other non-banking corporations. Rapidly, the largest US banks adopted the 'one bank holding company' status. These holding companies effectively permit the banks not only to hold equity shares in corporations, but also to offer new types of financial services as well as non-banking services to the corporations in whom they have a financial interest.

See also Index under Corporate Structure and Management.

home country. (Of foreign investment). Country from which a foreign investment originates and where the parent company of a multinational corporation is domiciled.

horizontal diversification. Corporate expansion through the manufacture of the same product in different countries.

horizontal expansion. *See* HORIZONTAL DIVERSIFICATION.

horizontal integration. The internalization of product lines that are at a similar level in the production chain. According to INTERNALIZATION THEORY, OWNERSHIP SPECIFIC ADVANTAGES lead to a multinational's decision to manufacture a product in a given country. If that product would otherwise have been marketed by a competitor, the diversification into its manufacture is known as horizontal integration.

See Index under Corporate Structure and Management.

host country. (Of foreign investment). Country receiving a foreign investment.

hot money. Capital shifted between countries in the short term because its owners fear losses if the funds stay where they are. Such capital movements are difficult to control and can precipitate actions, such as devaluations, that they are designed to avoid.

See Index under Financial and Risk Management.

I

IASC. *See* INTERNATIONAL ACCOUNTING STANDARDS COMMITTEE.

IBASE (Instituto Brasileiro de Analises Sociales e Economicas). Critical research and documentation centre providing consultancy service and information to worker- and community-based movements. Its data bank contains information on 1,000 major companies in Brazil. It publishes an English-language bimonthly, *Brasil Information*.

See Index under Data Sources.
Address: Rua Vicente Souza 29, 22251 Rio de Janeiro, Brazil.

ICFTU. *See* INTERNATIONAL CON-FEDERATION OF FREE TRADE UNIONS.

ICJ. *See* INTERNATIONAL COURT OF JUSTICE.

IFAC. *See* INTERNATIONAL FEDERATION OF ACCOUNTANTS.

IFPMA Code. A voluntary code of marketing practices promulgated by the International Federation of Pharmaceutical Manufacturers' Associations in 1981. The Code represents a bid on the part of the industry to pre-empt binding or more hostile codes from being adopted elsewhere. Following the success of the international baby foods campaign (*see* WHO/UNICEF CODE), both the INTERNATIONAL ORGANIZATION OF CONSUMER UNIONS (IOCU) and the World Health Organization had started to take a critical look at the drug industry's marketing practices in the THIRD WORLD. In 1981, the WHO adopted an action programme on essential drugs and vaccines which included a model list of 'essential drugs'. The WHO has also been active in trying to curb the cost of essential drugs to the Third World.

The substance of the IFPMA code is thin and does not go beyond a plea to the member multinationals to make information on their products both truthful and as widely available as possible.

See CODES OF CONDUCT, and Index under International Co-operation.

ILET (Instituto Latinoamericano de Estudios Transnacionales). An international, privately funded non-profit organization. Its object is the study of the transnationalization process of Latin America and its political, economic and cultural consequences. The Institute's work is broken down into a programme on communication and development, and political and social studies. ILET has affiliated institutes in Chile, Mexico, Argentina, Brazil, and Washington. Publications are mostly in Spanish.

See Index under Data Sources.
Address: Casilla 16637, Correao 9, Santiago, Chile.

IME Committee. *See* COMMITTEE ON INTERNATIONAL INVESTMENT AND MULTINATIONAL ENTERPRISES.

IMF. *See* INTERNATIONAL MONETARY FUND.

imperialism. A concept corroded by emotional usage and political sloganizing. Its most commonly accepted theoretical meaning denotes the practice in certain states of extending their sovereignty over other territories and peoples, for the purposes of economic exploitation and/or national glorification.

Imperialism has been a feature of state development in ancient as well as modern times. The difference appears to have been that whereas in the ancient world the conquered territories and people were normally integrated into an empire the modern variant has tended to adopt the 'colonial' form, whereby the subjected people are given inferior political, legal and social status.

In the 19th and early 20th century, the particular blend of nationalism, racism and commercial exploitation characteristic of European imperialism was expressed in a legitimizing ideology: it was the 'white man's burden' to assume a dual mandate, namely to offer civilization to 'backward' people, while opening up their territories for the benefit of the world. For a time, such apologetic beliefs and theories served to give the concept of imperialism a positive emotive content.

A turning point in the history of the concept came with J.A. Hobson's study (1902), in which he traced the cause of European expansionism to the underconsumptionist tendencies of modern capitalism and in which he criticized the powerful political lobbying of certain commercial elites. Hobson's radical-liberal views were soon taken up and expanded by Marxist writers. These writers differed on the particular causes of imperialism, but they all shared the view that modern imperialism is a necessary companion to capitalism and that it was responsible for rendering deep and lasting inequalities in economic development between the colonial powers and their subject colonies. Amongst these Marxist writers, Lenin's *Imperialism, the Highest Stage of Capitalism* (1916) undoubtedly made the greatest political impact, partly because of its success in incorporating different Marxist critiques of imperialism into one comprehensive theoretical framework, and partly because of its revolutionary message. Predicting that world wars were inevitable once the world was fully brought under the control of rival capitalist states, Lenin summoned true socialists to convert the war into a revolution at home.

The identification by Marxist writers of imperialism as an essentially economic process has permitted a continued preoccupation on their part with the phenomenon despite the ending of formal colonialism in the post-war period, when sovereign political control was handed over to the colonial peoples. 'Informal' imperialism, 'economic' imperialism, NEO-IMPERIALISM and even 'imperialism' without any such prefixes, became consonant with the 'neo-colonialism' defined by Nkrumah, first head of state of independent Ghana and leader of the Pan-African movement. By this definition, neo-colonialism is represented as a case in which the State is in theory independent and has all the outward trappings of international sovereignty, but where its economic – and thus its political – system continues to be directed from outside. (*See* Nkrumah, 1965).

In the age of 'informal' imperialism, it is the multinational corporation to which a crucial mediatory role is attributed in cementing the economic ties that bind the ex-colonies to the metropolitan centres. It is argued that the dismantling of direct colonial rule was accompanied by a vast increase in direct overseas investments by companies from the advanced countries (more especially US companies) in the former colonial territories. These investments have ensured continued access and control over resources and markets on terms advantageous to the metropolitan powers, at the expense of the local economies. The confidence of multinational corporate investors in the security of their overseas assets has in turn depended on the creation of international economic and financial institutions capable of steering the ex-colonial economies indirectly, as well as on the acceptance by the United States of the role of global policeman. Thus, in this view, the BRETTON WOODS MONETARY SYSTEM, the INTERNA-

TIONAL MONETARY FUND (IMF), the WORLD BANK and the GENERAL AGREEMENT ON TARIFFS AND TRADE (GATT) form the economic infrastructure of the post-war system of informal imperialism, just as the TRUMAN DOCTRINE, the American PL 480 food aid programme, the flexible response doctrine and American military involvement from Korea and Vietnam to El Salvador, are all political aspects of the post-war system of informal imperialism.

In recent years, Marxist theories of imperialism have undergone a reassessment, due to the apparent decline of US power and the rise of Third World ECONOMIC NATIONALISM, including the successful renegotiation of the terms of foreign capital participation in their economies and the obvious success of some Third World countries in achieving rapid industrialization and economic development under the auspices of foreign capital. There are now some social scientists who base their theories on an 'orthodox' position culled from Marx's own writings and view imperialism as a progressive historical force. Others continue to see imperialism as having a distortive effect on local economies, worsening domestic and global inequalities and deepening domestic poverty.

In the 1960s, the consolidation of the Soviet Union's position as a global superpower consequent on its achievement of nuclear parity with the United States contributed to a more aggressive Soviet foreign policy which soon earned the label, social imperialism, coined for the Chinese doctrine. Today, the word 'imperialism' has become part of a propaganda battle. There is now a tendency to regard as imperialism any form of more or less sustained aggressive action on the part of one political system toward another.

See also POST-IMPERIALISM; CORPORATE IMPERIALISM; SUPER-IMPERIALISM; INTER-IMPERIALIST COMPETITION; ULTRA-IMPERIALISM, and Index under Theoretical Issues.

import substitution. The replacement of an existing market for foreign goods and services by domestically produced commodities. It is most commonly associated with a strategy of industrialization which seeks to stimulate domestic infant industries through policies of TARIFF protection and tax concessions. Import-substitutive industrialization became a favoured development strategy of poor countries in the 1950s and 1960s, when it was realized that competition in finished manufactures from the already industrializd countries discouraged local entrepreneurs from investing in domestic industry.

See also ECONOMIC NATIONALISM, and Index under Development Policy.

imputation tax system. See under CORPORATE TAX SYSTEM.

Incoterms, 1953 (International Commercial Terms, 1953). A pamphlet published by the International Chamber of Commerce in Paris which lists common clauses used in international trade and their interpretation in 18 countries. Contracts can specify Incoterms, 1953 as a basis for their contract, by which they mean that there are minimum liabilities on the part of the seller, or 'Incoterms, 1953 plus' if the minimum terms are to be modified by the stated condition.

See EXPORTING TRADE TERMS, and Index under Trade.

indexation. Normally a term used to describe the pegging of domestic wages and incomes to the development of prices within the domestic economy, the term has also been applied to the field of international economic relations. There it denotes a method for adjusting the export price of unprocessed commodities from the developing countries against some indicator of the purchasing power of these exports. This indicator might be the costs of production of the exported commodities, world prices of manufactured products incorporating these commodities, or prices of imports into the developing countries.

A proposal for indexation was first unsuccessfully launched during the debate on the NEW INTERNATIONAL ECONOMIC ORDER (NIEO) in 1974. Third World countries claimed that since the Second World War the prices for their export commodities had declined consistently in relation to the prices of manufactured goods imported from the advanced countries. Indexation was proposed as one of a number of remedial measures within an Integrated Commodity Programme (ICP). More recently the idea of indexation was raised in the Organization of Petroleum Exporting Countries (OPEC).

Nevertheless, at the level of individual negotiations between host countries and multinational enterprises 'indexation' has sometimes been applied as a particular formula for determining the export price of a raw material extracted within the vertically integrated structure of a multinational company. It forms the basis for the calculation of the subsidiaries' income and profits tax and other duties payable to the host country where the extractive subsidiary is located. The formula involves the linking of the price of the raw material to the price of the final or semi-processed product: for instance, linking the price of bauxite to that of the ingot. Since the world market prices of these final or semi-processed commodities are known more and more through published sources and producers' councils, the policing of these agreements does not appear to present major problems for the host country.

See also REFERENCE PRICE SYSTEM; FAIR MARKET VALUE SYSTEM; NEGOTIATED PRICE SYSTEM; REALIZED PRICE SYSTEM; TRANSFER PRICE, and Index under Regulation and Tax.

indigenization. The statutory limitation of participation in a particular industry or sector of the economy to private individuals (indigenes). The term is relatively new and is associated with certain development strategies of newly emerging countries. Indigenization usually involves the EXPROPRIATION of foreign enterprise as government legislation compels the foreign owners to sell or divest. However indigenization does not always involve expropriation, as it also refers to the limitation of future and intended participation in the economy.

As is the case with NATIONALIZATION, the objective of indigenization policies is to gain national ownership over domestic economic resources and to assert national control over the direction of the economy. The choice between the two depends greatly on the dominant state ideology: those developing countries which are committed to a free-market, or at any rate a mixed, economy will prefer the indigenization option in the belief that this will stimulate the emergence of an expert, entrepreneurial bourgeoisie capable of taking charge of the economic life of the community.

Indigenization policies have been adopted in many developing countries but they have not often met with success. This is partly because in the absence of developed stock markets and a sufficiently broadly based middle class with the necessary investment capital, many foreign companies have found themselves with the State as owner or partner in the venture, making indigenization look very similar to nationalization. Foreign companies have managed at times, with the complicity of government officials, to defeat the indigenization objectives by using various devices such as 'fronting' and 'naturalizations', and other devices which enable formal compliance with the laws without a genuine transfer of ownership taking place. Even when such a genuine transfer does take place, the ultimate objective of 'control' may yet remain elusive. The extent to which operations of the indigenized firm are technologically and economically dependent upon transnational corporate operations will restrict the scope for independent domestic control.

See also EXPROPRIATION; CONFISCATION, and Index under Development Policy.

industrial free zone. *See under* FREE TRADE ZONE (FTZ).

industrial organization theory. *See* OLIGOPOLY MODEL.

inflation accounting. A method of constructing financial statements which takes into account the changes in the purchasing power of money resulting from the general inflation of a currency. True inflation accounting (known as 'current purchasing power' or 'general purchasing power' accounting) is based on the change in the general price index of the country concerned and has in the past been preferred by professional accounting bodies in the USA, UK and countries with similar regulatory structures. However, governmental intervention has frequently meant that where systems of accounting which incorporate inflation adjustments have been embodied in regulations, these have been on the basis of 'current cost' or 'replacement cost' accounting, which is based on the movements in price of specific assets owned by the company concerned. In countries that have experienced only moderate rates of inflation – perhaps with short periods of high inflation – there has been considerable opposition to incorporating price changes in accounting. Some countries that have experienced constant high rates of change in their currency, notably those of South America, have required inflation-adjusted accounts to be published by law. To date this has happened in Argentina, Brazil, Chile, Mexico and Uruguay. Index-linking of government bonds has also been a feature of some of these countries.

See also Index under International Accounting.

informal imperialism. *See under* IMPERIALISM.

Institute for Food and Development Policy. Independent critical research establishment focusing on AGRIBUSINESS and the political economy of food and hunger in Third World countries. It publishes its own documentation and issues a newsletter, *Food First News*.

See Index under Data Sources.
Address: 1885 Mission Street, San Francisco, California CA 94103, USA.

Institute for Policy Studies/Transnational Institute (IPS/TI). Radical research institute funded by church and other concerned social groups. 'Institute of Policy Studies' is the name for the American Institute in Washington, while the European branch, located in Amsterdam, is called the 'Transnational Institute'. The IPS/TI maintains a continual project of studies on transnational corporations and supports various TNC activist groups around the world (*See* TIE-EUROPE). It organizes international conferences on counterstrategies which bring together TNC activists and academics to evaluate anti-corporate campaigns. A major aspect of its work is to facilitate international trade union solidarity through the establishment of an information exchange. It produces reprint packets of articles on TNCs and – jointly with TIE-Europe – the *TIE-Report*, which it distributes to US subscribers.

See Index under Data Sources.
Address: 1901 Q Street NW, Washington DC 20009, USA and Paulus Potterstraat 20, 1071 Amsterdam, Netherlands.

Institute for Research on Multinational Enterprises (IRM). A foundation established in 1980 under Swiss law, which promotes and finances independent research on multinational companies and their impact on society. IRM is a successor foundation to the ECSIM (European Centre for Study and Information on Multinationals) which was set up in 1975 at the initiative of the Nestlé Company of Switzerland.

IRM's research is carried out by academics of various disciplines and institutions throughout the world. IRM publishes their findings and organizes conferences and meetings; occasionally it holds international competitions for the best university theses on multinationals. A bank of specialized documentation is being built up.

See Index under Data Sources.
Address: 45-47 Rue de Lausanne, 1201 Geneva, Switzerland.

inter-affiliate trade. *See* INTRA-FIRM TRADE.

Inter-American Development Bank. A bank established in 1959 to provide development capital for the countries of Central and Latin America. It currently has about 24 member states (including the USA, Canada and 5 Caribbean nations).
Address: 808 17th Street NW, Washington DC 20577, USA.

interest equalization tax. A tax charged on foreign security issues in the US capital markets during the period 1963 – 1974. It is probable that, by thus closing a rich source of lending to non-US borrowers, the policy contributed to the rapid expansion of the EUROBOND and similar instruments.

See also Index under Regulation and Tax.

interest rate parity. The theory of interest rate parity suggests that, if bonds issued in different countries are identical in both risk and time to maturity but differ in interest rates payable, then the difference between the interest rates will be exactly equal (excluding TRANSACTION COSTS) to the discount or premium of the currencies concerned in the forward exchange market (see HEDGE). Interest rate parity is maintained by the operations of arbitrageurs.

See also COVERED INTEREST ARBITRAGE, and Index under Theoretical Issues.

Interfaith Center on Corporate Responsibility. Sponsored by and closely connected with the National Council of Churches, this body researches and campaigns in the United States on the practices of corporations and business. It has helped church campaigns and boycotts against major companies, often during union struggles. It seeks to promote corporate accountability through shareholders' resolutions, congressional testimony and community education. It has also been active in international campaigns such as those against baby food marketing in the Third World, AGRIBUSINESS, arms trade and South Africa. It publishes a newsletter, *The Corporate Examiner*.

See Index under Data Sources.
Address: 475 Riverside Drive Rm 566, New York NY10115, USA.

inter-imperialist competition. A conceptual model of contemporary international political and economic relations predicated on the notion of rivalry between both international capitals and between the three major continental 'states' from which these capital flows originate: the United States, the European Community (EC) and Japan.

The model is an update of Lenin's original theory of imperialism and has proponents amongst such influential British writers as Michael Kidron, Robert Rowthorn and Mary Kaldor, and those of other nationalities, especially the Belgian writer Ernest Mandel.

It is argued that the uneven development of capital prevents the formation of an actual global community of interest for capital, as is for example espoused by the super-imperialist school (see SUPER-IMPERI-

ALISM). Whilst capital fusion is being achieved on a continental basis, thus replacing the larger number of independent imperialist powers of Lenin's day with a smaller number of imperialist superpowers, intercontinental rivalries are increasingly intensified. This rivalry is evidenced in the pursuance of independent and often conflicting policies in trade, and in foreign and military affairs. It is also witnessed in the weakening of the American economy vis-à-vis its competitors, Europe and Japan, and in the rapid overseas expansion of European and Japanese firms both inside the United States and inside the Third World.

Inter-imperialist struggle is thought likely to lead to the intensification of the Cold War between East and West as a means of keeping the capitalist world from falling apart. It is also thought to lead to local political rivalries and conflicts inside the THIRD WORLD, where the conflicts between East and West may be staged. Some writers, however, see positive benefits for the Third World arising out of inter-imperialist struggle (*see* Warren, 1980 and Cardoso and Faletto, 1967). They argue that those Third World countries able to 'play off' imperialist rivalries have good prospects for independent industrialization and development, as the competition between different multinationals permits them more scope for effective bargaining.

See also TRILATERAL COMMISSION; SUPER-IMPERIALISM; POST-IMPERIALISM; IMPERIALISM; ULTRA-IMPERIALISM, and Index under Theoretical Issues.

interlocking directorates. The widespread tendency of industrial, service and finance corporations to place directors on each others' boards. Interlocking directorates create opportunities for collusive practices such as price fixing and market sharing, which because of their unwritten nature may escape relevant anti-monopoly legislation.

For example, in the United States, Section 8 of the CLAYTON ACT expressly forbids any person from serving on the boards of two or more competing corporations, but this section has generally not been enforced.

There are direct and indirect interlocks: direct interlocks are those in which a single individual serves on the board of two companies, while indirect interlocks are constituted by the meeting of two directors from two different companies on the board of a third company.

See ANTI-TRUST LEGISLATION; CARTEL, and Index under Industry Structure.

intermediate technology. A term invented by E Schumacher (1973) who challenged the received economic wisdom which measures success in terms of output or income without considering the number of jobs. This doctrine he believed to be totally inapplicable to the developing countries where local FACTOR ENDOWMENTS (that is, labour and capital availability) are precisely the opposite of those pertaining in the advanced countries whose productive technology they import.

Defining the level of technology in terms of 'equipment cost per workplace', Schumacher argued for the invention of production techniques for the developing countries which are in between the indigenous £1 equipment cost per workplace and the modern £1,000 equipment cost per workplace.

See also APPROPRIATE TECHNOLOGY, and Index under Technology Transfer.

internal price. *See under* TRANSFER PRICE.

Internal Revenue Code Section 482. A provision in US tax law empowering the revenue authorities to inquire into and adjust TRANSFER PRICES between entities. Of considerable scope, it provides that: 'in any case of two or more organizations, trades, or businesses (whether or not incorporated, whether or not organized in the United States, and whether or not affiliated) owned or controlled directly or indirectly by the same interests, the Secretary or his delegate may distribute, apportion, or allocate gross income, deductions, credits, or allowances between or among such organizations, trades or businesses, if he determines that such distribution, apportionment or allocation is necessary in order to prevent evasion of taxes or clearly to reflect the income of any of such organizations, trades, or businesses'.

Regulations set out by the US Treasury in 1968 define how the US Internal Revenue will approach their judgment of transfer prices.

Three methods of creating a CONSTRUCTED PRICE are named: the 'comparable uncontrolled price' method, the 'resale price' method and the 'cost-plus' method. This is the authorities' order of preference, so that when the first fails the second is applied, and so on.

The first method is essentially one of ARM'S LENGTH price where comparable goods are traded between unconnected parties. Frequently for specialized internal transfers these will not exist. The next preferred method (retail price) is somewhat complex, but applies where the buyer appears to have added only a small markup to the international transfer price, and the buyer is also the seller. The third method ('cost-plus') adds a profit percentage to the seller's costs, and obtains evidence as to the appropriate rate from either sales by the seller in an uncontrolled market or, failing this, from others selling similar items in an uncontrolled market or, failing this, from others in the same industry. In practice this is believed to be the method most widely used because of the infrequency of the circumstances required for the previous two.

See Index under Regulation and Tax.

internalization theory. Theory of FOREIGN DIRECT INVESTMENT and INTERNATIONAL PRODUCTION which is at present gaining popularity. Originally developed to explain the growth of the multi-plant indigenous firm (*see* COASE THEOREM), the internalization concept is seen as equally relevant to the multinational firm. The theory takes as its point of departure the existing imperfections in markets which may make it less costly, or more profitable, for firms to undertake certain activities and transactions within their organizations, and to regulate such transactions by ADMINISTRATIVE FIAT rather than subject them to market processes. Whenever internalization processes occur across national frontiers, multinational enterprises are claimed to be generated. The first systematic attempt to incorporate the idea of internalization into a theory of foreign direct investment and multinational enterprise is credited to Buckley and Casson (1976).

Several kinds of market imperfections are usually identified as candidates for internalization:

1. Costs or benefits associated with uncertainties in external market transactions, for example finding suppliers, negotiating contracts, monitoring contractual obligations, uncertainty over future price developments (*see* TRANSACTION COSTS), and so on.

2. Costs or benefits associated with imperfections in markets for knowledge and information, as when a seller needs to protect the quality of his product by providing after-sales service, and/or by undertaking local production in technologically less advanced environments.

3. Benefits associated with the market imperfections generated by the size of the firm itself, as when a firm wishes to exploit oligopolistic advantages by controlling market outlets, supplies and conditions of sale, and engage in other restrictive business practices (*see* OLIGOPOLY).

4. Costs or benefits associated with government intervention, for example quotas,

tariffs, price controls, tax differences, and so on.

See Index under Theoretical Issues.

International Accounting Standards Committee (IASC). A body set up in June 1973 by the professional accounting bodies of nine countries. Its objectives, as contained in its constitution, are 'to formulate and publish in the public interest accounting standards to be observed in the presentation of financial statements and to promote their worldwide acceptance and observance; [and] to work generally for the improvement and harmonization of regulations, accounting standards and procedures relating to the presentation of financial statements'.

The number of bodies represented on the IASC has grown steadily since 1973, and at present 68 countries are represented by their professional accounting bodies .

At the time of writing the IASC had issued standards on the following subjects (in order of their issue): disclosure of accounting policies; valuation and presentation of inventories in the context of the historical cost system; consolidated financial statements; depreciation accounting; information to be disclosed in financial statements; accounting responses to changing prices; statement of changes in financial position; unusual and prior period items and changes in accounting policies; accounting for research and development activities; contingencies and events occurring after the balance sheet date; accounting for construction contracts; accounting for taxes on income; presentation of current assets and current liabilities; reporting financial information by segment; information reflecting the effects of changing prices; accounting for property, plant and equipment; accounting for leases; revenue recognition; accounting for retirement benefits in the financial statements of employers; accounting for government

grants and disclosure of government assistance; accounting for the effects of changes in foreign exchange rates; related party disclosure; capitalization of borrowing costs; and accounting for business combinations.

The power of the IASC is essentially a persuasive one. Hence there are three barriers to its recommendations being incorporated into national regulations and from there into financial statements. Firstly, member bodies are not obliged to recommend conformity to the standards (though they are strongly urged to do so). Secondly, even where the member professional bodies do endorse the standards, they may not be taken up by those with the authority to regulate accounting, which in most countries means the government. The power of professional bodies in this context is limited to persuasion, and many governments either fail to see any importance in such standards, or object to supranational control over their domestic affairs, or have more pressing matters to consider than accounting regulation. Thirdly, even where regulators are sympathetic and incorporate the IASC's standards into commercial codes or domestic accounting standards, the level of compliance may be low, since policing of compliance is time-consuming and expensive.

On the other hand there is considerable support for the activities of the IASC from those organizations who wish to see greater standardization and/or harmonization of financial reporting practices between countries. Such organizations include the United Nations, the ORGANIZATION FOR ECONOMIC CO-OPERATION AND DEVELOPMENT (OECD), the INTERNATIONAL FEDERATION OF ACCOUNTANTS (IFAC), national stock exchanges, and various regional groups of accountancy bodies. The activities of the IASC are complementary to those of the International Federation of Accountants.

See Index under International Accounting, and under International Co-operation.

Address: 41 Kingsway, London WC2B 6YU, UK.

international auditing firms. Large international partnerships of accountants that have grown over the past few decades. The largest of these, though formally in partnership form, rival large multinational corporations in size and income, and all the major nine would qualify for inclusion in the *Fortune* magazine's list of the 500 largest industrial corporations were they industrial companies and not private partnerships. There are two ways in which they may operate.

The first is to use a worldwide name for the firm, which has increasingly come to represent either an old-established name like Price Waterhouse and Co., or results from a merger across international borders of previously large but less internationally diversified firms (such as Ernst and Whinney). It is claimed by the firms themselves that this international integration is necessary if they are to offer a full set of specialist services to multinational clients; if it is to be possible for the same auditor to audit subsidiaries and parent companies rather than have to rely on other auditors overseas; and if auditor independence is to be assured, since no single client would constitute too large a proportion of total audit income so that the loss of such a client's custom would be so major as to prejudice such independence.

The nine international firms which dominate are: Coopers and Lybrand; Peat, Marwick, Mitchell; Arthur Andersen; Arthur Young; Klynveld Main Goerdeler (known in the UK as KMG Thomson McLintock); Price Waterhouse; Ernst and Whinney; Deloitte, Haskins and Sells; and Touche Ross. In 1981 they audited 493 of the *Fortune* Top 500 companies.

The second form of international audit relationship has been found among medium-sized audit firms which have not integrated or merged as such, but have affiliated across international boundaries. In such cases there is no international name: the extent to which such relationships differ from those of the largest firms will depend on the contractual arrangements made within the firms among the national partnerships.

See also Index under International Accounting.

International Bank for Reconstruction and Development (IBRD). *See* WORLD BANK.

international banking facility (IBF). A special status available to US banks under authorization from the Federal Reserve Board as from 3 December, 1981. They are separated in various ways from domestic banking activities, in particular by the stipulation that IBFs cannot lend to US residents, and by their exemption from normal reserve requirements and interest rate ceilings on deposits. IBFs have been allowed in order to permit US banks to offer time deposits to foreign residents and foreign banks. In particular, they have been designed to enable US banks to obtain eurocurrency business, offering the advantage of political security to non-resident depositors.

See Index under Regulation and Tax.

international bond. A bond raised in a country other than that of the borrower. There are two kinds of international bond: FOREIGN BONDS and EUROBONDS.

international cash management. *See under* CASH MANAGEMENT.

International Center for Settlement of Investment Disputes. An institution set up in 1966 at the WORLD BANK in Washington as a result of the signing of the CONVENTION ON THE SETTLEMENT OF INVESTMENT DISPUTES BETWEEN STATES AND NATIONALS OF OTHER STATES.

Established to provide a means of arbitrating between host nations and foreign investors (who tend to be multinational companies) the Centre offers a facilitating mechanism available to either country or company. It acts only when consent has been received from both parties, which may take place either at the time of original investment (as a result of a clause in a contract) or upon subsequent dispute.

See Index under Dispute and Settlement.

International Chamber of Commerce (ICC). An organization established in 1920 for the purpose of exchanging information between local chambers of commerce on matters of international interest. There are national committees of the ICC in over 40 countries and an additional 30 countries with associate members but without national committees.

The ICC was one of the first organizations to attempt to produce a CODE OF CONDUCT for international business. Its *Guidelines on International Investment*, published in 1972 and reflecting a clear business interest and free market approach, is noteworthy more for its existence than for its contents. The foreword acknowledges that the guidelines reflect a new approach: instead of the international convention concept focusing on the conditions to be fulfilled in a country seeking to attract foreign investments, the guidelines define the responsibilities which have to be accepted by all parties concerned, including the investors themselves. The guidelines are not meant as a rigorous code but as a set of practical recommendations arising from experience and aimed at facilitating consultation between investors and governments, and at promoting a better understanding of each others' needs and objectives. Many of the recommendations concerning host and home governments', as well as investors', attitudes to and responsibilities for investment, fiscal policies,

finance and balance of payments issues, labour relations, and technology, informed the subsequent production of the OECD Guidelines on Multinational Enterprises (1976). (*See under* DECLARATION AND DECISIONS ON INTERNATIONAL INVESTMENT AND MULTINATIONAL ENTERPRISES.)

The ICC has also operated for over 50 years a Court of Arbitration concerned with the resolution of conflicts between private parties and between governments and multinational enterprises. The Court of Arbitration does not itself settle disputes, but it appoints or confirms the appointments of arbitrators and it provides the rules by which disputes may be settled. To enhance the legal status of its conciliation and arbitration services, the ICC recommends all parties wishing to make reference to ICC arbitration in their foreign contracts to use a standard clause to the effect that all disputes arising in connection with the contract shall be finally settled under the Rules of Conciliation and Arbitration of the ICC.

In 1977, following the revelation of bribery and corruption cases involving multinational enterprises, the ICC adopted a code of conduct on Ethical Practices in Commercial Transactions.

See Index under International Co-operation, and under Corporate Structure and Management.

Address: 9 Boulevard Malesherbes, 75-Paris VIII, France.

International Committee for Accounting Co-operation. A discussion committee set up in 1966 – 7 by the American Institute of Certified Public Accountants, the Canadian Institute of Chartered Accountants, the Mexican Institute of Certified Public Accountants, the US Agency for International Development (AID), the Inter-American Development Bank and the International Finance Corporation. Its purpose was to improve professional accounting expertise in the Third World. Although it began with an attempt at a major project in Colombia, its activities have since declined.

See Index under International Co-operation.

International Confederation of Free Trade Unions (ICFTU). Established in 1949 after non-communist affiliates withdrew from the World Federation of Trade Unions, the ICFTU brings together the majority of national trade union centres in both industrialized and developing countries. At present it has 144 affiliates in 95 countries, with a total membership of 82 million. Supreme responsibility rests with Congress, which meets every three to four years and at which all affiliated organizations are represented; basic decisions are taken by the ICFTU Executive Board which meets biannually.

The ICFTU has a number of regional organizations and associated with it are 18 autonomous INTERNATIONAL TRADE SECRETARIATS (ITS). The AFL-CIO withdrew from the ICFTU in 1969 after a dispute.

The prime task of the ICFTU is to present a co-ordinated trade union viewpoint to international institutions, and to act as lobbyist on behalf of the labour movement in general. It differs from the international trade secretariats, whose job it is to represent workers at a specific industry or trade level and who may often have direct dealings with a particular multinational company.

At its sixth World Congress in 1959, the ICFTU adopted a statement calling upon multinational corporations to abide by fair labour standards. Further detailed attention to multinational companies and their control was given at the ICFTU World Economic Conference of 1971. Following this, the tenth World Congress in 1972 established a joint ICFTU/ITS Working Party on Multinational Companies to co-ordinate research and elaborate a common trade union strategy towards transnational enterprises.

The basic policy objectives of the ICFTU are contained in the *Multinational Charter* of trade union demands for legislative control of multinational corporations, which was formally adopted by the 11th World Congress held in Mexico in 1975. The Charter sets out the case for the supervision of multinational corporations and calls upon governments to co-operate in establishing legislative controls, both at national and international level. Specifically, the charter deals with the public accountability and social obligations of multinational enterprises, investments and takeovers, restrictive business practices, fiscal questions, transfer of technology and short-term capital movements. It also calls for legally binding international conventions which would have to be formally ratified by national governments.

The *ICFTU Development Charter*, adopted in 1978, has pressed for a mandatory CODE OF CONDUCT for the transfer of technology through negotiations within the UNITED NATIONS CONFERENCE ON TRADE AND DEVELOPMENT (UNCTAD). The ICFTU has also been regularly represented at the meetings of the UN Intergovernmental Working Group preparing the UN DRAFT CODE OF CONDUCT ON TRANSNATIONAL CORPORATIONS. Its views on the eventual implementation of such a Code are expressed in the *ICFTU 8-point procedure for UN Code*.

More recently, the ICFTU has devoted special attention to ways in which existing, voluntary, international codes of conduct can be implemented. Notwithstanding its preference for legally binding codes, the ICFTU's position is that the question of whether a code is voluntary or binding is perhaps less important than whether it can be made to work in practice. In order to encourage trade unions to make full use of existing codes (such as the OECD GUIDELINES and the ILO's TRIPARTITE DECLARATION ON MULTINATIONAL ENTERPRISES

AMD SOCIAL POLICY) it has published a *Checklist for Trade Unionists*. On the other hand, some international trade secretariats, in particular the International Metalworkers Federation (IMF) are sceptical of the utility of this strategy. They argue that the only effective long-term plan against multinational companies is to build up contacts between workers in the same multinational firm.

See Index under Labour, and under International Co-operation.

Address: Rue Montagne aux Herbes Potagères 37-41, B-1000 Brussels, Belgium.

International Convention for the Protection of Industrial Property. This convention is also known as the 'Paris Union' after the place where it was signed in 1883. It is the most important of all international PATENT treaties. Signatories include all the advanced western market economies and about a third of the developing countries. The Soviet Union and five other Eastern bloc countries are also signatories to the Convention.

The International Convention for the Protection of Industrial Property has so far been revised six times. Currently the Stockholm Act of 1967 is in force.

The key principle of the Convention is the NATIONAL TREATMENT principle, whereby all member countries agree to grant the same patent and TRADEMARK treatment to nationals of other member countries as they do to their own nationals. This is designed to eliminate discrimination against foreigners. However, each country is free to determine the scope of its own proprietary laws and the degree of protection arising from it. The Convention does not call for reciprocal treatment. It is possible therefore that nationals of a given country may receive less favourable treatment in other countries than is afforded to nationals of such other countries in their own country.

A second major provision of the Convention is the granting of the 'right of priority' to foreigners. This principle lays down that a patent owner has a twelve-month priority over any other applicant filing for the same invention in any other country belonging to the International Convention (six months in the case of trademarks). The grace period runs from the date of the filing of the application in the country of origin, not the date on which the patent was granted.

Since 1980 a Diplomatic Conference on the Revision of the Paris Convention has been under way. On the agenda of that conference have been included particular provisions of interest to developing countries, as well as a provision putting INVENTOR'S CERTIFICATES on an equal footing with patents. Amongst the provisions of interest to developing countries are a provision facilitating non-voluntary licenses in respect of patents not worked in developing countries and revocation of such patents, as well as provisions granting a preferential treatment to developing countries in respect of fees to be paid to industrial property offices and time limits to be respected in industrial property procedures.

See also PATENT; WORLD INDUSTRIAL PROPERTY ORGANIZATION (WIPO); EUROPEAN PATENT CONVENTION (EPC); PATENT CO-OPERATION TREATY (PCT), and Index under International Co-operation and under Technology Transfer.

international corporation/firm. *See under* MULTINATIONAL CORPORATION/ENTERPRISE.

International Court of Justice (ICJ). Founded in 1945, the Court is the principal judicial organ of the United Nations (UN). It succeeded the permanent Court of Justice, which had been set up as part of the 1919 Peace Settlement under auspices of the then League of Nations.

The Court has powers to decide disputes

between states only and its authority depends on the consent of the states concerned. This is the reason why very few cases of disputes between multinational companies and host states have ever been brought before the Court. (But see NOT-TEBOHM CASE and BARCELONA TRACTION CASE.) Such disputes are more commonly referred for arbitration to the INTERNATIONAL CENTER FOR THE SETTLEMENT OF INVESTMENT DISPUTES under the CONVENTION FOR THE SETTLEMENT OF INVESTMENT DISPUTES BETWEEN STATES AND NATIONALS OF OTHER STATES.

See Index under Dispute and Settlement and under International Co-operation.
Address: Peace Palace, Carnegielaan, The Hague, Netherlands.

International Development Association (IDA). Affiliate organization of the WORLD BANK, established in 1960 to provide assistance for the same purposes as the World Bank, but primarily to help the poorer developing countries on terms that would bear less heavily on their balance of payments than normal World Bank loans.

Membership of IDA is open to all members of the World Bank, and 131 had joined by 1984. The funds used by the IDA are called *'credits'* and come mostly in the form of subscriptions, general replenishments from IDA's more industrialized and developed members, and transfers from the net earnings of the World Bank. IDA credits are made to governments only and normally carry 10-year grace periods, 50-year maturities and no interest. In 1984 total credits outstanding amounted to US$33 billion.

As with the World Bank, the Association's lending is limited to member countries. Credits are normally granted for specific projects only and the decision to lend must be based on economic considerations. However the IDA's 'economic considerations' are less specific and narrowly

focused than those of the World Bank. Its present development strategy embraces projects that will mobilize domestic resources for faster economic growth by meeting the BASIC NEEDS of the poorest segments of the population. This strategy is increasingly evident in agriculture and rural development projects as well as in projects concerning education, family planning and nutrition.

See Index under International Co-operation.
Address: 1818 H Street NW, Washington DC 20433, USA; 66 Avenue d'Iena, 75116 Paris, France.

international division. A type of organizational structure found principally in US multinationals. In this structure the control of overseas activities is entrusted to a separate division; all subsidiaries abroad are responsible to the vice-president of the international division who is in turn responsible to the president for all foreign operations. This type of structure has been found far less frequently in multinationals based outside the USA, and indeed is often only a temporary device for US companies.

See also DIVISION, and Index under Corporate Structure and Management.

International Federation of Accountants (IFAC). An organization formed in 1977 by 63 professional accountancy bodies from 49 countries in order to pursue all areas of interest to those bodies, except for the setting of international accounting standards (*see* INTERNATIONAL ACCOUNTING STANDARDS COMMITTEE (IASC)). It has since grown so that now more than 80 bodies from 59 countries are represented.

The functions of IFAC are carried out by seven standing committees (on education, ethics, international auditing practices, international congresses, management accounting, planning, and regional organizations). Those activities of most importance to multinational enterprise are the Federation's recommendations concerning audit practice (for example, those which concern the relationships between auditors who audit different parts of the same corporation in different countries). To this end it has issued a number of international auditing and ethics guidelines, in addition to guidelines on the education of accountants.

See also Index under International Accounting, and under International Co-operation.

Address: 540 Madison Avenue, New York NY 10022, USA.

International Finance Corporation (IFC). Affiliate organization of the WORLD BANK, established in 1956 to supplement the Bank's activities by promoting and providing support for the private sectors in developing member countries. The IFC's role is to stimulate the flow of private capital into economic priority enterprises, whether private, public, or mixed. The corporation makes equity investments, usually in conjunction with long-term loans. Such loans need not have government guarantees. The IFC has today an investment portfolio of almost $2 billion on its own account. The purpose of the IFC's investment activities is to encourage other lenders and investors to follow suit. For every dollar it invested in 1984 it persuaded others to invest about US$5. The corporation generally limits its participation in an enterprise to under 25 per cent of the equity and is unwilling to be the largest shareholder. Just recently it has set up a new investment trust called the 'Emerging Markets Growth Fund' with the aim of channeling PORTFOLIO INVESTMENTS into the stock markets of some of the relatively advanced developing countries. For the present, this investment fund tries to attract institutional rather than individual investors.

In 1984, the IFC had an an authorized capital of US$1,300 million subscribed by 125 member countries. Membership of the corporation is limited to member countries of the World Bank. Although legally and financially the IFC and the World Bank are separate entities, they work closely together, and the corporation draws upon the Bank for administrative and other services. The IFC is responsible for the technical and financial appraisal and supervision of all projects relating to manufacturing industry, mining and development finance submitted to the World Bank group – irrespective of which member of the group (the World Bank, the INTERNATIONAL DEVELOPMENT ASSOCIATION (IDA) or the IFC) is to provide the financing. The President of the World Bank is also President of the IFC.

See Index under International Co-operation, and under Financial and Risk Management.

Address: 1818 H Street NW, Washington DC 20433, USA.

international firm. *See under* MULTINATIONAL CORPORATION/ENTERPRISE.

international Fisher effect. A derivation of the Fisher effect. The Fisher effect states that the nominal rate of interest will be equal to the sum of the real rate of interest and the expected inflation rate. From this it can be shown that the difference between nominal interest rates on otherwise comparable home and foreign securities should equal the difference between the expected inflation rates in the two countries. This is because ARBITRAGE operations tend to operate when disparities occur between securities of equal maturity and risk between countries. Government intervention may in practice modify this.

The international Fisher effect, derived from this, suggests that the difference between the nominal rates of interest offered for a given time period in two countries will constitute an unbiased predictor of the future change in the spot currency rate (*see* SPOT RATE). Put another way, it predicts that the spot rate will change to an equal extent, but in the opposite direction, to the offered interest rates in the countries concerned. Empirical research has tended to support the theory.

See Index under Theoretical Issues.

International Labour Organization (ILO). A specialized agency of the United Nations, with primary responsibility in the labour field. The ILO was founded in 1919 by the Treaty of Versailles as an affiliate of the then League of Nations. Its chief aim is to contribute to the establishment of universal and lasting peace based upon social justice by improving, through international action, labour conditions and living standards. The Organization was awarded the Nobel Peace prize in 1969.

The fundamental principles which guide the Organization's work were formulated in the *Declaration Concerning Aims and Purposes*, adopted in 1944. They are that labour is not a commodity; that freedom of expression and freedom of association are essential to sustain progress; and that the war against want is to be carried on by continuous and concerted effort in which the representatives of workers and employers, enjoying equal status with those of goverments, join with them in free discussion and democratic decision.

This last principle has led to the unique tripartite structure of the Organization, in which each member nation appoints to the International Labour Conference – which meets annually in Geneva [nd] two government delegates and one each from employers and from labour. The Organization today consists of some 150 member countries. Membership is voluntary and open to any sovereign country whose application receives two-thirds of the votes of the delegates at the Conference, including two-thirds of the government delegates.

Over the years the ILO has enacted conventions, which are draft multilateral treaties and which become binding upon ratification by member countries; recommendations, which are guides to member nations in establishing labour standards, and resolutions, memoranda and statements which have no binding effect on a nation. Together the conventions and the recommendations form the International Labour Code.

In 1977 the Organization pronounced a TRIPARTITE DECLARATION ON PRINCIPLES CONCERNING MULTINATIONAL ENTERPRISES AND SOCIAL POLICY. The secretariat of the ILO is the International Labour Office, which serves as administrative headquarters, research centre and publishing house.

See Index under Labour, and under International Co-operation.

Address: 4 Route de Morillons, 1211 Geneva 22, Switzerland.

International Monetary Fund (IMF). Specialized agency of the United Nations (UN), originating in the Bretton Woods Conference of 1944 and operating since 1947 (*see* BRETTON WOODS MONETARY SYSTEM). Its aims are to promote international monetary co-operation, exchange stability and to assist member countries in overcoming temporary balance of payments difficulties without resorting to measures destructive of national or international prosperity.

To further these aims, the Fund has since its inception operated a General Account, providing both a worldwide multilateral payments system and monetary reserves which enable member nations to overcome short run disequilibria in their BALANCE OF PAYMENTS.

The groundrules by which this general account has functioned are both ingenious and simple. They still survive – with modifications – today. Each member country is assigned a quota related to its national income, monetary reserves, trade balance and other economic indicators. Each member pays this quota into the Fund in a combination of 25 per cent gold (today 'SDRs'; *see* SPECIAL DRAWING RIGHTS) and 75 per cent of its own national currency. These resources enable the Fund to honour the *tranche* drawing rights which its members enjoy. When a member draws on the Fund, it purchases currencies of other member countries with its own currency. This results in an increase in the Fund's holding of the member's currency and a decrease in its holdings of the currencies that are purchased. The member normally has to repurchase its own currency within three to five years. A member can draw more than its quota (today up to 200 per cent) in 'credit *tranches*', but it will then have to satisfy the Fund that it is making reasonable efforts to overcome its financial difficulties. When borrowings occur in the 'upper' credit *tranches*, the IMF normally insists on recommending to the borrowing government a comprehensive stabilization programme under a 'standby arrangement', in which the right to draw is phased over the period of the standby arrangement and is subject to the member's observance of certain key policy indicators described by the programme (referred to as IMF conditionality).

Since the Fund, by its Articles of Agreement, exists to promote international monetary stability rather than economic development, its critics have argued that the BALANCE OF PAYMENTS orientation of the Fund's stabilization programme, with its strict adherence to deflationary demand management, often adversely affects the growth prospects and the social reform efforts of the developing countries. In the 1960s and 1970s, however, amendments to the Fund's articles enabled it to assist the developing countries with long-term financing of development programmes: these amendments included the introduction of the extended fund facility, the compensatory finance facility, the bufferstock facility, a trust fund and – most importantly – the linking of international liquidity creation through SDRs to development aid.

Whereas at the time of its inception in 1944 the number of member countries totalled only 39, by 1984 this number had increased to 146 and now includes the People's Republic of China. The USSR and other centrally planned economies of the Eastern bloc as well as Switzerland remain outside of the IMF. The increase in membership and the three increases in quota subscriptions introduced since 1944 have vastly enhanced the IMF's resources and by corollary its importance as an independent economic actor in the world economy. Critics, however, will argue that the unequal distribution of voting rights in the Fund, which are proportionate to the size of each member's quota, keep the Fund firmly under the control and direction of the richest nations in the world. The United States today has 23 per cent of the voting rights, sufficient – if it so wishes – to block any proposal to change the rules by which the Fund operates, since constitutional changes require a 85 per cent majority. The European Community (EC) countries together hold 19 per cent. Because the EC countries and the USA tend to be the creditor countries in the world economy as opposed to the less developed countries who are the debtor countries, it has been argued that the former extend informal imperial rule over the latter through the medium of the IMF (*see* IMPERIALISM). The mediating role of the IMF in recent years in respect of DEBT RESCHEDULING negotiations between creditor and debtor nations has fuelled these criticisms. Today, the economic intervention by the IMF in the debtor countries to safeguard multilateral public and short-term lending is also being regarded increasingly by private lenders like international banks and multinational corporations as a precondition of their willingness to extend long-term credit to these nations. To the extent that the implementation of IMF-imposed domestic economic policies tend to favour foreign creditors over the domestic poor, such criticism may be justified.

It is worth remembering, however, that the Fund's role as an 'economic policeman of the Western world' was never anticipated by its founders. Its primary function at the time of its inception was to supervise the Bretton Woods system of 'fixed but adjustable' exchange rates. It was the demise of this system in 1972, and the uncontrolled evolution of the international financial markets that has been responsible for the shift in focus of IMF activities towards co-ordination – in both an advisory and directive capacity – of global resource flows.

See Index under International Co-operation.

Address: 700 19th Street NW, Washington DC 20431, USA.

International Money Market of Chicago. *See* CHICAGO INTERNATIONAL MONEY MARKET.

International Multinational Directory. A publication by the Finance Publishing Corporation, New York, giving details of company relationships.

See Index under Data Sources.

International Organization of Consumer Unions (IOCU). Founded in 1960 in The Hague, Netherlands, this organization promotes and assists genuine efforts in consumer self-organization throughout the world, as well as governmental efforts to further the interests of the consumer. It promotes international co-operation in the comparative testing of consumer goods and services and in all other aspects of consumer information, including consumer laws and practices throughout the world. It maintains effective links with United Nations (UN) agencies and other international bodies, with a view to representing the interests of the consumer at the international level. The IOCU has a membership of over 120 consumer associations, government-financed consumer councils and other consumer bodies sponsored by family organizations, labour unions and similar groups.

Since its involvement with the International Baby Foods Action Network (IBFAN) campaign (*see under* WHO/UNICEF CODE OF MARKETING OF BREASTMILK SUBSTITUTES), the IOCU has been instrumental in getting two more citizens' campaigns off the ground: Health Action International and Pesticides Action Network. It has become increasingly critical of multinational corporate marketing practices in the Third World. Its most radical branch, the Consumer Association of Penang (Malaysia) which acts as the regional office for Asia and the Pacific has since 1981 administered Consumer Interpol, which is an international warning system to alert members to products that have been banned, restricted or recalled in any part of the world.

See Index under International Co-operation, and under Data Sources.

Address: Emmastraat 9, 2595 EG The Hague, Netherlands.

Regional Office for Asia and the Pacific: PO Box 1045, Penang, Malaysia

International Organization of Employers (IOE). Founded in November 1919 during the first International Labour Conference (*see under* INTERNATIONAL LABOUR ORGANIZATION (ILO)) as an organization of industrial employers, it changed to its present name and function in 1948, defending the interests of all employers, not merely industrial employers. The IOE aims to establish and maintain permanent contact between members, with a view to keeping them informed of developments in, and facilitating a common stance towards, social and economic problems that are discussed within the ILO and the United Nations Economic and Social Council (UNECOSOC) in particular, where it has consultative status. It comprises 94 members of national and other federations in 91 countries.

See Index under International Co-operation, and under Corporate Structure and Management.
Address: Chemin de Joinville 28, Case Postale 68, CH-1216 Geneva, Switzerland.

international production. Officially defined in 1973 by a United Nations (UN) commission on multinational corporations as 'production subject to foreign control or decision and measured by the sales of foreign affiliates of multinational corporations'.

Because there is considerable variation in national definitions of how much foreign equity is needed to classify a firm as foreign-controlled (*see* FOREIGN DIRECT INVESTMENT (FDI)), statistical estimates of the total value of international production are necessarily unreliable. Nevertheless it is worth noting that even using a conservative method based on an estimated 2:1 ratio of foreign sales to the historical book value of foreign direct investment, the Commission arrived at a statistical estimate which at the time of publication in 1973 put the total value of international production at a figure marginally greater than the total value of international trade. In other words international production seems to have become a more important vehicle for international economic exchanges than international trade. More recent estimates show that the gap between international production and international trade is still widening.

Contemporary theories of international production aim to provide a comprehensive explanation of the factors which determine a firm's FOREIGN INVOLVEMENT, including both trade and non-trade servicing of foreign markets (LICENSING, for example, and foreign direct investment).

See UN COMMISSION ON TRANSNATIONAL CORPORATIONS, and Index under Theoretical Issues, and under Corporate Structure and Management.

international subcontracting. A subcontracting relationship exists when a firm (the principal) places an order with another firm (the subcontractor) for the manufacture of parts, components, sub-assemblies or assemblies to be incorporated into a product which the principal will sell. Such orders may include the treatment, processing or finishing of materials or parts by the subcontractor at the principal's request. When the principal and the subcontractor are located in two different countries or when the principal is controlled by a foreign company, we speak of 'international subcontracting'.

Principals and subcontractors can either be independent production units or be linked in an association which may range from minority participation in the capital or in a JOINT VENTURE arrangement to a 100 per cent holding. However, in the latter case it is more common to speak of a WORKSHOP SUBSIDIARY.

Sometimes a distinction is made between 'commercial' and 'industrial' subcontracting. In the former case, subcontractors supply principals with a finished product and the principal only acts as a kind of trading company. In the latter case, the principal carries through part of the production process itself.

A different classification, proposed by Michalet (1980) is one by function.

1. *Economy subcontracting.* This applies to all instances where firms consider it more cost-effective to have a number of parts composing a product manufactured outside the country.
2. *Capacity subcontracting.* Here subcontracting occurs on a cyclical basis to allow the principal to expand or contract output in accordance with market demand.

3. *Speciality subcontracting*. This refers to a situation where the subcontractor's technical knowhow is of a higher order than that of the principal.

International subcontracting has grown very rapidly in recent years and is claimed to be largely responsible for the success of the NEWLY INDUSTRIALIZING COUNTRIES, especially those in Southeast Asia. International subcontracting marks a new development in the relationship between multinational companies, especially in the manufacturing sector, and host developing countries conscious of their ECONOMIC SOVEREIGNTY. International subcontracting permits the producing unit to be fully co-opted within the transnationally integrated system of international production and trade, while at the same time stressing the legal independence and national ownership of the subcontracting firm.

See also NEW INTERNATIONAL DIVISION OF LABOUR, and Index under Trade.

International Trade Secretariats (ITS). International trade union organizations based upon a federal structure of national trade unions in their respective trades or industries. The idea of international secretariats first took shape at a Labour Congress in Copenhagen in 1901. In the early years of their existence, the Secretariats were closely integrated with the International Federation of Trade Unions. This Federation was succeeded by the communist-dominated WORLD FEDERATION OF TRADE UNIONS (WFTU) in 1945, and the autonomy of the trade secretariats was threatened. In 1949, the withdrawal of the non-communist affiliates and the formation of the rival INTERNATIONAL CONFEDERATION OF FREE TRADE UNIONS (ICFTU) enabled the Secretariats to retain their independence while being closely associated with the International Confederation. Today there are 18 International Trade Secretariats

associated with the ICFTU.

Over the past decade, a number of Secretariats have begun to develop policies and instruments for dealing with multinational corporations. Among the more significant developments are:
(1) the setting up of *World Company Councils* pioneered by the International Metal Federation (IMF). World Company Councils provide constant links between trade unionists responsible for national and regional bargaining and plant level negotiations with the same worldwide employer. World Company Councils now exist for many car companies (General Motors, Ford, Chrysler, Datsun, Volkswagen) and also such varying companies as SKF, Nestlé, Woolworth and American Express.
(2) Where world company councils do not yet exist as permanent bodies, ITS have on occasion organized *World Company Conferences*.
(3) *Data banks* have been set up to pool information regarding TNCs in the relevant sector of industry. The best example is that of the International Union of Food and Allied Workers Association (IUF) which has an *IU File on TNCs* covering about 100 TNCs within its field of competence.
(4) *International solidarity strikes* and *international boycotts* have been organized on a number of occasions to defend trade union rights in countries where unions are in a weak position in relation to employers and governments.
(5) The International Transport Federation (ITF) has gone some way towards developing a mechanism for *international collective bargaining*. In one case involving the airline companies, the ITF has been successful in getting the COMMITTEE ON INTERNATIONAL INVESTMENT AND MULTINATIONAL ENTERPRISES of the OECD, responsible for the clarification and review of the OECD Guidelines, to make it clear that there is no obstacle to secretariats like the ITF being recognized as *bona fide* organizations of employees for the purposes of con-

sultations, and so on, as defined in the Guidelines. The International Textile, Garment and Leather Workers' Federation (ITGWF) have drawn up a common collective bargaining platform – the Asia Bata Charter – in an attempt to pursue industrial relations issues at transnational company level rather than (as the Bata company insists) at the level of each individual subsidiary.

Finally, ITSs have been active in the evolutionary process of international CODES OF CONDUCT such as the OECD Guidelines on Multinational Enterprises (*see under* DECLARATION AND DECISIONS ON INTERNATIONAL INVESTMENTS AND MULTINATIONAL ENTERPRISES). By making use of the clarification and review procedure of the OECD Guidelines and bringing cases of dispute to the attention of the OECD Committee on International Investment and Multinational Enterprises, they have contributed to a more precise formulation of such codes of conduct and they have, in one instance, added a new one. In a celebrated case concerning the Hertz car hire company, it was discovered that the Guidelines did not discourage the transfer of workers between different national subsidiaries during a dispute. This 'Hertz-gap' has been closed in the first review of the Guidelines.

See Index under Labour and under International Co-operation.

intra-firm trade. The exchange of goods and services between different branches, divisions or subsidiaries of the same enterprise. The term is applicable even when the subsidiaries are legally separate entities, although in such cases it is more common to speak of 'intra-group' trade. The decisive characteristic of intra-firm trade is that the transactions take place between units which are not economically independent agents and are therefore governed by ADMINISTRATIVE FIAT rather than free market forces or ARM'S LENGTH negotiations.

See also TRANSFER PRICE, and Index under Trade.

intra-group trade. *See* INTRA-FIRM TRADE.

inventor's certificate. An official state-issued document giving an inventor recognition of his invention and an entitlement to remuneration, depending on the use made of the invention. In force predominantly in countries with socialist planned economies, the inventor's certificate performs part of the function of the PATENT in capitalist market economies. But it is in fact very different from the patent, because it does not give the inventor the right to control the use of the invention.

Inventor's certificates are not wholly restricted to socialist planned economies. Some developing countries (Mexico is one example) have started to introduce inventor's certificates in a limited way and at the Diplomatic Conference on the Revision of the Paris Convention there are currently proposals on the agenda to put inventor's certificates on a par with patents.

See INTERNATIONAL CONVENTION FOR THE PROTECTION OF INDUSTRIAL PROPERTY, and Index under Technology Transfer.

Invest in Britain Bureau (IBB). A unit within the UK Department of Trade and Industry, set up in 1976 for the specific purpose of promoting the UK as a location for inward direct investment. It assists foreign firms with all aspects of locating or relocating in the UK or expanding existing facilities, and offers information on the national, regional and local incentives which are available to encourage investment. In its promotional activities, the Bureau operates overseas through Foreign Office accreditations and within the UK it works with the Department of Trade and Industry's network of regional offices in England, Scotland and Wales.

In addition, the IBB is also responsible

for co-ordinating the activities of the agencies which actively seek investment from overseas for particular parts of the country with a view to eliminating wasteful competition between them.

investment centre. A DIVISION of a company that is given the authority to make most decisions itself concerning inputs, outputs and capital expenditure (*see also* COST CENTRE; PROFIT CENTRE).

It is rare that authority of this kind is given within a multinational to a foreign subsidiary; usually some expenditure limit will be set beyond which all capital investment decisions must be referred to the parent. The profit centre is far more common. It is however difficult to draw a line between a profit centre and an investment centre. The extent to which investment authority is given may well affect the method of assessing the division's performance.

See Index under Corporate Structure and Management.

investment protection treaty. Intergovernmental agreement between home country and host country of foreign direct investors, enabling insurance cover of the investor to be extended by official agents of the home country. The US, for example, has concluded such agreements with some 90 developing countries, in order to extend political risk insurance for its investors through the OVERSEAS PRIVATE INVESTMENT CORPORATION (OPIC).

See Index under International Co-operation.

inward investment. The inflow of capital investments into a recipient, or HOST country. Its opposite is OUTWARD INVESTMENT.

irrevocable letter of credit. *See under* LETTER OF CREDIT.

J

Jane's Major Companies of Europe. Annual publication of Jane's Yearbooks, containing basic financial data on some 1000 leading companies throughout Western Europe. Each company has a profile which includes its assets and liabilities, turnover and income, exports, ownership and control, investments and subsidiary interests, output, brand names, and copyright.

See Index under Data Sources.
Address: Poulton House, 8 Shepherdess Walk, London N1 7LW, UK.

joint audit. Simultaneous examination programme, by the tax authorities of two countries or more, of multinational company accounts and tax returns. Pioneered by the US in 1977, joint audits may be considered to be an extension of the exchange-of-information provisions of DOUBLE TAXATION treaties.

See Index under Regulation and Tax, and under International Co-operation.

joint venture. A partnership of two or more companies in which they combine resources for production, marketing, financial and/or managerial reasons. A joint venture may be created for purposes of a limited activity or single transaction, but it can also be used as a form of enduring relationship between the parties. In international business, joint ventures between multinational companies and local state- or privately owned enterprises have become commonplace, particularly in less developed countries which often place statutory limitations on the degree of foreign ownership and control which is permissible, or offer special legal benefits to joint venture arrangements. The term 'joint venture' has become a generally used term

for a wide variety of foreign and domestic collaborative economic arrangements (*see* COPRODUCTION AGREEMENT, PRODUCTION SHARING AGREEMENT, LICENSING AGREEMENT and MANAGEMENT CONTRACT). These arrangements basically fall into two types: equity joint ventures and contractual joint ventures. In the former, ownership rights are shared between the foreign and domestic partners, while in the latter the ownership rights normally remain with the local partner, while the foreign partner supplies licensed technology and knowhow, management and/or marketing services on a contractual basis.

Apart from political considerations, there are also economic reasons why multinational companies, in entering a foreign market, may seek a joint venture participation rather than setting up a wholly owned foreign subsidiary. Local partners, having general knowledge of the local economy and of local politics and customs, are often perceived as useful in accessing local markets and local resource inputs as well as in dealing with local public authorities. Studies in this field have shown, however, that such joint venture preference or tolerance varies by type of activity, organizational structure and home country origin of the multinational enterprise.

See also CARTEL; WEBB – POMERANE ACT, and Index under Corporate Structure and Management, and under Technology Transfer.

junk bond. A high-yield fixed-interest bond issued by a borrower of low standing. The proliferate issue of these securities has been limited so far to the USA, where they have caused considerable concern. The high yield offered on junk bonds (generally three

137

to five per cent higher than 'investment grade' bonds) reflects the more than average chance of default on the bond obligations.

High-yield bonds have tended to come from three types of borrower: the large company which has in the past had a high credit rating from the two standard US rating agencies but has been downgraded by them; the growing, successful, but smaller company without a full track record; the corporate raider using the bonds to finance a disputed takeover (*see* ACQUISITION, MERGER).

High-yield bonds are unexceptionable in themselves, since they constitute just another type of security in the range from zero-risk low-yield government stock to high-risk high-return speculative equity. But much concern has been voiced over their issue because the need to pay interest on the bonds constitutes a high prior charge against profits and hence an increase in the financial risk of the borrower. High-yield equity does not involve this risk since the dividend can be foregone. The proliferation of junk bonds has two potential outcomes: it might jeopardize corporate health in a market downturn, which can have extensive socioeconomic consequences on a national scale; and the ensuing default on such bonds would endanger the financial institutions that have been taking up the issues to increase their profitability yields.

See Index under Financial and Risk Management.

L

Labor Education and Research Project. An American non-profit making research organization focusing on the American labour movement and the operations of multinational companies in the USA. It publishes the fortnightly *Labor Notes*.

See Index under Data Sources.
Address: PO Box 20001, Detroit, Michigan MI48220, USA.

Labor Research Association. Independent research group concerned with transnational corporations and international trade union activities. It seeks to facilitate international trade union solidarity by organizing annual conferences and acting as an information clearing house and communications network for trade unions negotiating with TNCs. It publishes a newsletter, *Economic Notes*.

See Index under Data Sources.
Address: 80 East 11th Street, Rm. 634, New York, NY 10003, USA.

lagging. *See* LEADING AND LAGGING.

LAIA. *See* LATIN AMERICAN INTEGRATION ASSOCIATION.

Lange – Gibbons Code. The *Draft Code of Principles for Multinational Enterprises and Governments* prepared by a joint European Parliament/US Congress delegation in September 1976 and agreed in a Resolution of the European Parliament on 16 April 1977. Popularly named after its two principal authors, Erwin Lange from the European Parliament and Sam Gibbons from the US Congress, the Code is also sometimes referred to as the Parliamentarians' Code.

The draft Code formulates a framework of law and responsibility for multinational enterprises and governments as the starting point for the development of internationally-agreed, legally enforceable norms. International agreements are to be concluded initially between the US and the European Community.

The Code divides into nine sections covering – besides an introduction and a general framework – information disclosure, competition, investment policy, fiscal policy, social and labour market policy, technology, and pernicious political activities. One of the novel contributions of the Code is its call in the competition section for much tighter co-operation on antitrust matters between the EC and the US.

Because the European Parliament is not a legislative body of the EC, the direct impact of the Resolution and the Code has been limited to providing a climate of support for many of the legislative ideas in respect of MNEs which the EC Commission was then and still is considering. In the US the Code was followed immediately with Mr Gibbons's own, unsuccessful, Bill to the House of Representatives on the regulation of multinational companies by American law.

See CODES OF CONDUCT, and Index under International Co-operation.

Latin American Free Trade Association (LAFTA). *See under* LATIN AMERICAN INTEGRATION ASSOCIATION (LAIA).

Latin American Integration Association (LAIA). An association of regional co-operation founded in 1980 as the successor to the Latin American Free Trade Association (LAFTA). Its long-term objective is the establishment of a common market through the creation of an area of economic preferences, based on regional tariff preference and regional and partial scope agreements. Established by the Montevideo Treaty of 1980, it differs in two key respects from the Montevideo Treaty of 1960 which set up LAFTA: it envisages the gradual and progressive establishment of an economic preferences and not of a free trade area, and it accepts in its objectives the need for differential treatments based on the classification of member countries into three main categories according to their economic structure: more developed (Argentina, Brazil, Mexico), intermediate (Colombia, Chile, Peru, Uruguay and Venezuela); and less developed (Bolivia, Ecuador and Paraguay).

See Index under International Co-operation.

Address: Cebollati 1461, PO Box 577, Montevideo, Uruguay.

Latin American Working Group (LAWG). Independent research group monitoring Canadian corporate investment in Latin America. Its Canada – Latin American Resource Centre houses extensive files on TNCs. It publishes the newsletter *LAWG Letter*.

See Index under Data Sources.

Address: Box 2207 Station P, Toronto M5S 2T2, Canada.

law of combined and uneven development. General historical-theoretical law postulated by Leon Trotsky as part of his theory of permanent revolution (1928). Trotsky argued that with the development of capitalism as a world system due to the global internationalization of capital, world history becomes a contradictory but concrete totality.

In this totality, countries develop at uneven pace in relation to one another. Within backward nations, advanced and primitive features of economy and society

coexist. This constitutes a unique historical situation which is ripe for socialist revolution. This more complex view of history enabled Trotsky to transcend the evolutionist conception of history as a succession of rigidly predetermined stages, which has been the received Soviet interpretation of Marx's theory of history since Stalin.

See Index under Theoretical Issues.

Law of the Sea Treaty. The common, if somewhat inaccurate, title of a series of conferences held under the auspices of the United Nations since 1958 and dealing with the exploitation of the mineral wealth of the oceans. The first took place in Geneva in 1958. The third and most important United Nations Conference on the Law of the Sea (UNCLOS III) was only completed in 1982 after negotiations which took more than eight years. This Law of the Sea Convention attracted 122 signatures of participating states, but for the present it remains of historical interest only because the United States voted against it and other leading mining states, such as the UK, West Germany and Italy, have all abstained.

UNCLOS III is of historical significance, because it represents a new and ambitious undertaking in international co-operation. It was intended to give effect to the Declaration of Principles of the United Nations General Assembly in 1970 that the seabed and its resources, beyond the limits of national jurisdiction, were the 'common heritage of mankind' (*see* GLOBAL COMMONS). This objective of internationalizing the seabed involved the setting up of an International Seabed Authority that would regulate, and tax, all mining of the international area, and even itself embark on such mining on mankind's behalf.

See Index under International Co-operation.

LDCC. *See* LESS DEVELOPED COUNTRY CORPORATION.

leading and lagging. A strategy by which firms involved in international operations can reduce their foreign exchange EXPOSURE by bringing forward or holding back payments that must be made in foreign currency. This is possible with payments to both SUBSIDIARIES and to other creditors. Companies will, therefore, pay early if they expect the denominated currency to rise (which would require them to pay more in local currency if they waited) and conversely attempt to delay payment if they expect the denominated currency to fall. Similar actions by non-multinational companies with foreign debts are also of course possible.

The practice of leading and lagging has implications for the pressure on a currency. If firms believe for example that a denominated currency will fall their delay in payment – that is, in purchasing that currency – will itself increase the pressure for that fall. As a result many countries have imposed legislative limits on export or import lagging, export or import leading, and/or netting (that is, the setting off against each other of intracompany debts).

See Index under Financial and Risk Management.

less developed country corporation (LDCC). A tax status available under US law to enterprises dealing with less developed countries. To qualify, a company must be a foreign corporation that receives 80 per cent or more of its gross income from less developed countries, and has at least 80 per cent of its assets there. In this context a less developed country is defined as any country except Australia, Canada, China, Japan, New Zealand, South Africa, the Soviet Bloc, and Western Europe. The advantage of this status is that a CONTROLLED FOREIGN CORPORATION can exclude dividends and interest received from a LDCC from its taxable income if these are reinvested in less developed countries.

See also Index under Regulation and Tax.

letter of credit. A document issued by a banker as part of the financing of international trade.

The most common type of letter of credit (often abbreviated to L/C) is the irrevocable letter of credit. This is issued by a bank at the request of an importer. It is needed where the exporter is unsure of the creditworthiness of the importer and hence requires some guarantee of payment. The importer ('the account party') requests a bank ('the issuing bank') to issue a letter of credit and pays a fee for the service. Once issued, the letter of credit obliges the bank to pay the exporter (the beneficiary) through the medium of his bank (the 'paying', or 'drawee' bank) on condition that all documentation required by the issuing bank and listed in the letter of credit is forthcoming. This will normally include at the very least a clean BILL OF LADING, an invoice and an insurance certificate. Other documents that may be specified include a customs invoice, packing list, consular invoice, certificate of origin, weight list, or certificate of analysis. In general, a bank's credit is better than an importer's, and therefore the issue of the letter of credit is a guarantee to the exporter that he will be paid. Once it is received, therefore, the goods may be shipped.

The exporter next draws a draft or BILL OF EXCHANGE on the bank which, assuming the accompanying documentation is in order, will honour the bill and pay the drawee bank which will in turn pay the beneficiary. The bank collects from the importer either immediately or at some future agreed date. It is necessary for the bank to collect or otherwise agree to deferral of collection, since the importer will need the bill of lading to be in the issuing bank's possession before he is allowed to take possession of the goods upon arrival.

There are however other types of letter of credit other than the basic documentary irrevocable letter of credit described above. A letter of credit may be 'revocable', in which case the issuing bank is not guaranteeing payment at all, but merely using the letter of credit as a means of making payment.

A particularly important variant is the 'confirmed' letter of credit where the exporter arranges for his domestic bank to confirm the letter of credit from the foreign bank. This means that the drawee bank also acknowledges an obligation to pay under the letter of credit and will itself honour the draft presented by the beneficiary, presenting it in turn for payment to the issuing bank. The beneficiary/exporter will seek confirmation where he has some reason to doubt the financial standing of the foreign bank, or where political/economic conditions make the honouring of the letter of credit more risky.

Although most letters of credit are once-only transactions, 'revolving' credits are also possible, whereby the issuing bank makes an agreed amount per set period (for instance, per week or per month) available to the beneficiary. Because of the lack of control over its obligations, the bank will normally agree to this only if the letter of credit is revocable.

A 'negotiable' letter of credit is one that is drawn up with its negotiability specifically stated on the face: this means the beneficiary can use any bank as a paying bank that is willing to do so.

A 'time' letter of credit requires that payment be made to the beneficiary, and hence by the account party, only after a specified period of time. This enables the exporter to extend credit to the importer while still retaining the credit guarantee of a major international bank.

A 'transferable' letter of credit is one where the role of beneficiary may be transferred (but only once). It can be used in one of two ways: a beneficiary who has sold the goods (as described earlier) may transfer the letter of credit as payment to a new beneficiary as settlement of a debt; or the original beneficiary may be a trading house which first arranges to find a buyer (the account party) and issuing bank, and only then seeks a seller, having the purchase and certain payment arranged, thus transferring beneficial rights to the seller proper.

The letter of credit system is a valuable means of enhancing international trade. It is helpful to importers, since it smooths the way for deals with exporters, who would otherwise have no indication of a firm's creditworthiness; to exporters, since it virtually guarantees that they receive payment; to bankers, since it represents a source of profit; and to the general public because it facilitates international trade.

See Index under Trade.

leverage. *See under* FINANCIAL STRUCTURE.

leveraged buyout. The acquisition of a company or a part of a company whereby the funds borrowed for the acquisition are secured on the assets of the target company. In recent years, leveraged buyouts have become a popular means for managers to buy out divisions of the companies for whom they work. The leveraged buyout has become better known as the MANAGEMENT BUYOUT.

Levy Group. The popular name for the OECD's Working Group on the Guidelines for Multinational Enterprises, so named after its Chairman, the Swiss diplomat Phillipe Levy.

See DECLARATION AND DECISIONS ON INTERNATIONAL INVESTMENT AND MULTINATIONAL ENTERPRISES.

LIBOR. *See* LONDON INTER-BANK OFFERED RATE.

licensing agreement. Contracts in which the licensor provides the licensee with access to one or a number of technologies (unpatented knowhow and TRADE SECRETS as well as PATENTS and TRADEMARKS), usually in exchange for an initial lump sum payment plus a percentage of sales or ROYALTIES or even a share of equity. In COUNTER PURCHASE or BUY-BACK deals, the payment also takes the form of goods bought by the licensor from the licensee at a discount.

In international business it is particularly important to distinguish a licensing agreement (which is only one of a variety of increasingly common contractual cross-border transactions) from both an export sale and from a FOREIGN DIRECT INVESTMENT (FDI).

Where an export sale involves spot market sales in which both ownership and control over the sold asset or technology passes from buyer to seller, and while foreign direct investment implies complete continued control over the asset by the investor as a function of equity ownership, a contractual agreement such as a license involves a *de facto* separation of ownership from control. The rights of control assigned to the licensor may be limited by the licensee and are moreover normally specified as being assigned for a given period of time. The licensing contract, for instance, may specify in some detail the requisite plant operation and the level of output; it may also place restrictions on export markets.

In respect of income, too, the contractual arrangement differs from an outright sale in that the licensor continues to have an interest in the future earnings derived from the use of the asset, and it differs from a foreign direct investment in that the right to this future income is not a function of the risk associated with the investment.

Both in terms of control over the use of the technology and in terms of the rights to income derived from that use, a licensing agreement represents a transaction at a point on a continuum from a direct investment at one extreme to an outright sale on the other.

See also FRANCHISE, and Index under Technology Transfer.

Licensing Executives Society. A professional organization aiming to link individuals engaged in the domestic and foreign licensing of technology and intellectual property or industrial property. The organization includes as members either individuals or national societies representing company or government officials, lawyers, patent agents, scientists, engineers and others engaged in some form of licensing activity. It publishes a monthly journal, *Les Nouvelles*.

See also LICENSING AGREEMENT.

link financing. *See* FRONTING LOAN.

liquidation. The dissolution or final extinction of corporate entity.

local incorporation. The establishment of operations in a host country by setting up a corporate entity within that country subject to its domestic law. The entity will be partly or wholly owned by the multinational parent: however the extent of control by the parent and responsibility for the entity's debts will vary from case to case.

See MONKEY LETTER; CENTRALIZATION, and Index under Corporate Structure and Management.

localization. The bringing together of as much of the production process as is possible in one domestic location. The policy of localization may form a part of an overall development programme.

See LOCAL VALUE ADDED, and Index under Development Policy.

local sourcing. The use of local (as distinct from foreign) inputs in industrial processes, be they local raw materials, locally produced components or services, or local skills and labour. Also referred to as 'domestic' sourcing.

See Index under Development Policy.

local value added. The difference between total revenue of a foreign affiliate (that is, quantity of goods sold multiplied by price) and the total cost of imported raw materials, components and services, including all payments made from net output to foreigners, such as royalties and dividends. As countries have become increasingly sensitive to the way in which foreign-controlled production affects the BALANCE OF PAYMENTS and the national income, so local value added has become a central tool for assessing this impact. Some countries have introduced specific local value added ratios as performance criteria for foreign-owned or controlled companies. Also referred to as 'domestic value added'.

See PERFORMANCE REQUIREMENTS, and Index under Development Policy.

location specific advantages. Advantages which a country may enjoy due to its specific location and which make it attractive to international direct investment. They include possession of certain natural resources, availability of cheap labour and proximity to large potential markets. In theories of international investment and trade, location specific advantages are distinguished from OWNERSHIP SPECIFIC ADVANTAGES which are possessed by firms.

See Index under Theoretical Issues.

location theory. Originally a theory explaining the territorial allocation of resources within a country, location theory has also been applied – with modifications – to international direct investments. For a country to be attractive to FOREIGN DIRECT INVESTMENT (FDI) the country should possess a number of LOCATION SPECIFIC ADVANTAGES, such as the availability of scarce natural resources or low labour costs, market characteristics such as potential size and growth, a certain level of national economic development, government-imposed barriers to trade which encourage the establishment of local production facilities to avoid exporting there, and other forms of government policy and a favourable political and economic 'climate'.

In academic literature the term 'location theory' also has a different meaning. It may also refer to a popular theory of the evolution of multinational enterprise developed by Stephen Hymer (1972). Hymer's location theory refers to the correspondence between on the one hand the evolution of a vertical division of labour within the firm by which more prestige and rewards are attached to the higher placed activities, and on the other a hierarchical division of labour between geographical regions. Hymer argued that the multinational enterprise will tend to centralize high level decision-making occupations in a few key cities in the advanced countries, surrounded by a number of regional subcapitals, and confine the rest of the world to lower levels of activity and income, that is to the status of towns and villages in a new imperial system. Income, status, authority and consumption patterns will radiate out from the centres along a declining curve, and the existing patterns of inequality and dependency between advanced and poor regions of the world will be perpetuated.

See Index under Theoretical Issues.

Lomé Convention. An agreement between the European Community (EC) countries and a large number of developing countries in Africa, the Caribbean and the Pacific (called the ACP STATES) intended to promote the social and economic development of the latter by giving them preferential trading access to the EC and by providing a Commodity Stabilization Fund (STABEX) plus other financial and technical aid channelled through the EUROPEAN DEVELOPMENT FUND (EDF). The Lomé Convention was first signed in the Tongolese capital in 1975 and is renegotiated every five years. The third Lomé Convention was signed in December 1984 between the 10 member states of the EC and 63 ACP states, plus Angola and Mozambique. The renegotiated versions have added only minor revisions to the original substance of the agreement.

The history of the Lomé Conventions is a controversial one and this is reflected in the protracted and often bitter quinquennial renegotiations. When the first Lomé Convention was signed in 1975 in the heydays of the demands for a NEW INTERNATIONAL ECONOMIC ORDER (NIEO), it was hailed as a unique experiment in international co-operation. Firstly, it differed from the more conventional bilateral trade and aid agreements between states in that it intended to create lasting co-operation between groups of developed and developing countries rather than individual states, and, moreover, on the basis of 'complete equality between partners'. Secondly, the Convention brought the novelty of combining aid and trade provisions in a single agreement, thus offering a 'new model for relations between developed and developing states, compatible with the aspirations of the international community towards a more just and more balanced economic order'.

The translation of the detailed schedules of the Convention into practice soon however dampened the initial enthusiasm. The fundamental principle of the Convention's trade regime, that ACP exports should have free access to EC markets, proved in reality to yield very few tangible benefits, when implemented in the context of the EC's other existing international and internal trade policies, and the Convention's own rules of origin and safeguard clauses.

For instance, while it is true that almost all of ACP exports to the EC enter the Community duty free, it can be argued that this is so only because trade barriers arising from the EC's Common Agricultural Policy and from the Rules of Origin and Safeguard Clauses, deter the entry of other ACP goods. Furthermore, most of the imports that do enter duty free would have done so in any case under the EC's GENERALIZED SYSTEM OF PREFERENCES (GSP).

The Commodity Stabilization Fund has also been criticized for its funding levels and eligibility rules, and for its objectives (stabilization of export earnings rather than stabilization of import capacity). But the deepest rift between the two 'equal' partners has undoubtedly been caused by the inequity implied in the donor-recipient relationship. This is especially acutely felt in conflicts over the Stabex transfers and EDF aid disbursements. While the EC countries take the view that as donors they should have some control over the distribution and allocation of Community aid, the ACP countries see this as an infringement on their sovereign right to determine their own development policies.

See Index under International Co-operation.

London Inter-Bank Offered Rate (LIBOR). The interest rate at which London banks lend to other first-class banks. This rate is in widespread use as a reference point for other loans, such as EUROCURRENCY deposits. Such loans are expressed at a rate which is a defined amount above LIBOR.

See Index under Financial and Risk Management.

low-context culture. *See under* HIGH CONTEXT CULTURE.

lump sum settlement. Compensation agreement between an expropriating state and the state of the investor(s) affected by the EXPROPRIATION. The claimant state collects the lump sum and settles the debt claims of the affected persons or companies.

Lump sum payments have been a common vehicle for compensation settlements since the Second World War, although they are not without precedent in earlier periods. While lump sum settlements are in a strict sense a departure from the principle of 'prompt, adequate and effective' compensation enshrined in international law relating to expropriation and the sanctity of private property abroad, such departure has in practice been accepted for political and economic reasons.

See also CONVENTION ON THE SETTLEMENT OF INVESTMENT DISPUTES BETWEEN STATES AND NATIONALS OF OTHER STATES, and Index under Dispute and Settlement.

M

majority-owned foreign affiliate (MOFA).
A classificatory term defined by the US
Bureau of Census and used by the US
Department of Commerce in its collection
and reporting of statistical data on the
extent and composition of US intra-firm
imports. Majority-owned affiliates are
defined as foreign affiliates of US firms in
which US equity interest is at least 50 per
cent. This US equity interest may be held
either directly by the parent company or
indirectly by another foreign affiliate of the
US parent firm. In the literature on multinational enterprise the term is more loosely
applied to any subsidiary in which a parent
company has more than 50 per cent interest.

See also FOREIGN DIRECT INVESTMENT
(FDI), and Index under Corporate Structure and Management.

managed float. A government-operated
system underpinning the value of a currency, and sometimes known as a DIRTY
FLOAT. Rather than a FREE FLOAT, where
market forces are allowed to prevail, the
government or governments concerned in a
managed float will be prepared to intervene
whenever it is felt necessary to protect a
desired exchange rate (for example, the
EUROPEAN MONETARY SYSTEM (EMS)). The
existence of the float however distinguishes
this exchange rate from the FIXED EXCHANGE
RATE. The managed float is perhaps the
most difficult of all exchange rate systems
for the multinational to forecast.

See Index under Financial and Risk
Management.

management buyout. A transfer of the
ownership of part of a large company to its
managers, usually financed by a package
put together by a specialist institution.

The management buyout (which may or
may not be highly levered) has become a
feature of the 1980s in both the USA and
UK. In 1985 it was estimated that these
transactions involved some £1 billion in the
UK and $20 billion in the USA. Although
some buyouts take place when a division or
factory is to be closed down, many others
are now taking place when the business is
thriving. The normal financing package for
a buyout involves the management itself
raising personal cash to pay for their equity
(frequently by personal borrowing), with
the balance being provided in the form of
debt and equity. This provision normally
comes from one of the specialist finance
houses that have sprung up solely to deal
with buyout packages, who finance the debt
issue using the company's assets as their
security. Although highly levered financing
(that is, a financing package with a high
debt proportion) is not yet common in the
UK, it is not unusual in the USA to find
debt constituting 90 per cent of the finance
raised: the buyout is consequently said to be
highly levered.

The advantage of high levering to the
equity holders and the management in particular is that, if the operations are successful, they can pay off the debt with the funds
generated by operations, and considerably
increase their personal holdings and hence
their wealth. This may in many cases eventually involve a refloating of the company so
that the management's stock becomes
tradeable. A further advantage is that interest is deductable against tax, thus reducing
its effective cost to the company. The
advantage to the financiers is at present that

the high interest charge acts as an incentive to management to cut costs and hence raise corporate profitability. Moreover, since at least part of the debt will be convertible into equity under certain conditions, the financiers have the opportunity to share in any reflotation profit.

The danger of high leverage is that those same high interest charges considerably increase the risk of the firm's failure in a market downturn.

See Index under Financial and Risk Management.

management contract. One of the many forms of cross-border economic co-operative ventures which have become commonplace in international business in the last 20 years. In a management contract a foreign company undertakes in exchange for a form of payment agreed in advance to manage a domestic enterprise for a fixed period of years. Often a management contract involves the startup of a new enterprise and the training of local personnel before handing over management authority after the set time period.

Management contracts may be concluded in the case of JOINT VENTURES where equity ownership of the domestic firm is shared with the foreign partner or in cases where equity ownership is entirely in the hands of the local partner. Frequently management contracts are a part of a more comprehensive agreement which includes technical, service and marketing agreements as part of the overall package (*see* TECHNICAL ASSISTANCE AGREEMENT).

Although in management contracts the managing agent is answerable to the board of directors where the local partner holds the majority voting stock, he must also be given the authority necessary to discharge his responsiblities. These typically include the running of the factories, the organization of marketing and the co-ordination of production, the purchase and installation of machinery and the acquisition of the materials appropriate for the operation and control of production processes. It also by corollary includes the right and the obligation to provide key personnel, whose salaries will be paid by the local enterprise. It will often be formally agreed in the contract that such decisions will not be interfered with by the board without full consultation.

For his part, the managing agent usually agrees to provide a variety of specified services to the local company. These may include making PATENT licenses and TRADE MARKS available, as well as information about processes, formulae and new technology. Usually such provisions are negotiated in separate agreements such as a technical or LICENSING AGREEMENT.

Management contracts usually specify the level and the form of payment for the services rendered. The foreign managing agent may receive any one or combination of the following:

a percentage of the profit earned;
a percentage of sales value;
a percentage of the purchase price of equipment for his purchasing services;
a fixed fee for specific services;
a lump sum or a fixed annual fee for specific services;
a fixed fee per unit of sales volume.

See Index under Technology Transfer.

Mandatory Control Program. A set of controls on direct investments abroad made by US companies in the period 1968 – 1974, set up to counter deficits in the balance of payments. The programme limited not only outward investment but also the reinvestment of overseas earnings. The same period saw the introduction of a parallel set of controls by the Federal Reserve System on foreign lending by US banks. The system was effectively ended in January 1974.

See Index under Regulation and Tax.

maquiladora. Mexican variant of the FREE

TRADE ZONE (FTZ). The *maquiladora* is a subcontracting company designed particularly for foreign industrialists and which enjoys freedom from customs duties. At first such firms could be set up only in the frontier zone, but legislative changes in 1970 and 1972 have given firms the freedom to set up anywhere in the country. The concept of the free trade zone has thus become one of status rather than territory.

Maquiladoras may be set up either by established foreign firms, which supply the domestic market and wish to orient their excess production capacity toward export activities, or by new foreign enterprises. The government's stated objective in the *maquiladora* legislation is to reduce unemployment.

See INTERNATIONAL SUBCONTRACTING; NEWLY INDUSTRIALIZING COUNTRIES, and Index under Trade.

market-in-hand contract. A variation on the typical TURNKEY CONTRACT which requires the contractor to give assistance in, or in some cases take responsiblity for, the sale of at least part of the project's output.

See Index under Technology Transfer.

market risk. *See* SYSTEMATIC RISK.

market segmentation This term has two quite distinct meanings.

As a term in marketing, the expression refers to the identification of separate sectors of the market for a company's products or services. The ability to segment effectively will lead to the appropriate commodity being supplied to the appropriate part of the market, and its advertising and distribution being targeted most cost-effectively.

The essence of the problem of market segmentation for the multinational lies in the question of specific product tailoring for individual markets. If a country, or part of a country's market, is identified as being sep-

arable in terms of tastes, needs, or any other appropriate criterion, then the company must make a judgement as to whether it is more cost-effective to tailor a product specifically to that market or to create an international brand identification such that the market sector takes on the characteristics of the rest of the market. Generalization is difficult in this area, since decisions will depend on the product type (consumer goods or capital goods, for example), the size of the segment, any special legal requirements, distribution costs, and so on.

As a term in international finance, however, the expression refers to differentiation in capital markets. If markets are homogeneous, then securities with similar expected risks and returns will be priced similarly after allowing for foreign exchange risk and political risk. If on the other hand the markets are segmented, then pricing between such similar securities will differ.

If investors had perfect information and there were free capital flows between capital markets, segmentation would be impossible because differences would vanish as a result of international ARBITRAGE transactions. In fact segmentation is common as a result of differences in available information (see DISCLOSURE IN ACCOUNTS, TRANSACTION COSTS) and the aforementioned exchange and political risk.

See COST OF CAPITAL, and Index under Corporate Structure and Management and under Financial and Risk Management.

matrix organization. An alternative to the more common and straightforward divisionalized organization that is found in most multinational enterprises (*see* DIVISION).

Although the characteristics of matrix designs for organizations vary from company to company, the basic structure can be identified fairly simply. It arises in many ways from the problems inherent in each of the two principal types of divisionalization.

If divisions are formed on a geographical basis, there are likely to be communication problems between managers who have responsibilities for similar products but are based in different regions of the world. On the other hand, the product-based divisionalized structure results in a lack of identification with the company's other operations in a given country or area of the world. In the matrix organization, each manager has a dual responsibility. Rather than be responsible only to the head of a product division, for example, he may be responsible to both a product head and an area head. The advantage of such a structure lies in improved communication. The disadvantages are principally the complexity that arises from the quantity of communication that takes place and the ambiguity that arises from reporting to two superiors concurrently. Matrix structures have been tried in a number of major multinationals, but many have subsequently reverted to other structures.

See Index under Corporate Structure and Management.

McCarthy's Information Service. Commercial organization offering a paper cutting service based on international financial weekly and daily newspapers. It collates the cuttings for each company. 'Back copies' may be obtained for all major companies from any one year onwards.

See Index under Data Sources.
Address: 19/19a Floral Street, London WC2, UK.

merger. The fusion of the assets of two or more companies with a view to forming a single company with both companies' consent. A merger is technically distinct from an ACQUISITION or takeover, which involves the purchase of shares of one company by another and which may occur without the consent of the targeted company. However, since any company that holds controlling share ownership in another can at any time merge the assets of the two, the distinction is more of form than of substance.

Nevertheless the distinction has been of great legal significance and practical consequence in the past. The CLAYTON ACT of 1914, which was intended to extend American ANTI-TRUST LEGISLATION to cover incipient monopolies, had granted the FEDERAL TRADE COMMISSION the authority under section 7 to prevent acquisitions of stock, but had failed to grant it the power to prevent the merging of assets. This omission made the law a dead letter until it was changed in the CELLER–KEFAUVER AMENDMENT of 1950, although even then not to much effect.

Mergers can be horizontal, absorbing direct competitors producing similar goods, or vertical, extending either backward to suppliers on the one hand, or forward into further fabricating facilities on the other. When mergers occur across sectors in unrelated businesses it is common to speak of CONGLOMERATE expansion.

There have been several periods of intensified merger activity in the history of capitalist development, but there appears to be a fundamental distinction between the causes of earlier merger movements and the more recent ones. In the turn of the century consolidation movement in the United States, and again in the wave of mergers before the Great Depression, the motivation for the mergers seems to have been largely rooted in operational considerations: to achieve economies of scale, to broaden product lines, to reduce costs and gain functional depth and /or to eliminate competition. But the merger mania of the 1960s and the 1980s is attributed by many critics less to economic or technological imperatives than to psychological factors and financial incentives.

The psychological motivation described in the literature is the quest on the part of corporate management for the status and power that accompanies size and monopoly: some firms take over others just to be bigger, and merging firms are often oriented more toward the interests of managers than toward profit maximization for their shareholders.

More serious is the charge that the present wave of conglomerate mergers seems propelled by tax incentives and questionable accounting practices, both of which may yield quick financial gains without reflecting real productive corporate growth. For instance, there is generally no taxation on the transfer of stock in the US or on the transfer of shares in the UK, and interest on debt instruments used to finance mergers are generally tax deductible. Among the accounting rules fuelling the present merger wave, 'pooling of interests' is the most important. By adding to its own assets only the book value of the acquired company (which is invariably less than the price actually paid) the merged corporation can exaggerate the declared value of its earnings for a number of years, thus securing a high price-earnings ratio (the ratio of estimated earnings from a company's stock to the price paid for it) and subsequently capitalize on a resulting rising securities market.

Some mergers may well be motivated by the belief that efficiencies will be realized by the final combination, but for the majority of present-day mergers this claim seems to be unsupported by the evidence. Mergers may also sometimes be pro-competitive; when, for example, an unproductive or failing company is resuscitated and re-enters the market with new vigour. But the overwhelming evidence points to the anti-competitive effects of mergers and their tendency to transform competitive industries into oligopolistic structures.

See CONCENTRATION; OLIGOPOLY; MONOPOLIES COMMISSION, and Index under Industry Structure.

Mergers Panel. *See* MONOPOLIES AND MERGERS COMMISSION.

MFA. *See* MULTIFIBRE ARRANGEMENT.

MFN clause. *See* MOST FAVOURED NATION CLAUSE.

M-form organization. One of two basic organizational structures identified and named by Williamson (1970). As such it is a theoretical formulation describing managerial practice. The M-form organization is multidivisional in contrast to the unitary U-FORM ORGANIZATION. It has been argued that this form was necessary to counteract the managerial limitations of the U-form organization once it grew beyond a certain size. Because of its suitability for large organizations, the M-form is probably the most common form of organization structure in the multinational enterprise.

See DIVISION, and Index under Corporate Structure and Management.

mining rent. All payments made to the owner of a mineable resource for the rights to exploration, exploitation and disposal of that resource. Today the ownership of mineable resources is usually vested in the State. In exchange for a CONCESSION or for another form of agreement to explore and exploit the resource, a multinational corporation will normally pay ROYALTIES per ton excavated and sold, annual rents for the lease of land, and income or profits taxes. Sometimes, as in PRODUCTION SHARING AGREEMENTS the payment consists of a share of the resultant product. Reference to 'mining' rent normally includes all such payments.

See also MODERNIZED CONCESSION AGREEMENT, and Index under Regulation and Tax.

.**MNC.** Abbreviation of 'multinational corporation'. *See* MULTINATIONAL CORPORATION/ENTERPRISE.

MNE. Abbreviation of 'multinational enterprise'. *See* MULTINATIONAL CORPORATION/ENTERPRISE.

mobilization fee. Euphemism for the payment of bribes. A foreign company may pay its local agents a mobilization fee to get a project through its pre-investment stages. Expenses incurred include bribes to relevant officials for the necessary permits and approvals. In the company's accounts such expenditure may be discreetly referred to as mobilization fees or FACILITATION FEES, or more commonly commission.

See also AGENCY AGREEMENT.

modernization. A central concept in the sociology of development, referring to the interactive processes of economic growth and social change through which underdeveloped societies of all periods are thought to become developed. Modernization studies typically deal with the effects of economic development on traditional social structures and values, and conversely with the manner in which traditional social structures and values can either hinder or facilitate successful economic development. For instance, modernization studies examine processes of secularization following the introduction of cash crops into traditional peasant communities, or the effect of industrialization on the prevailing family system.

Modernization has also come to stand for one particular, controversial and exclusively Western perspective on development and developing countries. Its critics claim it has even become an ideological apology for imperialist interference with, and exploitation of, developing countries since their independence from colonial rule. This claim is based on a critical analysis of the two intellectual origins of the concept. One of these origins was the practical advice of Western economic consultants to governments of newly independent countries. In the early 1950s these experts argued that policies of economic development could only be successful if they formed a part of a comprehensive plan affecting the entire social and cultural fabric into which the economic policies were injected. Western sociologists next began to underlay these practical observations with a theoretical framework consistent with mainstream Western sociological theories of society and of historical and social change. This theory was soon criticized for equating modernization with 'westernization'. Since westernization as a developmental ideology was seen to be partisan to Western commercial interests, modernization theory was entirely rejected by radical writers on Third World development.

See IMPERIALISM; DEPENDENCY; THIRD WORLD, and Index under Development Policy and under Theoretical Issues.

modernized concession agreement. During the 1970s most investment agreements between host governments and multinational corporations in the resource-based sector were reviewed, renegotiated and revised. Dissatisfied with traditional concession regimes which, it was argued, distributed the benefits of the concession unfairly between the parties, the renegotiated or 'modernized' concession agreements include more sophisticated mechanisms for assessing the gains from the venture, for maximizing the returns to the host governments, and for the exercise of control over the venture by the host government.

Most importantly, where traditional concessions were normally fixed for a very long period lasting between 50 and 100 years, the modernized agreements provide for greater flexibility by including review and renegotiation clauses. The inclusion of such clauses has been a major bone of contention between the contracting parties. Multinational companies have argued that their investment of substantial resources in projects is based upon careful long-term financial projections from which they determine their expected returns, and that the inclusion of review and renegotiation clauses subverts the stability of the venture. For their part, certain host governments have taken the view that far from subverting stability, renegotiation, as an alternative to expropriation or abrogation, ensures a longer lasting and more secure relationship between host government and the transnational corporation.

See CONCESSION; PRODUCTION SHARING AGREEMENT; RISK SERVICE CONTRACT, and Index under Regulation and Tax.

MOFA. *See* MAJORITY-OWNED FOREIGN AFFILIATE.

monkey letter. A term sometimes used to describe a 'moral' guarantee, as in cases where a parent refuses to give a legally binding guarantee of repayment to a bank that has been asked to lend to one of its foreign affiliates (and where, therefore, the parent as a shareholder is not in corporate law liable for the affiliate's debts) but is willing to write a letter acknowledging a moral commitment to honour the affiliate's debts.

Monopolies Commission. *See under* MONOPOLIES AND MERGERS COMMISSION.

Monopolies and Mergers Commission. Originally named the Monopolies Commission. Arising out of the Monopolies and Restrictive Practices (Inquiry and Control) Act of 1948, the Commission was set up with the powers to investigate and judge, in the light of public interest, any firm referred to it by the Board of Trade if such firm accounted for more than one third of market sales. The Monopolies and Mergers Act of 1965 widened these powers to include referral of mergers between firms involving a pool of £5m assets or over. The Fair Trading Act of 1973 again broadened the scope of the by now renamed Monopolies and Mergers Commission, including in the concept of 'monopoly' a market share of one quarter (instead of the previous one third) and permitting the affected market to be defined in relation to a local as well as national level. The Commission is also required to examine what types of market behaviour the enterprises concerned use to preserve and enhance their monopoly and to decide whether they operate or may be expected to operate against the public interest.

Under the Fair Trading Act of 1973, the Monopolies and Mergers Commission has no power to initiate enquiries itself, but has to await reference either from the Secretary of State for Trade and Industry or from the Director General of Fair Trading. The Commission also has no remedial powers and can only make recommendations to the Minister, at whose discretion action may or may not be taken.

At present mergers are normally only referred when there is a *prima facie* case for concern on the grounds of competition. However, the recent merger boom has caused anxiety in respect of both the extent of foreign takeovers of British manufacturing and retailing companies and the method of financing employed. At the time of writing a committee has been set up by the Department of Trade and Industry to review the referral policy and the role of the Commission.

Finally, it should be noted that the pragmatic and discretionary approach to British anti-trust legislation stands in contrast of both American and European Community (EC) legislation where even an attempt to monopolize constitutes in itself a breach of law.

See ANTI-TRUST LEGISLATION; SECURITIES AND EXCHANGE COMMISSION (SEC), and Index under Regulation and Tax.

monopoly. Strictly speaking this refers to a

market condition characterized by a complete absence of competition when one enterprise produces and sells the entire output of some commodity. This situation rarely occurs in practice, but the term is commonly used when a firm produces a sufficiently large proportion of total output to enable it to influence the market price of the commodity.

A market can equally be said to be monopolistic when a group of companies act in concert to maintain the price at a level above that which would prevail under normal competitive conditions. This is called 'monopolistic profit'. Such firms will displace their price competition with non-price or shadow competition, offering their customers attractive credit arrangements, personal services, or bonus gifts. This 'monopolistic competition' frequently takes the form of competition in diseconomies or disservices, that is in productive and commercial activities that are welfare-reducing instead of welfare-enhancing. Among these are frequent changes in design and planned obsolescence to accelerate the sale of commodities, illusory product differentiation (such as differences in wrapping paper, shape, colour and so on) and aggressive advertising campaigns.

Besides price-fixing, monopoly agreements between individual firms may be reached on restriction of output and on allocation of market shares (see OLIGOPOLY, CARTEL). Because such agreements need not be written agreements but may in fact amount to no more than a tacit understanding, ANTI-TRUST LEGISLATION is difficult to enforce. This is especially true in the world market, where multinational companies commonly agree on protected 'spheres of influence' and market shares.

According to the Marxist theory of CAPITALISM, monopolistic profits in the home market constitute one of the driving forces behind the international migration of capital. Thus, in this view, FOREIGN DIRECT INVESTMENT (FDI) comes from monopolistic competition. But the relationship between monopoly and foreign investment is more complex. It has also been argued that although foreign direct investment comes from monopolistic competition, it often breaks up local monopolies and thereby can improve efficiency in the country where it invests.

See IMPERIALISM, and Index under Industry Structure and under Theoretical Issues.

monopsony. A market structure in which a given commodity has only a single buyer, who can therefore strongly influence its price. Like MONOPOLY, monopsony reflects an extreme situation which rarely occurs in practice. But monopsonistic market characteristics, including price determination by buyers, do arise in the market for a homogeneous product in which a large number of competitive sellers offer their goods to a few large buyers. This is strictly speaking an 'oligopsony', but this term is never used. Many commodity markets, including petroleum, wheat, tobacco, sugar beet and bananas, are subject to monopsonistic market conditions.

See Index under Industry Structure.

Moodies Services. A commercial organization providing an extensive online and card reference service which gives information and extracts from press comments on major companies. It also publishes an annual *Investment Digest* with profiles of over 650 major companies, mainly in Britain, and an *Industrial Manual* with detailed information about American industrial corporations.

See Index under Data Sources.
Address: 68 Bonhill Street, London, EC2A 4BU, UK.

most-favoured nation (MFN) clause. Clause in bilateral trade agreements which stipulates that any trade concession offered by either of the two countries to a third party should be automatically extended to the other. In practical terms this means a reduction in the number of tariffs and other trade restrictions.

See GENERAL AGREEMENT ON TARIFFS AND TRADE (GATT), and Index under Trade.

multicurrency bond. Also known as a multiple currency bond. This is normally a bond denominated in a 'basket' of currencies such as the SPECIAL DRAWING RIGHTS (SDRs) of the INTERNATIONAL MONETARY FUND (IMF) or, increasingly, the EUROPEAN CURRENCY UNIT (ECU). It was estimated in 1986 that ECU-denominated bonds amounted to US$13 billion. (*See* CURRENCY COCKTAIL.) The term may also refer to various arrangements in which a bond is denominated in one currency with specified options to convert it to one or more currencies on redemption, and/or for the lender to specify the currency in which interest is paid.

See Index under Financial and Risk Management.

Multifibre Arrangement (MFA). An international agreement governing world trade in textiles and clothing. The agreement allocates total export QUOTAS for each producing country and sets its export quota to each importing country. The Agreement is organized under the aegis of the GENERAL AGREEMENT ON TARIFFS AND TRADE (GATT), even though the objectives of GATT are to liberalize trade, not restrict it. The original reason for this international sanctioning of protectionism was to give the advanced countries time to adjust their industrial structures while allowing new suppliers from developing countries to gain access to the domestic markets of the advanced countries in an orderly manner of measured expansion.

The first arrangement was negotiated in 1974, but hopes for orderly expansion of exports from developing countries were

dashed because of the worldwide recession which immediately followed. Instead, the renewed agreements of 1978 and 1982 formulated even tougher access rules which prejudiced the exports of a by then growing number of Third World suppliers. The fourth Agreement, reached in 1986, offers slightly higher growth targets for the poorest of the developing countries, but at the same time widens the coverage of the MFA to include, besides cotton, wool and manmade fibres, sisal, jute and ramie.

See Index under Trade.

multilateral netting. *See* NETTING.

multinational corporation/enterprise. The continually changing scope, organizational form and legal patterns of ownership of the multinational enterprise pose ever recurring definitional problems. Over the past 20 years, as different characteristics of companies operating internationally have attracted attention, the concept of the multinational enterprise has been variously redefined, and new concepts have been invented to give expression to perceived evolutionary developments in international corporate behaviour.

Although the terms 'international corporation' and 'multinational corporation' were used interchangeably in the 1960s, the term 'international corporation' was probably the more commonly used. Most definitions of the international corporation at that time stressed a feature which is regarded today as one particular evolutionary stage in international corporate expansion. This was the *national* character of the firm which, while operating extranationally, still insisted upon the primacy of the methods it used at home, and even of the laws of the home country. Such international firms typically would have strategic interest and expertise in an *INTERNATIONAL DIVISION*, but the functional expertise remained with the domestic divisions and with domestically-oriented staff departments. Control thus remained highly centralized and decisions had a heavy national bias. Home country nationals filled key positions overseas in what were for the most part wholly owned subsidiaries. The character of the international corporation corresponded to what Perlmutter (1969) has called the 'ethnocentric' phase in the evolution of multinational enterprise (see ETHNOCENTRIC).

The use of the term 'multinational corporation' as distinct from 'international corporation' seems to have become more popular since the early 1970s. By that time the typical pattern of international corporate activity involved a more complex, differentiated and arguably a more decentralized organizational structure: that of the multiproduct company with a product group organization for both home and foreign operations (see DIVISION). This worldwide multiproduct, multidivisional structure offered more scope to make decisions which were less nationally biased, to allow foreign subsidiaries to be managed by local managers and even to accommodate local equity participation and other forms of cross-border co-operation such as INTERNATIONAL SUBCONTRACTING and minority affiliation.

Definitions of the multinational enterprise of that period stressed the emerging dominant characteristic of a company or 'group' controlling many corporations of various nationalities, the emphasis being on a common strategy and a shared pool of financial and other resources rather than on legal ownership of the affiliated companies. Indeed, in its Guidelines for Multinational Enterprises (1976), the ORGANIZATION FOR ECONOMIC CO-OPERATION AND DEVELOPMENT (OECD) abandoned the search for a precise legal definition altogether:

'A precise legal definition of multinational enterprises is not required for the purposes of the Guidelines. These usually comprise companies or other entities whose ownership is private, state or mixed, established in different countries and so linked that one or more of them may be able to exercise a significant influence over the activities of others and, in particular, to share knowledge and resources with the others. The degree of autonomy of each entity in relation to the others varies widely from one multinational enterprise to another, depending on the nature of the links between such entities and the fields of activity concerned.'

The multinational character of the group was so important for some writers that they saw a certain amount of geographical spread as an essential part of their definition, excluding 'a parent with a stake in only a country or two outside its home base'. As an empirical if not logical corollary, size became an equally important criterion for inclusion: 'Size is important as well: a cluster of this sort with less than $100 million of sales rarely merits much attention', wrote Raymond Vernon (1971, p. 4) whose work with the Harvard project on American multinational enterprises probably contributed most to making the concept of 'multinational enterprise', with its connotation of size and many nationalities, a household word.

Others took a more literal view, defining a multinational as an enterprise with productive facilities in at least two countries. This view was shared by the UN Group of Eminent Persons in their report, *The Impact of Multinational Corporations on Development and on International Relations*:

'Multinational corporations are enterprises which own or control production or service facilities outside the country in which they are based. Such enterprises are not always incorporated or private; they can also be co-operatives or state-owned entities' (see UNECOSOC, *Transnational Corporations in World Development, a Re-examination*, 1978 p.158).

Similarly, the 1973 Guidelines of the

European Community (EC) state that a multinational undertaking is an undertaking with production facilities in at least two countries.

One characteristic of the multinational enterprise which has surfaced in all definitions is that the multinational is an undertaking which owns or controls 'productive' or 'service' facilities in more than one country, thus excluding mere exporters, even exporters with established sales subsidiaries abroad, as it does mere licensers of technology.

The combination of the increasingly multinational character of worldwide enterprises and the pervasive common strategy of their operations, has led many writers to try and invent a novel concept that would capture both these characteristics and stress the extent to which multinational corporations have 'outgrown' the nation state, including the home nation from which it sprang. 'Supra-national firms', 'global corporation', 'cosmocorp' and TRANSNATIONAL CORPORATION have all been proposed to describe a centrally organized structure of multinational economic activity which is geared to the maximization of profits on a global basis and which is beyond the effective reach of the national policies of any one country.

As was the case with the evolution from the 'ethnocentric' to the 'polycentric' multinational corporation, the present search for a new concept reflects real and novel tendencies in the evolution of multinational enterprise. These new tendencies are centralizing in their effects, giving the enterprise a GEOCENTRIC orientation when the perceived commercial advantages of worldwide integration of operations outweigh the political and social advantages of decentralization (*see* CENTRALIZATION).

The fact, however, that in recent years the term 'transnational corporation' has become widely used, often in preference to 'multinational corporation' does not completely follow on from these developments.

Instead it has been the United Nations' official adoption of this terminology that has had such a major impact. The Group of Eminent Persons' Report mentioned above, while giving a definition of multinational corporations, expressed a preference for the word 'transnational' because it was felt that it would convey better the notion that such firms operate from their home bases across national borders and are not set up and do not operate jointly under the auspices of more than one nation state. That is to say, they illustrate the opposite of certain joint state-owned companies of the ANDEAN PACT COUNTRIES in Latin America. Thus, in 1974, the United Nations' Commission on *Trans*national Corporations was set up. In the course of its work on the UN DRAFT CODE OF CONDUCT ON TRANSNATIONAL CORPORATIONS the Commission, after many years of deliberation, has now finally come up with an agreed definition of what a transnational corporation is (*see under* TRANSNATIONAL CORPORATION).

Finally, a word about the tail end of the concept. In the literature, one finds the words 'corporation', 'enterprise', 'company', and 'firm' used interchangeably and indiscriminately, although some writers will try to qualify their choice. 'Corporation' and 'company' are effectively interchangeable. Historically, the former has tended to be a US term and the latter British. The term 'enterprise' is sometimes preferred in order to underline the fact that the precise legal form (that is, whether the company is incorporated or not) is of no significance, and to ensure that the definition includes private-owned and state-owned as well as public companies. Others prefer the term 'corporation' because they wish to reserve the concept of transnational or multinational corporation for enterprises originating in the private sector of market economies. Strictly speaking, 'firm' is broader than 'corporation' or 'company' since it includes partnerships too (*see* INTERNATIONAL ACCOUNTING FIRMS), but since these entities are rarely linked with the term 'multinational' the distinction is unimportant in practice.

See Index under Corporate Structure and Management and under Theoretical Issues.

Multinational Monitor. Bimonthly magazine published by the Corporate Accountability Research Group. It includes analytical reports on developments in the global economy, the activities of multinational companies and up-to-date news and information on such issues as plant closures, violations of union rights, and health and environmental issues.

See Index under Data Sources.

Address: PO Box 19405, Washington DC 20036, USA.

multiprocessing. Pattern of international production in which different components of a product are produced by affiliates of a parent company located in several different countries, and then assembled in yet another country or countries. Multiprocessing forms the basis for the use and the manipulation of TRANSFER PRICES.

See Index under Corporate Structure and Management.

N

national contact point. As part of the establishment of follow-up procedures for their Guidelines on Multinational Enterprises, the OECD has encouraged the member countries to set up, normally within their respective Ministries for Trade and Industry, an office which would deal with promotion of the guidelines and encourage their practical application by providing facilities for handling enquiries and for discussions with the parties concerned on matters relating to them. The UK national contact point is housed in the International Trade Policy Division of the Department of Trade and Industry.

See DECLARATION AND DECISIONS ON INTERNATIONAL INVESTMENT AND MULTINATIONAL ENTERPRISES (OECD), and Index under International Co-operation and under Dispute and Settlement.

national registry of technology. A national regulatory body found in many Latin American countries. It monitors foreign technology contracts and ensures that contractual provisions work in favour of licensees as far as possible.

See Index under Regulation and Tax.

national treatment. A rule of international economic law normally embodied in commercial treaties. It defines a basic standard of treatment accorded to aliens. The national treatment standard stipulates that the treatment of aliens within the territories of a given state should be upon terms no less favourable than the treatment accorded there in similar situations to subjects of the state, their companies, products, vessels, or other possessions.

The national treatment principle was adopted in a multilateral agreement by the Organization for Economic Co-operation and Development (OECD) member countries in 1976 as one of three instruments for the treatment of international investment. The other two instruments adopted at the time were the Guidelines for Multinational Enterprises and the Incentives/Disincentives Instrument (*see* DECLARATION AND DECISIONS ON INTERNATIONAL INVESTMENT AND MULTINATIONAL ENTERPRISES).

The National Treatment Instrument obliges the member countries to treat enterprises operating in their territory and controlled by nationals of another member country no less favourably than domestic enterprises in similar situations. Member countries also agreed to notify the Organization of all government measures constituting exceptions to national treatment.

The national treatment principle has important consequences in the areas of fiscal obligations, government aids and subsidies, access to local bank credits and capital expansion of foreign affiliates through further investment activities.

Since its adoption, and because of the need to improve the 'transparency' of member countries' existing policies and measures relating to national treatment, the OECD has had to clarify the scope and coverage of the National Treatment Instrument further. In particular, it has now been agreed that the Instrument applies only to foreign investments already in existence, including additional investments by already established local SUBSIDIARIES, but not to new INWARD INVESTMENTS and additional investments by an overseas parent company.

There are indications that the national treatment principle is being adopted more widely in negotiations on international codes of conduct.

See UNITED NATIONS DRAFT CODE OF CONDUCT ON TRANSNATIONAL CORPORATIONS; CODES OF CONDUCT, and Index under International Co-operation and under Dispute and Settlement.

nationalization. As with EXPROPRIATION, a term with which it is often interchangeably used, nationalization involves the acquisition by the State of private property out of public necessity and for public use. International law recognizes the right of a state to nationalize foreign-owned property only if it is in the public interest and if compensation is paid.

The term 'nationalization' has in recent times become the more commonly used term because it permits the contrast with INDIGENIZATION, which may also involve a process of expropriation.

See CHARTER OF ECONOMIC RIGHTS AND DUTIES OF STATES, and Index under Dispute and Settlement.

negotiated price system. In order to be able to bargain over the distribution of future profits which the multinational corporation will make in its natural resource sector, host governments must find a formula for computing the value of the commodities such corporations produce. The negotiated price system is one such formula. The value of the product is assessed on the basis of the prices negotiated between the company and long-term contractual buyers.

See also REALIZED PRICE SYSTEM; REFERENCE PRICE SYSTEM; FAIR MARKET VALUE SYSTEM; TRANSFER PRICE, and Index under Regulation and Tax.

neo-classical trade theory. *See* HECKSCHER – OHLIN THEOREM.

neo-factor trade theory. A modification of the neo-classical theory of trade to give it greater relevance in view of the phenomenon of the international firm. Where the HECKSCHER–OHLIN THEOREM had embraced only two factors of production (capital and labour), neo-factor theories include other location specific endowments, notably natural resources, and they differentiate between different 'quality of labour' inputs. These are on the one hand 'human capital' such as managerial, professional and highly skilled labour, and unskilled labour on the other.

See Index under Theoretical Issues.

neo-imperialism. The economic exploitation of poor countries by rich countries without direct military intervention or formal state control. The term 'neo-imperialism' has often been used by writers in the Marxist tradition to describe a situation in which the resource sector of developing countries is controlled even after political independence by large multinationals from the advanced countries. Through this control, the interests of the multinational's home country may be furthered. Another term used to describe the same phenomenon is 'informal imperialism'.

See IMPERIALISM; DEPENDENCY; POST-IMPERIALISM; ULTRA-IMPERIALISM; INTER-IMPERIALIST COMPETITION; SUPER-IMPERIALISM, and Index under Theoretical Issues.

neo-technology trade theory. Like NEO-FACTOR TRADE THEORY, neo-technology trade theory is an attempt to modify neo-classical theories of trade to account for the phenomenon of international direct investment. By differentiating between capital and technology the theory introduces new explanatory variables for international trade flows, which focus not on the specific resource endowments of countries, but rather on the exclusive possession of certain assets (such as patented technology) by enterprises.

See Index under Theoretical Issues.

net exchange position. A term sometimes used to describe the net holding of, or liability in, a currency.

netting. Frequently the affiliate of a multinational will owe debts to an affiliate in a different country (*see* AFFILIATE COMPANY). The settlement of such debts can incur expensive TRANSACTION COSTS. If however the second affiliate also owes money to the first, the two debts can be 'netted' off, thus avoiding such costs.

In addition to this bilateral netting, more complex netting can be managed by a central treasury which integrates the information on the whole web of such intracorporate debts, and issues instructions on netting the debts of all the affiliates as far as possible. It has been argued that the ability to net in this way, with its associated cost savings, constitutes an advantage of the multinational over its exporting or importing domestic competitor. Some countries, notably Japan and Italy, limit or prohibit netting.

See also LEADING AND LAGGING, and Index under Financial and Risk Management.

new international division of labour. An expression current since the mid-1970s which refers to a process through which industrial production is relocated from the traditional centres of world industrial activity to newly emerging centres. These new centres are located in Southern Europe, parts of Latin America, parts of Southeast Asia, and even in some parts of Eastern Europe (*see* NEWLY INDUSTRIALIZING COUNTRIES). The term is however most commonly associated with the participation of newly industrializing countries from the developing world in global industrial pro-

duction and trade. This is seen to contrast with the 'old' international division of labour in which such countries essentially merely figured as suppliers of primary products, markets, and occasionally as providers of cheap labour. There is substantial controversy in the academic literature about the degree to which industrial production has been moved to new sites, and the extent to which new centres of industrial production also become new centres of independent capital accumulation. In the view of many, the new international division of labour is simply another expression for the globalization process of industrial production under the aegis of multinational companies. As a part of this process, certain developing countries are increasingly integrated as sites for world market competitive manufacturing production. Such transnational integration is thought to hinder rather than advance the potential of these countries for independent industrial development.

See also FREE TRADE ZONE (FTZ); SPLIT-SITE PRODUCTION; U-TURN INVESTMENT, and Index under Trade and under Theoretical Issues.

New International Economic Order (NIEO). At its sixth special session (the first ever to be held exclusively on economic issues) the United Nations General Assembly adopted without a vote a Declaration on the Establishment of a New International Economic Order, and a companion Program of Action.

The Declaration and the Program were the culmination both of the evolution of THIRD WORLD solidarity in international organizational fora, and of the expression of that solidarity in ideological terms. The concept of a new international economic order arose out of the Third World view of the world economy. This view argues that the colonially imposed 'old' international division of labour coupled with the free –

that is, unregulated – operations of the world markets systematically disadvantages the poorer, ex-colonial countries of Africa, Asia and Latin America.

The demand for a new international economic order therefore rests on an appeal to the advanced countries to redress the inequities in world economic arrangements by intervening, politically and bureaucratically, in the world's free market system.

The Declaration and the Program were simply a minimal draft and have been expanded, detailed and further negotiated in numerous international conferences and global negotiations following the adoption of the Declaration in 1974. The term 'New International Economic Order' has thus come to refer to the totality of demands for GLOBAL REFORMS made since that time.

The demands deal with six areas: trade, industrialization, international finance, food and agriculture, science and technology, and co-operation amongst the Third World countries themselves. For example, in the field of trade, index-linking and price stabilization measures have been proposed to help Third World countries improve their earnings from unprocessed export commodities. In the field of industrialization, the demands hinge on preferential access for manufactured goods from the Third World to the domestic markets of the advanced countries. In respect of science and technology, calls have been made for a legally binding code to regulate the conduct of multinational companies, and for a review and a revision of the international PATENT system (*see* INTERNATIONAL CONVENTION FOR THE PROTECTION OF INDUSTRIAL PROPERTY).

Ten years after the NIEO Declaration and many rounds of global negotiations later, few changes in the world economy can be attributed to these demands and negotiations. Where progress has been made, such as in the rapid industrialization of a handful of NEWLY INDUSTRIALIZING COUNTRIES, this progress owes more to the free restructuring of the world economy during the crisis of the 1970s than to any globally planned and managed reform.

See also NEW INTERNATIONAL DIVISION OF LABOUR; CHARTER OF ECONOMIC RIGHTS AND DUTIES OF STATES; CODES OF CONDUCT; and Index under International Co-operation.

newly industrializing countries (NIC). This label came into vogue during the recessionary years of the 1970s, when, as a consequence of a general restructuring of world markets and world industrial production, the old industrial centres of Europe and North America experienced a rapid import penetration from relatively new suppliers including Japan, Eastern Europe, Southern Europe and some Third World countries. By 1977 all these 'new' sources together accounted for 50 per cent of US and European Community (EC) imports of non-chemical manufactures, while US – EC trade itself accounted for just 20 per cent of each import market. Of these new sources the import penetration by Japanese manufactured products has been by far the most significant in volume (Bradford, 1982).

Nevertheless, the official classifications of newly industrializing countries tend to exclude Japan from their lists. They also specify varying criteria for inclusion, and the number and kinds of countries included consequently differs from definition to definition.

The OECD has a top list of 10 NICs and a second list of another 13, selected on the basis of 3 criteria: rapid penetration of the world market of manufactures, a rising share of industrial employment and an increase in real per capita GDP in relation to the more advanced countries. Its top list of 10 is made up of Singapore, South Korea, Hong Kong, Taiwan, Brazil, Mexico, Spain, Portugal, Yugoslavia and Greece (*see* Organization for Economic Co-operation and Development, 1979). The WORLD BANK, on the other hand, restricting itself to defining as newly industrializing countries where manufacturing accounts for 20 per cent of total GDP, has come up with a list of 16 'semi-industrialized' countries. To the OECD's 10 countries it adds Colombia, Egypt, the Philippines, Turkey, Argentina and Israel (World Bank, 1979).

Britain's Foreign and Commonwealth Office uses an even wider list, which includes Israel and Malta from the Mediterranean, and Poland, Romania and Hungary from Eastern Europe (Foreign and Commonwealth Office, 1979).

The inconsistency of the classification practice is confusing because, throughout these official documents, source data are presented referring to the NICs as a group, often without reference to the original selection of countries.

Newly industrializing countries, especially those from the Third World, are generally thought to owe their success in improving their share of world industrial production and trade to their OPEN DOOR policies *vis-à-vis* foreign investment and trade. Their vigorous incentive policies attract foreign direct investment in manufacturing industry, and these are combined with low wages and little if any restrictive legislation in the areas of industrial relations, environmental protection, or economic protectionism. This has made them a preferred location for so-called SPLIT-SITE production by multinational manufacturers. Many large industrial corporations have in the past two decades found it profitable to relocate the more labour-intensive parts of their industrial production in the newly industrializing countries. It could be argued that well over half of these countries' manufacturing exports to the advanced countries originate in firms controlled by multinational corporations.

See Index under Development Policy.

NIEO. *See* NEW INTERNATIONAL ECONOMIC ORDER.

nominal exchange rate. The visible exchange rate between two currencies as measured by the current values of the currencies, and quoted in the foreign exchange markets. This is contrasted with the REAL EXCHANGE RATE.

non-discrimination rule. Generally accepted principle in international law which holds that persons residing within the territory of a foreign state are entitled to the same protection of their person and property as afforded by the local law to the nationals of that state (*see also* NATIONAL TREATMENT).

In the early years of EXPROPRIATION of foreign property by newly emerging countries, the offended parties often invoked the non-discrimination rule.

See also CALVO CLAUSE, and Index under Dispute and Settlement.

non-tariff barrier. Indirect government measure to protect the domestic market against competitive imports and to assist domestic producers in export expansion. The more important categories of such measures are: government subsidies to domestic producers; various forms of taxation in addition to customs duties such as excise and processing taxes; national and local authority procurement policies; and a vast array of technical regulations imposing safety, health, and quality control standards which are sometimes deliberately formulated to make it difficult for foreign producers to comply with the regulations. Last but not least, the pressure on exporting countries to apply VOLUNTARY EXPORT RESTRAINTS is also an important variant of non-tariff measures.

Non-tariff barriers have become increasingly common amongst the industrialized countries, all of whom subscribe to the GENERAL AGREEMENT ON TARIFFS AND TRADE (GATT). Indeed, while the GATT rules have had some success in liberalizing world trade by lowering tariff barriers and by ensuring that where such barriers exist they should apply on a non-discriminatory basis (*see* MOST FAVOURED NATION (MFN) CLAUSE) non-tariff barriers have steadily increased. Non-tariff barriers are difficult for organizations like GATT to detect and police, especially when the barrier can legitimately be claimed to be the unintentional result of a policy not directly related to trade, such as maintaining domestic health and safety standards, or supporting regional development programmes. (*See also* TARIFF.)

It is sometimes argued that non-tariff barriers give a competitive edge to multinational companies and discriminate against national exporters. Because of their size, their institutional sophistication, and their product development, multinational companies are typically better placed to deal with complexity and a variety of requirements than relatively small-scale exporting entities, especially those from developing countries.

See Index under Trade.

Northwest Transnationals Project. A critical study and campaign group whose objectives include the facilitation of international links between workers at shopfloor or workplace level. It links the domestic questions which trade unionists face with international issues, and encourages trade union education stressing the international perspective. It also produces company profiles on particular transnational companies in the UK, and publishes the bimonthly *International Labour Reports*.

See Index under Data Sources.

Address: 2/4 Oxford Road, Manchester M13 9NS, UK.

Nottebohm case. A celebrated case of nationality in relation to diplomatic protection brought before the INTERNATIONAL COURT OF JUSTICE (ICJ) in 1955. Nottebohm was a German citizen who had applied for, and obtained, Liechtenstein nationality in addition to his German nationality. When Guatemala entered the war with Germany in 1943, Nottebohm's assets in that country were seized under Guatemalan law. The state of Liechtenstein claimed the restitution of the confiscated property and damages for the deterioration of the property on Nottebohm's behalf. The Court established the absence of a 'genuine connection' and a 'real and effective' nationality test which precluded Liechtenstein from extending its protection to Nottebohm, and hence the Court held its claim for compensation after CONFISCATION to be inadmissible (*see* EXPROPRIATION).

The Nottebohm case is considered an important milestone in the international law of foreign property because it affirms that any exercise of the right of diplomatic protection is a serious international act which must be justified on cogent legal and factual grounds. States claiming such a right must establish a genuine and substantial link with the individual whose claims they seek to assert. Without this requirement there is a danger that states may abuse the right to determine who are their nationals entitled to protection abroad.

See also BARCELONA TRACTION CASE, and Index under Dispute and Settlement.

O

obsolescing bargain. A term coined by Raymond Vernon (1977) to describe the development of bargaining relations between host countries and foreign companies in the natural resource sector. Initially, before an investment is made, the risk and uncertainty associated with the investment is high because production costs are still unclear and markets need to be established. Bargaining power rests with the company, which needs to be induced to invest by an agreement which promises handsome returns if the project proves successful.

But once the investment is made and the project is properly established, the bargaining power tilts in favour of the host country. This is partly a result of the dissipation of risk and uncertainty, and partly because of a kind of 'hostage' effect: the company cannot credibly threaten to withdraw once its investment has been sunk. This offers the host countries the possibility of effective renegotiation of the contracts in their favour to include higher taxes, local processing, joint marketing, more employment of nationals, joint management and so on.

See Index under Theoretical Issues.

OECD. *See* ORGANIZATION FOR ECONOMIC CO-OPERATION AND DEVELOPMENT.

OECD Guidelines on Multinational Enterprises. *See under* DECLARATION AND DECISIONS ON INTERNATIONAL INVESTMENT AND MULTINATIONAL ENTERPRISES.

Office of Foreign Direct Investment. *See* FOREIGN DIRECT INVESTMENT PROGRAM.

offsets. A term used in a wide variety of international trade and investment contracts. It refers to the stipulation by the purchaser in such contracts that the monetary value of the contract must be 'offset' in full or in part by the contractor through a COUNTER PURCHASE or BUY BACK DEAL; or through investment performance which will guarantee increased export levels; or through the purchase of some inputs from domestic suppliers (*see* BACKWARD LINKAGE).

The term is used mainly in the US, where the government – while nominally an adversary of COUNTERTRADE – has in fact operated a sizeable 'offset' programme in aerospace and other defence-related industries since the early 1950s. Its offset programme involves the stipulation to US multinationals under contract to the US Defense Department to purchase goods from overseas customers. The programme has been justified on the grounds that it gives allies of the United States a capacity for self-defence and helps create a multinational defence force.

See Index under Trade and under Technology Transfer.

offshore assembly. The joining together, in an overseas SUBSIDIARY or AFFILIATE COMPANY of mechanically linked prefabricated components of a product. Since the assembly stage of production typically involves low-skill manual tasks, such assembly is frequently a favourite candidate for industrial relocation to low income countries.

See COMPLETELY KNOCKED DOWN (CKD); FREE TRADE ZONE (FTZ), and Index under Corporate Structure and Management.

offshore finance subsidiary. A subsidiary of a multinational that is formed, usually in a

165

TAX HAVEN, to raise funds from foreign lenders, normally using such funds to finance foreign operations. The dealings of these affiliates have been aided by the development of markets in EUROCURRENCIES and EUROBONDS, and they in turn have fostered these markets. A principal advantage of using an offshore finance subsidiary is that it avoids the WITHHOLDING TAX that would be levied under the tax laws of many countries on the interest payable to foreign lenders if the parent company raised the bond directly.

See Index under Financial and Risk Management.

offshore financial centre. An international financial market in which foreign borrowers and foreign lenders are brought together. The world's principal financial markets deal in all four possible configurations of foreign and domestic lending: domestic borrowing from domestic lenders, domestic borrowing from foreign lenders, foreign borrowing from domestic lenders, and foreign borrowing from foreign lenders. An offshore financial centre deals only with foreign borrowing from foreign lenders. Examples include the Bahamas, Bahrain, Hong Kong, Luxembourg, the Netherlands Antilles and Singapore.

See Index under Financial and Risk Management.

offshore market. The transactions between foreign borrowers and lenders conducted in an OFFSHORE FINANCIAL CENTRE.

Oklahoma letter. *See* MONKEY LETTER.

oligopoly. The domination of a market by a few large firms surrounded by smaller firms who fill various niches, often in specialized production, bespoke work, distribution and so on.

In its ideal form, oligopolistic competition should take the form of a price war,

the development of newer methods of production and the invention of new commodities. If oligopolists in this way were to keep each other on their toes, oligopoly could be a most progressive form of industrial structure. Instead, oligopoly is unstable. More often than not it lapses into monopolistic competition (*see* MONOPOLY) when the giant firms prefer to avoid ruinous competition and engage in various forms of tacit collusion (*see* CARTEL) allowing each other a more or less regular share of the market and a level of return that they regard as adequate for themselves. As a consequence, oligopolistic competition often takes the form of such non-price competition as advertising and the term becomes practically indistinguishable from monopolistic competition.

It is sometimes argued – particularly by writers in the Marxist tradition – that restrictions on enlarging shares in the domestic market, coupled with the monopolistic profits obtained there, drive the giant firms to invest abroad. They are forced to seek new market outlets and to compete with one another in securing new sources of raw materials. And empiricial evidence does indeed suggest that the larger part of FOREIGN DIRECT INVESTMENT (FDI) springs from large firms sharing an oligopolistic industry structure in their home markets.

See also ANTI-TRUST LEGISLATION; OLIGOPOLY MODEL, and Index under Industry Structure and under Theoretical Issues.

oligopoly model. An influential theory of FOREIGN DIRECT INVESTMENT (FDI), first developed by Stephen Hymer in a doctoral thesis in 1960, which was belatedly published in 1976 (Hymer, 1976). In the meantime, the theory had become a dominant approach to the subject.

The essence of Hymer's approach was that oligopolistic market structures (*see* OLIGOPOLY) set the conditions for foreign expansion. Large firms which dominate their domestic markets are characterized by the ownership of specific assets unique to the firm which can be transferred at a relatively low cost within the organization but which cannot be easily acquired by any other domestic or foreign companies because markets for these assets are either imperfect or absent. This allows the firm owning the assets to exercise monopoly power at home and to exploit its advantage abroad by internalizing the BARRIERS TO ENTRY which exist for other firms (*see* INTERNALIZATION).

The identification and evaluation of these OWNERSHIP SPECIFIC ADVANTAGES which are at the same time barriers to the entry of other firms commanded much of the attention of economists in the late 1960's and early 1970's. They typically include economies of scale, technological expertise in product and process development, a successfully differentiated product and managerial and marketing skills.

Because Hymer was the first to try and explain foreign direct investment from a perspective of traditional industrial organization theory, his oligopoly model is also often referred to as the 'industrial organization theory' of foreign direct investment or the 'industrial economics' approach. It acquired a new and important dimension in Vernon's PRODUCT CYCLE THEORY.

See Index under Theoretical Issues.

oligopoly reaction. *See* FOLLOW THE LEADER THEORY.

OPEC. *See* ORGANIZATION OF PETROLEUM EXPORTING COUNTRIES.

open door policies. National economic policies on foreign trade and capital movements which involve a minimum of protection and regulation, permitting the relatively free transfer of goods, services and capital across borders. Open door policies are the opposite of AUTARCHY in international economic relations.

See Index under Development Policy.

OPIC. *See* OVERSEAS PRIVATE INVESTMENT CORPORATION.

option. The right to trade in a security at or before a specified date and at a specified price. A *call* option is a right to buy a security at the agreed price, a *put* option is a right to sell at an agreed price, a *European* option is exercisable only on the date agreed, and an *American* option can be exercised on or before that date. The names refer only to the terms of the option, not the place where it is traded.

Although we tend to think of options as denoting securities more generally, options in foreign currencies are now heavily traded. The multinational's corporate treasurer can insure against the adverse movement of a currency in which the company has future obligations by taking out an option in that currency. This is done by paying a premium to the seller or 'writer' of an option who will then be obliged to provide the agreed amount of the currency concerned at the agreed price at the exercise date if asked to do so. This premium is in effect an insurance premium against loss if the currency should move.

The growth of options can be traced to the opening of the Chicago Board Options Exchange in 1973 – by the 1980s it was the world's second largest securities market – and the 1982 commencement of business in currency options by the Philadelphia Stock Exchange. At present currency options are traded on the Chicago, Montreal, Amsterdam and Sydney stock exchanges as well as the London Stock Exchange and the London International Financial Futures Market.

See Index under Financial and Risk Management.

Organization for Economic Co-operation

and Development (OECD). An international organization set up by Convention in 1960 (with effect from 1961) to succeed the Organization for European Economic Co-operation (OEEC) of 1948. The OEEC had been established to foster common action amongst the European countries receiving American post-war recovery aid under the so-called Marshall Plan. The reconstituted OECD of 1960 included the USA and Canada as member countries, and subsequently the remaining advanced market economies of the world (Japan, Australia, New Zealand) were invited to join. Membership of the Organization today totals 24 countries.

The Organization's chief aims as set out in Article 1 of the Convention are to promote polices designed (1) to achieve the highest sustainable economic growth and employment and a rising standard of living in member countries, while maintaining financial stability, and thus to contribute to the development of the world economy; (2) to contribute to sound economic expansion in member as well as non-member countries in the process of economic development; and (3) to contribute to the expansion of world trade on a multilateral, non-discriminatory basis in accordance with international obligations.

The formulation of these aims reveals the Organization's underlying economic philosophy, namely that the continued economic growth of the advanced countries, coupled with trade liberalization and financial stability, will have an expansionary effect on the world economy and contribute to the economic development of the less developed countries.

The Organization is primarily a body of consultation, co-ordination and joint policy formulation among member countries. It represents a major effort on the part of the advanced Western nations to harmonize their internal and their foreign economic policies. But its legal personality falls short of that of for example the EUROPEAN COM-MUNITY (EC). Co-operation remains purely voluntary in character.

Apart from the Council, which meets about once a week, the Organization has an Executive Committee and such subsidiary bodies, working parties and committees, as it may deem necessary to set up in order to achieve the aims of the Organization. The most important of these from the point of view of multinational enterprise are the COMMITTEE ON INTERNATIONAL INVESTMENT AND MULTINATIONAL ENTERPRISES (IME COMMITTEE), the Development Assistance Committee, which co-ordinates aid programmes to developing countries and works towards enhancing the flow of resources to those countries, the Economic Policy Committee, which recommends policies to encourage economic expansion, the Trade Committee, which aims to resolve trade issues, and a Restrictive Business Practices Committee. The total number of specialized committees and working parties currently stands at over 200. Important decisions relevant to multinational enterprise which have been taken by the OECD are the CODE OF LIBERALIZATION OF CAPITAL MOVEMENTS (1960) and the DECLARATION AND DECISIONS ON INTERNATIONAL INVESTMENT AND MULTINATIONAL ENTERPRISES (1976).

In terms of international economic relations, the Organization is sometimes portrayed as a rich man's club: membership is by invitation and only after a unanimous decision. Within the framework of wider international organizations, such as the United Nations and its subsidary organizations, the OECD countries form a natural caucus group (*see* GROUP B COUNTRIES).

Although the efficacy of the OECD as a policy co-ordinating body is waning in view of the protracted economic recession of the 1970s, which has engendered conflicting national policies for dealing with economic stagnation (protectionism, diverging interest rates) the continued usefulness of the Organization as an information gathering and processing institution is not in doubt. Its regular surveys (such as *Economic Survey*, annually for each member country, and *Main Economic Indicators*, monthly), specialized reports and monographs, are widely respected as primary source material for academic research as well as for national policy making bodies.

See Index under International Co-operation.

Address: 2 rue André Pascal, 75775 Paris, France.

Organization of Petroleum Exporting Countries (OPEC). Historically the first example of a CARTEL of countries producing the same commodity, the Organization was set up in 1960 with the aim of co-ordinating and unifying the petroleum policies of member countries and the protection of their individual and collective interests. The formation of OPEC was prompted by the cuts in the posted price for crude oil imposed by the oil companies in the late 1950s, itself an example of cartel behaviour. The five founding countries were soon joined by another seven, all located in the THIRD WORLD.

In 1973 the Organization succeeded in co-ordinating international action by its members sufficiently to cause a quadrupling of oil prices. This in turn resulted in a massive transfer of resources from the developed to the less developed countries, both directly to the oil producing countries themselves, and indirectly to oil-importing Third World countries through the recycling of the capital surpluses of some OPEC member countries (so-called 'petrodollars') by the international banking system. It is in this period that the composition of the flow of resources from rich to poor countries changes from predominantly FOREIGN DIRECT INVESTMENT (FDI) to indirect investment or bank lending. This contributed substantially to the debt crisis of the 1980s. OPEC has also been successful in pursuing policies of NATIONALIZATION of oil extraction and in forcing the oil companies to relocate some of their refining activity in the petroleum-producing countries themselves.

Although membership of the Organization is open to any country which is a substantial net exporter of crude and which has fundamentally similar interests to those of member countries, the major exporters of the advanced countries have failed to join. It is this fact which has in part been responsible for the decline of OPEC's power in recent years.

See Index under International Co-operation.

Address: Obere Donaustrasse 93, 1020 Vienna, Austria.

outright forward rate. The exchange rate at which a currency may be bought or sold for future delivery. An 'outright' quotation is expressed directly (for example, US$1.50=£1); the alternative is a quotation expressed as a premium or discount from the spot rate.

outward investment. The outflow of capital investments from a particular domestic economy, or HOME country.

Overseas Private Investment Corporation (OPIC). An agency of the US government which aims to facilitate and mobilize the use of US private capital and expertise in the development of the developing countries through two programmes: the co-financing of projects sponsored by US investors, and the insuring of US private investment in developing countries against political risks, including the risk of EXPROPRIATION. OPIC, however, discriminates against enterprises which might have adverse effects on the domestic job market. Such discrimination is based on a case-by-case evaluation of the possible effect of the proposed project on the US balance of payments and employment.

See also AGENCY FOR INTERNATIONAL DEVELOPMENT (AID), and Index under Financial and Risk Management.

ownership specific advantages. Competitive advantages accruing to an enterprise and arising from its possession of intangible assets which are – at least for a period of time – exclusive or specific to the firm possessing them. Examples are TRADEMARKS and proprietary technology protected by PATENT legislation; production management and organizational and marketing systems; monopolistic and monopsonistic power; research and development capacity, and so on. In theories of international direct investment and trade, ownership specific advantages are thought to be a variable which positively affects a firm's involvement in foreign markets. They are distinguished from so-called LOCATION SPECIFIC ADVANTAGES, which are thought to be characteristics of the country or location receiving the investment.

See also PRODUCT CYCLE THEORY; APPROPRIABILITY THEORY; OLIGOPOLY MODEL, and Index under Theoretical Issues.

P

Pacific Studies Centre. A research and documentation centre with extensive documentation on AGRIBUSINESS, auto, chemical and electronics industries, particularly in Asia and the Pacific. As part of its Global Electronics Information Project it publishes the *Global Electronics Information Newsletter.*

See Index under Data Sources.
Address: Pacific Studies Centre, 867 West Dana St. 204 Mountain View, CA 94041, USA.

pacta sunt servanda. General rule of international law. Its literal meaning in Latin is that contracts are binding and should be observed. It is the principle which establishes the legal basis on which treaties constitute binding contracts between signatory states. The implication of this principle is that, in the absence of an international enforcement agency, each member of the international community has the responsibility to keep its agreements.

The principle of *pacta sunt servanda*, while in the first instance applicable to agreements between sovereign states, has frequently been invoked in disputes between multinational companies and the countries hosting their investments. Thus for example it has been argued that where a state has undertaken by an international (for example, BILATERAL INVESTMENT) treaty to protect foreign owned private investments against EXPROPRIATION or other forms of interference, a breach of such an undertaking will be an international tort. The home state of the multinational will demand restitution on behalf of its nationals, the owners of the company.

There is also a legal view which argues that the principle of *pacta sunt servanda* must also be applicable to a state's own contracts with aliens such as CONCESSION agreements between states and aliens. In disputes arising over the termination or mid-term revision of concession agreements, multinational companies have argued this view against that usually held by host states, that relations between it and private foreign parties are governed *not* by international but by domestic law (*see* CALVO CLAUSE). Sometimes, however, the applicability of the *pacta sunt servanda* rule is implicitly admitted by the offending states when they invoke another principle of international law, *CLAUSULA REBUS SIC STANTIBUS*, which sanctions the revision of agreements on the grounds of changing circumstances.

See also CONVENTION ON THE SETTLEMENT OF INVESTMENT DISPUTES BETWEEN STATES AND NATIONALS OF OTHER STATES, and Index under Dispute and Settlement.

parallel loan. Also sometimes referred to as a BACK TO BACK LOAN. It is a means whereby multinational companies can avoid restrictions on remittances of currency between countries. Two companies based in different countries each lend funds to the other's SUBSIDIARY in their own countries on an agreed basis. For instance, if the head office of a company in country A needs to transfer funds for expansion to its subsidiary in country B but is prevented by foreign exchange regulations from doing so, it may reach an agreement with a company in country B such that the second company lends the necessary funds to the subsidiary of the first, while at the same time the head office of the first in country A lends a similar amount to a subsidiary of the second. Each has lent money to the other in such a way that the foreign exchange markets are not used directly, and normally no governmental approval will be necessary for the transaction.

See also CURRENCY EXCHANGE AGREEMENT, and Index under Financial and Risk Management.

para-tariff barrier. *See* NON-TARIFF BARRIER.

parent company. The ultimate holding company of a group. The location of a multinational's parent is important because it governs the laws and taxes to which the company is subject.

See also HOLDING COMPANY, and Index under corporate structure and management.

parent guarantee. An undertaking by the PARENT COMPANY of a group to a bank lending to one or more of its foreign affiliates that it will honour specified or unspecified debts in the event of the affiliate's inability to pay. Such a guarantee is made necessary because under most countries' corporate law the nature of limited liability means that the liability of the parent (which is just a shareholder of the affiliate) is limited to the nominal value of the shares it owns in the affiliate.

See also MONKEY LETTER.

Paris Club. Common parlance name for the group of negotiators representing the advanced industrial countries in multilateral DEBT RESCHEDULING negotiations. The negotiations take place in Paris.

Paris Union. *See* INTERNATIONAL CONVENTION FOR THE PROTECTION OF INDUSTRIAL PROPERTY.

Parliamentarians' Code. *See* LANGE-GIBBONS CODE.

patent. An exclusive grant by a national government to an inventor, giving the right to exclude others from making, using or selling the invention in the domestic market for a specified number of years (17 in the US, and 20 in the UK).

The inventor may be an individual or a company and the patent applies to any new machine, design, process, composition, substance, or plant variety. Patents are not granted for improvements upon existing inventions.

The patent holder normally derives from the patent the associated rights to impose price, as well as output, quality and market restrictions on the invention. A patent holder may either work the patent himself or license another individual or firm to use the patent, imposing these restrictions on the licensee if he so wishes and if the buyer agrees. When the buyer resides in another country, it is essential that the foreign government recognizes and protects the patent rights. To this effect, various international unions have been established by multilateral treaties, and international organizations such as the INTERNATIONAL CONVENTION FOR THE PROTECTION OF INDUSTRIAL PROPERTY, the PATENT CO-OPERATION TREATY (PCT), and the EUROPEAN PATENT CONVENTION (EPC) exist to centralize the administration of such unions and the registration of international patent rights.

While patents are clearly a source of MONOPOLY power, they have generally been exempted from anti-monopoly or ANTITRUST LEGISLATION. But patent licenses can easily become the pretext for otherwise illegal restraints on trade. An example is 'patent suppression', when a local subsidiary of a multinational company registers a patent not with a view to working it locally but to prevent others from doing so, and in this way safeguard market access for the product via imports from the parent or another subsidiary of the parent located in another country.

In the advanced countries, where fairly developed national systems for monitoring illegal trade practices exist, the authorities are usually competent to judge whether particular restraints form a legitimate extension of basic patent rights or not. In the developing countries this is not always the case.

Patent rights represent a particular form of property rights, and have always been considered as the backbone of the development of capitalist enterprise. International patent rights are equally seen as an essential turnpike regulating, and hence contributing to, the vast expansion of international production and trade.

However, the extremely uneven distribution of patents between advanced and developing countries, with latter holding today only six per cent of the world total, has called into question the role of patents in the transfer of technology from rich to poor countries. Developing countries have become increasingly frustrated both with the constraining impact of international patents on the development of their own domestic markets and technological base, and with the punitive loss of foreign exchange arising from ROYALTIES, licensing fees, and other payments for proprietary knowhow. In the last decade these costs have mounted in inverse relation to the success with which developing countries have held down traditional profit remittances by foreign investors as a result of their policies of NATIONALIZATION and other forms of local participation in the ownership of foreign enterprises (*see* JOINT VENTURES).

To secure continued control over, and future earnings from, their divested overseas subsidiaries, multinational enterprises have typically codified their relationship with the overseas firm in detailed technical, service and LICENSING AGREEMENTS, often using their original patent rights as the lynchpin of an elaborate set of contractual obligations. As a precaution against future developments in the ECONOMIC NATIONALISM of host countries, it is now common practice for multinational enterprises to codify in licensing agreements even their relationship with wholly owned SUBSIDIARIES. It would therefore seem that with economic nationalism and legal decentralization of multinational companies, patents and international patent rights are becoming more important than ever.

International organizations, in particular the UNITED NATIONS CONFERENCE ON TRADE AND DEVELOPMENT (UNCTAD) are currently preparing draft codes for the Transfer of Technology. These pay particular attention to the use and abuse of patents.

See also TRANSFER OF TECHNOLOGY (TOT) CODE; TRADE SECRET; TRADEMARK; FRANCHISING, and Index under Technology Transfer.

Patent Co-operation Treaty. A patent application system, in force since 1978, which enables multinational companies to file a single application for PATENT searches among all participating nations. While the treaty does not protect patents, it is meant to speed up the process of application and preliminary examination in different countries.

See also INTERNATIONAL CONVENTION FOR THE PROTECTION OF INDUSTRIAL PROPERTY; EUROPEAN PATENT CONVENTION, and Index under International Co-operation.

patent pool. An accommodation between different firms dealing with patents of theirs which may be technically complementary or connected in a sequential production process. To secure access to the patents possessed by others, firms may decide to share some or all of their own. Such accommodation may also happen in the event of parallel research into a new invention which is still in the patent application stage. Although it is the task of the patent office to determine who has been first in discovery, it is not uncommon for companies to make this decision themselves. They may reach an agreement among themselves that each shall be licensed under the patent, and all but one of them will withdraw their patent applications. In such a case there is no controversy before the Patent Office and the patent automatically issues. While such patent licensing arrangements are theoretically preferable to pure MONOPOLY situations, they may contain provisions designed to restrict competition.

See ANTI-TRUST LEGISLATION; CROSS-LICENSING, and Index under Industry Structure.

patent revision. *See under* INTERNATIONAL CONVENTION FOR THE PROTECTION OF INDUSTRIAL PROPERTY.

Pease Bill. An international labour rights bill incorporated in US trade legislation since 1985, when Congress renewed the United States' membership of the GENERALIZED SYSTEM OF PREFERENCES (GSP), which it had joined in 1975.

The Bill declares any developing country ineligible for designation as a beneficiary of the generalized system of preferences if that country has not adopted laws which extend internationally recognized worker rights to its workers and is not enforcing those laws. The Bill defines internationally recognized worker rights as including the freedom of association, the right to organize and bargain collectively, a prohibition on the use of any form of forced or compulsory labour, the prohibition and elimination of discrimination in respect of employment and occupation, the establishment of a minimum age for the employment of children, and the delineation of acceptable conditions of work with respect to minimum wages, hours of work, and occupational safety and health.

While the passage of the Pease Bill came after intense lobbying and campaigning on the part of church and human rights groups, its success in Congress may also have resulted from domestic economic pressures, particularly from companies and unions whose trade is affected by the giving of GSP benefits.

See GENERALIZED SYSTEM OF REFERENCES, and Index under Regulation and Tax.

performance guarantee. Guarantee issued to the purchaser of a development project by a commercial bank in the country of the project's contractor. The provisions of the performance guarantee enable the purchaser of the project to invoke the guarantee should the contractor default on his obligations without having to obtain the contractor's concurrence, an arbitration decree, or an order form from a court of competent jurisdiction.

In a performance guarantee the coverage in the case of default is normally between 10 per cent and 15 per cent of the contract price. In the US it is customary for BONDING COMPANIES to issue a performance bond.

performance requirements. In an attempt to influence positively the impact of foreign investment projects on their economy and society, some developing countries, most notably in Latin America, have introduced comprehensive regulations governing the inflows of such investments. Such regulations require the foreign investor to 'perform' in certain prescribed ways.

Although performance requirements differ from country to country, certain common elements may be identified:

1. Directing investment projects to certain priority economic activities and to certain priority geographical areas;

2. Achieving more local ownership and control of foreign investments;

3. Achieving a given level of LOCAL VALUE ADDED over a certain period of time;

4. Requiring the introduction of local staff training programmes with a view to indigenizing the management staff over a period of time and phasing out foreign personnel;

5. Encouraging certain capital/labour ratios with a view to increasing the employment effect of the enterprise;

6. Requiring a given level of exports to improve the balance of payments position;

7. Regulating the repatriation of profits and encouraging the reinvestment of earnings.

In the developed countries, on the other hand, the imposition of performance requirements as a condition for AUTHORIZATION of inward foreign investment is rare. Performance requirements do, however, play an important role in qualifying inward foreign investors for host government incentives (such as financial grants, tax exemptions, and government contracts). This happens notwithstanding the declared commitment of the member countries of the ORGANIZATION FOR ECONOMIC CO-OPERATION AND DEVELOPMENT (OECD) to resist 'beggar thy neighbour' policies in relation to international capital (*see* DECLARATION AND DECISIONS ON INTERNATIONAL INVESTMENT AND MULTINATIONAL ENTERPRISES). Recent years have seen an increase in the use of both incentives and disincentives, inducements and performance criteria. In a sophisticated application of the carrot and stick approach, governments try on the one hand to attract inward foreign investors with a range of incentives, and on the other to use these same incentives as a means to channel such investments into desired economic and social directions. These performance requirements include location, employment, output, sales, and export criteria and sometimes transfer of technology, industrial relations, and environmental commitments (*see* OECD, 1983).

The European Commission has become increasingly concerned over the 'beggar thy neighbour' contest between the European Community (EC) Governments and it has started to enforce a legal clampdown on all state aids to investors which contravene the fair competition terms of Article 93 of the Treaty of Rome.

See Index under Development Policy.

petrodollar. The hard currency earned by the oil-exporting companies after the October 1973 oil price rise and left in investments in the developed world's financial markets rather than used to import goods into the countries concerned. Although some of this money has been held in dollar deposits in the USA, rather more has been invested in the EUROCURRENCY and EUROBOND markets.

See also ORGANIZATION OF PETROLEUM EXPORTING COUNTRIES (OPEC); EURODOLLAR; ASIADOLLAR.

phase-in policy. Another name for FADEOUT POLICY, viewed from the perspective of a government receiving foreign direct investment.

piggybacking. *See* CO-OPERATIVE EXPORTER.

political risk assessment. *See* COUNTRY RISK

ASSESSMENT.

polycentric. A term devised by Howard Perlmutter to describe a managerial attitude taken by certain kinds of multinational. The polycentric multinational has relatively low centralization of decision making at head office, permits standards of performance evaluation to be determined by local conditions, has a low extent of communication within the corporation, and identifies with the host country for each subsidiary. The other types of attitude defined by Perlmutter are ETHNOCENTRIC, GEOCENTRIC and REGIOCENTRIC.

See Index under Corporate Structure and Management and under Theoretical Issues.

populism. A general term covering a great variety of political movements from the Russian Narodnik groups and the American People's Party of the late 19th century, to the national socialist movements in Western Europe and the Peronist and other developmentalist ideologies in Latin America in the 20th century.

What these diverse movements have in common is a style of politics rather than a specific programme. Recognizable common elements of this style are the personal appeal of a leader to the 'people-as-a-whole'; the portrayal in emotional and moralistic, rather than intellectual, terms of a society divided between 'good but powerless' ordinary folk and the 'evil and all-powerful' forces that dominate the state; a belief in a conspiracy against the ordinary man in the street; and a rhetoric aimed at rapid (and usually remarkably successful) mobilization of all underprivileged groups regardless of class or social status.

In many less developed countries, but particularly in Latin America, populist movements have forged an alliance between a weak national bourgeoisie on the one hand, and workers and peasants on the other, against agrarian oligarchies and foreign capitalist interests. Such populism has often become the official state ideology and has combined with a developmentalist strategy which has tended to emphasize import substitutive industrialization and has included policies of NATIONALIZATION and other forms of domestic control over foreign capital.

See Index under Development Policy.

portage. One of the means by which banks can finance their corporate clients. It involves supplying funds through the purchase of ordinary shares, as opposed to the extension of a loan. While US bank regulation limits this method of financing to venture capital for small enterprises, many US banks use portage in the foreign countries in which they are established.

See EDGE ACT CORPORATION (EAC).

portfolio investment. The investment in a foreign asset where management control is not exercised. In this essential aspect it differs from FOREIGN DIRECT INVESTMENT (FDI). Although a company may hold a portfolio investment as a precursor to direct control, it has been argued that it is less efficient than FDI since the company loses such benefits as information sharing and the more general benefits of internalization (*see* INTERNALIZATION THEORY).

See Index under Corporate Structure and Management.

portfolio theory. A theoretical model which, it is claimed, aids the construction of the optimal portfolio of securities which should be held by an investor. It has been used both to analyse the desirability of holding shares in multinational corporations for investors, and as an attempted explanation of FOREIGN DIRECT INVESTMENT (FDI) by multinationals.

Modern portfolio theory (MPT) is based on the assumption that investor needs can be summarized within two parameters: the return expected to be earned on an investment and the risk of the investment as measured by the variance of the returns. Because investors are risk-averse, more risky securities provide higher yields. If the investor holds only one security the choice is therefore between high return, high risk and low return, low risk.

Since security prices do not move together exactly, it can be mathematically proved that they may be combined so as to give a return that is the weighted average return of the securities but at a risk that is less than their average. The logical outcome of this theory is the recommendation that investors should diversify their investments to such an extent that each should hold securities in exact proportion to the market as a whole (the 'market portfolio'). This can be achieved approximately through investing in unit trusts or mutual funds. Combining this holding of risky assets with either borrowing or lending at a risk-free rate will enable the investor to create an optimal portfolio that suits his or her own risk preference.

This diversification does not eliminate risk altogether. The risk remaining is that of the market portfolio, and is called SYSTEMATIC RISK, since it is the risk of the system as a whole.

The theory is relevant to international investment because securities markets in different countries do not move together. As a result, a further reduction in risk can be achieved by diversifying the holding of securities across national boundaries. MPT suggests that the individual investor should attempt to do this rather than any multinational corporation: however as there are frequently barriers to investing in the securities markets of foreign countries, this DIVERSIFICATION may only be possible for the individual by investing in domestic multinationals that themselves are benefiting from international diversification.

It has also been suggested (although not substantiated) that this advantage to international diversification might explain the internal diversification of multinationals. Since subsidiaries in different countries experience different risks, it is thought that multinationals should therefore wish to expand into a number of other countries.

See also DIVERSIFICATION, and Index under Theoretical Issues and under Financial and Risk Management.

possessions corporation. A favourable tax status that may be enjoyed by a US company that carries on business principally in a US possession. In essence, the qualifying requirements for this status are: that the company is a domestic US corporation; that it derives at least 80 per cent of its gross income from within a US possession; and that it derives at least 50 per cent of that gross income from active trading or business in the possession. The income must not be received within the US.

Possessions for this purpose include Guam, the Panama Canal zone, Puerto Rico, American Samoa and the Wake and Midway Islands. The US Virgin Islands are excluded.

See Index under Regulation and Tax.

post-imperialism. The conception, formulated by a school of Marxist thought, of the most recent and still nascent phase in the evolution of world capitalism. In this phase, according to the theory, relations of dominance and dependency between nations (the defining characteristic of IMPERIALISM) have been relegated to a secondary status. Instead, relations of capitalist domination and exploitation are conceptualized in terms of global class relations, which transcend national class structures.

Transnational enterprises are, it is claimed, integrating the world economy and in the process they create an international bourgeoisie alongside an exploited international proletariat. Nation states mediate in the process of exploitation, but no one state is a critical part of it. The members of the corporate international bourgeoisie are united by mutual interests which transcend those of the states whose passports they happen to carry. They no longer need the imperialist power of their home states to gain access to resources and markets in the peripheral areas of the world. Instead, they negotiate this access by professing to an ideology which separates the political from the economic sphere. This ideology, which is expressed in the DOCTRINE OF DOMICILE, holds that there is no innate antagonism between the global economic interests of the TNCs and the national economic aspirations of host or home countries. Transnational corporations are believed to transcend both: their subsidiaries are instructed to behave as 'good citizens' in any country where they do business. As good citizens they are thought to be able to observe national laws and regulations and accommodate national economic and social interests.

The corporate hegemonic world view which reduces the nation state – including the home nation – to a degree of irrelevancy, opens up domestic, social and economic opportunities that did not previously exist in the colonial and neo-colonial areas: the global profit orientation of the contemporary transnational firm, coupled with a growing indifference to its national roots, implies a continuous recalculation of optimal production and profit locations. This view implies that developing host countries, offering lower wage rates and competitive tax concessions, can achieve rapid industrialization and economic progress under the auspices of transnational capital.

To the extent that the corporate national bourgeoisies in developing countries are able to consolidate these advances through informed state action, including improved bargaining with TNCs in the national economic interests, the current international division of labour will not remain fixed forever. Although world capitalist development is uneven, some peripheral countries may one day attain metropolitan status and some present metropoles may decay to peripheral status without contravening the fundaments of the international order (Becker, 1984 and Sklar, 1976).

See also IMPERIALISM; SUPER-IMPERIALISM; ULTRA-IMPERIALISM; INTER-IMPERIALIST COMPETITION; NEO-IMPERIALISM, and Index under Theoretical Issues.

preproduction grant. Whereas traditional concession agreements tended to automatically link exploration rights with mining rights, in MODERNIZED CONCESSION AGREEMENTS the two tend to be separated. In a preproduction grant, preliminary prospecting or exploration rights are granted and the company is offered an exclusive option to negotiate a mining agreement in the event of successful exploration. The state undertakes to refrain from negotiating with any third party while serious negotiations proceed with the first party. A preproduction grant also carries the commitment to reimburse the mining company for its exploration expenses in the event of mining rights being granted to a third party.

See also CONCESSION; RISK SERVICE CONTRACT; PRODUCTION SHARING AGREEMENT, and Index under Technology Transfer.

product cycle theory. A theory of FOREIGN DIRECT INVESTMENT (FDI) closely connected with Vernon (1966) and Hirsch (1976). The theory appeared to explain the foreign expansion of US industrial corporations in the 1960s. It argued that because American firms operate in high-income and high-wage markets, they have a strong incentive to develop products for leisure and to save labour. New products are typically first introduced by large firms with extensive research programmes. If the product proves successful, output expands and cost per unit falls. The firm then begins to export.

At first, foreign markets for such goods are small and local competition is undeveloped, making exporting a preferred method for supplying foreign demand. However, as time passes and the technology of production stabilizes, it becomes easily imitable, both at home and abroad.

As foreign competition grows, foreign direct investment in productive facilities becomes necessary to defend a market already built up through export. It allows the firm to average overhead and R&D costs over larger production runs, thus giving it much-needed competitive strength against the formidable advantages at the disposal of local competitors who have local knowhow, no transportation costs, and who can lobby for domestic protective tariffs. In this theory of foreign direct investment, therefore, it is the OWNERSHIP SPECIFIC ADVANTAGES of the firm which are the principal determinants.

Studies of US corporate expansion carried out by Vernon and his colleagues at the Harvard Business School in the mid-sixties found overwhelming evidence in support of this theory. On the other hand it has been successfully argued by Franko (1976) and others that this model does not apply to the foreign expansion of European and Japanese multinationals, which have expanded overseas for diverse historical reasons and which have been propelled by quite dif-

ferent profit strategies and concerns.

Product cycle theory has not only been used to explain the shift from exporting to foreign production over the product's life-span. Put in the context of a world of nations at different levels of economic development and technological sophistication, it has also been used as an optimistic model of economic progress through the steady diffusion of technology from advanced to less advanced areas.

While product cycle analysis has proved a reasonably adequate tool for describing foreign expansion of US multinationals in the 1960s, its continuing applicability to foreign direct investment flows in the 1970s is seriously in doubt, as Vernon himself (1979) admits. Firstly, the model does not account for the recent trend in foreign investment, namely the location in low-income countries such as those of Southeast Asia of low-skill, labour-intensive processes or for the production or assembly of components and spare parts in a vertically-integrated multinational firm. Secondly, the model of planning products for one market before selling them abroad does not adequately describe the complex activity of market SEGMENTATION in different countries, which underlies much of present-day multinational corporate practices. And thirdly, the theoretical premise of the relationship between OLIGOPOLY in domestic markets and foreign expansion which had been observed in the sixties seems recently to have become weaker, as today smaller firms are increasing the amount of cross-border production facilities.

See also OLIGOPOLY MODEL; APPROPRIABILITY THEORY; INTERNALIZATION THEORY, and Index under Theoretical Issues.

product-in-hand contract. A variation on the typical TURNKEY CONTRACT which takes the responsibility of the contracting company beyond the delivery of the ready-to-operate plant into the stage of initial operations. This contract is meant to ensure that the design of the plant, its adaptation to domestic conditions and the training of local staff will result in the ability of the client to operate the plant independently. Also referred to as a 'turnkey-plus' contract.

See also MARKET-IN-HAND CONTRACT, and Index under Technology Transfer.

production sharing agreement. A relatively recent development in JOINT VENTURE arrangements between multinational corporations in the resource-based sector and the companies of the host country, normally state-owned ones. First developed in Indonesia in the 1960s, production sharing agreements are now widely in use in the petroleum sector and also from time to time in mining. In a production sharing agreement, the foreign company undertakes exploration and if the oil or mineral is found it undertakes production jointly with the host country's state-owned company for a specified period of time in return for a predetermined share of the physical output. In the petroleum sector this share is normally a share of the 'profit' oil, namely that part of the crude oil production which remains after the contracting company has received its share of the 'cost' oil, which in turn is that part of production that has been set aside for the recovery of exploration, development and operating costs.

See Index under Technology Transfer.

product sharing agreement. Often used as a synonym for PRODUCTION SHARING AGREEMENT, product sharing arrangements are limited more strictly to the manufacturing sector. For example, in JOINT VENTURE arrangements between Japanese companies and Chinese state-owned companies, the foreign supplier of plant and technology

may receive a predetermined part of the physical output as a form of 'dividend'.

See also COPRODUCTION AGREEMENT; BUY-BACK DEAL; COUNTERTRADE, and Index under Technology Transfer.

profit centre. A DIVISION of a company that is held responsible for its profits (and not merely for costs; *see* COST CENTRE). To this end, it is given authority to make pricing, output, and other marketing decisions. It is very common for multinational subsidiaries to be treated as profit centres.

See also INVESTMENT CENTRE, and Index under Corporate Structure and Management.

public utility rule. International legal principle which acknowledges the right of a sovereign state to expropriate any property within its territory provided this right is exercised for a public purpose or in the public interest.

See EXPROPRIATION, and Index under Dispute and Settlement.

purchase power parity (PPP). In its absolute form, purchase power parity refers to an exchange rate between the currencies of two countries that is exactly equal to the ratio of the price levels in those countries. In its relative form, it refers to an exchange rate that makes the ratio of the exchange rates in two time periods equal to the relative ratios of the price levels in the two countries in the two time periods, where the base period was one of equilibrium.

The theory of purchase power parity (PPP) states that the equilibrium exchange rate tends towards one of the two rates above. It was first put forward in a rigorous form by the Swedish economist Gustav Cassel in 1916 and widely advocated after the

First World War, when there was uncertainty about the exchange rates which ought to prevail after the wartime interruption of the operation of the foreign exchange markets. In its absolute form it proposes that when the currency markets are in equilibrium, and there are no restrictions on the operations of the market, the exchange rate at that time R(t), will be equal to the ratio between the price level in country A, P(a) and the price level in country B, P(b): that is, R(t) = P(a)/P(b). In this form it is made problematic by the restrictive conditions that apply, since it ignores transport costs, product differentiation, import duties, and other market imperfections. Thus the ARBITRAGE mechanism that would cause it to occur is obstructed.

In its more commonly accepted relative form, the theory is concerned with changes rather than absolute amounts. Suppose we define t(0) as the time at which there was an equilibrium, and R(0) as the exchange rate at that time, then R(t)/R(0) = R(c) will be the relative change in the exchange rate. Next, we similarly define P(At) and P(A0) as the price level in country A at times t and 0 respectively, so that P(Ac) is the relative change P(At)/P(A0). Finally, P(Bc) is the similar change in price level for country B. Then the relative form of PPP theory states that R(c) = P(Ac)/P(Bc).

The mechanism that supposedly leads to the operation of PPP is that of ARBITRAGE. If we suppose that two countries A and B begin in equilibrium, but A experiences a higher inflation rate than B, then exports become less competitive and imports into A are cheaper than home-produced goods. In these circumstances a balance of payments deficit arises. This leads to a demand for country B's currency at the expense of that of country A, and this in turn leads to a fall in the value of currency A. At the same time, so long as currency A has not fallen as far as PPP suggests that it should, arbitrageurs can identify potential profits to be gained by buying goods in country B and

selling them in A for higher monetary prices. They will continue to do so until equilibrium is reached, when profits can no longer be made (this is of course limited by the costs of transporting the goods, by any import restrictions introduced by A, and so on). The theory, developed for a pair of currencies, can be generalized to all currencies so that in equilibrium all currencies should, according to the model, reflect the proposed relationship.

For PPP theory to hold true, a number of conditions must be fulfilled. All goods and services must be traded internationally, there must be no barriers to trade, and no transport costs. None of these conditions can be said to hold. Moreover, the existence of massive multinational investment in addition to the international trade envisaged in the theory adds further imperfections, since administered decisions within multinationals need not conform to the behaviour of arm's length trade (see TRANSFER PRICE; ARM'S LENGTH). For these and other reasons, empirical tests of the theory have tended to point to the conclusion that it holds over the long but not over the short term. Testing the theory however presents a number of problems. Tests use price indices that include non-traded goods; factors other than price levels affect the balance of trade – changes in productivity, for example; governments frequently intervene in currency markets, so the markets are not free to respond as the theory would require; and one of the causes of price level changes is probably the change in exchange rates, and hence it is difficult to separate cause from effect.

The practical implications of PPP theory extend particularly to the forecasting of exchange rates. This is an important matter for the multinational, particularly over the short term, which is the very term over which the theory is least applicable. Thus although inflation rates can be and are used in helping multinationals and others to predict future exchange rates, they must be used with caution (*see* Officer, 1976).

See also Index under Theoretical Issues and under Financial and Risk Management.

purchasing agent. An agent who acts on behalf of a (usually large) overseas buyer to purchase goods of a price and quality specified by his principal.

See also AGENCY AGREEMENT.

Q

quality circle. A management technique for improving human relations and productivity on the shop floor, originally developed by the Tavistock Institute of Human Relations in London in the 1950s. While this experiment in industrial democracy was not widely adopted by British companies at the time, it was soon seized upon by Japanese multinationals. Quality circles are now being re-introduced into Britain on a wide scale by both Japanese and American multinationals.

A quality circle is an 'involvement group' of workers, often selected by management, who – after some initial training – meet from time to time in 'brainstorming' sessions to identify creative ways of improving production and cutting costs. The basic idea is that workers have a much closer knowledge than management of the actual workings of the production process.

Proponents of quality circles argue that they lead both to significant cost savings for the firm and to greater job satisfaction for the employees. Opponents argue that, depending on the state of the economy, creative suggestions are soon likely to hinge on pay cutting and other contracting activities, conveniently proposed and supported by the workforce itself. There is some evidence that quality circles have been a percursor of campaigns for the withdrawal of union recognition.

quasi-cartel. *See under* CARTEL.

quota. A government-imposed share of imports or exports serving as a quantitative restriction on external trade. Import quotas may be termed unilateral when they are adopted without prior discussion or negotiation with another country, and bilateral or multilateral when the importing nation negotiates with the various supplying nations before declaring the allotment of the quota by defined shares. TARIFF quotas provide for the importation of a specified quantity of a product which may be imported at a given rate of duty or even duty-free. Export quotas are less common but occur in cases where a government's adoption of VOLUNTARY EXPORT RESTRAINT results in the need to allocate shares of the export trade to various domestic producers.

Quotas may also be used in another context, namely when producers allocate production quotas to members of a CARTEL, the purpose of which is to restrain competition. Producer cartels may be formed either among governments or among firms.

See Index under Trade.

R

Raw Materials Group. A non-profit organization which collects, analyses and publishes information on global raw materials, as well as other articles dealing with corporate control of raw materials. Founded in 1971, the group numbers specialists in various fields from geology and mining to political science, international economy and transnational corporations. The group specializes in giving information on output, trade, consumption, ownership structure, property and uses of minerals, both processed and unprocessed. The group carries out contract projects giving specially compiled information and data to a variety of clients, including trade unions, government bodies and international organizations. It publishes the quarterly *Raw Materials Report*.

See Index under Data Sources.
Address: PO Box 5195, S-102 44 Stockholm, Sweden.

RBP Code. *See* RESTRICTIVE BUSINESS PRACTICES CODE.

real exchange rate. The NOMINAL EXCHANGE RATE adjusted for any changes in the purchasing power of the two currencies concerned since a defined base point in time. It is intended that this rate should measure the underlying changes in TERMS OF TRADE between countries. The idea of the real exchange rate arises from the theory of PURCHASE POWER PARITY: if the latter holds, so that changes in the nominal exchange rate have been exactly offset by changes in the relative price levels in the countries concerned, then it is said that there has been no change in the real exchange rate.

See also Index under Financial and Risk Management.

realized price system. A formula for computing the value of a resource (such as petroleum) for purposes of negotiating the distribution of gains from the exploitation and sale of the resource between producing host country and multinational corporation. In the 'realized price' system the value of the resource is the amount actually received by the operator when he sells the resource.

See REFERENCE PRICE SYSTEM; FAIR MARKET VALUE SYSTEM; NEGOTIATED PRICE SYSTEM; INDEXING; TRANSFER PRICE, and Index under Regulation and Tax.

red multinationals. An expression coined to describe enterprises from the Soviet Union and from other Eastern European countries established as capitalist-based firms in the Western market economies. These firms are either companies wholly owned by the socialist countries' FOREIGN TRADE ORGANIZATIONS (FTOs) or, more commonly, equity shared JOINT VENTURES with Western multinationals.

The setting up of these red multinationals is frequently an outcome of the complex COPRODUCTION AGREEMENTS between Western companies and state-owned enterprises inside the CMEA countries, which provide for the obligatory export of the output of the coproduction venture. In order to facilitate the export of this output to the capitalist economies of the West, socialist countries have set up a variety of marketing, assembly and refinery operations both in Europe and in the Americas. For example, the Soviet-owned Nafta oil company has a wholly owned refinery in Antwerp, and a distribution network for oil products in the UK. Scalda-Volga is a 95 per cent Soviet-owned auto assembly plant in Belgium. Satra Corporation of New York is a joint marketing venture importing Soviet cars and hydrofoils. There are also CMEA country subsidiaries and joint ventures in the less developed countries.

The most significant CMEA presence in Western capitalism is in the banking sector, for example the Moscow Narodny Bank in London and the Eurobank in Paris. The Eurobank in Paris is the largest foreign banking house and its activities are generally agreed to have led to the development of the EURODOLLAR market. 'Red' banks can be found in TAX HAVENS around the world (Levinson, 1979). (*See* Index under Trade.)

reference price system. A method of calculating the value of a resource (such as petroleum) for purposes of negotiating the distribution of gains from the exploitation and sale of the resource between producing host country and transnational corporation. The reference price system uses the published price of a comparable product, adjusting it according to quality and freight differentials.

See REALIZED PRICE SYSTEM; INDEXATION; FAIR MARKET VALUE SYSTEM; NEGOTIATED PRICE SYSTEM; TRANSFER PRICE, and Index under Regulation and Tax.

regiocentric. A term coined by Wind, Douglas and Perlmutter (1973) to describe a particular attitude by multinational management. It is essentially a modification of Perlmutter's notion of the GEOCENTRIC attitude; but whereas in the latter the total worldwide corporate activity is seen as an integrated whole, regiocentrism takes one particular region of the world and seeks integrated marketing and production policies for that region.

See also ETHNOCENTRIC; POLYCENTRIC, and Index under Corporate Structure and Management and under Theoretical Issues.

Registrar of Companies. The UK government officer with whom all company financial statements and certain other information required under corporate law must be filed. Companies must send this information annually within defined time limits. The resulting information is publicly available on payment of a small fee.

See Index under Data Sources and under Regulation and Tax.
Addresses: Companies Registration Office, Cardiff/ Companies House, 55-71 City Road, London EC1.

Regulation Q. A now defunct regulation which limited the interest that US banks could pay on deposits. The regulation was an important stimulus to the EURODOLLAR market because it did not apply there. The movement of foreign loans out of US domestic dollar deposits into Eurodollar deposits was accelerated when the commercial lending rate reached the Regulation Q ceiling. Regulation Q was suspended in 1974.

See also Index under Regulation and Tax.

reinvoicing centre. A tax avoidance device used by multinational enterprise. It sets up a subsidiary in a TAX HAVEN, which nominally purchases goods from one part of the firm, selling them to another part of the firm at a higher price, thus extracting profit which attracts a low tax rate. The goods do not physically travel via the tax haven. A further advantage to a reinvoicing centre is that pricing and currency decisions can be implemented quickly because all contracts pass through the one centre, rather than being bilateral between different parts of the MNC. Against this there are the expenses and communication costs of such a centre.

See also TRIANGULAR TRADE, and Index

under Financial and Risk Management and Regulation and Tax.

related company. First defined in the UK Companies Act of 1981 as a company other than a group company in which an investing company holds, on a long-term basis, a qualifying capital interest (usually 20 per cent or more of equity share capital), and carrying voting rights for the purpose of securing a contribution to the investing company's own activities by the exercise of any control or influence arising from that interest.

See also ASSOCIATED COMPANY; AFFILIATE COMPANY; RELATED PARTY TRADE, and Index under Corporate Structure and Management.

related party imports. Since a 1974 tariff classification issued by the Foreign Trade Division of the US Bureau of Census, related party imports are defined as those imports which originate in firms in which five per cent or more of voting stock is owned by the other party to the transaction. This classification goes beyond the published statistics of the US Department of Commerce on export sales by so-called MAJORITY OWNED FOREIGN AFFILIATES (MOFAs). It reflects new trends in the cross-border arrangements of multinational enterprises.

See Index under Trade.

relay subsidiary. Subsidiary which is largely engaged in the manufacture or the assembly of finished products for local or worldwide marketing by the parent company. The range of goods is copied from the parent's range, and is manufactured according to specifications laid down by the parent company. Sometimes relay subsidiaries in their turn establish a subcontracting relationship with local firms.

See also BRANCH PLANT.

rent. In the vernacular, the term refers to the price paid for the use of a durable good such as land or buildings. In economic theory, the concept has been both widened and refined as 'economic' rent, meaning the payment made for any productive resource (whether land, labour or technology) beyond that which is needed to bring or keep the resource in production in the long run. This incremental, unearned gain is the outcome of restrictions on the supply side of the productive resource coupled with the private ownership of such resource, restricting access to it. For example, good fertile land is scarce in nature, and when privately owned, permits its owners to charge a rent higher than that paid for other land which is not so fertile but still producing the same crop. The essence of the theory of rent is that rent is not a cost of production but a function of the demand for the product resulting from the use of the land. As Ricardo wrote in a well-worn passage: 'Corn is not high because rent is paid, but a rent is paid because corn is high'.

Modern economic analysis has shown that the theory of economic rent applies not only to land but to other special facilities of production which are not accessible to all. Some writers in the Marxist tradition even speak of 'technological' rents. Mandel (1978, p.192), for example, defines 'technological' rents as 'surplus profits derived from the monopolization of technical progress, from discoveries and inventions which lower the cost price of commodities but cannot (at least in the medium run) become generalized throughout a given branch of production and applied by all competitors, because of the structure of monopoly capital itself: difficulties of entry, size of minimum investment, control of pat-

ents, cartel arrangements and so on'. ROY-
ALTIES and other payments for proprietary
knowledge, TRADEMARKS or patented technologies granted under license, are in this
view a form of rent or unearned income.

See also PATENT; ROYALTY; TRANSFER
PRICE, and Index under Theoretical Issues.

requisition. The acquisition of private property without compensation by the State, for
the time being and for its own use.
Although the term 'requisition' is reserved
in legal language for a state's legal right to
take possession without compensation in
such emergencies as war, the state may of
course at its own discretion decide to pay
compensation after all. For instance, during
the Falklands war the UK government paid
compensation for ships 'requisitioned' from
private firms.

See EXPROPRIATION; NATIONALIZATION;
CONFISCATION.

resource consortium. A collaborative
arrangement, between a number of companies operating in a particular resource
sector, for the purposes of sharing the risks
and the benefits associated with large-scale
resource development projects. Resource
consortia have become an increasingly common variant of JOINT VENTURE arrangements
as the costs and risks associated with modern technologically sophisticated mining
and mineral processing ventures have come
to exceed any one or two companies' abilities to manage and control.

See Index under Industry Structure.

resource equity. *See* FREE EQUITY.

Restrictive Business Practices (RBP) Code.
Formally adopted by the UN General
Assembly in 1980, this voluntary code was
drawn up under the auspices of the UNITED
NATIONS CONFERENCE ON TRADE AND
DEVELOPMENT (UNCTAD) under the full

title of *Set of Multilaterally Agreed Equitable Principles for the Control of Restrictive
Business Practices.* In comparison with
other draft UN codes of conduct, negotiations on the RBP Code were concluded relatively swiftly. This owes much to the fact
that from the outset the negotiating group
of developed countries (*see* GROUP B
STATES) recognized an advantage in for-
mulating internationally agreed principles
of competition, many of them in line with
existing anti-trust provisions in the
advanced countries. But it is also substantially due to the fact that the Code is voluntary and is formulated to apply to RBPs in
general, whether perpetrated by domestic
private enterprises or state-owned enterprises, or multinational corporations.
Indeed, the Code excludes from its scope
restrictive business transactions occurring
within multinational groups of companies,
except in so far as they are deemed to adversely affect competition ouside such groups.

Although the final text is a loosely
worded statement which can mean all things
to all men, there is nevertheless some educational merit in its listing of those practices
that may produce adverse effects on international trade and competition. These are:
price fixing agreements; collusive tendering; market or customer allocation arrangements; allocation by quota as to sales and
production; collective action to enforce
arrangements (for example, by concerted
refusal to deal); concerted refusal of supplies to potential importers; collective
denial of access to an arrangement or association which is crucial to competition; pre-
datory behaviour to competitors when in a
dominant position; and discriminatory pricing when in a dominant position.

Last but not least, in describing international measures of co-operation and information exchange and in giving the
UNCTAD secretariat a watching brief on
developments in restrictive business practices worldwide as well as a task in advising
developing countries in the formulation and

administration of their national RBP legislation, the Code further institutionalizes intergovernmental concern with the abuses of concentration of economic power. Following the adoption of the RBP Code, the UNCTAD secretariat has prepared a draft Model Law on Restrictive Business Practices which is at present being considered by the Intergovernmental Group of Experts on Restrictive Business Practices.

See also CODES OF CONDUCT, and Index under International Co-operation.

retrocession clause. *See* GRANT BACK PROVISION.

reverse engineering. A method of acquiring technical skills and developing technological capability through disassembling purchased (including imported) technological products. This technique of 'learning by undoing' has proved very successful in the development of Japan, and it is hence frequently advocated as a means of technological development for contemporary developing countries. The technique, however, has its limitations in cases where the product and process technology has been 'systems' integrated and not 'mechanically' integrated, as for example in the case of COMPUTER AIDED DESIGN (CAD), and COMPUTER AIDED MANUFACTURING (CAM) processes.

See Index under Technology Transfer.

revolver. *See* REVOLVING LOAN.

revolving loan. A loan with a floating interest rate which is periodically renegotiated along with the amount of the loan within a given line of credit. Such loans are frequently found in the EURODOLLAR market. Also known as 'revolvers' or 'rollover credits'.

risk premium. For financial securities, the risk premium is the difference between the expected return on the security and the expected return on a risk-free security such as a treasury bond. In a slightly different context the term is used in COUNTRY RISK ASSESSMENT, where the return required from an investment will vary depending on the perceived risk of the host country: the risk premium is the difference between the return required from the foreign investment and the return required from an equivalent domestic investment.

See Index under Financial and Risk Management.

risk service contract. A novel contractual arrangement between foreign multinationals operating in the resource sector and a company of the host country, often a state-owned one. Risk service contracts are similar to PRODUCTION SHARING AGREEMENTS except that payment to the foreign contractor is in cash rather than in physical output. It is called a 'risk' contract because the foreign contractor carries the risk of the venture by providing investment capital for exploration and production. This capital is reimbursed, together with interests and a risk fee, out of production revenues.

See Index under Technology Transfer.

rollover credit. *See* REVOLVING LOAN.

Roundtable of European Industrialists. A group of European businessmen from both publicly and privately owned major enterprises, which was formed in 1983. The Roundtable first met in April of that year and has had a number of meetings since. Its principal aim is to act as a pressure group in and towards the European Community (EC) to remove obstacles to business enterprise in the Community. It intends to be project-based and has selected the lack of European venture capital as its first issue. It has taken action by forming a company to offer venture capital with initial funds of US$100m.

See Index under International Co-operation and under Corporate Structure and Management.

royalty. Formerly a term for those royal rights which could not be granted away with any piece of land except by special mention in the grant or charter by which the land was given. The term subsequently came to refer to the share accruing to any landlord from the exploitation of a resource in his property. This is still one of the meanings of the concept. For example, besides other payments, such as surface rentals and profits tax, multinational companies operating in the mineral resource sector will typically pay royalties to host governments (or private land owners) for the right to mine the land. Such payment is normally a fixed percentage of the physical or monetary value of the output, or sometimes of the profit. With the progression from traditional to modernized concession regimes (*see under* CONCESSION *and under* MODERNIZED CONCESSION AGREEMENT) the composition of the financial returns to host governments has typically involved a declining contribution of royalties in favour of an increasing share of profit taxes. This has had implications for the inter-nation distribution of the returns from such ventures, since the existence of DOUBLE TAXATION AGREEMENTS between nations coupled with the higher rate of taxation usually applicable in developing host countries has often secured zero tax obligations at home for multinationals on profits earned from overseas operations (*see* TAX CREDIT).

In modern times, the term has acquired a much wider application. It is a share of a product or profit reserved by an owner for permitting another the use of his property. This property may include, besides land and natural resource, patented inventions or trademarks which are granted under license, or copyrighted material. Royalty payments for licensed technology or trademark products are currently a controversial issue in the transfer of technology to developing countries.

See also PATENT; TRADEMARK; LICENSING AGREEMENT; RENT, and Index under Technology Transfer.

runaway shop. A term used particularly in trade union circles to describe a business concern that moves to another region or country to escape union demands. A number of multinational corporations operating in the industrial sector have relocated a sizeable part of their activities from their traditional sites in the advanced countries to less developed regions in Europe, in Central and Latin America and in Southeast Asia. (*See* NEW INTERNATIONAL DIVISION OF LABOUR; NEWLY INDUSTRIALIZING COUNTRIES.) However, the motives for such relocation are open to dispute. While those in labour circles are prone to use the runaway shop argument, management will often insist that the primary reasons for the move were tax concessions, better access to raw materials or greater proximity to new markets.

See Index under Corporate Structure and Management.

S

samurai bond. A FOREIGN BOND issued in Japan and denominated in yen.

See also YANKEE BOND.

scale economies. When expansion of the productive capacity of a firm or industry causes total production costs to increase proportionately less than the rise of output, economies of scale have been created. Consequently, long-run average costs of production will fall. There are many ways in which economies of scale may be created. Some scale economies result from managerial and organizational capabilities, others stem from the technical and engineering characteristics of plant and machinery. An important corollary for theories of international direct investment is that the scale economies of large firms present an OWNERSHIP SPECIFIC ADVANTAGE which may make it attractive for such firms to compete in foreign markets.

See OLIGOPOLY MODEL; PRODUCT CYCLE THEORY; APPROPRIABILITY THEORY, and Index under Theoretical Issues.

scout. A currency hedging instrument recently developed by Midland Montagu Investment Bank. The term is an acronym for a shared currency OPTION under tender, and is designed for companies tendering for foreign contracts. The instrument gives the buyer specified in the tender the right to sell the base currency of the contract against the tenderer's domestic currency at a nominated price.

See HEDGE, and Index under Financial and Risk Management.

SDR. *See* SPECIAL DRAWING RIGHTS.

SEC. *See* SECURITIES AND EXCHANGE COMMISSION.

second world. A term normally only used in the contrasting context of THIRD WORLD and FIRST WORLD. The Second World consists of the centrally planned economies of the Eastern bloc countries. The term 'second' refers to the fact that industrialization in that part of the world followed the industrialization in the advanced countries of Northwest Europe and the United States.

secret reserves. Items which are not disclosed in corporate financial statements but nevertheless have value to the company. Secret reserves can be created in a company's accounts in many ways. The classic method is to undervalue an asset in some fashion, so that the asset continues to generate revenue and yet does not appear in full on the balance sheet. This has the consequence of overstating the apparent return on assets, since the profits generated by the undisclosed assets are still reported as normal. It also may permit the company to write the asset back into the accounts in a subsequent year. Similarly, profits can be concealed in good years and brought into poor ones, thus 'smoothing' the apparent trend of earnings. Well-known methods of creating secret reserves are the over-zealous depreciation of assets (that is, writing them out of the accounts before they actually cease to exist) and the overestimation of doubtful debt provisions.

The history of secret reserves in the accounts of UK and US companies shows that an early support of them as protectors of companies against the ignorance or wilfulness of shareholders has given way to a general disapproval. In most cases they are legislated against. The holding of secret reserves is however still endemic in the financial statements of many other countries, and the result is that such statements cannot be relied on in the same way that, for example, British, Dutch or US accounts can.

See also Index under International Accounting.

Section 485, Income and Corporation Taxes Act. UK tax legislation which empowers the Inland Revenue to adjust a TRANSFER PRICE in calculating corporate profits for tax purposes. The Act provides that the section will apply where either the buyer controls the seller, the seller controls the buyer, or both are controlled by a third party.

The section is specifically designed for those cases where tax revenue is likely to be lost to the UK exchequer: the deeming provision only applies where the TRANSFER PRICE is considered to be artificially high and the buyer is in the UK, or the transfer price is artificially low and the seller is in the UK. The touchstone to be applied is a price at which the trade would have taken place if it had been between independent persons dealing at ARM'S LENGTH. Where no benchmark market price exists, the appropriate price to be used for tax purposes is subject to estimation and, on occasion, negotiation.

Application of Section 485 is not automatic. It only applies where the Board of Inland Revenue so directs.

See also INTERNAL REVENUE SERVICE CODE 482, and Index under Regulation and Tax.

Securities and Exchange Commission (SEC). A regulatory body set up and funded by the US government under the Securities Exchange Act, 1934, for the purpose of investor protection. Since that time its powers and duties have been extended and it is now one of the major Federal regulators

of commercial activity in the USA.

In addition to the disclosure requirements of the 1934 Act (*see* DISCLOSURE IN ACCOUNTS), the SEC also oversees the provisions of the Securities Act, 1933. Its activities are also governed by a number of later acts including the Public Utility Holding Company Act, 1935; Bankruptcy Act, 1938; Trust Indenture Act, 1939; Investment Company Act, 1940; Investment Advisers Act, 1940; the Securities Investor Protection Act, 1970, and the Securities Acts Amendments of 1975.

The SEC consists of five commissioners, one of whom is chairman. They are appointed for five-year terms on a rolling basis so that one retires each year. Both commissioners and chairman are appointed by the US President, and confirmed by the Senate. There is in addition a large permanent staff of lawyers, acccountants, economists and others.

The activities of the SEC are widespread, including the day-to-day collection of information, the regulation of a large number of activities and organizations, and the conducting of *ad hoc* investigations and reports. They include:
(a) Overseeing the regulation of security dealers, the detail of which is normally delegated to the US stock exchanges and the National Association of Securities Dealers (the latter being concerned with over-the-counter trading).
(b) Investigating particular instances of possible abuse of position such as insider trading, for which purpose it regularly monitors volume of trading and prices just before the announcement of significant events such as bids. Recently the SEC has extended its definition of insider dealing to include dealing with the knowledge that a share is about to be recommended by an influential newspaper tipster. This has caused controversy.
(c) Requiring regular information from companies subject to its auspices (see the discussion of Form 10-K below). The SEC

publishes a *Directory of Companies filing Annual Reports with the Securities and Exchange Commission* which classifies these companies according to Standard Industrial Codes.

(d) Receiving information on new issues, principally under the terms of the Securities Act, 1933. Such prospectus requirements are very detailed. Moreover, the SEC will generally require a 'reasonable waiting period', which is usually 20 days.

(e) Receiving and approving registration applications from intending brokers and security dealers.

(f) Ensuring that the requirements of the Acts are complied with in connection with share manipulation and fraud. This applies not only to stock exchange members but also over-the-counter dealers, corporate insiders and others.

(g) Issuing particular regulations over securities trading. For example, it has banned short selling in cases where the market for a security is falling, on the grounds that this might exacerbate the situation and cause panic. In a different vein, it has required the US securities exchanges to consolidate share quotations through an electronic network (the Consolidated Quotations Service) so as to give brokers' clients access to the most competitive prices.

(h) Undertaking *ad hoc* special studies into the securities markets and other institutions under its auspices.

(i) Regulating the financial reporting and disclosure standards of large US companies. However, as with the stock exchanges, this duty has normally been delegated, the Commission having stated that the 'principles, standards, and practices promulgated by the FASB (FINANCIAL ACCOUNTING STANDARDS BOARD) in its statements and interpretations, will be considered by the Commission as having substantial authoritative support' (*see Accounting Series Releases* No 150, 1973). The SEC has however overruled the FASB

on occasion.

(j) Reporting in detail on its activities each year to Congress.

There are three principal documents that large public US corporations have to file with the SEC. The rules apply to those listed on stock exchanges, those whose securities are sold over the counter, and in addition, those with over 500 shareholders and assets of more than US$ 1 million. All these forms are made publicly available, and many share analysts tend to prefer them to the published financial statements.

Form 10-K. A 10-K report must be filed annually with the SEC by every company that comes under its jurisdiction. The rules that govern the content of the 10-K files are listed in the SEC's publication *Regulation S-X*. In general the information required is similar to that contained in companies' annual financial statements, but it is more detailed. Regulation S-X sets out what are considered by the SEC to be acceptable accounting principles: these tend to be the same as the statements of the FINANCIAL ACCOUNTING STANDARDS BOARD (FASB). The information contained in the 10-K report must be laid out in a standard format.

Form 10-Q. The same companies must file form 10-Q quarterly. This gives its (unaudited) quarterly results.

Form 8-Q. Significant events, such as mergers or major asset disposals, have to be reported to the SEC on form 8-Q.

Although there has been a steadily increasing tendency among large firms and particularly multinationals to widen the number of securities markets worldwide on which they are quoted, since this is generally agreed to reduce their cost of capital, many non-US companies have baulked at making their shares and bonds available in the United States because of the SEC's comparatively stringent disclosure requirements (for an instrument that bypasses this problem, *see* AMERICAN DEPOSITORY RECEIPT (ADR)). This is for reasons both of commercial confidentiality (when such companies are unaccustomed to high disclosure in their own countries) and expense. The latter arises both from the cost of employing accountants to restate accounts in terms of US accounting principles and from the cost of translating narrative documentation.

As a result of representations and a steadily evolving policy, the SEC has at the time of writing agreed that in a number of respects the disclosure requirements for foreign firms whose securities are traded in the USA should be less onerous than those for US firms and for other north American companies; those based in Canada or Mexico, for example. As a result, the form on which foreign companies make a return is different. They may file a return annually on form 20-F instead of the domestic form 10-K, and there are a number of other special forms for foreign firms.

Although the basic disclosure requirements for textual material are similar to those for US companies (as set out in Regulation S-K) and for financial statements are the same as in Regulation S-X, certain concessions are allowed. The following list is for guidance only: reference to the detailed requirements of the SEC is advised for fuller information and exceptions.

Foreign companies may use foreign accounting principles in their financial returns, but they should quantify the effects of major material differences from US principles.

In certain circumstances foreign firms are exempt from filing information on segmented results (*see* SEGMENTATION).

Certain other information, such as remuneration paid to management and disclosure of management transactions, need only be disclosed to the SEC if it has already been communicated to shareholders or otherwise made public.

See Index under Regulation and Tax, and under Data Sources.

Securities and Investments Board (SIB). As a result of pressure arising both from the government's dislike of the restrictive practices it felt were endemic in the securities community and from well-publicized frauds and scandals in the City, the Financial Services Bill was published in December 1985. This was designed to regulate the investment business. One key aspect of the Bill (which had not become law at the time of writing) is the ability of the Secretary of State for Trade and Industry to delegate most of his powers to a self-regulatory agency. The Securities and Investments Board (SIB) and Marketing of Investments Board Organizing Committee (MIBOC) proposed themselves and the government indicated that it would accede to this. Since then it has been agreed that, with government approval, they will merge.

Financed by those it will regulate, the SIB will have wide powers in controlling the investment community. It will recognize Self-Regulating Organizations (SROs) which will be responsible for particular investment sectors. Three of these seem certain to be authorized (the Stock Exchange, the International Securities Regulation Organization and the Association of Futures Brokers and Dealers), having been suggested in the White Paper which preceded the Bill. Four others have had talks with the SIB although they are being encouraged to merge into just two associations.

The overall philosophy is one of self-regulation: the UK government does not wish to follow the example of the USA with its SECURITIES AND EXCHANGE COMMISSION (SEC). The regulating institutions are not only being given wide powers but also immunity from prosecution for negligence. How effectively they will operate when they come onstream in 1987, given the new atmosphere that will come from the DEREGULATION of the City in October 1986 and the internationalization of the various City institutions (banks, dealers, and brokers) in the wake of the BIG BANG, is at the time of writing unclear.

See Index under Regulation and Tax.
Address: 3, Royal Exchange Buildings, London EC3V 3NL, UK.

securitization. A process by which financial intermediaries such as banks are bypassed as companies trade in each others' securities, borrowing directly from financial markets instead of from banks. It has accelerated in the mid-1980s.

The process of securitization or disintermediation has grown from the realization by major US companies that they can borrow more cheaply by issuing commercial paper (that is, short- to medium- term fixed-interest borrowing) themselves than by arranging loans from commercial banks.

Although at present not practised in the UK, securitization may well become common there too given the UK government's announcement that it is to remove restrictions under the Banking Act that forbade the issue of sterling commercial paper (EUROCOMMERCIAL PAPER has been traded for some time). Any doubt that currently remains in the UK over this latter market stems from the greater flexibility the UK overdraft system gives to companies and the relatively small number of issuers who have sufficiently high credit ratings to be attractive to lenders.

See also DEREGULATION, and Index under Financial and Risk Management.

segmentation. The breaking down of corporate financial statements into their constituent parts on some predefined basis. For example, profits, sales and/or assets may be segmented by geographical region, by product, or by both together.

See Index under International Accounting.

Self Regulating Organization (SRO). *See under* SECURITIES AND INVESTMENTS BOARD.

self-reliance. The theory of self-reliant development probably originated in the People's Republic of China during the Great Leap Forward of 1957. But it owes its popularity to the Arusha Declaration (1967) when President Nyerere of Tanzania used the term in a salute to the aspirations of his own nation and those of the entire THIRD WORLD.

Upon independence, most Third World countries had found themselves deeply entangled in a system of international specialization and trade which, they argued, increasingly blocked their chances of independent development and industrialization. Self-reliance immediately became a political force uniting the ex-colonial countries as well as a programme of independent development strategies.

As a political ideology, it complemented the concept of 'neo-colonialism' which had already begun to bring the emerging Third World countries into one camp in the international political arena. The idea of neo-colonialism was in essence only an anti-ideology, but self-reliance held out the promise of something positive, inspiring the Third World to believe it could do things for itself.

As a development strategy, self-reliance has two main planks. The first of these is DELINKING, a gradual disengagement from the international specialization which had left so many countries dependent on the export earnings of one or two primary agricultural commodities. This is complemented by diversification of agricultural production with an emphasis on self-sufficiency in food production, and by import-substitutive industrialization to reduce dependency on manufacturing imports from the technologically advanced countries. More generally there is an emphasis on a reduction of dependency on imported capital, technology and commodities from the advanced countries, coupled with an emphasis on LOCAL SOURCING and LOCALIZATION of productive activities.

Secondly, there are rural 'self-help' programmes, especially important in the original Tanzanian self-reliant development plan. It was planned to build viable socialist communities in the rural areas (the so-called 'Ujamaa' villages) not by direct government intervention and tutelage, but based on a democratic system of self-government.

See DEPENDENCY, and Index under Development Policy.

service contract. *See* RISK SERVICE CONTRACT.

Seven Sisters. The historical nickname for the seven major oil companies who together dominated and controlled the world oil industry. They were called sisters because for all the rivalry between them, they operated a worldwide informal but unbreakable CARTEL. The seven companies were: Exxon, Shell, BP, Gulf, Texaco, Mobil and Socal (Chevron). Today their power is arguably reduced by the oil producing countries (*see* ORGANIZATION OF PETROLEUM EXPORTING COUNTRIES (OPEC)) and competition from new oil companies.

Sharia court. An Islamic court which can be found in various Middle Eastern countries. Operating under strict Islamic law, which forbids the charging of interest, these courts have recently been finding against lenders who seek to enforce contracts that involve interest payments. This has been particularly important for international bankers who have experienced difficulty, in the wake of falling oil prices, in recovering loans to borrowers.

Sherman Act. *See under* ANTI-TRUST LEGISLATION.

SIB. *See* SECURITIES AND INVESTMENTS BOARD .

SIBOR. *See* SINGAPORE INTER-BANK OFFERED RATE.

Singapore Inter-Bank Offered Rate (SIBOR). An interest rate based on, and closely tied to, the LONDON INTER-BANK OFFERED RATE (LIBOR). As with LIBOR, it is an inter-bank rate which acts as a touchstone, other commercial rates then being quoted at a premium above SIBOR.

SITC. *See* STANDARD INTERNATIONAL TRADE CLASSIFICATION.

snake. The commonly used name for the European Joint Float Agreement, set up in April 1972. Under the agreement, the currencies of member countries (who were not limited to the EUROPEAN COMMUNITY) were to be held to within 2.25 per cent of each other. Because the original agreement also included a provision that these float within a 4.5 per cent band of the US dollar the whole became known as the 'snake within the tunnel'. The snake had a stormy history; various countries left it (including the UK, Denmark, and Italy) and Denmark rejoined. The tunnel (that is, the band tied to the US dollar) disappeared with the advent of free floating.

The snake was all but dead by 1978, and it was effectively superseded by the EUROPEAN MONETARY SYSTEM (EMS).

See Index under International Co-operation.

social imperialism. *See under* IMPERIALISM.

socialism. A system of production and distribution in which social ownership of the means of production replaces private property, and allocation of resources is subject to central planning and control rather than to the determination of individuals pursuing their private interests in a free market as in CAPITALISM.

Today about a third of the world population lives in countries which call themselves socialist but their systems of socialism vary greatly. This variation is chiefly due to differences both in the degree and in the scope of central planning and control, and also in the interpretation of what constitutes social ownership.

Some countries are characterized by strictly centralized and comprehensive state control which affects all areas of civic life including culture, religion, and the arts as well as economy and polity (North Korea is one example). Other countries allow for more decentralization, conceding a measure of autonomy and planning to lower level organizations, be they local government bodies or economic organizations like factories, as for example in Yugoslavia. Sometimes such decentralization goes hand in hand with a restricted scope of planning which leaves certain sectors of the economy (small-scale industry and agriculture) to develop a measure of free enterprise. In some cases state control affects the economy and polity but only marginally touches upon school curricula, religion or recreation, etc. The concept of social ownership too can range considerably: from national state ownership to local collectives, co-operatives or communes (as, for example, in Tanzania).

Not only do socialist systems vary as between societies, they also vary within one and the same society over a period of time. The People's Republic of China is a good example of continuous reassessment of the virtues of socialist organization in the process of development and this reassessment is accompanied, time and again, by quite dramatic shifts towards greater decentralization, market-oriented forms of resource allocation, free enterprise and even private ownership.

These shifts in socialist organization are an empirical testimony to something which has always been a deeply controversial theoretical dilemma, that is, whether socialism is a historical stage of societal organization which must await the full completion of the development of productive forces under capitalism, or whether it can be a transitional form in which such productive development can be undertaken in tandem with the achievement of the socialist ideals of equality, solidarity, and the satisfaction of human needs instead of the pursuit of profit.

It is in this context that continually changing attitudes of socialist countries towards international capital and multinational corporations in particular must be understood. While multinational companies are anathema to all socialisms and regarded as the acme of capitalist and imperialist exploitation, nearly all socialist countries seek some form of collaboration with multinational enterprise in order to gain access to technology, knowhow, organizational efficiency, foreign exchange or export markets. Since FOREIGN DIRECT INVESTMENT (FDI) with its implied private ownership of productive facilities runs counter to the ideological commitment to social ownership, socialist countries have pioneered many new forms of contractual JOINT VENTURES with multinationals in order to circumvent the need for foreign equity participation in the domestic economy (*see under* COPRODUCTION AGREEMENT; COMPENSATION AGREEMENT).

In some cases where foreign equity joint ventures are permitted, care is taken to direct and concentrate such investments into specially designated geographical areas, so as to minimize the full impact of the compromise with capitalism on the society and economy as a whole. This is for example the formula used in China today (*see under* SPECIAL ECONOMIC ZONE). Another means of participating in the Western capitalist world without fear of such compromise in the domestic economy is to set up, as the Soviet Union has done, capitalist trading companies and even joint equity industrial ventures in Western countries *(see* RED MULTINATIONALS).

See also IMPERIALISM, and Index under Theoretical Issues.

socialist common enterprise. Co-operative venture between socialist (CMEA) enterprises in two or more Eastern bloc countries, mostly concerned with improving co-ordination and specialization in the power and extractive industries. Examples are Interatomergo, covering atomic nuclear energy and equipment, and the Adriatika and Friendship Oil Pipelines.

While socialist common enterprises are as yet quite rare, both Soviet and other Eastern Bloc countries have established quite a few capitalist-based enterprises in the Western market economies, either as wholly owned companies or, more commonly, in equity-shared JOINT VENTURES with Western multinationals.

See also RED MULTINATIONALS.

Societas Europaea. Name used for the proposal of the EUROPEAN COMMUNITY (EC) that a corporate entity should be created which is a Community company, governed by Community law and not registered in any individual member state. First mooted in 1959, its progress has been slow, and it is expected to be many years before the Community adopts the proposal.

See also EUROPEAN ECONOMIC INTEREST GROUPING (EEIG).

Société à responsibilité limitée (Sarl). One of seven forms of commercial association in France (the name is also used in the commercial law of Luxembourg). It differs from the SOCIETE ANONYME in a number of ways, chiefly that the minimum number of shareholders is two; transfer of shares must be restricted; it cannot raise capital from the public; annual financial statements need not be filed with the government or made public; the minimum share capital is only F20,000; and an auditor is only necessary if the capital exceeds F300,000 or 20 per cent of the members request the court to nominate one. Either this or the Société Anonyme would be the normal method of incorporation for a foreign investor: it would be normal to begin as a Société à responsabilité limitée and convert to a Société Anonyme later. The Société à responsabilité limitée is denoted by a suffix Sarl after the company name.

soft currency. A currency that is expected to fall in value in relation to the major stable currencies within the short to medium term, or one that is being artificially supported by the direct intervention of its government in the foreign exchange market.

See also HARD CURRENCY.

sogo sosha. Very large Japanese general trading companies. Because of their tremendous size, global spread and CONGLOMERATE diversification into manufacturing and finance, the *sogo soshas* rank amongst the world's top multinational corporations. However, they differ from the Western type of multinational conglomerates in that their core business is trading, not manufacturing. While they own hundreds of small subsidiaries and large JOINT VENTURES in Japan and elsewhere, engaging in resource prospecting and development, manufacturing, assembly, construction, financing and leasing, they are still run primarily for the purpose of buying and selling. They have made their mark on the world as giant commercial institutions, being principally active as agents, commission merchants, brokers, retailers and wholesalers in domestic and foreign trade.

The *sogo sosha* trade spans the entire

gamut of products; each of the larger *sogo soshas* is said to handle over 26,000 product lines from instant noodles to missiles.

CONCENTRATION is a characteristic feature of the *sogo soshas*. The top nine account for over half of Japan's foreign trade. Within Japan itself, the *sogo soshas* have intricate ties with Japan's large industrial and financial concerns, serving their respective conglomerate groups as supply and marketing agents and as co-ordinators of joint projects within the conglomerate group. Their intimate financial and business ties with these groups give the *sogo soshas* access to sources of funds at preferred rates, and assure them of both markets and supplies.

As trade intermediaries the *sogo soshas* engage in a variety of multi-product as well as third country transactions, putting together 'package' sales of plant, equipment, technology and consulting services from numerous manufacturers and delivering them to a third party without the direct involvement of Japan as either source of supply or market.

But the *sogo soshas* also play a vital role in Japan's FOREIGN DIRECT INVESTMENTS. This took off in a big way in the mid-sixties when a shortage of labour at home and rising competition from developing countries threatened Japan's light manufacturing industry. In a bid to save their established business, the *sogo soshas* encouraged the small Japanese firms whose products they exported to move to the labour-abundant neighbouring countries. They provided them with the necessary organizational and managerial assistance and would typically share two-thirds of the equity with them, while selecting local partners to participate with the remaining third.

See also ZAIBATSU, and Index under Corporate Structure and Management.

SOMO (Stichting Onderzoek Multinationale Ondernemingen). An independent Dutch research institute set up to investigate the behaviour and the socioeconomic impact of multinational companies. Established in 1973 by interested parties from the trade unions, the universities and local citizen campaigns lobbying on behalf of the Third World, the initial research activities of SOMO focused on the role of multinationals in the relocation of industrial activities from advanced to poor countries. Currently the Institute's scope of research has widened to include the resulting patterns of reorganization in home country affiliates of Dutch parent companies. Through its work SOMO aims to strengthen the bargaining position of the workforce.

The institute numbers six full-time research staff and has a well-developed documentation library.

See Index under Data Sources.
Address: Paulus Potterstraat 20, 1071 DA Amsterdam, Holland.

space arbitrage. The purchase of a currency in one market and the simultaneous sale of the same currency in another market where its price is higher. This is frequently just referred to as ARBITRAGE.

See also Index under Financial and Risk Management.

special drawing right (SDR). A new internal account and reserve asset created by the INTERNATIONAL MONETARY FUND (IMF) in 1970. SDRs are distributed among the participating countries in proportion to their IMF quota. The value of the SDR in terms of national currencies was initially set by the convention that one SDR equalled one thirty-fifth of an ounce of gold, so that until the increase of the dollar price of gold in 1971 one SDR equalled one dollar. As a consequence of the breakdown of the BRETTON WOODS MONETARY SYSTEM when the dollar was effectively delinked from gold, the value of the SDR has varied proportionately with a basket first of 16, and since

1981, 5 national currencies (the US dollar, sterling, deutschmark, French franc and the yen).

Under the SDR facility, member countries of the IMF may use their SDRs either bilaterally to buy back their own currency from another member country if that country is willing to sell, or through the Fund. In this case the Fund designates other participants to whom the SDRs may be transferred for any national currency.

The aim of the SDR scheme is to provide the international monetary system with a means of creating liquidity which is independent both of the production of gold and of the unregulated state of the United States balance of payments both of which were problematic under the Bretton Woods monetary system.

The original intention of the SDR scheme was to be neutral on international resource transfers. However the allocation of a basket of HARD CURRENCIES to the less developed member countries on the basis of their quota subscription of inconvertible domestic currencies has resulted in a real transfer of resources from rich to poor countries, albeit a small one. It is not surprising, therefore, that advocates of multilateral official aid to poorer countries have proposed many schemes for enhancing the SDR allocations to them with a view to linking SDR-based international liquidity creation to development assistance. So far none of these schemes has materialized.

See Index under International Co-operation.

Special Economic Zones. Specially designated areas in the People's Republic of China, mostly in regions contiguous to Hong Kong and Macao (such as Shanzhen and Zhuhai). They have been set up since 1979 with the specific objective of attracting Hong Kong and other overseas direct investment for purposes of processing and COMPENSATION TRADE, and for production

for the domestic market (*see* COUNTERTRADE and COPRODUCTION AGREEMENT).

The Zones offer investors not only lower tax rates than those prevalent elsewhere in China, but also more scope for private initiative and greater flexibility in the choice of investment contract. This may even include equity JOINT VENTURES. The Zones moreover were turned into showplaces of efficient administration where workers could be recruited from all over China. However, in the mid-eighties their utility is subject to controversy and debate.

The introduction in the new Chinese constitution of 1982 of the concept of 'self-administration areas' in which the capitalist system can be maintained is particularly relevant for some of these zones in view of their proximity to Hong Kong and Macao. It is to these two areas in particular that the 'self-administration' concept is meant to apply in the future. Furthermore, since 1983 fourteen cities along the coast have been designated as 'open cities' with Special Economic Zone status, although following the debate about the usefulness of the first generation zones, it has been decided by the authorities to concentrate capital and efforts for the present on just four of these fourteen. Shanghai is among the four chosen for special attention.

See SOCIALISM, and Index under Trade and under Technology Transfer.

specific duty. An import duty that is levied on the basis of some physical quantity of weight or volume as opposed to value.

See also AD VALOREM DUTY and COMPOUND DUTY.

spillover effect. Indirect beneficial effect of foreign multinational enterprise on a nation's industry as a whole, stemming from the diffusion of knowledge, skill in management and international marketing, and the opening up of new markets.

split-site production. The manufacturing in BRANCH PLANTS located at different sites (whether national or international) of a mechanically complex product, such that each site contributes a part of the final output but not the whole.

See also RUNAWAY SHOP; WORKSHOP SUBSIDIARY; RELAY SUBSIDIARY, and Index under Corporate Structure and Management.

spot rate. The currency exchange rate at which a deal is struck for immediate delivery. By convention, immediate delivery in fact normally means 'in two working days' time' to allow the necessary paperwork to be completed.

It is possible to have delivery the day following the deal, or even (for sterling into US or Canadian dollars) the same day.

See also Index under Financial and Risk Management.

square position. The status of a person or company dealing in the foreign currency markets who has bought forward a given currency and sold forward the same currency, both for delivery on the same date. In such a case they are said to be 'square' in that currency.

See also SWAP POSITION, and Index under Financial and Risk Management.

SRO. *See* SELF-REGULATING ORGANIZATION.

STABEX. A Commodity Stabilization Fund set up in 1975 within the framework of the LOMÉ CONVENTION, which was signed by the member states of the European Community (EC) and a number of developing countries in Africa, the Caribbean and the Pacific (ACP STATES).

The objective of the Fund is to stabilize the earnings from certain unprocessed agricultural commodities which contribute significantly to the export income of the ACP countries. Most ACP countries depend heavily on the exports of a few primary commodities and they are therefore particularly vulnerable to fluctuations in world market prices. The idea of the Stabilization Fund is to make good the loss in normal export earnings in any one year in which these earnings fall below the average of the previous four years.

The STABEX Fund has tended to benefit the ACP countries very unevenly: it has been criticized for its strict rules of eligibility and for its general underfunding. But more fundamentally it has been criticized for its objectives: it is an attempt to stabilize export earnings rather than import capacity, and discourages agricultural diversification and industrialization by supporting traditional agricultural production against market trends.

See Index under International Co-operation.

Standard International Trade Classification (SITC). A commodity classification system for reporting international trade statistics. The list was first drawn up by the United Nations (UN) Secretariat in 1950. Since then it has been adopted by a large number of countries and by all international organizations for whom international trade is relevant. Some countries have also used it as a basis for their customs nomenclature. The adoption by the Customs Co-operation Council in 1955 of the BRUSSELS TARIFF NOMENCLATURE (BTN) occasioned a first revision of the SITC in 1960 to enable the regrouping of BTN recorded data into SITC. The SITC was revised for a second time in 1974.

The SITC, Rev. 2, identifies some 2,000 basic items, gathered into 786 subgroups. These subgroups are in fact all commodities of international trade. The subgroups in turn are summarized into 233 groups, which provide the data most usually sought in international compilations of external trade statistics (the so-called SITC 3-digit level). The groups, in their turn, are assembled into 63 divisions and these divisions are finally consolidated into 10 sections which divide the trade aggregate according to broad economic categories.

See Index under Trade.

stepping stone company. A new name for an intermediary HOLDING COMPANY in a country which is not a TAX HAVEN, sometimes set up by multinational companies for the exclusive purpose of dodging taxes.

It is not uncommon for the financial administration of international activities to be managed by holding companies based in tax havens, where taxes on profits earned abroad are minimal or non-existent. However, the country where these profits originate is able to tax them before they leave the country. This tax can be avoided by routing the profits via a 'stepping stone' company in a third country with which the country where the profits originate has signed a DOUBLE TAXATION AGREEMENT. Provided that the profits are transferred to the tax haven country as soon as they arrive in the third country, the tax authorities in the third country will normally leave them alone. Stepping stone companies therefore make an improper use of the international regulations which are aimed at avoiding double taxation.

See Index under Financial and Risk Management and under Regulation and Tax.

Stiftung. A legal form of organization in the principality of Liechtenstein. It is popular as a vehicle for personal, rather than corporate, tax avoidance with non-Liechtenstein nationals. The *Stiftung* is not normally a business trading form, and is closest to the Anglo-Saxon concept of the trust. Its advantages for foreign nationals seeking a TAX HAVEN are that anonymity can be preserved, and particulars do not need to be entered in the commercial register.

See also ANSTALT, and Index under Regulation and Tax.

subcontracting. *See* INTERNATIONAL SUBCONTRACTING.

subpart 'F' income. A provision of the US Revenue Act, 1962, which amended the Internal Revenue Code to limit the effective use of TAX HAVENS by US companies.

Under the normal provisions of US tax law, foreign subsidiaries of US parent companies are taxed only on earnings which are repatriated in the form of dividends. This concession was granted to enable foreign subsidiaries to grow under conditions of equality with multinationals based outside the US which gained from favourable home-country tax provisions. It was however exploited by the use of specially set up SUBSIDIARIES in tax havens which received profits from other subsidiaries, escaped with little or no tax, and then used these tax-free funds for further expansion.

Subpart 'F' was designed to overcome this avoidance procedure. As amended in 1976, it provides that a special type of subsidiary is defined as a CONTROLLED FOREIGN CORPORATION (CFC) if certain conditions are fulfilled. Basically these are that more than half the voting shares are owned by US shareholders, though only holdings of ten per cent or more are counted. The CFC will then be taxed on undistributed income if that income is 'passive income' such as dividends, rents, interest, and fees received from other subsidiaries. Various minor exceptions may be made to this rule (for instance, where the passive income constitutes less than ten per cent of the subsidiary's gross income).

See Index under Regulation and Tax.

subsidiary. A company in which a significant proportion of the equity share capital is owned by another company, called the PARENT. There is no technical or universally accepted definition of what constitutes a subsidiary as opposed to an AFFILIATED or ASSOCIATED COMPANY. There are usually two criteria. The first is that the parent should own at least 50 per cent of the voting shares in the company, in which case control is normally assumed. The second criterion is that the parent is able to exercise a strong control even though it may not own a majority shareholding. A subsidiary is distinguished from a branch in that a branch is not separately incorporated and hence is legally part of the parent; a subsidiary, on the other hand, has a separate legal identity.

The overseas subsidiary of the multinational differs from the domestic subsidiary in a number of ways:
(1) Although the potential for close control may exist as a result of the parent's property rights, such control may be exercised with caution as a result of nationalist pressures.
(2) Even though a subsidiary may be 100% owned by a parent, its LIQUIDATION need not be accompanied by the willingness of the parent to honour the subsidiary's debts, since the doctrine of limited liability applies. However national company laws will 'lift the veil' to a certain extent where they feel it is appropriate.
(3) There are different rules in different countries as to the extent to which subsidiaries are recognized as sufficiently intertwined with the parent for their financial results to be consolidated with those of the parent (*see* CONSOLIDATED ACCOUNTS). US and UK overseas subsidiaries tend to be consolidated: those in West German multinationals tend not to be.

See Index under Corporate Structure and Management.

substitution effect. The impact of the choice of technology by an investing firm on the employment position of the host country. By opting for capital-intensive technology the firm is said to substitute capital for labour; by opting for labour-intensive technology the firm is said to substitute labour for capital.

Sullivan Principles. Set of voluntary, non-governmental guidelines for US investors in South Africa. The Principles are named after the Reverend Leon Sullivan, who first developed and promoted them amongst American multinationals in 1977. From an initial endorsement by 12 major companies, the Principles have now become accepted by over 150 companies, about half of the total number of US companies operating in South Africa.

The Principles are concerned with the application of equal rights in industrial relations with a view to providing a platform in this way from which more far-reaching changes may be achieved, both inside and outside the workplace. The desired changes include government policies, practices and laws, and particularly the full enfranchisement of all of South Africa's people. In content very similar to the EC CODE OF CONDUCT FOR COMPANIES WITH SUBSIDIARIES, BRANCHES OR REPRESENTATION IN SOUTH AFRICA, the Sullivan Principles include non-segregation of the races at the place of work; equal and fair employment practices for all employees; equal pay for all employees doing equal or comparable work; provision of training programmes that will prepare blacks and other non-whites in substantial numbers for supervisory, administrative, clerical and technical jobs; the appointment of increasing numbers of blacks and other non-whites in management and supervisory positions; improving the quality of employees' lives outside the work environment in such fields as housing, transportation, schooling, recreation and health facilities, and recognizing the right of black workers to form their own trade unions or to be represented by existing unions. The Sullivan Code has unique reporting requirements, which include verification of the reports by independent auditors. It has a follow-up procedure which involves the 'ranking' of reporting companies into three categories. Category I denotes that the company is making good progress in organizing its structure along the Sullivan Principles. Category II denotes that the company is making progress, and Category III that it needs to become more active.

While the Sullivan principles have yet to prove a major force in South African industrial relations (the 1982 report showed only 34 of 144 reporting companies 'making good progress') they have in a small way contributed to a change in the working environment for black workers throughout South Africa. They have led to the formulation and development of new policies, practices and activities that without them probably would not have happened.

In order to make the Principles more effective still, Reverend Sullivan has called for them to be made mandatory by the United States government, and to be backed up with sanctions, embargos, tax penalties and loss of trading licenses.

At the time of writing the revolutionary events in South Africa have led to a massive DIVESTMENT by overseas companies and they have made codes of conduct such as the Sullivan Principles of limited interest at the moment.

See also CODES OF CONDUCT, and Index under International Co-operation.

super-imperialism. A conceptual model of contemporary relations between international capital and nation states on the one hand, and of the ensuing hierarchical relations of dominance and submission between states on the other. The super-imperialism model is argued by such prominent American Marxist writers as the editors of the influential *Monthly Review* (Paul Sweezy and Harry Magdoff) and by influential European writers like Pierre Jalée and Nicolas Poulantzas.

According to this school of thought, the key factor in contemporary imperialism is that the largest number of the largest multinational companies today are American companies. They argue that whatever intervention in the world economy is undertaken by the American state is done to serve the interests of American capital abroad. In opposition to the INTER-IMPERIALIST COMPETITION model, they doubt the ability of big European and Japanese companies to provide effective competition to their American counterparts in the long run, either for economic reasons, such as lack of technological sophistication, capital strength or managerial skills, or for political reasons – the fear that such effective competition might undermine the military and political centre of contemporary world imperialism with dire consequences for themselves. Rather, American super-imperialism, in this view, is thought to have successfully imposed its ruling ethos on its European and Japanese 'satellites' or 'junior partners'. Because of this, and despite certain internal rivalries between European and Japanese multinationals, where the THIRD WORLD is concerned the unity of international capitalism is seen as essential to the survival of the world capitalist system. The reason for this unity is that the advanced countries today are thought to be more and not less dependent on supplies of energy and critical minerals from the Third World. This global community of interest on the part of international capital is argued to be shown in the harmonious operation of international consortia involving capital of American, Japanese and European origin in the extractive sectors of the less developed countries.

In this view therefore the primary contradiction in the world today is between the imperialist bloc and the Third World bloc (or between North and South). Consequently, supporters of this view favour generalized anti-imperialist type struggles in the Third World and radical DELINKING policies, of the type that are also advocated by some DEPENDENCY theorists.

See also POST-IMPERIALISM; ULTRA-IMPERIALISM; IMPERIALISM, and Index under Theoretical Issues.

supra-national firm. *See under* MULTINATIONAL CORPORATION/ENTERPRISE.

swap. There are three uses of the term that are significant. It can be used to denote a purchase in the FORWARD EXCHANGE MARKET combined with a simultaneous sale in the SPOT MARKET (or vice versa). In the US, it refers to the simultaneous sale of a bond by a lender and the substitution of a different bond. More recently, it has come to denote an arrangement between two borrowers through which each takes on the other's debt obligations, either principal or interest. For example a foreign debt can be swapped for a domestic one, or a floating rate obligation for fixed. Combined with the increasing internationalization of the securities markets (for instance the increasing use of EUROBONDS and EUROCOMMERCIAL PAPER) the growth of swaps has helped to break down the barriers between national and international capital markets. It has been estimated that between 1983 and 1985 swaps grew from US$5 billion to US$150 billion.

See Index under Financial and Risk Management.

swap position. A position in the foreign exchange markets in which an equal amount of a currency has been bought and sold forward, but at different times. This contrasts with a SQUARE POSITION, where the maturities of the purchase and sale are at the same date.

See Index under Financial and Risk Management.

swap rate. The premium or discount in a forward exchange contract expressed in terms of the difference between the forward price and that of a spot contract.

See also FORWARD EXCHANGE MARKET; SPOT MARKET, and Index under Financial and Risk Management.

switch trade. In COUNTER PURCHASE transactions between Western multinationals and Eastern bloc countries or between Western multinationals and less developed countries, the Western firms often have to take a wide variety of goods in payment, many types of which they find hard to sell. This can be all the more true because these products may be quite unrelated to their own line of business. Therefore they turn to a trading house (a 'switch house') which specializes in finding customers for such goods at an appropriate discount. The *SOGO SOSHAS* are past masters in this particular line of business.

See also COUNTERTRADE, and Index under Trade.

syndicated loan. A very large loan to a private or public borrower, made by a syndicate of bankers. These loans are organized by a major international bank (the 'lead bank'), which receives a fee in return. It invites other banks to join the syndicate and normally charges a variable interest rate based on a premium over the LONDON INTER-BANK OFFERED RATE (LIBOR). Syndication has proved necessary because the size of the loans involved have made them too risky for any one lending institution.

The threatened default of a number of developing countries such as Argentina, Bolivia, Mexico and Poland over the past few years as a result of mounting foreign debts and an inability to repay them has led to rescheduling of these loans. In view of the size of the loans, true and permanent default would threaten the stability of the whole international banking system. As a result, power has shifted from the lenders to the borrowers, and the delicate negotiations that have resulted have involved the intervention of governmental agencies in the developed countries.

See DEBT RESCHEDULING, Index under Financial and Risk Management.

systematic risk. The risk of a well-diversified selection of securities in a risky market. Also sometimes known as 'market risk'.

The concept of systematic risk is important to the CAPITAL ASSET PRICING MODEL (CAPM), which forms one of the principal cornerstones of modern finance theory. Measuring risk as the variance of the returns received from a share or a portfolio of shares, modern PORTFOLIO THEORY implies that the investor should diversify the holding of securities over a large number. By doing so, the risk of the portfolio can be decreased because the securities in a market do not move up and down in perfect synchronization. However, there is a limit to the extent to which diversification can reduce risk: this comes when the investor has diversified in such a way that he or she holds all the securities in the market in proportion to their value weights. This fully diversified risk is known as 'systematic' risk or 'market' risk. It exists because there are still forces that cause a country's security market as a whole to move up and down (measured approximately by indices such as the Dow Jones Index or the FT Index).

This market risk can be reduced still further by diversifying across national securities markets so that the investor holds a portfolio of shares across the world's financial markets. This strategy is helpful because individual countries' securities markets do not move together exactly. Eventually a limit will be reached once again which will be a 'world market risk'.

The capital asset pricing model purports to explain the pricing of any individual risky security as a simple linear function of the systematic risk, riskless interest rate, and the security's BETA.

See Index under Theoretical Issues and Financial and Risk Management.

T

takeover. *See* ACQUISITION.

tap certificate of deposit. *See under* CERTIFICATE OF DEPOSIT.

tariff. A tax on imported commodities. Tariffs may be levied either as a specific amount per unit, or as a certain percentage of value (*see* AD VALOREM). Sometimes their purpose is solely to raise revenue, but more often it is to implement a domestic economic policy, such as protecting key or infant industries at home, retaliating against similar restrictions to trade in other countries, or protecting the BALANCE OF PAYMENTS position.

Tariffs may be either non-discriminatory and apply to all nations, or preferential, in which a distinction is made in favour of nations and groups of nations with which the country has specific bilateral or multilateral agreements. Since the establishment of the GENERAL AGREEMENT ON TARIFFS AND TRADE (GATT) in 1948, the international community has regularly negotiated in order to achieve non-discriminatory tariffs and a reduction of tariff levels worldwide. The use of tariff policies in the inter-war and post-war period, especially in the less developed countries today, is generally thought to have contributed to the growth of FOREIGN DIRECT INVESTMENT (FDI) and the expansion of multinational enterprises. Foreign companies sometimes have to 'jump' tariff barriers and set up local subsidiaries in order to protect their former export markets.

See INTERNALIZATION THEORY; ECLECTIC THEORY, and Index under Trade.

tariff preference. A scheme in which certain classes of goods from certain countries are charged lower or zero tariffs when imported. It is diffcult to speak generally about the field of tariff preferences, but a particularly important set of such provisions is the GENERALIZED SYSTEM OF PREFERENCES (GSP) which is granted by most of the advanced countries to goods imported from developing countries. This is the major exception to the MOST FAVOURED NATION (MFN) treatment under GATT rules. Tariff preferences are normally non-reciprocal.

See TARIFF; GENERAL AGREEMENT ON TARIFFS AND TRADE (GATT), and Index under Trade.

tariff schedules 806.30 and 807.00. Two very important value added tariff provisions created in 1966 by the US government. Items 806.30 and 807.00 of the tariff require that duties on imports should only be paid on foreign value added when imports originate in the US itself. (*See* LOCAL VALUE ADDED.)

The very rapid growth in the use of these provisions since 1966 has often been cited in academic literature as evidence both of the rapidly expanding phenomena of INTRA-FIRM TRADE and INTERNATIONAL SUB-CONTRACTING, and of the crucial role of the US Government's tariff policy in stimulating these developments.

Firstly, the NEWLY INDUSTRIALIZING COUNTRIES (Mexico, Taiwan, Singapore, and Hong Kong in particular) account for the largest share of American imports under the tariff schedules. Secondly, value added abroad constitutes a significantly smaller proportion of the value of this trade in the case of developing countries as compared with the developed countries. Finally, the spectacular growth of the newly industrializing countries' participation in world manufacturing trade appears to date roughly from the introduction of the tariff schedules. In other words, the evidence suggests that the US tariff schedules have played an important role in encouraging American firms to engage in industrial relocation, exporting the labour-intensive parts of their production processes to affiliates or subcontractors overseas with a view to importing the final assembled product back into the US.

See also SPLIT-SITE PRODUCTION; NEW INTERNATIONAL DIVISION OF LABOUR; FREE TRADE ZONE (FTZ), and Index under Trade.

Taskforce on the Churches and Corporate Responsibility. An ecumenical coalition of major church groups in Canada, established in 1975. It addresses human rights and social justice in the area of corporate and banking activity, as well as Canadian foreign and domestic policies influencing such activity. Issues related to Southern Africa and Latin America are high on its agenda. While much of the work centres on corporate and bank contacts, management discussions and shareholder actions, there are also regular meetings with various government departments.

The Taskforce compiles press articles from Canadian and international newspapers and journals. These, plus some other occasional papers, constitute a monthly mailing package available to subscribers.

See Index under Data Sources.

Address: 129 St Clair Avenue, West Toronto, Ontario M4V 1N5, Canada.

tax credit. Although this term has various uses in a domestic context, in an international context it refers to the amount of credit that is allowed in respect of corporation taxes paid on profits or WITHHOLDING TAXES paid on dividend remittances by for-eign subsidiaries to their host nations.

There are two ways in which such a credit can be given. The first method is for the profits of the host country to be assessed to home country tax, deducting tax up to the amount of home country tax before striking the balance that has to be paid. For example, if the host country has a corporate tax rate of 35 per cent and the home country a rate of 50 per cent, then on profits of £1000 the host country will take £350 in tax. The home country will assess tax on the full £1000 (that is, £500) but deduct the £350 already paid and require payment of only £150. If the rate of tax in the host country is higher than that of the home country, it is normal to limit the relief to the tax charge by the home country. This is the method used in both the UK and USA.

The second method is known as 'deduction relief'. In this case the home country assesses the profits of the foreign subsidiary after the foreign tax charge, applying the usual rate of tax to that net amount. Taking the previous example, the host country tax charge would be as before, but the home country would assess the 50 per cent charge on the net of (£1000 - £350) = £650; that is, tax of £325 would be demanded. It will be seen that the total burden on the company is higher in the second case.

All such methods are normally subject to the provisions of DOUBLE TAXATION AGREEMENTS; no further general principles exist.

See Index under Regulation and Tax.

tax harmonization. Differences in tax systems and tax rates distort world trade flows. Despite many pleas to reduce such distortion by tax harmonization, progress has been slow. The only success has been in the field of direct taxes in the European Community (EC). All member states now use VALUE ADDED TAX as the principal indirect tax. No harmonization of the VAT rate has yet been achieved, since it would remove a potent fiscal weapon from the armoury of the national economic authorities.

See Index under Regulation and Tax, and under International Co-operation.

tax haven. A country, usually a small one, which has very low or non-existent corporate tax rates on the foreign earnings of expatriate companies. Tax havens include the Bahamas, Bermuda, the British Virgin Islands, the Cayman Islands, the Channel Islands, the Dutch Antilles, Hong Kong, Liberia, Liechtenstein, and Panama. The reason for such favourable tax treatment may be a deliberate policy on the part of the country concerned to boost a flagging economy at no effective cost, by attracting companies which do not trade in the country but contribute to its exchequer. However some tax havens do not discriminate in favour of foreign companies: they simply have low taxes for domestic companies and do not prevent foreign companies from taking advantage of them.

Tax havens may be used by multinationals as a channel for overseas earnings by other SUBSIDIARIES (*see* BRASS PLATE COMPANY, BASE COMPANY, CONTROLLED FOREIGN CORPORATION, HOLDING COMPANY, TRANSFER BOOKING, TRANSFER PARKING, TRIANGULAR TRADE). They are also used as a base for OFFSHORE FUNDS.

Tax authorities are well aware of the potential use of tax havens and the regulations governing the tax of overseas business will generally take their existence into account (*see* SUBPART 'F' INCOME). Thus both the USA and UK have provisions for adjusting TRANSFER PRICES where the authorities are satisfied that they are not similar to ARM'S LENGTH prices (*see* SECTION 485, INCOME AND CORPORATION TAXES ACT and INTERNAL REVENUE CODE SECTION 482). They are also prepared to inquire into where the 'real' management control of the company resides, thus ignoring the operations of 'brass plate' companies.

Although a tax haven can be used for

manufacturing, the term is not commonly used for such activity. Instead, reference would normally be made to a 'low tax' environment.

See also STIFTUNG, and Index under Regulation and Tax.

tax holiday. A tax incentive offered to a potential inward investor by a country (*see* INWARD INVESTMENT). The normal method is to specify a fixed number of years during which the new facility will not be chargeable to any direct corporate taxes by the host nation. In addition there may be exemption from property taxes. Tax holidays are often negotiated as an integral part of a wider package of incentives. As with other types of investment incentive, the danger to the host nation is that bargaining between investment-hungry countries leads to an escalation of offers so that the benefits to the country from the investment are substantially reduced, even nonexistent or negative.

See NEWLY INDUSTRIALIZING COUNTRIES, FREE TRADE ZONE, and Index under Regulation and Tax.

tax shelter. *See* TAX HAVEN.

tax sparing. A reduction of tax by a host country to encourage INWARD INVESTMENT. Such tax incentives may be largely ineffective to those multinationals with headquarters in countries such as the USA where credit for taxes spared is not allowed against group taxes.

The normal way of avoiding double taxation (*see* DOUBLE TAXATION AGREEMENT) in the absence of a formal bilateral agreement is to deduct foreign tax paid in the form of a TAX CREDIT from the group tax assessment. If no special provision is made, it follows that tax sparing will be ineffective, because the spared tax will be automatically charged by the home country's tax authorities. However some double taxation agreements between developed and developing countries are now beginning to recognize the need to incorporate tax sparing clauses.

See also TAX HOLIDAY, and Index under Regulation and Tax.

tax spinning. Sometimes used to describe a means of reducing the short-term liability of an oil company to tax. Where tax is charged on oil production, a revenue to the company is needed to produce a value for the oil which the revenue authorities might suppose is the market value. If the company is a major that owns its own refining capacity, it can produce 'evidence' for the authorities that the value is lower than otherwise might be supposed by selling some of the oil into the market at a lower than average price.

It has been argued that this practice, when adopted in a market downturn, can cause panic by apparently signalling further expected decreases by the majors, who are thus DUMPING oil at low prices in the market.

See Index under Regulation and Tax.

tax treaty. *See* DOUBLE TAXATION AGREEMENT.

technical assistance agreement. Together with the MANAGEMENT CONTRACT, with which it is often linked in one comprehensive agreement, a technical assistance agreement is one of many relatively new forms of contractual co-operation between host governments of developing countries and multinational corporations. Under a technical assistance agreement, a multinational corporation is engaged to provide technical services for the execution of a project for a specified fee, without any immediate or ultimate proprietary interest in the production of the enterprise. The technical assistance agreement does not impose any obligation on the multinational to provide capital for the project. The host government owns the natural resource, the entire production and the equipment and other facilities related to the project. The company merely provides technical assistance in all aspects of the execution of the project from design through operating and maintenance procedures, training programmes, personnel recruitment and a plan for the implementation of the various phases of the project. Technical assistance typically includes the use of proprietary knowledge and inventions, but not a responsibility for the disposal or marketing of the output of the project. The multinational company is renumerated in the form of fees, consisting of stipulated amounts in the period preceding the commencement of production, and a prescribed percentage of the sales value of the output for a stated period with effect from the commencement of commercial production. While the national agency or state-owned enterprise will through its own managing director have full power, authority and responsibility for the project, the multinational will second its own technical staff to a general manager, to whom all necessary managerial powers will be delegated.

See Index under Technology Transfer.

technological fixity. A characteristic of many production processes in which the factors of production – capital and labour – are not easily substituted. For example, to substitute labour-intensive techniques of production for capital-intensive techniques may be costly, requiring more and better supervisors, more materials which are wasted by less precise or unreliable hand methods, and more working capital because of greater need for inprocess inventory.

The concept has bearing on the debate concerning APPROPRIATE TECHNOLOGY or INTERMEDIATE TECHNOLOGY, where the substitution of labour for capital is often assumed to be a matter of political will rather than economic constraints.

technological rent. *See under* RENT.

terms of access. The conditions under which a country allows the importation of foreign goods. Such terms include restrictions on quantity or quotas, import duties (TARIFFS) and foreign exchange regulations.

territorial limitation. *See under* EXTRATERRITORIALITY.

Third World. A designation with five main meanings. Geographically, it refers – somewhat imprecisely – to the countries on the continents of Africa, Asia and Latin America. Economically, it refers equally loosely to all the poor countries of the world. Ideologically, it captures the self-awareness of newly emerging nations on these continents wishing to develop an economy and society different from the 'models' presented by the Western capitalist countries (FIRST WORLD) and the state socialist countries of Eastern Europe (SECOND WORLD). Institutionally, it refers to the association of countries on these continents, beginning with the 1955 Bandung Conference of African and Asian countries which laid the foundation for the non-aligned movement. This was consolidated by the formation of a caucus group of Third World countries at the first UNITED NATIONS CONFERENCE ON TRADE AND DEVELOPMENT (UNCTAD) (1964) when Latin American countries joined with those of Asia and Africa in presenting advanced countries with a determined negotiating 'bloc', known as the GROUP OF 77. Politically, the term refers to a third force in international political relations against the backdrop of the cold war between East and West.

Recent economic division of the Third World into rapidly growing economies such as OPEC and the NEWLY INDUSTRIALIZING COUNTRIES on the one hand, and stagnating or declining economies (now known as the FOURTH WORLD) on the other has eroded the institutional cohesion of the member countries. This has in turn shed doubt on the usefulness of the concept as an analytical and descriptive term.

See Index under International Co-operation, and under Theoretical Issues.

Third World multinationals. Multinational companies originating and headquartered in the developing countries. In 1985, 42 out of the top 500 non-American industrial corporations listed in *FORTUNE'S* annual league table were from the THIRD WORLD, with no less than 9 featuring amongst the top 50. In a combined ranking of American and non-American industrial corporations, the Third World contributes 25 companies. With 10 in the top 500, South Korea in fact has greater corporate muscle on the international scene than countries like France, Switzerland, or Italy. The emergence of multinationals from the Third World has occasioned some writers to argue that we are now entering a phase of POST-IMPERIALISM.

A characteristic feature of Third World multinationals is their para-statal character. Many are state-owned enterprises, or enterprises in which the state has a large stake. A second common feature, particularly amongst the giant companies of developing Asia and those of South Korea in particular, is that they are fashioned after the model of the giant trading companies of Japan, the *SOGO SOSHAS*. A third characteristic feature is their predilection for JOINT VENTURES in regional and international coalitions with other multinationals.

See also GLOBAL INDUSTRIAL SYSTEMS CONSTELLATION (GISC), and Index under Corporate Structure and Management.

TIE – Europe (Transnationals Information Exchange – Europe). Formed in 1978 and jointly sponsored by the World Council of Churches and the TRANSNATIONAL INSTITUTE, TIE is a network of some 40 action and research groups and workers' organizations. These include trade unions, shop stewards' committees, Third World groups, church organizations, and labour research centres. The strengthening of contacts between workers from transnational subsidiaries in different countries is a major aim of TIE – Europe.

A bulletin, *TIE – Report*, is published four times a year. It contains company case studies, information requirements from TIE affiliates and a comprehensive review of new publications.

See Index under Data Sources.
Address: Paulus Potterstraat 20, 1071 Amsterdam, Netherlands.

tied purchase clause. *See* TIE-IN CLAUSE.

tie-in clause. Clause in a FOREIGN DIRECT INVESTMENT (FDI) contract and/or LICENSING AGREEMENT which requires the subsidiary or licensee to purchase intermediate or spare parts and capital goods from the parent corporation which supplied the basic technology.

See TRANSFER OF TECHNOLOGY (ToT) CODE, and Index under Technology Transfer.

Times 1000. Annual publication of Times Newspapers Ltd, concerning the 1,000 leading companies in Britain and overseas. It is a statistical guide to the performance of the leading industrial and financial companies and the largest building societies, and ranks them according to sales, profits, and assets. It covers the UK, Europe, the USA, Canada, Japan, Australia, South Africa and Ireland. It gives data on acquisitions and mergers as well as on nationalized industries. It offers international comparisons of industrial performance and an index to the companies which includes the full postal addresses.

See Index under Data Sources.

TNB. *See* TRANSNATIONAL BANK.

TNC. *See* TRANSNATIONAL CORPORATION.

trademark. Any visible sign or device used by a business enterprise to identify its goods and distinguish them from those made or carried by others. The original function of trademarks was as an indication of origin. In the Middle Ages trade marks were used by the Guilds to guarantee quality and control entry to particular trades. Their use was compulsory, and could be considered to have constituted a liability for the producer in the sense that they could be used to trace the workman who made or sold defective goods. Modern trademarks date from the second half of the 19th century, when several countries enacted their first trademark legislation.

The objectives of modern trademark legislation are different from those of mediaeval times. Firstly, legal protection of trademarks is meant to protect one manufacturer against the possibility that another manufacturer will try to fraudulently present his products as his own. It therefore serves to foster fair competition. Secondly, trademark legislation today is said to secure quality identification for the consumer, thus protecting the consumer against confusion in the market place. Furthermore, the registration of trademarks today is not compulsory, as it was in mediaeval times. Generally, it is up to the seller to use or not to use a trademark. Thus, modern marks are an asset for the producer instead of a liability. They are legally protected as industrial property.

Although in modern legislation trademarks are understood as fostering fair competition, over time this protection permits the creation of market power for trademark holders. This power over price is achieved through persuasive advertising aimed at creating brand loyalty. In this way, trademark protection has an anti-competitive effect.

Most countries in the world today have enacted national trademark legislation.

While the registration of trademarks is a feature common to all national legislation, the effect of registration may differ. There is a broad division between countries where trademark rights are held to accrue to the first user of the mark (the United States and Canada) and those countries where the first registrant acquires exclusive rights (the Benelux countries and France). National laws, furthermore, vary in their regulation of the nature of granted titles, duration of rights, renewals, assignments and licensing.

At the end of the last century, when most national trademark laws were being enacted, trademarks were included with PATENTS in the INTERNATIONAL CONVENTION FOR THE PROTECTION OF INDUSTRIAL PROPERTY, which was concluded in 1883.

As in the case of PATENTS, developing countries have become increasingly aware and critical of their disadvantaged position *vis-à-vis* the advanced countries in a world of internationally protected trademarks, where through persuasive advertising such trademarks have become a major source of market power. Of the trademarks granted by developing countries some 50 per cent are owned by foreigners, and 95 per cent of foreign trademarks in developing countries are owned by nationals, mostly multi-national companies, of developed market economy countries. These trademarks are used in some cases to cover imported goods and more generally products made in the host countries by foreign manufacturing subsidiaries and licensees (*see* LICENSING AGREEMENT). In a trademark licensing agreement, the licensor has the right to control the products made under the licensed trademark in order to ensure that quality standards associated with the trademark are maintained. However, the contractual specifications as to the precise method of production required to meet the quality implied in the use of the trademark frequently involve tying clauses (*see under* TIE-IN CLAUSE) for the purchase of imputs, which in turn creates further DEPENDENCY

on the foreign supplier.

The developing countries have argued that foreign-owned trademarks place a burden on their balance of payments through remittances of fees paid (*see* ROYALTY) and through the implied dependence on imports; that the enormous advertising expenditures are borne by the consumers of the developing countries while the accrual in goodwill (and therefore profit) is for the benefit of the non-resident owner of the intangible asset; and finally, that foreign-owned trademarks shape consumption patterns in favour of the foreign product, leading to a misallocation of resources in the production of goods and services which are less than optimally suited to the BASIC NEEDS of the population. For example, in many regions of the world Pepsi-Cola is more readily available than safe drinking water.

The concern of the developing countries has been reflected both in new laws and policies on trademarks being enacted in countries like Mexico, Brazil, Argentina, the ANDEAN PACT COUNTRIES and India, and in current international efforts to revise the Paris Convention of 1883 (*see under* INTERNATIONAL CONVENTION FOR THE PROTECTION OF INDUSTRIAL PROPERTY). For example, the Mexican Law on Inventions and Trademarks of 1976 has introduced the concept of the 'combined trademark' as a means of sharing the benefits of the development of the goodwill between licensor and licensee. Article 127 states that any licensee of a trademark which is foreign-owned or of foreign origin cannot be authorized unless such a mark will be used jointly and equally prominently with a mark originally registered in Mexico, and whose owner is the licensee. Moreover, according to Article 91, marks originally registered in Mexico may not consist of words of a live foreign language or their corresponding phonetic equivalent, or in the combination of two or more words of a live foreign language. Article 127 applies only to those goods made in Mexico. Imported goods may still be sold with foreign-owned trademarks without any linkage to a domestic mark. Finally, some developing countries have also placed a ceiling on royalty payments for the use of foreign-owned trademarks and/or prohibit payments between subsidiaries and parent companies of multinational corporations for the use of foreign-owned trademarks (Brazil, India, and the Andean Pact countries).

See Index under Technology Transfer.

trade secret. Any industrial property not protected by PATENT. It may consist of any formula, pattern, device, or compilation of information which is used in a business, and which gives an opportunity to obtain an advantage over competitors who do not know or use it. While the owner of a trade secret cannot prevent others from developing and using his possession of technology, he can prevent wrongful disclosure and improper use by persons with whom a fiduciary or confidential relationship has been established. Success in a common law suit following unauthorized disclosure (by an employee, for example) depends however on the fiduciary or confidential relationship having been clearly established before the disclosure and also on the discretion of the courts, since there are no specific statutory laws for the protection of trade secrets.

The decision on whether to protect a new invention through patent or through the practice of the trade secret principle depends on a number of considerations: the cost of patent protection (which multiplies in direct proportion to the number of countries in which a multinational company markets its products), the economic strength of the company, and the rate or speed of the technological development affecting the invention or process. A most important consideration in favour of the trade secret option is that once a patent has expired, normally after 20 years, the secret is lost.

Even the mere issue of the patent may alert potential competitors to the existence of the new invention. A celebrated example of the preferred use of trade secret over patent is that of the Coca-Cola formula.

See Index under Technology Transfer.

Trade Union Advisory Committee (TUAC). An advisory body recognized within the ORGANIZATION FOR ECONOMIC CO-OPERATION AND DEVELOPMENT (OECD) as the official vehicle for expressing trade union views. TUAC comprises 38 national trade union federations from 22 OECD member countries, as well as affiliations from the INTERNATIONAL CONFEDERATION OF FREE TRADE UNIONS (ICFTU), the WORLD CONFEDERATION OF LABOUR (WCL), the EUROPEAN TRADE UNION CONFEDERATION (ETUC), and INTERNATIONAL TRADE SECRETARIATS (ITS).

TUAC's priorities are economic and employment policies, transnational corporations, and energy and education questions. There is a special permanent TUAC Working Group for Multinational Enterprises, where trade union views are prepared and co-ordinated. Since 1978 this working party has met jointly with the ICFTU Working Party on Multinationals. The trade union views on multinationals are presented to the OECD in consultative meetings with the OECD's IME COMMITTEE.

See Index under International Co-operation and under Labour.

Address: 26 Avenue de la Grande Armee, 75017 Paris, France.

transaction costs. Costs arising from the process of exchange in the market. For example, costs are generated by the search to find appropriate suppliers; associated with the drawing up of contracts, or monitoring the adherence to such contracts. Transaction costs have become an important concept in theories of the growth of firms, including the growth of multinational firms, since it is argued that firms tend to internalize market transactions which give rise to costs.

See INTERNALIZATION THEORY; COASE THEOREM; APPROPRIABILITY THEORY, and Index under Theoretical Issues.

TransAfrica. The major black American foreign policy lobby for Africa and the Caribbean. Its focus is on the impact of United States corporations on the economic development of African and Caribbean states. It monitors corporations which invest in South Africa, and publishes the newletter *TransAfrica Forum*.

See Index under Data Sources.
Address: 545 8th Street SE, Washington DC 20003, USA.

transfer booking. In international banking, the selective siting of loans and deposits. Transfer banking serves much of the same purpose for TRANSNATIONAL BANKS (TNBs), as transfer pricing does for other multinational corporations (*see* TRANSFER PRICE).

By placing their EURODOLLAR loans on the books of their TAX HAVEN subsidiaries, transnational banks can minimize their global tax liabilities. This is made possible by the existence of double taxation relief provisions in many advanced countries where the TNBs are located. The US government, for example, allows banks to earn tax credit from areas where they have had to pay a higher level of tax to a foreign government than they would to the US government. But such tax credits would be wasted if banks did not set them off against the normal level of US taxes, topping up the charge in a low tax area.

The selective siting of loans is also practised by small-scale US banks, though for different reasons. They place loans on the books of their companies in tax haven countries in order to comply with US restrictions on their participation in the EURODOLLAR market.

Transfer booking is not the same as transfer pricing, since it does not involve the administrative allocation of a price – the foreign exchange value of the currency, or the interest rate – to the commodity in question. But *see* TRANSFER PARKING.

See also DOUBLE TAXATION AGREEMENT, and Index under Financial and Risk Management.

Transfer of Technology (TOT) Code. Since 1977 there have been intense and protracted negotiations for an international code of conduct on the transfer of technology, conducted under the auspices of the UNITED NATIONS CONFERENCE ON TRADE AND DEVELOPMENT (UNCTAD). Because the positions of the technology exporting countries (the advanced, industrialized countries, or GROUP B STATES in UN parlance) and the technology importing countries (the less developed countries or GROUP OF 77, plus the Communist bloc or GROUP D STATES) are diametrically opposed, the outcome of the negotiations is still uncertain. This uncertainty persists even though one of the most contentious issues, the Code's formal legal status, has been resolved in favour of a voluntary code. It has been agreed that it should take the form of a proposed UN General Assembly resolution and include follow-up machinery which will require states which have accepted the Code to take appropriate steps at the national level to meet their commitment to it.

The draft Code defines technology transfer as the transfer of systematic knowledge for the manufacture of a product, for the application of a process or for the rendering of a service. Transactions involving technology transfer which are within the scope of the draft Code include the sale and licensing of all forms of industrial property, provision of knowhow and technical expertise and provision of technological knowledge necessary for the installation, operation and functioning of plant and equipment, and

TURNKEY projects. It does not extend to transactions involving the mere sale or lease of goods.

Areas of substantial agreement include the identification of and provisions for dealing with 12 restrictive business practices: GRANT BACK PROVISIONS; challenge to validity of patents; exclusive dealing; restrictions of research; restrictions on the use of personnel; price fixing; restrictions on adaptations; exclusive sales or representation agreements; tying arrangements; patent pool or CROSS-LICENSING agreements; restrictions on publicity; and payments and other obligations after expiration of industrial property rights. There is still disagreement on export restrictions and restrictions after expiration of the arrangement, and on six additional restrictive practices identified by the Group of 77 and the Group D states, but not recognized by Group B.

More fundamental is the disagreement between the negotiating groups of countries over the issue of transfers of technology between companies in common ownership. This issue was conveniently excluded from the successfully negotiated RESTRICTIVE BUSINESS PRACTICES (RBP) CODE. Developing countries argue that the identification and the control of restrictive practices in technology transfer transactions should also apply to transactions between parent companies and their cross-frontier subsidiaries. They insist that for the purposes of the Code a parent and its subsidiary should be considered as legally separate entities. Group B countries however have maintained that technology transfer transactions between parent and subsidiary should be considered to fall within the Code's provisions if they are concluded as part of a process of rationalization or reasonable allocation of functions, and if they do not constitute an abuse of a dominant position of market power within the relevant market.

There is also fundamental disagreement over the extent to which the provisions of the draft Code should apply to transactions within national boundaries that might have an international content. Group B countries wish to see the draft Code applied by means of national legislation to all technology transfers within their national boundaries (including transactions between domestic enterprises). Group D and the Group of 77 propose in contrast that the draft Code should apply to transactions between parties residing or established in the same country only if in the latter case at least one of them is directly or indirectly controlled by a foreign entity, and the technology transferred has not been developed in the acquiring country by the supplying party.

A final issue which remains to be resolved is the text on applicable law and settlement of disputes.

See also CODES OF CONDUCT; UNITED NATIONS DRAFT CODE OF CONDUCT ON TRANSNATIONAL CORPORATIONS, and Index under International Co-operation and under Dispute and Settlement.

transfer parking. The practice of transfer pricing (*see* TRANSFER PRICE) in the field of international banking. It involves the setting of administered or internal prices for foreign exchange values, and the realization of the gains of such pricing in low tax areas. Thus, a TRANSNATIONAL BANK (TNB) headquartered in New York may instruct its Nassau branch to sell £1 million to its Frankfurt branch at the rate of US$1.60. A few hours later that day the Frankfurt branch will be instructed to sell £1 million to the Nassau branch at US$1.555. By this transaction, the Frankfurt branch takes a taxable loss in a high income tax country (in this case, West Germany) while the Nassau branch registers a gain in a low or near zero tax rate country. At the same time, in the internal books of the TNB, the Frankfurt branch is credited back with the same amount to compensate for the apparent reduction in earnings.

Unlike the practice of transfer pricing of physical commodities in multinational corporations, where often as not no true market prices exist for the transferred commodities, and the manipulation of such pricing for tax purposes frequently remains open to dispute, in transfer parking the practice, though limited in scale, is undoubtedly carried on for tax avoidance purposes only.

See Index under Financial and Risk Management.

transfer price. The concept of the transfer price is probably the most controversial in the theory and practice of multinational enterprise. The development of the concept, in particular its increasingly wide scope, has reflected both the changing organizational structure of multinational business and its heightened political sensitivity.

Originally, the term transfer price was better known as 'accounting' or 'internal' or 'administered' price. Firms which had developed into organizationally complex structures encompassing different divisional subsidiaries faced the problem of having to assign prices to transactions between their different subsidiaries; as, for example, when half-finished goods produced in one subsidiary were transferred for final processing to another (*see* PROFIT CENTRE). The setting of such transfer prices reflected a decision internal to the firm, and as such it was distinct from (though not necessarily independent of) the setting of market or ARM's LENGTH prices between independent producers. As firms developed into still more elaborate structures with separate research, finance and other central service divisions, the definition of transfer price widened to include all internal transactions including services and financial transactions. A still broader definition emerged with the development of new cross-border transactions involving firms which are not wholly owned but are minority affiliates or subcontracted parties. The concept has now, therefore, simply come to refer to all transactions between related parties for which the price is not the result of competitive market or arm's length negotiations.

The expanding market share of cross-frontier INTRA-FIRM TRADE which now encompasses an estimated four-fifths of all international trade in raw materials and one quarter of all international trade in manufactures, has catapulted the practice of transfer pricing into the political arena. The ability of multinational enterprises to adjust transfer prices arbitrarily may affect the international distribution of income between nations. Less developed countries in particular have become sensitive to the way in which overpricing of imports or underpricing of exports can adversely affect their BALANCE OF PAYMENTS and national income. Much of their strident nationalism on the issue of ownership over foreign-controlled activities and resources stems from this awareness (*see* ECONOMIC NATIONALISM).

In assessing the magnitude of the problem of transfer pricing and in deciding what if anything nation states can or should do about it, it is important to distinguish between transfer pricing as an accounting problem for the firm and transfer pricing as a manipulative tool for maximizing its global post-tax profits.

Addressing the accounting problem first, there are basically two guidelines that management work by in assigning transfer prices: cost-based systems and market-based systems. In cost-based systems the price of the transferred commodity is based on either the average unit cost of production (whether that is a historical actual average or a standard average cost) or on the marginal cost of production. Cost-based systems have the advantage of being relatively straightforward to operate and easy to justify to tax authorities. The disadvantage of the cost-based system is that in the absence of competitive market forces there is no incentive to improve cost performance, nor is there a means for the firm to distinguish between profitable and unprofitable operations. In the case of production technology there is the additional problem that once the initial research and development expenditure for the technology has been recovered in the sales of the resulting output, the technology strictly speaking no longer 'costs' anything. Less developed countries have sometimes taken this view in respect of intra-firm technology transfers from advanced countries, arguing that ROYALTY payments for such transfers are RENTS and should be classed as profits. For example, under Decision 24 of the ANDEAN PACT, royalty payments between subsidiaries and their overseas parent companies are disallowed, as they are in Brazilian legislation for TRADEMARKS and PATENTS.

Market-based systems link the price of the product, technology or service to its equivalent in a relevant existing market. While market-based systems do provide a meaningful criterion for evaluating performance and hence can assist management in distinguishing between profitable and unprofitable operations, they are difficult to implement because competitive markets seldom exist externally for transactions between related parties. Again, this is especially the case in respect of technology and of both producer and intermediate goods, though much less so in the case of finished manufactures and unprocessed raw materials. Nevertheless, the US tax authorities in particular try very hard to develop valuation standards based on comparable market prices in order to curb the abuse of transfer pricing (*see* CONSTRUCTED PRICE).

Given that the assignation of realistic transfer prices (that is, based on market or cost prices) is in many cases an elusive goal,

it is not surprising that multinational enterprises have turned this accounting problem into an instrument of profit maximization. With an intelligent use of transfer pricing, a multinational can channel its global profits into the country where its tax rate is lowest and reduce its tax exposure in countries where it is higher.

But the circumnavigation of differential tax rates, structures and administrations between countries is only one objective in setting transfer prices. There are other fiscal and financial gains to be made. Customs duties, for example, also vary between countries. The higher the import duties in country A, the more it pays a multinational to lower the value of its transactions to its subsidiary in A, provided the tax rate in country B from which it exports, is equal to or higher than that in country A. Export subsidies too may be a factor affecting the calculation of transfer prices, and so may be multiple currencies and variable exchange rates. Judicious administration of transfer prices can minimize the exchange risk for multinationals as well as offer speculative gains, provided the transfer price manipulations are complemented by corresponding changes in the timing of the payments, that is by LEADING AND LAGGING.

It is a matter of continuing political controversy and academic dispute whether the universalization of the nation state, with its attendant multiplication of differential national policies (TARIFFS, taxes, subsidies and currencies) has in fact induced companies not only to use transfer pricing as a central tool of global profit maximization, but also to deliberately plan their global operations in such a manner as to maximize the gains arising from the trading off of one set of public policies against another. What is in less doubt is that many policies flowing from economic nationalism have forced multinational companies to use transfer pricing as a defensive mechanism in securing their return on capital. Demands for local shareholdings, pressures from local trade unions, exchange control restrictions, profit remittance limitations and threats of outright EXPROPRIATION may all combine to make the multinational identify a particular location as an undesirable area in which to declare high profits and thus induce it to use the transfer pricing mechanism as a means of substituting direct trade earnings for the traditional 'invisible' earnings (like dividends and royalties).

Multinational companies are not exclusively interested in maximizing short-term return on investments. Long-term growth and expansion strategies also play a role in the manipulative use of transfer pricing. Such strategic reasons may include the desire to support a new infant industry with supplies of cheap subsidized imports, or the need to penetrate a new market against competitive rivals (see CROSS-SUBSI-DIZATION).

As the opportunities for the gainful abuse of transfer prices have multiplied, so have constraints on them. It is common to distinguish between two types of limitations on the manipulation of transfer prices: internal and external limitations. Internal restrictions are those organizational and managerial limitations within the enterprise which inhibit the successful exploitation of transfer pricing techniques in the pursuit of fiscal, financial and strategic objectives. The conflicting demands of these objectives coupled with the diversity of public policies in a world of 120 or more competing nation states, yields variables of such complexity that only the largest of corporations can process this information, formulate rational decisions and execute them. Only they have the necessary advanced computational facilities, the experience and knowledge of world conditions and – most importantly – the ability to exercise tight centralized control over overseas operations. And while some analysts would argue that the evolving structure of management has indeed tended toward increasing control from the centre, others point to the decentralizing forces

also in evidence (see CENTRALIZATION).

External constraints on transfer pricing are those enforced with varying degrees of success by public authorities. Enhanced scrutiny by tax and customs authorities can, and has, curbed pricing abuses, especially in the transfers of finished manufactures and primary commodities, where external markets often do exist to help the authorities determine 'arm's length' prices. But this is not the case with the transfer of technology.

It is difficult to estimate whether or not transfer pricing is a problem that is increasing or declining. This is because the evidence as to whether intra-firm trade in intermediate goods and technology is growing faster than that in finished manufactures and unprocessed raw materials is contradictory. It is however generally agreed that transfer pricing has become a less contentious issue in some respects than it was 20 years ago, due to the nationalist policies which some developing countries pursue in their resource sectors, as well as to the development of various pricing systems based on market and cost figures (see INDEXATION; REFERENCE PRICE SYSTEM; FAIR MARKET VALUE SYSTEM). But such success has not been achieved in the transfer of technologies, intermediate products and producer goods. It is in this area that much of the attention of international regulatory efforts is focused (see for example the UN DRAFT CODE OF CONDUCT ON TRANSNA-TIONAL CORPORATIONS).

See Index under Corporate Structure and Management, under Financial and Risk Management.

translation. The conversion of the financial results of a multinational's overseas SUB-SIDIARIES into the home currency, usually for the purpose of consolidation into a set of group accounts (see CONSOLIDATED ACCOUNTS). Translation problems arise as a result of fluctuating exchange rates.

Four basic methods of translation have

been commonly used in the UK and USA. These have all involved some combination of the 'closing rate', that is, the rate of exchange obtaining at the date of the balance sheet and the 'historical rate', which for an asset is the rate of exchange at the date of acquisition and for a liability is the rate prevailing on the date when the liability arose.

The four methods are:

the *closing rate* method. This method translates all items at the closing rate. It was popular in the UK in the past when exchange rates were less volatile than they have since become.

The *current non-current* method. This method distinguishes between current and non-current assets and liabilities. The former are translated at the closing rate, the latter at the historical rate.

The *monetary non-monetary* method. This translates monetary items at the closing rate and non-monetary items at the historical rate.

The *temporal* method. Identical to the monetary non-monetary method except for items which are subject to a choice of valuation method. For example, inventory may be valued at either cost (a historical valuation) or market valule (a current valuation), whichever is lower. These are consequently translated differently, valuations at cost being translated at the historical rate and market valuations at the current rate.

Currency translation is a complex technical process, involving further detailed choices of method. For example, translation may take place at the closing rate as defined above, or at an average rate for the year in question. Again, the charges to reserves allowed under some methods may be limited, if they are losses, to charges against previous translation profits that have been credited to reserves, or this limit may not apply.

The most significant aspect of currency translation comes in its implication for prof-

its declared. A requirement that all losses in a period should be charged against the profit for that period was the cause of the controversy at the heart of FINANCIAL ACCOUNTING STANDARD No 8 (FAS 8) in the United States, which resulted in its withdrawal and replacement by FINANCIAL ACCOUNTING STANDARD No 52 (FAS 52). The current UK standard, SSAP 20, uses a method involving a choice between the current rate method (which takes exchange differences to reserves) and the temporal method (which charges them to income) depending on the nature of the subsidiary. It is effectively the same as FAS 52 as a part of a deliberate policy to seek harmonization of standards (*see* HARMONIZATION POLICIES).

Worldwide the current rate method is the most prevalent method, but this may cnange now that the INTERNATIONAL ACCOUNTING STANDARDS COMMITTEE (IASC) has adopted the UK/US method in International Accounting Standard No 21, *Accounting for the Effects of Changes in Foreign Exchange Rates.*

See FINANCIAL ACCOUNTING STANDARDS BOARD (FASB), and Index under International Accounting.

transnational bank (TNB). A relatively new designation for a bank with worldwide international operations. The term has become current since the mid-seventies. Its popularity is owed in part to the parallel naming of the TRANSNATIONAL CORPORATION, which also dates from that time.

The preferred usage over the previous designation 'international' bank, however, also reflects an awareness of new trends in international banking, including offshore funds (*see* OFFSHORE FINANCIAL MARKET) and deepening integration between finance and industrial capital; of the accelerated pace of internationalization of banks worldwide and particularly the very rapid expansion of their overseas activities by banks headquartered in the US; and of the growing concentration of bank capital through MERGERS and TAKEOVERS.

See also EDGE ACT CORPORATION; AGREEMENT CORPORATION, and Index under Corporate Structure and Management.

transnational corporation (TNC). A recent addition to the vocabulary of terms used interchangeably with MULTINATIONAL CORPORATION. Its precise definition has been the outcome of many years of international negotiations and deliberations within the framework of the drafting of a code of conduct on transnational corporations under auspices of the United Nations. The term as used in the draft Code 'means an enterprise, comprising entities in two or more countries, regardless of the legal form and fields of activities of these entities, which operates under a system of decision-making, permitting coherent policies and a common strategy through one or more decision-making centres, in which the entities are so linked, by ownership or otherwise, that one or more of them may be able to exercise a significant influence over the activities of others and, in particular, to share knowledge, resources and responsibilities with others'. The most controversial part of this definition is the phrase 'regardless of the legal form'. The term, like the Code, is meant to apply just as much to state-owned enterprises from the socialist countries which have foreign undertakings as it is to private companies and state-owned enterprises originating in capitalist countries (*see* RED MULTINATIONALS and FOREIGN TRADE ORGANIZATIONS (FTO)).

The term 'transnational corporation' is the preferred term in United Nations and trade union circles, as well as amongst activist groups engaged in campaigns of opposition. For the evolution of this term *see under* MULTINATIONAL CORPORATION/ENTERPRISE.

See also UN DRAFT CODE OF CONDUCT ON TRANSNATIONAL CORPORATIONS, and Index under Corporate Structure and Management.

Transnational Corporations Research Project. A research group at the University of Sydney, studying transnational corporations in Australia, Southeast Asia and the Pacific with the aim of providing documentation on them. It has made studies of minerals and energy, finance, and of the labour movement in the region.

See Index under Data Sources.
Address: Department of Economics, University of Sydney, Sydney, Australia.

Transnational Institute. *See* INSTITUTE FOR POLICY STUDIES (IPS).

Transnationals Information Centre (TIC). An independent resource centre, originally supported financially by the Greater London Council. Its aim is to make information about transnational companies more widely available. It plans to build a campaign which will encourage greater awareness of the effect of transnational companies in London; to develop a discussion on ways of controlling transnational corporations; and to work towards extending international solidarity amongst trade unions, Third World organizations, migrant workers, women and action, research and solidarity groups outside the UK. TIC provides information and organizes education for relevant groups on industries and transnationals in order to increase the understanding of transnationals' current strategies in the context of their global operations.

See Index under Data Sources.
Address: 9 Poland Street, London W1V 3DG, UK.

Treaty of Rome. *See under* EUROPEAN COMMUNITY.

triangular trade. A particular form of INTRA-FIRM TRADE involving a subsidiary located in a low tax or tax exempt country. Exports are sold to the subsidiary at a price less than the market price. From the TAX HAVEN they are next exported again at a higher value to their final destination. Sometimes, depending on the laxity or corruptibility of the customs officials in the countries of final destination, the triangular trade transaction may amount to no more than a paper transaction, with the physical trade being direct between the exporting and importing countries.

See Index under Trade.

Trilateral Commission. A private committee set up in 1973 at the initiative of David Rockefeller, championing the cause of inter-continental co-operation between the USA, Europe and Japan. The membership of the Commission is exclusive and consists of some 200 representatives of the world's most powerful multinational corporations, banks, communications conglomerates, international organizations, and a few of the biggest Trade Unions. As a result, some critics have dubbed the Commission the 'executive committee of transnational finance capital'. They contend that its ideological perspective represents the transnational outlook of multinational capital, seeking to subordinate territorial politics to non-territorial economic goals.

The full commission meets only once a year; its work is made up of task-force reports (normally commissioned from leading academics and specialists) on contemporary problems in need of 'global management'. These include energy, relations with the Third World, international monetary reform and international trade.

See Index under International Co-operation, and under Corporate Structure and Management.

Tripartite Declaration of Principles Con- cerning **Multinational Enterprises and Social Policy.** Non-mandatory code of conduct adopted by the governing body of the INTERNATIONAL LABOUR ORGANIZATION (ILO) in 1977. The unique tripartite structure of the ILO, which is reflected in the representation of governments, employers' organizations and employee organizations on the governing body, gives this voluntary code a degree of political authority in the absence of legal force. This authority rests upon the agreement of all parties to the tripartite structure, and it ensures that at the very least promotional measures are taken in the relevant contexts and that some machinery may be set up at a national level for tripartite consultations about the code's substantive problems and effects. Furthermore, although a follow-up obligation cannot arise automatically from a non-binding Declaration, the ILO has established its own follow-up procedure involving a three-yearly questionnaire for government reporting and an ad hoc committee which assesses in a general way the degree of acceptance of the terms of the Declaration, considers the difficulties or inadequacies in the light of experience and evolves procedures for the examination of disputes about the application of the Declaration.

The Declaration is addressed to national governments, employers' organizations and trade unions, as well as to the multinational enterprises themselves. The principles cover areas of specific concern to the ILO relating to the social aspects of multinational enterprise activity, and include the following.

General policies. MNEs are urged to harmonize their activities with the national development priorities and social aims of the countries in which they operate; governments are urged to ratify the ILO conventions regarding freedom of association, collective bargaining and non-discrimination in employment.

Employment. MNEs should endeavour to increase employment opportunities and standards, and give priority to the employment and occupational development of nationals of host countries; in developing countries they should have regard to the importance of using technologies which generate employment, directly and indirectly.

Training. MNEs should provide relevant training for all levels of their employees with a view to meeting the needs of the enterprise as well as those of the host country.

Conditions of work and life. Wages, benefits and conditions of work should not be less favourable than those offered by comparable local employers. Where such comparable local employers may not exist, as in developing countries, these conditions of work should at the minimum satisfy the basic needs of the workers and their families. In such countries MNEs are recommended to become 'leading' employers, offering 'best prevailing' wages and benefits.

Industrial relations. MNEs should observe the best existing practices of the host countries, but also respect the principles of freedom of association and the right to organize. Limitations on the latter must not be included by governments as special incentives to attract foreign enterprise. In the context of bona fide negotiations, MNEs should not threaten to utilize a capacity to transfer operations from a country in order to influence unfairly those negotiations or to hinder the exercise of workers' right to organize.

Although sections of the ILO membership, including labour representatives in general as well as certain states, would prefer a mandatory instrument in the form of an International Labour Convention, there is a view which ascribes potential legal significance and efficacy to the Declaration, in that it is, however slowly, helping to establish internationally accepted and recognized standards. Already the text of the ILO Code is fully compatible with the rele-

vant subsections of the OECD Guidelines (*see under* DECLARATION AND DECISIONS ON INTERNATIONAL INVESTMENT AND MULTINATIONAL ENTERPRISE) and it has also been adopted by the UN Intergovernmental Working Group as the appropriate text for the specialized subsections of the more comprehensive UN DRAFT CODE ON TRANSNATIONAL CORPORATIONS, which is still being negotiated. And finally, the objectives enshrined in the Declaration are also adopted in the VREDELING DIRECTIVE, which is on the European Community (EC) agenda for eventual mandatory status in EC countries.

See Index under International Co-operation and under Dispute and Settlement.

Truman Doctrine. The first major US foreign policy statement after the Second World War, announced by President Harry Truman on 12 March 1947. Following the withdrawal of British troops from the crisis-torn states of Greece and Turkey, Truman went before Congress and successfully sought military and economic aid for the two countries. He justified American military involvement in the region by proclaiming the existence of a world division between the 'free' West and the 'totalitarian' East, and by pledging US support to 'free people who are resisting subjection by armed minorities or outside pressures'. The Truman Doctrine effectively set the US on course in its role as global policeman.

turnkey contract. A contract in a country lacking relevant technical knowledge between a purchaser (normally a government or state-owned enterprise) and an overseas contractor. The contractor agrees to construct a complete, ready-to-operate, production facility for a predetermined fee and the turnkey operator will generally receive staged payments, with a final payment made when the facility is operating satisfactorily.

There are variations in the turnkey contract depending on the degree of participation in the project on the part of the purchaser. In a 'turnkey-plus' contract the responsibilities of the contractor go beyond the stages of commissioning and startup of the production facility into the initial stages of operation (*see* PRODUCT-IN-HAND AGREEMENT) or even into selling the output (*see* MARKET-IN-HAND AGREEMENT).

In a 'semi-turnkey' contract, on the other hand, the supply of the plant and equipment is the responsibility of the contractor, but the civil engineering and erection is undertaken by the purchaser or his subcontractors. When the participation of the purchaser increases still further, for example in taking responsibility for choosing and purchasing the plant and equipment himself, the contract ceases to be referred to as turnkey and becomes a COST-REIMBURSABLE CONTRACT.

Because turnkey contracts are an increasingly common and important form of technology transfer from advanced to less developed countries, the UNITED NATIONS INDUSTRIAL DEVELOPMENT ORGANIZATION (UNIDO) has begun to develop model forms of turnkey contracts, beginning with the fertilizer industry. The UNIDO model contracts are the product of intensive discussions with experienced contractors from developed countries and purchasers from less developed countries. They are aimed at striking a balance between the needs and the industrial reality of developing countries and the established commercial practices in this field.

See Index under Technology Transfer.

turnover tax. An indirect tax levied on the sales revenue of an organization. There may be one of two basic philosophies behind the imposition of such a tax.

The first is to be found in developed countries where turnover taxes are seen as inexpensive to assess and collect. They are charged at some stage of the process from production to sale to final consumer. In Canada, for example, they are charged when production is completed, in the USA when the final sale takes place. In West Germany they were at one time charged at all stages of the process. This meant that each successive link in the chain accumulated further tax, and hence such a tax was known as a 'cascade tax'.

The second is more likely to be found in a less developed country. Suspicious of the ability of companies, and in particular foreign companies, to manipulate earnings, they are unwilling to base corporate tax on profits. Therefore the tax is charged on the company's turnover on the grounds that this is less susceptible to manipulation. In this case, therefore, the underlying philosophy is one of a direct rather than an indirect tax.

See Index under Regulation and Tax.

U

UEC (Union Européenne des Experts Comptables Economiques et Financiers). A body founded in 1951 by 12 national associations of professional accountants. Its membership now covers not only the countries of the European Community (EC) but also Scandinavia and Yugoslavia, amounting to 29 bodies in some 20 countries. It has in the past issued recommendations on accounting reporting methods, but has since acknowledged the more recently formed INTERNATIONAL ACCOUNTING STANDARDS COMMITTEE (IASC) as the appropriate body for this.

It now numbers among its activities recommendations on audit practice, co-ordinating this with the activities of the INTERNATIONAL FEDERATION OF ACCOUNTANTS (IFAC); the holding of triennial congresses; and the issue of international publications such as an eight-language accounting dictionary. At the time of writing proposals were in train to merge the UEC with the GROUPE D'ETUDES DES EXPERTS COMPTABLES DE LA CEE.

See Index under International Accounting and under International Co-operation.
Address: 8 München 80, Worthstrasse 42/1, West Germany.

U-form organization. One of two basic organizational structures as identified and named by Williamson (1970). The U-form organization is unitary; that is, it is not broken down into seperate divisions. It contrasts with the multidivisional M-FORM ORGANIZATION and preceded it historically. It is still a more appropriate organizational form for the smaller company, but lacks the growth potential and flexibility of the multidivisional structure.

See DIVISION, and Index under Corporate Structure and Management.

ultra-imperialism. A model of world politico-economic relations formulated by Karl Kautsky in 1914 and revived more recently by some modern writers on IMPERIALISM.

In opposition to Lenin's theory of imperialism, which was predicated on the rivalry between imperialist nations, Kautsky envisaged a gradual weakening of imperialist rivalries as a consequence of the growing CENTRALIZATION and CONCENTRATION of capital. Through MERGERS and takeovers, multinational companies would simply outgrow the nation state. They would become indifferent to their national roots, and in consequence, the nation state would for its part relinquish its role as an instrument of inter-imperialist competition. Instead, the organization of the world capitalist economy would be the function of a world state: that is, a coalition of nations in international organizations.

More recently, and taking up this theme in the context of the post-war establishment of international economic organizations such as the INTERNATIONAL MONETARY FUND (IMF) and the WORLD BANK, some Eastern European writers (Varga, 1963) have argued that there is now evidence of the existence of such an ultra-imperialist world state. The causes and objectives of these organizations in the age of 'supra-national' monopoly capitalism are seen to be identical to those of state monopoly capitalism on a national scale, namely to preserve the capitalist social system, to secure high monopoly profits, and to mediate between conflicting interests of monopoly capitalists and contain their contradictions.

See also SUPER-IMPERIALISM; POST-IMPERI-

224

ALISM; INTER-IMPERIALIST COMPETITION; NEO-IMPERIALISM, and Index under Theoretical Issues.

unbundling. Conventionally, FOREIGN DIRECT INVESTMENT (FDI) by multinational enterprises has involved a 'bundle' consisting of capital, technology, equipment, management, servicing, and market access. By combining all the elements in a single package, critics argue, additional premiums or RENTS may be obtained over and above the total costs of the elements if acquired separately. This would be so particularly if competition for each element were more active than for the package as a whole.

Recipient host countries, particularly host developing countries, have therefore started to experiment with unbundling. This means that they have started to negotiate and pay separately for each component, often seeking to obtain the money capital from a different source (bank credit, for instance, or foreign aid). Unbundling in the sense described thus far is also sometimes referred to as 'depackaging'.

The term is also used in international financial management. Here it denotes the separation of remittances from a foreign affiliate to its parent company into their constituent parts (dividends, royalties, management fees, etc.). This may be advantageous to the multinational for two reasons: it may facilitate the remittance of funds, since countries banning or limiting the amount of dividend remittances may allow ROYALTIES or other fees that can be justified on a rational basis. There may also be tax advantages, because these fees are charges against income in the accounts of the affiliate, whereas dividend remittances are distributions of profit. The disadvantage to the multinational may be a reduction of motivation or confidence within the subsidiary, where the charging of these fees reduces earnings and signals continual dependence on head office expertise and other services.

See Index under Technology Transfer, and under International Accounting.

UNCLOS. Abbreviation of 'United States Convention on the Law of the Sea'. *See* LAW OF THE SEA TREATY.

UNCTAD. *See* UNITED NATIONS CONFERENCE ON TRADE AND DEVELOPMENT.

UNCTC. *See* UNITED NATIONS COMMISSION ON TRANSNATIONAL CORPORATIONS.

underwriter. An organization in the securities markets which aids companies seeking to sell their shares or bonds by guaranteeing, for a fee, to take up any shares that remain after a sale to the public. Most securities issues are underwritten because it is important to the issuing company to ensure as far as possible that all the funds it wishes to raise by the issue do materialize.

UNICE. French acronym for the Union of Industries of the European Community (EC). It is the official vehicle for the combined views on European policy of the national employers' confederations of the EC member countries. Although it is often regarded as the employers' counterpart of the EUROPEAN TRADE UNION CONFEDERATION (ETUC) it is not of equal importance as a channel of influence on issues affecting multinational companies. This is so because UNICE has no special brief for multinationals but also because it does not speak at all for the non-EC multinationals which are amongst the major economic operators in the Community.

See Index under International Co-operation and under Corporate Structure and Management.
Address: Rue de Loxum 6 (bte 21), 1000 Brussels, Belgium.

UNIDO. *See* United Nations Industrial Development Organization.

uniform accounting. An approach to corporate financial statements which emphasizes the form of accounts rather than the content. It originated in pre-war Germany, and was taken up in France. Essentially, it is a means of enforcing uniformity in the appearance of corporate accounts by specifying in detail the headings under which balance sheet and income statement items are shown. Uniform accounting has never affected the USA or the countries heavily influenced by US or UK accounting, but it has since 1981 been a fundamental aspect of UK financial reporting as a result of Britain's adoption of the principles of the Fourth Company Law Directive of the EUROPEAN COMMUNITY (EC) in the Companies Act, 1981.

See Index under International Accounting.

unitary taxation. A corporate tax system imposed by individual States in the USA whereby a corporation's activities throughout the world may be treated as a single unit. If they are, the State levies a tax upon the corporation based on some proportion of that income. The method of assessing the proportion varies from State to State. The result of the system has been, for example, that some companies making a loss in a particular year in a US State have found themselves nevertheless assessed to pay tax because the corporation has shown a profit worldwide.

The system is not confined to companies with a head office in the State concerned: the presence of a SUBSIDIARY is sufficient to make the corporation liable to such an assessment. It dates back to 1926, but has recently become more controversial as more States have attempted to impose the system and foreign multinationals have found that it is being applied to them.

By 1984 the system was being operated by Alaska, California, Colorado, Florida, Idaho, Indiana, Illinois, Massachusetts, Montana, New Mexico, North Dakota, Oregon, and Utah, and a further seven states were seen as likely to adopt it. Foreign government pressure, including the threat of retaliation via fiscal legislation, forced the US federal government to set up a working party to examine the system of unitary taxation. The working party recommended that States should only apply the system to operations within the USA but was not prepared to legislate federally against them. In view of this pressure many States have abandoned the system and at the time of writing it was only in full operation in Alaska, California, Montana and North Dakota, having been ruled illegal in Massachusetts. Unitary taxation has proved a political embarrassment to the US government, particularly in view of the recent threats of retaliation (including a clause in the UK's 1985 Finance Act) and the interest of some THIRD WORLD countries to follow suit.

See also CORPORATE TAX SYSTEM, and Index under Regulation and Tax.

United Nations Center on Transnational Corporations (UNCTC). A research and information centre set up in 1975 under the aegis of the UN Economic and Social Council (UNECOSOC). Its chief task is the provision of substantive and administrative services to the UNITED NATIONS COMMISSION ON TRANSNATIONAL CORPORATIONS. Additionally, by collecting and disseminating pertinent information on key issues of state-company relations such as restrictive business practices, transfer pricing and taxation, the unit helps to strengthen the capacity of developing countries, in particular in dealing with multinational corporations; to improve their capacity to formulate policies; to evaluate the impact of transnational corporations on their economies and to ensure that the activities of TNCs are consistent with national interests and development objectives.

The Center's research studies are issued as reports to the Commission and as general publications. It also produces a biannual publication, *The CTC Reporter*. The Center is also widely known for the development of its *Comprehensive Information System on Transnational Corporations*, which includes a computerized and regularly updated corporate profile database.

See Index under International Co-operation, and under Data Sources.

Address: United Nations, Room BR-1066, New York NY 10017, USA.

United Nations Commission on Transnational Corporations. A permanent Commission set up in 1974, following the recommendations of an *ad hoc* Group of Eminent Persons appointed by the UN Economic and Social Council (UNECOSOC) in the preceding year to study the role of multinational corporations and their impact on the process of development.

The Commission today consists of 48 members who each serve for a three-year term, and who are selected, as is usual in the UN, on the basis of broad geographical representation from both developed and developing home and host countries. Additionally the selection of commission members reflects relevant backgrounds, from politics and public service through to business, labour and consumer interests.

The Commission attempts to further understanding of the nature of transnational corporate activity in home and host countries, and of the political, legal, economic and social effects of those activities, particularly where the international relations between developing and developed countries are concerned. It tries also to secure effective international arrangements for the operation of transnational corporations so as to promote their contribution to national developmental goals and world economic growth while controlling and eliminating their negative effects. Thirdly,

it attempts to strengthen the negotiating capacity of host countries, in particular the developing countries, in their dealings with transnational corporations.

The Commission reports to the UN Economic and Social Council. It is serviced by a special research and administrative body, the UN CENTER ON TRANSNATIONAL CORPORATIONS (UNCTC) which was established in 1975, also on the recommendation of the Group of Eminent Persons.

The Commission meets annually in different locations. So far it has published two main general reports on transnational corporations in world development, in 1979 and 1983. Its chief preoccupation at present is the formulation of a UN DRAFT CODE OF CONDUCT ON TRANSNATIONAL CORPORATIONS.

See Index under International Co-operation.

United Nations Conference on the Law of the Sea (UNCLOS). *See* LAW OF THE SEA TREATY.

United Nations Conference on Trade and Development (UNCTAD). A permanent organ of the United Nations General Assembly, set up in 1964. UNCTAD developed from a one-off conference on international trade and development which had been called for at the behest of the non-aligned countries in a resolution of the United Nations General Assembly in 1962. The unique mandate of UNCTAD is to deal with global economic issues in terms of their impact on the self-sustaining growth of the less developed countries. From the beginning, therefore, it has served as a forum for such countries to formulate their demands for certain reforms in the world economic order. Moreover, the decision to make UNCTAD directly responsible to the General Assembly, which implies the opportunity to bring resolutions and recommendations directly to the Assembly (where the Third World holds a majority of two-thirds) proved advantageous. The developing countries could view UNCTAD as a means of circumventing the developed countries' control of the various UN sub-organizations and affiliated organizations, such as the INTERNATIONAL MONETARY FUND (IMF) and the WORLD BANK, where this control is ensured through weighted voting. Membership of the Conference now totals over 160 countries.

Since its establishment the machinery of UNCTAD has grown to impressive dimensions, consisting of the periodic Conference (held every four years) as the apex, the Trade and Development Board and its main committees. To these are added a number of continuing or *ad hoc* intergovernmental groups, special or negotiating conferences, and the like. There are main committees on commodities, manufactures, invisibles and finance related to trade, shipping, transfer of technology and economic co-operation among developing countries (*see* COLLECTIVE SELF-RELIANCE) and a special committee on trade preferences.

The process of setting up expert groups, sessional committees, *ad hoc* intergovernmental groups and working groups over a period of time has reflected a complex process of negotiation within UNCTAD, involving the extension and definition time and again of new areas of study, deliberation and negotiation. There were for example groups on each of the international development strategies, on supplementary finance, on debt operations and international monetary reform, on reverse transfer of technology and on an integrated programme for commodities.

Of crucial importance to the world economy and to UNCTAD's work has been the rise of the transnational corporation as the dominant institution in world trade and development. The transnational corporation has therefore assumed an important role in UNCTAD's work programme, and it has influenced UNCTAD's analysis of the global complex of power that dominates the world economy. This perception of the global role of the transnational corporation is clearly seen in certain key UNCTAD studies on commodities and commodity markets.

In many of these pioneering studies, notably those on bananas, tobacco, fibres, textiles and services – UNCTAD's methodology has departed from more traditional approaches. By studying the commodities in their totality and highlighting intersectoral connexions, it has analysed and laid bare the role of corporate power at each specific link of production and trade in the commodity chain.

See also TRANSFER OF TECHNOLOGY (TOT) CODE; RESTRICTIVE BUSINESS PRACTICES (RBP) CODE; PATENT REVISION, and Index under International Co-operation and under Trade and under Data Sources.

Address: Palais des Nations, ch-1211, Geneva 10, Switzerland.

United Nations Draft Code of Conduct on Transnational Corporations. A draft CODE OF CONDUCT still being negotiated under auspices of the UNITED NATIONS COMMISSION ON TRANSNATIONAL CORPORATIONS.

Work on the Code was started in 1977 by the Intergovernmental Working Group, a subsidiary body of the Commission which was established in 1975, and consisted of delegates from 48 states. Although the Working Group submitted a draft Code after its 17th session in 1982, there were still so many areas of disagreement that doubts were raised as to whether a final text could ever be agreed upon.

However, at the behest of the General Assembly, negotiations have been resumed with a view to finding an overall solution to the remaining issues and completing work on the Code in 1986.

The draft Code consists of six main parts. The first part, which has not yet been drafted, is to contain a preamble and a statement of objectives. The second part consists of a set of provisions on the definition of transnational corporations and the scope of the Code's application. The Commission on Transnational Corporations, which has had an item relating to the definition of TNCs on its agenda since its inception in 1974, decided to deal with the matter in the context of the Code of Conduct. While the intergovernmental working group has reached agreement on the main characteristics of a TNC (*see* TRANSNATIONAL CORPORATION), a fundamental issue persists as to whether the Code should apply to all enterprises falling within the scope of the definition 'regardless of their ownership' (state-owned or public enterprises being included, for example) and 'regardless of their country of origin' (including those from Eastern bloc countries).

The third and longest section deals with the activities of transnational corporations and their attitudes towards their host countries. The provisions in this section have obtained considerable consensus and include respect for host country social and cultural values; co-operation with national objectives for local equity participation and adoption of local recruitment policies; consideration of the financial interests of host countries, particularly their balance of payments and currency situation; the abandonment of those TRANSFER PRICING methods not based on the ARM'S LENGTH principle; the public disclosure in the countries in which they operate not only of information on their subsidiaries but also of full and 'comprehensible' information on structure, policies, activities and operations of the corporation as a whole. The fourth part of the Code deals with the treatment that transnational corporations are to receive from the governments of host countries. This section includes the major outstanding issues of international law, NATIONALIZATION, State contracts, NON-DISCRIMINATION and fair and equitable treatment, free choice of law and the means of settlement of any dispute, and

non-interference in internal affairs. On all of these issues consensus has so far eluded the Commission. The fifth part of the Code defines the co-operation necessary among governments for the application of the Code, while the sixth deals more specifically with the action needed at the national and international levels for its implementation. On both of these sections there is a fair amount of agreement.

The history of the Code negotiations is probably of greater interest and lasting importance than its eventual outcome. The initial conception of the Code on the part of many delegations, especially those from the less developed (GROUP OF 77) countries, was that it should be an instrument governing the whole range of activities of transnational corporations, and that it should be legally binding rather than voluntary. However, in the course of the negotiations the advanced (GROUP B STATES), WHO HAD INSISTED THROUGHOUT UPON A VOLUNTARY CODE, GOT ACCEPTANCE IN PRINCIPLE THAT THE CODE SHOULD BE COMPREHENSIVE AND INCLUDE A SECTION ON THE NATIONAL TREATMENT of TNCs. It was agreed that this section might include references culled from established international law regarding the protection of foreign property, full or adequate compensation in the event of expropriation, non-discrimination, choice of law in case of dispute and so on.

The acceptance on the part of the Group of 77 countries of the inclusion in principle of a section on national treatment (however finally worded) has indirectly and paradoxically affected their stance on the status of the Code. For the reference to established international laws regarding NATIONAL TREATMENT contravenes the CALVO CLAUSE upon which much of their claim to absolute national sovereignty *vis-à-vis* the treatment of alien enterprises rests. In their view, to make such a comprehensive Code legally binding would be to weaken the same national sovereignty which they originally sought to enhance with the Code. This paradox may open up possibilities for a successful conclusion of the negotiations by fundamentally altering the approach to the them and the expectations of the final text.

Firstly, there is now a generally shared emphasis on the primary need for the Code to be 'effective', 'generally accepted' and 'universally adopted', and this is coupled with an understanding that effectiveness does not necessarily depend on its legal form. Secondly, it is generally understood to follow from this that there is therefore no longer a need for all provisions in the Code to be couched in precise legal terms, thus making it possible to resolve the difficulties relating to some formulations especially involving those concepts on which there is basic agreement. Thirdly, it is seen to follow that the Code in fact does not need to embody a 'final' text, but that instead certain issues can be taken up in later negotiations, either separately or as part of the Code follow-up process. Finally, continually changing historical circumstances argue in favour of an instrument that is flexible, not fixed for all time, and capable of being reformulated and refined in the course of time. As a result, there is now a generally shared view that the Code should itself be an evolving and evolutionary document rather than a final and definitive text.

See CODES OF CONDUCT, and Index under International Co-operation, and under Dispute and Settlement.

United Nations Industrial Development Organization (UNIDO). Established as an organ of the United Nations General Assembly in 1966, the organization has had – since 1979, but with effect from 1985 – the status of a UN specialized agency. The purpose of the organization is to promote and accelerate the industrialization of the developing countries, with particular emphasis on the manufacturing sector. It is empowered to undertake operational activities as well as action-oriented studies and research programmes.

Of particular interest to multinational corporations are its global negotiations branch and its technology transfer section, which provide a forum for consultations and negotiations among developing countries and between developing and industrialized countries. A vast body of knowledge about patterns and practices of technology contracts in developing countries has been accumulated (*see under* TURNKEY CONTRACT).

Operational activities include the provision of short-term and emergency aid to help solve urgent technical problems and the provision of expert personnel and consultants.

The organization fosters links between potential investors and business people in developed countries, and enterprises in developing countries. To this end, it has set up investment promotion offices in Western financial centres such as Brussels, Cologne, New York and Zurich.

The organization's publications include the quarterly journal *Industry and Development* and the annual *Industrial Development Survey*.

See Index under Technology Transfer and under International Co-operation.

Address: Vienna International Center, PO Box 300, 1400 Vienna, Austria.

usance. The time period of a draft or BILL OF EXCHANGE; that is, the period before it becomes due for payment.

U-turn investment. A relatively new pattern of investment, in which labour-intensive production processes previously thought to be suitable for investment in the less developed countries are instead established in the advanced countries. The U-turn or 'relocation back North' investment pattern occurs because the development of labour saving innovations and automation has rendered the competitive wages prevailing in Third World countries obsolete. Examples of U-turn investments can be found in the garment industry and in the electronics industry.

See NEWLY INDUSTRIALIZING COUNTRIES; NEW INTERNATIONAL DIVISION OF LABOUR, and Index under Trade.

V

value added tax (VAT). Sometimes known as 'added-value tax'. An indirect tax, originally developed by the US for Japan during the post-war occupation, but now forming the central plank of indirect taxes in the EUROPEAN COMMUNITY (EC) among other countries.

VAT is assessed on the output or sale value of all goods or services that are defined by the law or commercial code as being subject to it. Each person assessed to VAT may however deduct from the amount due to the authorities the amount of input tax paid by him. This ensures that the inequities of so-called 'cascade taxes' are not perpetuated. In a cascade tax system there is no deduction for inputs, so that the larger the number of stages in the production process, the higher the tax charge. The tax is relatively inexpensive to collect (although dearer than simple sales taxes) but can leave itself open to fraud since some traders are 'zero rated' and hence are net recipients of the tax from the taxing authorities. For many years the tax has provided an export incentive available to countries under the GENERAL AGREEMENT ON TARIFFS AND TRADE (GATT) rules in that it could be rebated for export sales, when many other taxes could not.

See TURNOVER TAX, and Index under Regulation and Tax.

vertical integration. The control and ownership of more than one stage of the extraction, production and sales process by one company. According to INTERNALIZATION THEORY, TRANSACTION COSTS lead to a multinational's decision to incorporate the different stages of the production process, thus eliminating uncertainties in the market in its own interest at the expense of suppliers and customers. Vertical integration may lead to the abuse of monopolistic advantages, including the ability to manipulate TRANSFER PRICES and benefit from leads and lags in intracorporate remittances (*see* LEADING AND LAGGING).

See also HORIZONTAL INTEGRATION, and Index under Corporate Structure and Management, and under Industry Structure.

voluntary export restraint. The restraint of exports by nationals of one country to the domestic market of another country or countries at the request of the government of the importing country. Voluntary export restraints have become an increasingly popular form of NON-TARIFF BARRIER in the advanced countries. Beginning in the late 1950s with the voluntary restraint on Japan's exports of textiles to the US and spreading in the 1960s to some West European countries, voluntary export restraints have been extended during the following decades to cover a wide range of developing countries and products.

See Index under Trade.

Vredeling Proposal. A term generally used to refer to the EUROPEAN COMMUNITY (EC)'s *Draft Directive on Procedures for Informing and Consulting the Employees of Undertakings with Complex Structures in Particular Transnational Undertakings*. This proposal of the European Commission, first proposed in 1980 and revised in 1983, has met with strong opposition even in its revised form from corporate interests in the EC, from non-EC multinationals operating in the EC, and from some governments, such as that of the UK.

Named after Henk Vredeling, the Dutch

EC Commissioner for Social and Labour Affairs, it is concerned with the disclosure of information about business enterprises to their employees. The terms of the proposal have changed in the successive drafts and overlap to some extent with the employee representation proposals of the Draft Fifth directive on company law (*see under* EURO-PEAN COMMUNITY (EC).

The revised proposal makes several recommendations for multinational undertakings with 1000 employees or more. It states that employees have the right to receive information annually from the corporate parent concerning employment, investment prospects and other economic and financial matters, the right to prompt information about any proposed changes liable to have serious consequences for the interests of the employees of the company's subsidiaries in the European Community, and the right to be consulted over these changes and a minimum 30 days' delay in their implementation after consultations have begun.

Neither this proposal nor the fifth directive is likely to reach the statute books in the next few years.

See also CODES OF CONDUCT, and Index under International Co-operation and under Labour.

W

War on Want (WoW). An independent radical organization campaigning against world poverty. Recent campaigns have increasingly focused on the relationship of transnational corporations to poverty and underdevelopment.

See Index under Data Sources.

Address: 1 London Bridge Street, London, SE1 9SG, UK.

Webb – Pomerane Act. This Act of 1919 was intended to exempt from the provisions of the Sherman anti-trust Act those associations 'entered into for the sole purpose of engaging in export trade' provided they do not restrain the export trade of any domestic competitor or enter into any agreement, understanding, or conspiracy to artificially or intentionally enhance or depress prices within the United States. In practice very few 'Webb' trusts have been set up, because the courts have excluded foreign subsidiaries, whether wholly or jointly owned. Webb associations therefore make it impossible to follow an export success with a FOREIGN DIRECT INVESTMENT (FDI) in the associate's firm. Nevertheless, the Webb – Pomerane Act represented an important step in the trend toward the use of contractual international JOINT VENTURES which have become important vehicles for collective action by oligopolistic firms in a number of key industries.

See CARTEL, OLIGOPOLY, ANTI-TRUST LEGISLATION, and Index under Regulation and Tax.

Western Hemisphere Trade Corporation (WHTC). A special tax status available to US companies that traded exclusively within the Western hemisphere and derived at least 95 per cent of their gross income from sources outside the USA. Such companies were taxed at a lower rate than domestic companies. The status of WHTC was dropped from 31st December 1979.

See Index under Regulation and Tax.

WFTU. *See* WORLD FEDERATION OF TRADE UNIONS.

wholly owned subsidiary. A subsidiary that is 100 per cent owned by its parent. For many years there was a strong feeling among many multinationals, and particularly US multinationals, that it was desirable or even essential to insist upon 100 per cent ownership of overseas operations. There is some evidence that the extent of ownership preferred was more a function of the industry the company operated in than its home country. The pressures of the ECONOMIC NATIONALISM of host nations, the growth of JOINT VENTURES, the recognition of the advantages of at least some local ownership to aid access to foreign capital markets, and the development of new control methods such as INTERNATIONAL SUBCONTRACTING have all contributed to the recognition by many that full ownership is not necessary for the exercise of control. Full ownership, however, retains the advantage that there is no conflict of interest when the parent wishes to act in a way that might be unpalatable to local or other minority shareholders.

See Index under Corporate Structure and Management.

Who Owns Whom. A series of company relationship directories, published annually by Who Owns Whom Ltd, London. The directories are compiled on the basis of annual reports and questionnaire surveys. The North American edition contains an alphabetical list of parent companies in the USA and Canada, giving addresses, industrial sectors, subsidiaries and associated companies, including the countries in which these are located. It also gives a list of all foreign subsidiaries in the USA and Canada, and the names of their parent companies.

The continental edition gives an alphabetical list of parent companies by country, an alphabetical list of all European subsidiaries throughout the continent, including a list of such subsidiaries and associated companies by country, and the names and country of origin of their respective parent companies. The UK and Ireland edition does the same for all parent companies and subsidiaries and associated comanies located in the British Isles.

See Index under Data Sources.
Address: 24 Tufton Street, London SW1P 3RA, UK.

WHO/UNICEF Code of Marketing of Breastmilk Substitutes. The first code of its kind to evolve out of an international grassroots campaign against a particular multinational company and industry. The Nestlé Baby Food campaign was started in 1974 by WAR ON WANT in the United Kingdom, and was followed by a libel suit brought by Nestlé in the Swiss courts when German activists translated the original monograph *The Baby Killer* under a new title, *Nestlé Kills Babies*. The judge ultimately ruled that the translators were technically guilty of libel, but imposed a token fine and admonished Nestlé to change its advertising practices.

At issue was the question of whether the industry's milk powders designed for bottle feeding became lethal in areas where the population lacks access to safe water, money to buy the requisite amount of the product and are not at the necessary level of literacy to follow the printed instructions. The campaign broadened in 1977 when the United States Infant Formula Action Coalition (INFACT) began a boycott of the products of Nestlé, and American churches joined in with stockholders' campaigns and other forms of protest. Through the International Baby Food Action Network (IBFAN) the campaign became still more international, mobilizing at its height some 100 groups in 65 countries. The campaign also propelled the INTERNATIONAL ORGANIZATION OF CONSUMER UNIONS (IOCU) into a new activist role, in which it began to focus on the marketing practices of certain multinationals in less developed countries and on the suitability of their products for these markets.

In 1978, the industry itself, aware that it had lost the propaganda battle, turned to the World Health Organization (WHO) with the request that it act as a forum for informed debate on the subject. A meeting of doctors, industry representatives and corporate critics was held under joint WHO/UNICEF auspices to examine the whole issue of infant nutrition. Out of this meeting a compromise formulation emerged which was to become the basis for the Code, which in turn was passed after numerous drafts by the WHO assembly in 1981. The compromise formula recognized breastfood substitutes as legitimate products and also allowed the right of the industry to market its product, but still heavily circumscribed the prevalent marketing practices. Advertising and promotion were for the most part to be stopped. Labelling of the product would have to state clearly the superiority of breast feeding and the health hazards of inappropriate preparation.

The Code was passed by 118 member countries with only the USA voting against. Although the Code is a recommendation and not a binding international regulation and many countries have failed to take action on it, the fact that Nestlé eventually implemented it and made a public display of this implementation, resulted in the weakening of the boycott and finally its suspension. The history of this Code is of importance because it demonstrates how the development of a Code of Conduct under the auspices of international organizations can legitimize the practices of multinational corporations and disarm their critics. The success of this particular Code has prompted the IOCU to press the WHO for a voluntary code of pharmaceutical marketing practices.

See IFPMA CODE; CODES OF CONDUCT, and Index under International Cooperation.

WHTC. *See* WESTERN HEMISPHERE TRADE CORPORATION.

WIPO. *See* World Intellectual Property Organization.

withholding tax. A tax levied by a government on dividends or interest paid to foreign investors. In many systems withholding taxes are a natural result of the tax system rather than a punitive measure to discriminate against foreigners: under the classical system of corporation tax, for example, companies deduct income tax at the standard rate before remitting the net amount to all shareholders. Domestic shareholders can then set this off against their personal tax assessments as a credit: overseas recipients, not of course being assessible by the host nation, cannot. It is normal to include provisions concerning withholding taxes in DOUBLE TAXATION AGREEMENTS.

See also CORPORATE TAX SYSTEM, and Index under Regulation and Tax.

workshop subsidiary. Normally a foreign subsidiary of a parent company which manufactures parts or components for the parent only. It is distinct from a RELAY SUB-SIDIARY which also supplies third parties. Workshop subsidiaries are also known as 'branch plants'.

See Index under Corporate Structure and Management.

World Bank. Specialized agency of the United Nations originating in the Bretton Woods Conference of 1944, and established since 1945.

Originally called the International Bank for Reconstruction and Development (IBRD), it was set up to help nations recover from the ravages of the Second World War and to promote economic development. Since 1949 the Bank's activities have focused increasingly on the less developed countries. As a sister organization of the INTERNATIONAL MONETARY FUND (IMF), also instituted at the Bretton Woods Conference, membership of the World Bank is open only to those countries who have joined the IMF. These now number 146, including China but excluding the USSR, the Eastern bloc socialist countries and Switzerland.

The Bank's resources consist of its capital stock, the member countries' paid up and callable subscriptions, and of funds raised through borrowing in the world's capital markets. A substantial contribution to the Bank's resources also comes from its retained earnings and the flow of repayments on its loans. In 1984 its assets expressed in US dollars totalled $60 billion.

The World Bank mostly lends capital for infrastructural and productive investment projects on a medium- or long-term basis at interest rates which are closely linked to the Bank's own cost of borrowing. Repayment of principal is normally phased over 5 – 15 years with an initial grace period of 5 years. Loans are extended to member governments or must be guaranteed by them; the World Bank's affiliate, the INTERNATIONAL FINANCE CORPORATION (IFC) was set up in 1956 specifically to complement the Bank's lending in the private sector of developing countries.

In recent years, as a consequence of the 'debt crisis' which has tended to slow down the flow of commercial lending to developing countries, the Bank has become involved in complex co-financing arrangements with official aid organizations and international banks in an attempt to encourage commercial lenders to loan funds on the long maturities appropriate for development finance. To encourage the increase of FOREIGN DIRECT INVESTMENT flows to developing countries it has recently set up the Multinational Investment Guarantee Agency. Furthermore, in an important departure from its previous lending practices, it has since 1980 engaged in so-called 'structural adjustment lending' programmes. The purpose of these nonproject long-term loans is to assist developing nations with severe short-term balance of payments difficulties lest these should jeopardize the implementation of current investment programmes and activities productive of foreign exchange. In order to qualify for such structural adjustment loans, however, the recipient countries need to satisfy the Bank that they are developing specific policy, industrial and other changes designed to strengthen their balance of payments position. This novel practice of World Bank 'conditionality' has invited criticisms of 'imperialist' intervention similar to those levelled at the IMF's 'stabilization' programmes.

Besides offering financial assistance, the World Bank also undertakes broad technical assistance programmes to help prepare the ground for appropriate loans and to help recipients make effective use of the loans once granted. Its advisory and consultancy work has expanded into longstanding policy dialogues with borrowing member countries .

As is the case with the International Monetary Fund, the governing structure of the World Bank reflects the proportionate share of member countries' subscriptions in that the larger subscribers hold more of the votes. Today the USA has 20.5 per cent of the voting strength, the UK 6.5 per cent. The President of the World Bank has always been an American citizen. The general operations of the Bank are delegated to a Board of Executive Directors, each of whom is appointed by either a single member country or a geographic group of member countries depending on the size of subscription.

The World Bank publishes the annual and much acclaimed *World Development Report*, as well as numerous staff papers and country studies.

See also INTERNATIONAL DEVELOPMENT ASSOCIATION; INTERNATIONAL FINANCE CORPORATION; IMPERIALISM, and Index under International Co-operation and under Financial and Risk Management.
Address: 1818 H Street NW, Washington DC 20433, USA/and 66 Avenue d'Iena 75116, Paris, France.

World Council of Churches Programme on Transnational Corporations. Established in 1977 at the World Council's Nairobi Conference, this programme provided for a series of regional consultations, gathering experiences and opinions on the activities of transnational corporations in the Third World as well as in industrialized countries and socialist economies. The programme culminated in a second 'worldwide' consultation on TNCs in November 1981. The TNC programme aims to develop alternative postures towards TNCs from an ecumenical point of view. It supports studies on the impact of TNCs in the Third World, support which involves financial help, and actions which seek to remedy TNC domination. The Programme publishes the newsletter *Sharing*.

The TNC programme has had an awakening effect in many national churches, and questions are now being raised about TNCs in ways that have not previously been used. Many church bodies have become involved in campaigning on particular issues related to TNCs, ranging from the Nestlé boycott by the Methodists and others in the USA, to the advocacy of the ending of bank loans to South Africa by the Dutch, Canadian, British and US churches. The US churches have also tackled Coca-Cola on its activities in Guatemala, while the Canadian churches have confronted mining companies on their activities in Namibia.

See Index under Data Sources.
Address: 150 Route de Ferney, 1211 Geneva 20, Switzerland.

World Directory of Multinational Enterprises. A publication by Macmillan (Globe), London. Compiled biannually by John Stopford , it gives an alphabetical register of the 500 largest TNCs and the countries in which their headquarters are located. Each company is described in two or more pages giving history, organization, structure, production, and financial details.

See Index under Data Sources.

World Federation of Trade Unions (WFTU). Set up as an international trade union in 1945 to replace the International Federation of Trade Unions, the WFTU has from its inception been dominated by communist influence. Failure to get recognition from the United Nations, together with the pro-Soviet leanings of its leadership and internal differences over the acceptance of Marshall Aid, led in 1949 to a withdrawal of non-communist trade union organizations and the formation of the rival international trade union organization, the INTERNATIONAL CONFEDERATION OF FREE TRADE UNIONS (ICFTU).

The WFTU has over 155 million members drawn in the main from affiliations with unions in the Soviet Union, though affiliated organizations also exist in France, India and some developing countries in Africa.

See Index under International Co-operation and under Labour.
Address: Mamesti Curreovych 1, 11688 Prague 1, Czechoslovakia.

World Intellectual Property Organization (WIPO). Established by international Convention in Stockholm in 1967 to succeed the United International Bureau for the Protection of Intellectual Property of 1893. WIPO started its operations in 1970 and became a specialized agency of the United Nations in 1974.

The organization's main objectives are to promote the protection of intellectual property throughout the world, to centralize the administration of the various multilateral treaties dealing with industrial or artistic and literary property, and to give legal and technical assistance, especially to developing countries in the formulation of modern industrial property and copyright systems.

See also INTERNATIONAL CONVENTION FOR THE PROTECTION OF INDUSTRIAL PROPERTY; PATENT, and Index under International Co-operation and under Technology Transfer.
Address: 32 Chemin de Colombettes, 1211 Geneva 20, Switzerland.

The World's Largest Industrial Enterprises. Directory published by Gower Press/ Farnborough, UK. Prepared by John Dunning and Robert Pearce, it presents an alphabetical register of companies giving history, structure and financial details.

See Index under Data Sources.

X

X-efficiency A concept developed by Leibenstein (1966). He noted the considerable literature in neo-classical economics that argued, following the pioneer work of Harberger (1954), that the diminution of allocative efficiency of an economy for instance results from MONOPOLY or OLIGOPOLY, is of relatively little importance in terms of welfare loss. Leibenstein postulated that an alternative conception of efficiency, the efficiency within the firm which was under the control of management, was of far greater significance. Organizational theorists had for some time known this concept as 'organizational slack'. Leibenstein called it 'X-inefficiency'. It is concerned with the skills of management in allocating resources to the firm's processes. The X-efficient firm uses those resources to the best advantage. The validity of the concept has been challenged by those who argue that market competition will tend to drive out X-inefficiency. Nevertheless the concept has been found to be fruitful by industrial economists.

More recently the concept of X-efficiency has been used to explain the success of the developing economies such as those of Hong Kong and Singapore. It is generally accepted that X-efficiency is greater in more competitive markets: and the markets of these countries are exceptionally competitive, with few BARRIERS TO ENTRY or oligopolistic structures. It has been argued that one reason for this is the presence of foreign companies in these markets, which have stimulated competition without at the same time introducing oligopoly.

See Index under Theoretical Issues.

Y

yankee bond. A FOREIGN BOND sold in the USA and denominated in US dollars.

See also SAMURAI BOND.

yen company. Japanese subsidiary of a foreign company which has been established without specific government approval owing to the parent company's willingness to forego the Japanese government's explicit guarantee of repatration of principal and profits. Yen companies date from 1956 when the Japanese Government relaxed its strict screening requirements of all inward foreign direct investment.

See Index under Regulation and Tax.

Z

zaibatsu. Giant family-controlled trading companies that, before the Second World War, dominated the Japanese economy. There was considerable concentration, and this was regarded as unacceptable by the US occupying forces after the war. Basing their thinking on US ANTI-TRUST LEGISLATION, they broke up the largest of the *zaibatsu*.

Since the occupation ended three of the leading *zaibatsu* – Mitsui, Mitsubishi and Sumitomo – have taken some steps to reassemble themselves. Nevertheless it is considered unacceptable to refer to them as *zaibatsu*, and indeed some of the complex cross-holdings are far weaker than they then were.

See also SOGO SOSHA.

zero coupon bond. A relatively recent innovation among financial instruments, also sometimes known as a 'deep-discounted bond'. They have been popular mainly for their tax advantages, and were no special tax provision to be made for them they would avoid tax until the capital gain was realized on maturity. However as a result of legislation both in the USA and the UK, there are provisions for spreading the discount over the period of the bond on an actuarial basis. Although popular in the USA, such bonds had not, at the time of writing, proved very popular in the UK, even though tax experts consider they have marginal advantages over conventional bonds.

See Index under Financial and Risk Management.

APPENDIX I

REFERENCES

ACCOUNTING STANDARDS COMMITTEE
Accounting Standards Committee. 1983. *Foreign Currency Translation (SSAP 20)*. London: Accounting Standards Committee.

AGRIBUSINESS
Versluysen, Eugene L. 1981. *The Political Economy of International Finance*. London: Gower Publishing Co. Ltd.

United Nations Conference On Trade and Development (UNCTAD). 1985. *Handbook of International Trade and Development Statistics, 1985 Supplement. Geneva: UNCTAD*.

ANDEAN PACT COUNTRIES
Mytelka, Lynn K. 1977. Regulating direct foreign investment and technology transfer in the Andean group. In *Journal of Peace Research* XIV (2), pp.155-184.

APPROPRIABILITY THEORY
Magee, Stephen P. 1977. Information and the multinational corporation: an appropriability theory of direct foreign investment. In J.N. Bhagwati, *ed The New International Economic Order, the North-South Debate*. Cambridge, Mass.: MIT Press.

BALANCE OF PAYMENTS
Bell, Phillip W. 1962. Private capital movements and the US balance of payments position. In *Factors Affecting the United States Balance of Payments; a compilation of studies prepared for the Joint Economic Committee*. Washington, DC: US GPO.

Stopford, John M. and Turner, Louis. 1985. *Britain and the Multinationals*. Chichester and New York: IRM/John Wiley and Sons.

Bos, H., Sanders, M. and Secchi, C. 1974. *Private Foreign Investment in Developing Countries: A Quantitative Study of the Evaluation of the Macro-Economic Effects*. New York: Reidel Publishing Co.

Lall, Sanjaya andStreeten, Paul, 1978. *Foreign Investment, Transnationals and Developing Countries*. London: Macmillan.

BARRIERS TO ENTRY
Bain, J. 1956. *Barriers to New Competition; their Character and Consequences in Manufacturing Industries*. Cambridge, Mass.: Harvard University Press.

BARRIERS TO EXIT
Caves, E. and Porter M.E. 1976. Barriers to exit. In R.T. Masson and P.D. Qualls, *eds, Essays on Industrial Organization in Honor of Joe Bain*. Cambridge, Mass.: Ballinger.

BASIC NEEDS
Herrera, A. D. et. al. 1976. *Catastrophe or New Society?*. Ottawa: International Development Research Centre.

BENCHMARK SURVEY
US Department of Commerce Bureau of Economic Analysis. 1981. *US Direct Investment Abroad, 1977*. Washington DC: US GPO.

BRANDT COMMISSION
Brandt Commission. 1980. *North-South, A*

Programme for Survival. The report of the independent commission on international development issues under chairmanship of Willy Brandt. London: Pan Books.

Brandt Commission. 1983. *Common Crisis. The report of the independent commission on international development issues under the chairmanship of Will Brandt.* London: Pan Books.

CAPITALISM
Weber, Max. 1927. *General Economic History.* London: Allen and Unwin.

Parsons, Talcott. 1971. *The System of Modern Societies.* Englewood Cliffs, NJ: Prentice-Hall.

CLUB OF ROME
Meadows, D. et. al. 1974. *The Limits to Growth.* London: Pan Books.

COASE THEOREM
Coase, Ronald H. 1937. The nature of the firm. In *Economica, 4, pp.386–405.*

CORPORATE IMPERIALISM
Girvan, N. 1976. *Corporate Imperialism: Conflict and Expropriation.* New York: Monthly Review Press.

COUNTERTRADE
Organization for Economic Co-operation and Development 1985. *Countertrade; Developing Countries' Practices.* Paris: OECD.

COUNTRY RISK ASSESSMENT
Knudsen, H. 1974. Explaining the national propensity to expropriate: an ecological approach. In *Journal of International Business Studies,* Spring 1974, pp. 51-71.

DECLARATION AND DECISIONS
Organization of Economic Co-operation and Development (OECD). 1976. *International Investment and Multinational Enter-prises: Guidelines for Multinational Enterprises, National Treatment, International Investment Incentives and Disincentives, Consultation Procedures.* Paris: OECD. (Revised edition Paris, 1984).

DEPENDENCY
Prebisch, R. 1950. *The Economic Development of Latin America and its Principal Problems.* New York: Economic Commission for Latin America.

Furtado, C. 1958. The external disequilibrium in the underdeveloped Economies. In *The Indian Journal of Economics,* April 403–410.

Baran, P. 1957. *The Political Economy of Growth.* New York: Monthly Review Press (trans 1967).

Frank, A. 1967. *Capitalism and Underdevelopment in Latin America.* New York: Monthly Review Press.

Warren, B. 1980. *Imperialism, Pioneer of Capitalism.* London: New Left Books.

Cardoso, F.H. and Faletto, E. 1967. *Dependency and Development in Latin America.* Berkeley and Los Angeles: University of California Press (trans 1979).

DIVISION
Penrose, E. 1959. *The Theory of the Growth of the Firm.* Oxford. Blackwell.

DUALISM
Boeke, J. 1953. *Economics and Economic Policy of Dual Societies.* New York: Institute of Pacific Relations.

ECLECTIC THEORY
Dunning, J. 1977. Trade, location of economic activity and the multinational enterprise: a search for an eclectic approach. In Ohlin, B., Hesselborn, P.O. and Wijkman,

P.M. (eds), *The International Allocation of Economic Activity*. London: Macmillan. Reprinted in Dunning, J. H. *International Production and the Multinational Enterprise*. London: George Allen and Unwin, 1981.

ETHNOCENTRIC
Perlmutter, H.V. 1969. The Torturous Evolution of the Multinational Corporation. In *Columbia Journal of World Business* Jan-Feb pp. 9–18.

EUROPEAN COMMUNITY
European Community (EC). 1973. *Multinational Undertakings and Community Regulations*. Luxembourg: COM (73) 1930/1973.

EXTERNALITIES
Pigou, A.C. 1924. *The Economics of Welfare*. London: Macmillan.

FEDERAL CHARTERING
Nader, R., Green, M. and Seligman, J. 1976. *Taming the Giant Corporation*. New York: Norton and Co.

FOOTLOOSE INVESTMENT
Frobel, F., Heinrichs, J. and Kreye, D. 1980. *The New International Division of Labour*. Cambridge: Cambridge University Press.

FOREIGN DIRECT INVESTMENT
International Monetary Fund (IMF). 1964. *Balance of Payments Yearbook – Concepts and Definitions*. Washington: IMF.

GLOBAL INDUSTRIAL SYSTEMS CONSTELLATION
Perlmutter, H.V. 1972. The multinational firm in the future. In *Annals of the American Academy of Political and Social Science*, September, pp. 139–152.

HECKSCHER-OHLIN THEOREM
Heckscher, E. 1919. The effect of foreign trade on the distribution of income. Reprinted in Ellis, H.S. and Metzler, L.A. (eds) *Readings in the Theory of International Trade*. London: Allen and Unwin, 1950.

Ohlin, B. 1967. *Interregional and International Trade, Revised Edition*. Cambridge, Mass.: Harvard University Press.

HIGH-CONTEXT CULTURE
Hall, E.T. 1976. *Beyond Culture*. New York: Doubleday.

IMPERIALISM
Hobson, J.A. 1902. *Imperialism: A Study*. London: Allen and Unwin.

Lenin, V.I. 1916. *Imperialism, the Highest Stage of Capitalism*. London: Lawrence and Wishart.

Nkrumah, K. 1965. *Neocolonialism, the Last Stage of Imperialism*. London: Thomas Nelson and Sons.

INTER-IMPERIALIST COMPETITION
Cardoso, F.H. and Faletto, E. 1967. *Dependency and Development in Latin America*. Berkeley and Los Angeles: University of California Press (trans. 1979).

Warren, B. 1980. *Imperialism, Pioneer of Capitalism*. London: New Left Books.

INTERMEDIATE TECHNOLOGY
Schumacher, E.F. 1973. *Small is Beautiful: a Study of Economics as if People Mattered*. London: Blond and Briggs.

INTERNALIZATION THEORY
Buckley, P.J. and Casson, M. 1976. *The Future of Multinational Enterprise*. London: Macmillan.

INTERNATIONAL CHAMBER OF COMMERCE
Organization of Economic Co-operation

and Development (OECD) 1976. *International Investment and Multinational Enterprises: Guidelines for Multinational Enterprises, National Treatment, International Investment Incentives and Disincentives, Consultation Procedures.* Paris: OECD. (Revised edition Paris, 1984).

INTERNATIONAL SUBCONTRACTING
Michalet, A. 1980. International Subcontracting: A State-of-the-Art. In Germidis, D. *(ed) International Subcontracting.* Paris: OECD Development Centre.

LAW OF COMBINED AND UNEVEN DEVELOPMENT
Trotsky, L. 1928. *The Permanent Revolution* (new edition). New York: Merit Publishers, 1969.

LOCATION THEORY
Hymer, S. 1972. The multinational corporation and the law of uneven development. *In* Bhagwati, J.N. *(ed) Economics and World Order from the 1970s to the 1990s.* London: Collier Macmillan.

M-FORM ORGANIZATION
Williamson, O. 1970. *Corporate Control and Business Behavior.* Englewood Cliffs, Prentice-Hall.

MULTINATIONALCORPORATION/ ENTERPRISE
Vernon, R. 1971. *Sovereignty at Bay.* New York: Basic Books.

UNECOSOC. 1978. *Transnational Corporations in World Development – a Re-examination.* New York: United Nations.

European Community. 1973. *Multinational Undertakings and Community Regulations.* Luxembourg: Com (73) 1930/1973.

Perlmutter, H.V. 1969. The Torturous Evolution of Multi-national Corporation. In *Columbia Journal of World Business* Jan.

pp.9-18.

Organization of Economic Co-operation and Development 1976. *International Investment and Multinational Enterprises: Guidelines for Multinational Enterprises, National Treatment. International Investment Incentives and Disincentives, Consultation Procedures.* Paris: OECD.

NEWLY INDUSTRIALIZING COUNTRIES
Bradford, C. 1982. The rise of the NICs as exporters on a global scale. *In* Turner, L. and McMullen, N. *(eds) The Newly Industrializing Countries, Trade and Adjustment.* London: Allen Unwin.

Organization for Economic Co-operation and Development (OECD). 1979. *Report of the Secretary-General.* Paris: OECD.

World Bank. 1979. *World Development Report.* Washington, DC: IBRD.

Foreign and Commonwealth Office. 1979. *The Newly Industrializing Countries and the Adjustment Problem.* London: Foreign and Commonwealth Office.

OBSOLESCING BARGAIN
Vernon, R. 1977. *Storm over the Multinationals: The Real Issues.* London: Macmillan.

OLIGOPOLY MODEL
Hymer, S. 1976. *The International Operations of National Firms: A Study of Direct Foreign Investment.* Cambridge, Mass.: MIT Press.

PERFORMANCE REQUIREMENTS
Organization of Economic Co-operation and Development (OECD). 1983. *International Investment and Multinational Enterprises: Incentives and Disincentives and the International Investment Process.* Paris: OECD.

POST-IMPERIALISM
Becker, D. 1984. Development, democracy and dependency in Latin America: a post-imperialist view. *In Third World Quarterly*, 6(2)411–431.

Sklar, R.L. 1975. *Corporate Power in an African State*. Berkeley and Los Angeles: University of California Press.

PRODUCT CYCLE THEORY
Vernon, R. 1966. International investment and international trade in the product cycle. In *Journal of Economics* 80 190–207.

Hirsch, S. 1967. *Location of Industry and International Competitiveness*. London: Oxford University Press.

Franko, L.G. 1976. *The European Multinationals: A Challenge to American and British Big Business*. New York: Harper and Row.

Vernon, R. 1979. The product cycle hypothesis in a new international environment. In *Oxford Bulletin of Economics and Statistics* November 255–267.

PURCHASE POWER PARITY
Cassel, G. 1916. The present situation of the foreign exchanges. In *Economic Journal* XXVI 62–65.

Officer, L.H. 1976. The purchasing-power-parity-theory of exchange rates: A review article. *IMF Staff Papers*, March 1–60.

RED MULTINATIONALS
Levinson, C. 1979. *Vodka-Cola*. London: Gordon and Cremonesci.

REGIOCENTRIC
Wind, Y., Douglas, S.P. and Perlmutter, H.V. 1973. Guidelines for developing international marketing strategy. In *Journal of Marketing* 37 April 14–23.

RENT
Mandel, E. 1978. *Late Capitalism*. London: New Left Books (Verso edition).

U-FORM ORGANIZATION
D. Williamson 1970. *Corporate Control and Business Behavior*. Englewood Cliffs, Prentice-Hall.

Williamson, O. 1970. *Corporate Control and Business Behaviour*. Englewood Cliffs, Prentice-Hall.

ULTRA-IMPERIALISM
Kautsky, K. 1970. Der Imperialismus. In *Die Neue Zeit* 11 September 1914. Trans. as Ultra-imperialism. *New Left Review* (59).

Varga, E. 1963. *Twentieth Centry Capitalism*. Moscow: Foreign Languages Press.

X-EFFICIENCY
Leibenstein, H. 1966. Allocative efficiency vs. X-efficiency. In *American Economic Review* June 392–415.

Harberger, A.C. 1954. Monopoly and resource allocation. In *American Economic Review Papers and Proceedings* 44 77–87.

APPENDIX II

SELECT LIST OF BIBLIOGRAPHIES ON MULTINATIONAL ENTERPRISE

(Note: We have not been able to trace bibliographies of more recent date than those here. We believe that this is due to the prohibitive costs of production of such bibliographies, coupled with today's easy availability of library computer search facilities. Nevertheless, the present list, while limited to literature produced before 1982, will be of use to those readers not within easy access of computer search facilities.)

Michael. Z. Brooke, Mary Black and Paul Neville
International Business Bibliography
International Business Unit, University of Manchester Institute of Science and Technology
London: Macmillan 1977, 480 pp.

Comprehensive bibliography including books published in the previous 20 years, and articles and papers in the previous 5 years, one-half of which are briefly summarized. Subjects covered are international trade theory; international investment theory and currency exchanges; writings on the management process in international companies, and comparative management; politics and the interface between company and governments.
The alphabetical bibliography is indexed by subject headings and entries are prefixed with a number, enabling readers to put together booklists on any aspect of international business.

Eric Browndorf, Scott Reimer and Kenneth

R. Simmonds
Bibliography of Multinational Corporations & Foreign & Direct Investment
Oceana Publications, 1980

Gerard Ghersi and Jean-Louis Rastoin et. al.
Multinational Firms and Agro-Food Systems in Developing Countries: a Bibliographic Review
Paris: OECD Development Centre, 1981, 85pp

Consists of an analytical section and a selected bibliographic section. Bibliography of 400 references from 1970 onwards assembled around the proposition that food problems have to be analysed in a systems context. References classified under the following headings: nutrition, consumption and food distribution; agricultural development; agro-food industries; agro-food technology and its transfer; food policy; government policies *vis-à-vis* multinational firms and international trade; multinational firms and the developing countries: general aspects.

H. Gunter, with M. Gaudier
Multinational Corporations and Labour: a selected and annotated bibliography
Geneva: International Institute for Labour Studies, 1973, 37 pp.

Abstracts of 170 contributions from English and French literature covering different aspects of the labour problems associated with multinational enterprise.

Roger Hilbert and Christiane Oehlmann
Foreign Direct Investments and Multi-national Corporations in sub-Saharan Africa: a bibliography
Frankfurt/New York: Campus Verlag, 1980, 699 pp.

Friedrich von Kirchbach
Annotated Bibliography on Transnational Corporations in the ASEAN region
Joint CTC/ESCAP Unit on Transnational Corporations/Bankok: United Nations Economic and Social Commission for Asia and the Pacific, 1980, 60pp.

Sanjaya Lall
Foreign Private Manufacturing Investment and Multinational Corporations: an Annotated Bibliography
New York/London: Praeger Publishers, 1975, 195 pp.

While limited to the manufacturing sector, this fully annotated guide covers a wide range of literature from pure theory and Marxist critiques to vocationally oriented business school texts. The 1044 references are alphabetically listed in 16 chapters, covering *inter alia*: causes and effects of foreign direct investment; legal issues; technology; labour; restrictive practices. Entries are numbered and cross-referenced by number.

Edgardo Lifschnitz
Bibliografia analitica sobre empresas transnacionales (Analytical Bibliography on Transnational Corporations)
Mexico: Intstituto Latinoamericano de Estudios Transnacionales (ILET), 1980, 607 pp.

Joseph D. Mekeirle
Multinational Corporations: The ECSIM Guide to Information Sources
Brussels: ECSIM, 1977, 454 pp.

A very comprehensive guide to worldwide and regional company directories, business and financial services, research establishments and other information sources. It includes a bibliography of bibliographies and of review articles. Some of these are summarized or abstracted. It contains an ambitious index system of great help to diligent users only.

Organization of American States. Executive Secretariat for Economic and Social Affairs
Annotated Bibliography on Transnational Enterprises with Emphasis on Latin America
Washington: Organization of American States, Pan American Union Building, 1974

Taghi Saghafi-Nejad and Robert Belfield
Transnational Corporations, Technology Transfer, and Development: a Bibliography
New York: Pergamon Press, 1980, 145 pp.

A bibliography of readings assembled around the basic proposition that science and technology are crucial to development, and that TNCs are key actors in the international trade in technology. Includes material concerning the modes, appropriateness, costs and consequences of the technology transfer for the development process – especially for the technological self-reliance of nation states.

Harry Strharsky and Mary Riesch, with Bill Arnold and Colleen O'Connor
Bibliographical Notes for Understanding Transnational Corporations and the Third World
Washington, D.C.: CoDoc International Secretariat, 1975, 231 pp.

With contributions from a number of campaigning organizations, this CoDoc (Cooperation in Documentation and Communication) bibliography contains a total of 1300 references. Many of these are critical documents, reports and pamphlets which one would not normally encounter in the standard bibliographies on multinational enterprise. The majority of entries cover the years 1970–1974. The entries do not provide summaries, but are annotated with key-word descriptors: capital, labour, government, mining, working conditions and so on.

UNIPUB
Technology Transfer
New York: Unipub, 1977

Comprehensive listing of texts relating to international technology transfer. Unipub is the US clearing house for publications by the United Nations and other international organizations. The bibliography includes abstracts of relevant documents by international organizations, including some on themes such as investment legislation, licensing agreements and development programmes.

United Nations Centre on Transnational Corporations
Bibliography on Transnational Corporations

United Nations, 1979, 426pp. (ST/CTC/4-Sales NoE/F.78.II.A.4)
The first computer-produced bibliography on transnational corporations compiled by the Centre on Transnational Corporations as a continuing project. The alphabetical unannotated listing totals 4200 references and includes, besides books and journal articles, government publications, dissertations and unpublished papers. Entries are numbered, and there is a complex classication system appended at the back of the volume, which gathers entries by their numbers into subject groups.

The bibliography is one part of a directory of information sources on transnational corporations, which also comprises a *Survey of Research on Transnational Corporations* (United Nations publications, Sales No. E.77.II,A,16); a *list of Company Directories and Summary of Their Contents* (United Nations publication, Sales No. E.77.II.A.8) and an *International Directory of Data Bases Relating to Companies* (United Nations publication, Sales No. E.79.II.A.1).

APPENDIX III

ORGANIZATIONS

Andean Pact countries
Council for Mutual Economic Assistance (CMEA)
European Community (EC)
European Trade Union Confederation (ETUC)
Financial Accounting Standards Board (FASB)
Food and Agriculture Organization (FAO)
General Agreement on Tariffs and Trade (GATT)
International Accounting Standards Committee (IASC)
International Center for the Settlement of Investment Disputes
International Chamber of Commerce (ICC)
International Confederation of Free Trade Unions (ICFTU)
International Court of Justice (ICJ)
International Development Association (IDA)
International Federation of Accountants (IFAC)
International Finance Corporation (IFC)
International Labour Organization (ILO)
International Monetary Fund (IMF)
International Organization of Consumer Unions (IOCU)
International Organization of Employers (IOE)
Latin American Integration Association (LAIA)
Organization for Economic Co-operation and Development (OECD)
Organization of Petroleum Exporting Countries (OPEC)
United Nations Conference on Trade and Development (UNCTAD)
United Nations Industrial Development Organizations (UNIDO)
World Bank
World Federation of Trade Union (WFTU)
World Intellectual Property Organization (WIPO)

INDEX

Note: For an explanation as to how to use this index see page xi.

1. CORPORATE STRUCTURE AND MANAGEMENT

administrative fiat *see also* Financial and Risk Management
affiliate company
agency problem
arm's length *see also* Financial and Risk Management
associated company
binational enterprise
branch plant
Business and Industry Advisory Committee (BIAC) *see also* International Co-operation
captive market
centralization *see also* Theoretical Issues; Industry Structure
competence centre
conglomerate *see also* Industry structure
cost centre
cross-subsidization *see also* Financial and Risk Management
consolidated accounts *see also* International Accounting
diversification *see also* Theoretical Issues; Financial and Risk Management
division
double sourcing
ethnocentric *see also* Theoretical Issues
expatriate management
footloose investment
geocentric *see also* Theoretical Issues
global scanning
global strategy
high context culture *see also* Theoretical Issues
holding company *see also* Financial and Risk Management
horizontal integration
International Chamber of Commerce

(ICC) *see also* International Co-operation
international division
international production *see also* Theoretical Issues
International Organization of Employers (IOE) *see also* International Co-operation
investment centre *see also* Financial and Risk Management
joint venture *see also* Technology Transfer
local incorporation
M-form organization
majority-owned foreign affiliate (MOFA)
market segmentation *see also* Financial and Risk Management
matrix organization
multinational corporation/enterprise *see also* Theoretical Issues
multiprocessing
offshore assembly *see also* Trade
parent company
polycentric *see also* Theoretical Issues
portfolio investment *see also* Financial and Risk Management
profit centre *see also* Financial and Risk Management
regiocentric
related company *see also* Theoretical Issues
Roundtable of European Industrialists *see also* International Co-operation
runaway shop *see also* Labour
sogo sosha see also Industry Structure
split-site production
subsidiary
Third World multinationals
transfer price *see also* Financial and Risk Management; Regulation and Tax; Theoretical Issues
transnational bank (TNB)

251

transnational corporation (TNC)
Trilateral Commission *see also*
    International Co-operation
U-form organization
UNICE *see also* International
    Co-operation
vertical integration *see also* Industry
    Structure; Theoretical Issues
wholly-owned subsidiary
workshop subsidiary

2. DATA SOURCES
Asia Monitor Resource Center (AMRC)
Australia Asia Worker Links (AAWL)
Banker (the)
benchmark survey
Bottin International
Britain's Top Private Companies
Business Environment Risk Index (BERI)
    see also Financial and Risk
    Management
Center for Alternative Industrial and
    Technological Systems (CAITS) *see
    also* Technology Transfer
Corporate Data Exchange
Counter Information Services (CIS)
Data Center
Data Star
Dialog Information Services
Directory of Social Change
Disclosure Incorporated
East-West Center Project on Women and
    TNCs
Ethical Investment Research and
    Information Service
Extel Information Service
Financial Times International Business
    Yearbook
Forbes
Fortune
IBASE (*Instituto Brasiliero Analises
    Sociales y Economicas*)
ILET (*Instituto Latinoamericano de
    estudios transnacionales*)
Institute for Food and Development
    Policy
Institute for Policy Studies/Transnational
    Institute (IPS/TI)

Institute for Research on Multinational
    Enterprises (IRM)
Interfaith Center on Corporate
    Responsibility
International Multinational Directory
International Organization of Consumer
    Unions (IOCU) *see also* International
    Co-operation
Jane's Major Companies of Europe
Labor Education and Research Project
Labor Research Association
Latin American Working Group
    (LAWG)
McCarthy's Information Service Ltd
Moodies Services Ltd
Multinational Monitor
Northwest Transnationals Project
Pacific Studies Center
Raw Materials Group
Registrar of Companies *see also*
    Regulation and Tax
Securities and Exchange Commission *see
    also* Regulation and Tax
SOMO (*Stichting Onderzoek
    Multinationale Ondernemingen*)
Taskforce on the Churches and Corporate
    Responsibility
TIE-Europe (Transnationals Information
    Exchange-Europe)
Times 1000
TransAfrica
Transnational Corporation Research
    Project
Transnationals Information Center
United Nations Center on Transnational
    Corporations (UNCTC) *see also*
    International Co-operation
United Nations Conference on Trade and
    Development (UNCTAD) *see also*
    Trade; International Co-operation
War on Want
Who Owns Whom
World Council of Churches Programme
    on Transnational Corporations
World Directory of Multinational
    Enterprises
World's Largest Industrial
    Enterprises

3. DEVELOPMENT POLICY

autarchy
backward linkages
balance of payments *see also* Regulation
    and Tax
basic needs
collective self-reliance *see also*
    International Co-operation
debt rescheduling *see also* International
    Co-operation
delinking *see also* Trade
dependency *see also* Theoretical Issues
economic nationalism *see also* Theoretical
    Issues
expatriate management quota *see also*
    Corporate Structure and Management
forward linkages
import substitution
indigenization *see also* Dispute and
    Settlement
localization
local sourcing
local value added
modernization *see also* Theoretical Issues
newly industrializing countries *see also*
    Trade
open door policies
performance requirements *see also*
    Regulation and Tax
populism
self-reliance

4. DISPUTE AND SETTLEMENT

Badger case *see also* Labour
Barcelona Traction case
Calvo clause
Charter of Economic Rights and Duties of
    States *see also* International
    Co-operation
choice of law clause
clausula rebus sic stantibus
codes of conduct *see also* International
    Co-operation
comity principle
concession *see also* Regulation and Tax
confiscation
Convention on the Settlement of
    Investment Disputes between States

and Nationals of Other States *see also*
    International Co-operation
doctrine of domicile
economic sovereignty
effects principle
estoppel principle
expropriation
extraterritoriality *see also* Regulation and
    Tax
International Center for the Settlement of
    Investment Disputes
International Court of Justice (ICJ) *see*
    also International Co-operation
lump-sum settlement
national contact point *see also*
    International Co-operation
national treatment *see also* International
    Co-operation
nationalization
non-discrimination rule
Nottebohm case
pacta sunt servanda
public utility rule
Transfer of Technology (TOT) Code *see*
    also International Co-operation
Tripartite Declaration on Multinational
    Enterprises and Social Policy *see also*
    International Co-operation
United Nations Draft Code of Conduct on
    Transnational Corporations *see also*
    International Co-operation

5. FINANCIAL AND RISK MANAGEMENT

administrative fiat
arbi-loan *see also* Theoretical Issues
arbitrage, and arbitrage pricing theory *see*
    also Theoretical Issues
back to back loans
base company *see also* Regulation and
    Tax
beta *see also* Theoretical Issues
blocked funds
brass plate company *see also* Regulation
    and Tax
business environment risk index *see also*
    Data Sources
capital asset pricing model (CAPM) *see*

also Theoretical Issues
captive insurance company
cash management
certificate of deposit (CD)
Chicago International Money Market
Code of Liberalization of Capital
  Movements *see also* International
  Co-operation
convertible bond
corporate tax system *see also* Regulation
  and Tax
cost of capital *see also* Theoretical Issues
country risk assessment *see also*
  Theoretical Issues
covered interest arbitrage *see also*
  Theoretical Issues
credit swap
creeping expropriation *see also* Dispute
  and Settlement
cross default clause *see also* International
  Co-operation
currency cocktail
currency exchange agreement
debt service ratio *see also* Development
  Policy
diversification *see also* Theoretical Issues;
  Corporate Structure and Management
dividend repatriation *see also* Regulation
  and Tax
efficient market *see also* Theoretical
  Issues
eurobond
euro-commercial paper
eurocurrency
European currency unit (ECU) *see also*
  International Co-operation
exchange controls
Export Credits Guarantee Department
  (ECGD)
financial structure
fixed exchange rate
Foreign Credit Insurance Association
foreign exchange risk
fronting loan
hedge
hot money
interest rate parity *see also* Theoretical
  Issues

International Finance Corporation (IFC)
  see also International Co-operation
international Fisher effect *see also*
  Theoretical Issues
junk bond
leading and lagging
link financing
London Inter-Bank Offered Rate
  (LIBOR)
managed float
management buyout *see also* Corporate
  Structure and Management
market segmentation *see also* Corporate
  Structure and Management
multicurrency bond
netting
offshore finance subsidiary *see also*
  Regulation and Tax
offshore financial centre
option
Overseas Private Investment Corporation
  (OPIC)
parallel loan
portfolio theory *see also* Theoretical
  Issues
purchase power parity *see also* Theoretical
  Issues
real exchange rate
reinvoicing centre *see also* Regulation and
  Tax
risk premium
scout
securitization
space arbitrage
spot rate
square position
stepping stone company *see also*
  Regulation and Tax
swap
swap position
swap rate
syndicated loan
systematic risk *see also* Theoretical Issues
transfer booking
transfer parking
transfer price *see also* Corporate Structure
  and Management; Regulation and Tax;
  Theoretical Issues

World Bank *see also* Regulation and Tax
zero coupon bond *see also* International
  Co-operation

6. INDUSTRY STRUCTURE
acquisition
aggregate concentration
agribusiness *see also* Development Policy
business reciprocity
cartel
concentration *see also* Theoretical Issues
cross-licensing
forbearance
global industrial systems constellation
  (GISC)
interlocking directorates
merger *see also* Regulation and Tax
monopoly *see also* Theoretical Issues
monopsony *see also* Theoretical Issues
oligopoly *see also* Theoretical Issues
patent pool
resource consortium
vertical integration *see also* Corporate
  Structure and Management;
  Theoretical Issues

7. INTERNATIONAL ACCOUNTING
Accounting Standards Committee (ASC)
accounting principles
auditing
compliance accounting
consolidated accounts *see also* Corporate
  Structure and Management
convenience financial statements
disclosure in accounts
exposure
Financial Accounting Standard No.8
  (FAS 8)
Financial Accounting Standard No.52
  (FAS 52)
Financial Accounting Standards Board
  (FASB)
financial reports
functional currency
inflation accounting
International Accounting Standards
  Committee (IASC) *see also*
  International Co-operation

international auditing firms
International Committee for Accounting
  Co-operation *see also* International
  Co-operation
International Federation of Accountants
  (IFAC) *see also* International
  Co-operation
secret reserves
segmentation
translation
UEC (Union Européenne des Experts
  Comptables) *see also* International
  Co-operation
unbundling *see also* Technology Transfer
uniform accounting

8. INTERNATIONAL CO-OPERATION
ACP states
Agency for International Development
  (AID)
Andean Pact countries *see also* Regulation
  and Tax; Technology Transfer
Berne Union
bilateral investment agreement
Brandt Commission
Bretton Woods monetary system
Business and Industry Advisory
  Committee (BIAC) *see also* Corporate
  Structure and Management
Caborn Report *see also* Dispute and
  Settlement
Charter of Economic Rights and Duties of
  States *see also* Dispute and Settlement
Club of Rome *see also* Corporate
  Structure and Management
Code of Liberalization of Capital
  Movements *see also* Financial and Risk
  Management
codes of conduct *see also* Dispute and
  Settlement
collective self-reliance *see also*
  Development Policy
Committee on International Investment
  and Multinational Enterprises
Common Fund *see also* Trade
Convention on the Settlement of
  Investment Disputes *see also* Dispute
  and Settlement

Council for Mutual Economic Assistance (CMEA)
customs union *see also* Trade
debt rescheduling *see also* Development Policy
Declaration and Decisions on International Investment and Multinational Enterprises *see also* Dispute and Settlement
double taxation agreement *see also* Regulation and Tax
EC Code of Conduct for Companies with Subsidiaries, Branches or Representation in South Africa *see also* Dispute and Settlement
European Community (EC) *see also* Regulation and Tax
European currency unit (ECU) *see also* Financial and Risk Management
European Investment Bank (EIB)
European monetary system (EMS)
European Patent Convention *see also* Technology Transfer
European Trade Union Confederation (ETUC) *see also* Labour
Food and Agriculture Organization (FAO)
General Agreement on Tariffs and Trade (GATT) *see also* Trade
Generalised System of Preferences *see also* Trade
global reforms
Group of 77 (G-77) *see also* Development Policy
harmonization policies *see also* Regulation and Tax
Havana Charter *see also* Trade
IFPMA Code *see also* Dispute and Settlement
International Accounting Standards Committee (IASC) *see also* International Accounting
International Chamber of Commerce (ICC) *see also* Corporate Structure and Management
International Committee for Accounting Co-operation *see also* International Accounting

International Confederation of Free Trade Unions (ICFTU) *see also* Labour
International Convention for the Protection of Industrial Property *see also* Technology Transfer
International Court of Justice (ICJ) *see also* Dispute and Settlement
International Development Association (IDA) *see also* Development Policy
International Federation of Accountants (IFAC) *see also* International Accounting
International Finance Corporation (IFA) *see also* Financial and Risk Management
International Labour Organization (ILO) *see also* Labour
International Monetary Fund (IMF) *see also* Financial and Risk Management
International Organization of Consumer Unions (IOCU) *see also* Data Sources
International Organization of Employers (IOE) *see also* Corporate Structure and Management
International Trade Secretariats (ITS) *see also* Labour
investment protection treaty
joint audit *see also* Regulation and Tax
Lange-Gibbons Code *see also* Dispute and Settlement
Latin American Integration Association (LAIA)
Law of the Sea Treaty
Lomé Convention *see also* Development Policy
national contact point *see also* Dispute and Settlement
national treatment *see also* Dispute and Settlement
New International Economic Order (NIEO)
Organization for Economic Co-operation and Development (OECD)
Organization of Petroleum Exporting Countries (OPEC)
Paris Club
Patent Co-operation Treaty

Restrictive Business Practices (RBP)
Code *see also* Dispute and Settlement
Round Table of European Industrialists
see also Corporate Structure and
Management
snake
special drawing rights
STABEX *see also* Trade
Sullivan Principles *see also* Dispute and
Settlement
tax harmonization *see also* Regulation and
Tax
Third World *see also* Development Policy;
Theoretical Issues
Trade Union Advisory Committee
(TUAC) *see also* Labour
Transfer of Technology (TOT) Code *see
also* Dispute and Settlement;
Technology Transfer
Trilateral Commission *see also* Corporate
Structure and Management
Tripartite Declaration on Multinational
Enterprises and Social Policy *see also*
Dispute and Settlement; Labour
UEC (*Union Europeenne des Experts
Comptables*) *see also* International
Accounting
UNICE *see also* Corporate Structure and
Management
United Nations Center on Transnational
Corporations (UNCTC) *see also* Data
Sources
United Nations Commission on
Transnational Corporations
United Nations Conference on Trade and
Development (UNCTAD) *see also*
Trade; Data Sources
United Nations Draft Code of Conduct on
Transnational Corporations *see also*
Dispute and Settlement
United Nations Industrial Development
Organization (UNIDO) *see also*
Technology Transfer
Vredeling Proposal *see also* Labour
WHO/UNICEF Code of Marketing of
Breastmilk Substitutes *see also* Dispute
and Settlement
World Bank *see also* Development Policy;

Financial and Risk Management
World Federation of Trade Unions
(WFTU) *see also* Labour
World Intellectual Property Organization
see also Technology Transfer

9. LABOUR
combine committee
European Trade Union Confederation
(ETUC) *see also* International
Co-operation
International Confederation of Free
Trade Unions (ICFTU) *see also*
International Co-operation
International Labour Organization (ILO)
see also International Co-operation
International Trade Secretariats (ITS) *see
also* International Co-operation
Trade Union Advisory Committee
(TUAC) *see also* International
Co-operation
Vredeling Proposal *see also* International
Co-operation
World Federation of Trade Unions
(WFTU) *see also* International
Co-operation

10. REGULATIONS AND TAX
agreement corporation *see also* Financial
and Risk Management
American depository receipt (ADR)
Andean Pact countries *see also*
International Co-operation;
Technology Transfer
Anstalt see also Financial and Risk
Management
Anti-Trust Division
anti-trust legislation *see also* Industry
Structure
authorization procedures
avoir fiscale
balance of payments *see also*
Development Policy
Burke-Hartke Bill
capital export neutrality *see also*
Theoretical Issues
Celler-Kefauver Amendment *see also*
Industry Stucture

Clayton Act *see also* Industry Structure
comfort letter *see also* Industry Structure
commissaires aux comptes see also
    International accounting
concession *see also* Dispute and
    Settlement
constructed price
corporate tax system *see also* Financial
    and Risk Management
deregulation
dividend repatriation *see also* Financial
    and Risk Management
domestic international sales corporation
    (DISC) *see also* Corporate Structure
    and Management
double taxation agreement *see also*
    International Co-operation
Edge Act corporation (EAC) *see also*
    Corporate Structure and Management
European Community (EC) *see also*
    International Co-operation
European economic interest grouping
    (EEIG) *see also* Corporate Sructure
    and Management
Export Administration Act
fadeout policies *see also* Development
    Policy
fair market value system
Fair Trading Act
Federal Trade Commission (FTC)
Foreign Corrupt Practices Act
Foreign Direct Investment Program
Gonzalez Amendment *see also* Dispute
    and Settlement
harmonization policies *see also*
    International Co-operation
Hickenlooper Amendment *see also*
    Dispute and Settlement
indexation
interest equalization tax
Internal Revenue Code Section 482
international banking facility (IBF) *see
    also* Corporate Structure and
    Management
joint audit *see also* International
    Co-operation
less developed country corporation
    (LDCC) *see also* Corporate Structure

and Management
Mandatory Control Program
mining rent
modernized concession agreement *see also*
    Development Policy
Monopolies and Mergers Commission *see
    also* Industry Structure
national registry of technology *see also*
    Technology Transfer
negotiated price system
Pease Bill *see also* Trade; Labour
possessions corporation *see also*
    Corporate Structure and Management
realized price system
reference price system
Registrar of Companies *see also* Data
    Sources
Regulation Q
Section 485, Income and Corporation
    Taxes Act
Securities and Exchange Commission
    (SEC) *see also* Financial and Risk
    Management; Data Sources
Securities and Investment Board (SIB) *see
    also* Financial and Risk Management
Stiftung see also Financial and Risk
    Management
subpart 'F' income
tax credit *see also* Financial and Risk
    Management
tax harmonization *see also* International
    Co-operation
tax haven *see also* Financial and Risk
    Management
tax holiday *see also* Financial and Risk
    Management
tax sparing *see also* Financial and Risk
    Management
tax spinning *see also* Financial and Risk
    Management
turnover tax
unitary taxation
value added tax (VAT)
Webb-Pomerane Act *see also* Industry
    Structure
Western Hemisphere Trade Corporation
    (WHTC) *see also* Corporate Structure
    and Management

withholding tax
yen company *see also* Corporate Structure and Management

11. THEORETICAL ISSUES
appropriability theory
arbitrage *see also* Financial and Risk Management
arbitrage pricing theory (APT) *see also* Financial and Risk Management
barriers to entry
barriers to exit
capital asset pricing model (CAPM) *see also* Financial and Risk Management
capital export neutrality *see also* Regulation and Tax
capitalism
centralization *see also* Corporate Structure and Management; Industry Structure
Coase theorem
concentration *see also* Industry Structure
contagion hypothesis
corporate imperialism
country risk assessment *see also* Financial and Risk Management
covered interest arbitrage *see also* Financial and Risk Management
dependency *see also* Development Policy
diversification *see also* Corporate Structure and Management; Financial and Risk Management
dualism *see also* Development Policy
eclectic theory
efficient market *see also* Financial and Risk Management
enclave economy *see also* Development Policy
ethnocentric *see also* Corporate Structure and Management
externalities
factor mobility
follow the leader theory
foreign direct investment (FDI) *see also* Technology Transfer
geocentric *see also* Corporate Structure and Management
Heckscher-Ohlin theorem
high context culture *see also* Corporate

Structure and Management
imperialism
inter-imperialist competition
interest rate parity *see also* Financial and Risk Management
internalization theory *see also* Corporate Structure and Management
international Fisher effect *see also* Financial and Risk Management
international production *see also* Corporate Structure and Management
law of combined and uneven development
location specific advantages
location theory
modernization *see also* Development Policy
monopoly *see also* Industry Structure
multinational corporation/enterprise *see also* Corporate Structure and Management
neo-factor trade theory
neo-imperialism
neo-technology trade theory
new international division of labour *see also* Trade
obsolescing bargain
oligopoly *see also* Industry Structure
oligopoly model *see also* Industry Structure
ownership specific advantages
polycentric *see also* Corporate Structure and Management
portfolio theory *see also* Financial and Risk Management
post-imperialism
product cycle theory
purchase power parity *see also* Financial and Risk Management
regiocentric *see also* Corporate Structure and Management
rent
scale economies
socialism
super-imperialism
systematic risk *see also* Financial and Risk Management
Third World *see also* International Co-operation

transaction cost
ultra-imperialism
x-efficiency *see also* Industry Structure

12. TRADE
agency agreement
American selling price
barter *see also* Technology Transfer
bilateral clearing arrangement
bill of exchange
bill of lading
bonded warehouse
buy-back deal *see also* Technology
    Transfer
certificate of analysis
co-operative exporter
combination export manager (CEM)
Common Fund *see also* International
    Co-operation
compensation trade *see also* Technology
    Transfer
correspondent bank
counter purchase *see also* Technology
    Transfer
countertrade *see also* Technology Transfer
countervailing duty
covering
customs union *see also* International
    Co-operation
drawback
dumping
export broker
Export Import Bank (EX-IM Bank)
exporting trade terms
foreign freight forwarder
Foreign Trade Organization (FTO) *see
    also* Technology Transfer
forfaiting
free trade zone (FTZ) *see also*
    Development Policy
General Agreement on Tariffs and Trade
    (GATT) *see also* International
    Co-operation
Generalised System of Preferences (GSP)
    see also International Co-operation
Incoterms, 1953 (International
    Commercial Terms, 1953)
international subcontracting

intra-firm trade *see also* Corporate
    Structure and Management
letter of credit
maquiladora see also Development Policy
most favoured nation (MFN) clause
Multifibre Arrangement (MFA)
new international division of labour *see
    also* Theoretical Issues
non-tariff barrier
offsets *see also* Technology Transfer
quota
red multinationals
related party imports
Special Economic Zones *see also*
    Development Policy; Technology
    Transfer
Standard International Trade
    Classification (SITC) *see also* Data
    Sources
switch trade *see also* Technology Transfer
tariff *see also* Development Policy
tariff preference
tariff schedules 806.30 and 807.00 *see also*
    Corporate Structure and Management
triangular trade *see also* Financial and
    Risk Management
United Nations Conference on Trade and
    Development *see also* International
    Co-operation; Data Sources
U-turn investment
voluntary export restraint

13. TECHNOLOGY TRANSFER
appropriate technology
barter *see also* Trade
brain drain
buy-back deal *see also* Trade
Coproduction agreement *see also*
    Corporate Structure and Management
compensation trade *see also* Trade
completely-knocked-down (CKD)
computer aided design (CAD) *see also*
    Corporate Structure and Management
computer aided manufacture (CAM) *see
    also* Corporate Structure and
    Management
cost-reimbursable contract *see also*
    Corporate Structure and Management

cross-border transactions
counter purchase *see also* Trade
countertrade *see also* Trade
franchising
intermediate technology
inventor's certificate
International Convention for the
    Protection of Industrial Property *see*
    also International Co-operation
joint venture *see also* Corporate Structure
    and Management
licensing agreement *see also* Corporate
    Structure and Management
management contract *see also* Corporate
    Structure and Management
market-in-hand contract *see also*
    Corporate Structure and Management
offsets *see also* Trade
patent
preproduction grant *see also* Corporate
    Structure and Management
product-in-hand contract *see also*
    Corporate Structure and Management

product sharing agreement *see also*
    Corporate Structure and Management
production sharing agreement *see also*
    Corporate Structure and Management
reverse engineering
risk service contract *see also* Corporate
    Structure and Management
royalty
Special Economic Zones *see also* Trade
technical assistance agreement *see also*
    Corporate Structure and Management
tie-in clause
trademark
trade secret
turnkey contract *see also* Corporate
    Structure and Management
unbundling *see also* Financial and Risk
    Management; Development Policy
United Nations Industrial Development
    Organization (UNIDO) *see also*
    International Co-operation
World Intellectual Property Organization
    see also International Co-operation